Scottish History in 15 Violent Crimes

History in 15

This pioneering new series offers lively perspectives on regional and global histories. Adopting an innovative thematic approach, each title is structured around 15 items, concepts or sources through which the history of a particular region, or the entire world, can be illuminated. From food to films, from cities to songs, this series brings history into focus for students and interested readers.

These approachable books use a consistent set of themes or sources as a lens through which to view the broader history, transforming how the reader understands these items while imparting critical lessons about historical context and analysis. For example, a book on *US History in 15 Foods* would use 15 foods to examine the history of the nation, covering key topics and themes in US history.

Series Editors: Laura A. Belmonte (Virginia Tech, USA)

Editorial Board

Maria Montoya, NYU-Shanghai, China
Kyle Longley, Chapman University, USA
Anne Foster, Indiana State University, USA
Julia Irwin, University of South Florida, USA
Fabian Hilfrich, University of Edinburgh, UK
Justin Hart, Texas Tech, USA
Kelly Shannon, Florida Atlantic University, USA
Holly M. Karibo, Oklahoma State University, USA
Ellen Hartigan O'Connor, UC-Davis, USA
Andrew Rotter, Colgate University, USA

PUBLISHED

US History in 15 Foods, Anna Zeide
A History of Canada in 15 Moments, Jeff Keshen and Raymond B. Blake
US History in 15 Photographs: 1865 to the 21st Century, Rebecca S. Wingo and Lauren Tilton

FORTHCOMING

Global History in 15 Epidemics, Andrew Robarts

Queer History in 15 Lives, Laura A. Belmonte

Global History in 15 Latin American Foods, Elizabeth Newman

Atlantic History in 15 Slave Revolts: Resistance, Rebellion and Abolition from Below, Christian Høgsbjerg

South Asian History in 15 Films, Talat Ahmed

Global History in 15 Disasters: Urban Catastrophes and Reconstruction since 18th Century, Pierre Purseigle

Scottish History in 15 Violent Crimes

Gender, Society and the Law

LOUISE HEREN

BLOOMSBURY ACADEMIC
LONDON • NEW YORK • OXFORD • NEW DELHI • SYDNEY

BLOOMSBURY ACADEMIC

Bloomsbury Publishing Plc, 50 Bedford Square, London, WC1B 3DP, UK
Bloomsbury Publishing Inc, 1359 Broadway, New York, NY 10018, USA
Bloomsbury Publishing Ireland, 29 Earlsfort Terrace, Dublin 2, D02 AY28, Ireland

BLOOMSBURY, BLOOMSBURY ACADEMIC and the Diana logo are trademarks of
Bloomsbury Publishing Plc

First published in Great Britain 2026

Copyright © Louise Heren, 2026

Louise Heren has asserted her right under the Copyright, Designs and Patents Act, 1988,
to be identified as Author of this work.

For legal purposes the Acknowledgements on p. xiii constitute an
extension of this copyright page.

Cover image: diane555 via Getty Images

All rights reserved. No part of this publication may be: i) reproduced or transmitted in
any form, electronic or mechanical, including photocopying, recording or by means of
any information storage or retrieval system without prior permission in writing from the
publishers; or ii) used or reproduced in any way for the training, development or operation
of artificial intelligence (AI) technologies, including generative AI technologies. The rights
holders expressly reserve this publication from the text and data mining exception as per
Article 4(3) of the Digital Single Market Directive (EU) 2019/790.

Bloomsbury Publishing Plc does not have any control over, or responsibility for, any
third-party websites referred to or in this book. All internet addresses given in this
book were correct at the time of going to press. The author and publisher regret any
inconvenience caused if addresses have changed or sites have ceased to exist,
but can accept no responsibility for any such changes.

A catalogue record for this book is available from the British Library.

A catalog record for this book is available from the Library of Congress.

ISBN: HB: 978-1-3504-3722-7
PB: 978-1-3504-3721-0
ePDF: 978-1-3504-3723-4
eBook: 978-1-3504-3724-1

Series: History in 15

Typeset by Newgen KnowledgeWorks Pvt. Ltd., Chennai, India
Printed and bound in Great Britain

For product safety related questions contact productsafety@bloomsbury.com.

To find out more about our authors and books visit www.bloomsbury.com
and sign up for our newsletters.

For Bill, always ... and for Louis, forever to excel.

*In memory of
Rufus of Reybridge*

Contents

List of Illustrations xi
Acknowledgements xiii

Introduction: Scottish exceptionalism 1

1 John Martine 1709: Incest, relations and the law 15

2 Janet Horne 1727: Widow, misogyny, marginality and witch 27

3 Barbara Malcolm 1808: Mother, 'monster' and murderer 43

4 Tron Rioters 1811–12: Protest, murder and class conflict 61

5 Burke and Hare 1828: Multiple murder, vulnerability and the law 81

6 Dobie and Thomson 1830: Misogyny, female agency and rape 99

7 Madeleine Smith 1857: Class, gender and sexual morality 117

8 Patrick Higgins 1895: Lodger, same-sex child abuse and syphilis 133

9 Oscar Slater 1909: Murderer, 'other' and justice 149

10 Susan Newell 1923: Murderess, evidence and insanity 167

11 Robert Handley 1926: Lover, murderer and culpability 185

12 Thomas Lutton 1928: Stepfather, rapist and the law 201

13 Peter Manuel 1958: 'Serial killer', mind and motive 215

14 Henry John Burnett 1963: Murderer, state execution and abolition 231

15 *S. v. HM Advocate* 1989: Marriage, rape and abuse 243

Conclusion 255

Glossary 261
Further and Extended Reading 263
Bibliography 267
Index 281

Illustrations

1.1 Verdict of Assize, Elspeth Martine 19

2.1 Stone commemorating Janet Horne's place of execution 38

3.1 Indictment for Barbara Malcolm, 5 January 1808 51

4.1 Grassmarket, Old Edinburgh 66

5.1 Frontispiece, *Trial of William Burke and Helen M'Dougal: Before the High Court of Justiciary, Edinburgh, on Wednesday, December 24, 1828, for the murder of Margery Campbell, or Docherty* (Edinburgh, 1829) 88

6.1 Latin extract describing Margaret Paterson's ordeal 107

7.1 Frontispiece, *Trial of Miss Madeleine H. Smith before the High Court of Justiciary, Edinburgh, June 30 to July 9, 1857, for the alleged poisoning of M. Pierre Emile L'Angelier at Glasgow* (Edinburgh, 1857) 121

7.2 Madeleine offers Emile a cup of chocolate from her bedroom window 128

8.1 Declaration of Patrick Higgins 139

9.1 Oscar Slater (Edinburgh, 1910) 151

9.2 West Princes Street (Edinburgh, 1910) 153

9.3 Dining Room, 15 Queen's Terrace (Edinburgh, 1910) 155

9.4 On trial, High Court of Justiciary, Edinburgh (Edinburgh, 1910) 157

9.5 Plan of Marion Gilchrist's home (Edinburgh, 1910) 162

10.1 Telegram confirming Susan Newell's execution,
10 October 1923 176

11.1 List of Forensic Evidence Productions at the trial of
Robert Handley 192

12.1 Street conditions Glasgow's central districts, early 1900s 204

13.1 *The Trial of Peter Manuel: The Man Who Talked Too Much*
(London, 1959) 221

14.1 Craiginches Prison, Aberdeen 1963 240

Acknowledgements

While this book is not a collaboration, it would not have come together without the support, encouragement and the reading of draft chapters by several academic historians and legal friends.

First, my sincere thanks are extended to Dr Robert Shiels, retired solicitor and a legal academic, with a keen eye for precise writing and therefore precise meaning. He has read more draft chapters of this book than either he or I would care to reflect on, and he has contributed greatly to sharpening my arguments.

Second, huge gratitude to Dr Bill Knox who has been reading my work since I used to present him with handwritten scrawls in the days before students ever owned laptops. He has seen me through two graduations at the University of St Andrews, Scotland, and will never be rid of me!

Professor Lindsay Farmer and Professor Anne-Marie Kilday have offered historical legal and criminal expertise and interpretations. Thank you for continuing to fit in my requests among all the other demands on your time. Brian Dempsey at the University of Dundee and Dr Ashlyn Cudney at the University of Edinburgh – thank you for your specific insights on nineteenth-century same-sex child abuse and late Scottish witchcraft trials.

And as always, Alison Lindsay and her team at the National Records of Scotland have come up trumps, anticipating my completion of one bundle of pink, string-bound documents, producing a conveyor belt of legal archive for days on end.

At Bloomsbury, Maddie Smith – no, not the nineteenth-century poisoner of Chapter 7 – has been a patient commissioning editor, with a friendly and supportive team – Meg and Niamh, thank you for keeping me and this book on track.

Lastly, Eric and Louis … there's much I could still endlessly tell you about violent crime. Thank you for listening so far.

Introduction: Scottish exceptionalism

Scotland is different from the constituent countries that comprise the UK. Even after the Parliamentary Union of 1707, it has historically behaved differently from the rest of Britain, although that difference is rarely acknowledged in 'British' histories.

Until 1707, Scotland was an independent country north of England, with which since 1603, it had shared its Stuart monarch. However, on 1 May 1707 the Act of Union between Scotland and England united the governments of both countries under the single governance of Parliament at Westminster, finalizing the two countries' connection that had begun with the union of the crowns and ended with the creation of a new country – Great Britain. At the time, it was hoped that the Union would end seven centuries of intermittent warfare and border skirmishes, and that Scotland would become 'north Britain', while others protested against this second political union seeing it as the subsumption of Scotland into England. In the immediate aftermath of the public announcement, protests broke out in some of Scotland's urban centres, notably Edinburgh and Glasgow. They had much to protest against.

First, the Union of 1707 was a response to Scotland's virtual bankruptcy caused by the catastrophic failure of the Darien Scheme. Witnessing the success of the English East India Company in London, in the late 1690s, the Company of Scotland was formed as an opportunity for Scots to exploit Atlantic trade opportunities. Immediately, the Company faced English opposition because of its potential threat to the English monopoly on East India and West Indies trade, and from the Spanish already established in the New World. Thus, when contributions from English investors were withdrawn, the Company's Scottish financiers in London turned to those at home. Pledges were received from across all Scottish social strata, with everyone from tradesmen to farmers, academics, lawyers and aristocrats down to students financially involved. Thus, when the Company's Darien adventure eventually failed, the impact affected the whole of Scotland. With the country now bankrupt, the Union of 1707 was effectively the reflotation of Scotland. Thus, political and economic union was not inevitable, but circumstances at home and on the continent, as the costs of the English war with France increased and Queen Anne failed to produce an heir, made negotiating a Scottish–English settlement pressing.[1]

Second, the Union removed the prospect of King James VII (II of England) and his heirs from the royal succession under article 2, which precluded Roman Catholics from inheriting the crown. Instead, the throne was secured for the Hanoverian, and Protestant, line. Thus, Jacobite hopes of a return of the Catholic Stuart monarchy were dashed, and Jacobite rebellions in 1715 and 1745 were crushed. Defeat at the Battle of Culloden resulted in thousands of deaths, executions and transportation to America, as well as the abolition of the office of the Secretary of State for Scotland at Westminster. That office's duties were absorbed by the Lord Advocate, Scotland's chief state law officer working with the Solicitor General, both of whom were answerable to the Home Secretary.[2]

It might appear that Scotland benefitted little from the Act of Union, having lost its king to an absentee monarchy in England and political control of its people to Westminster. In 1708, further injury was meted out when Scotland's Privy Council was abolished, thereby denying 'Scottish administrative autonomy'. However, Brian Levack comments that the abolition of the Privy Council stopped the operation of local 'conciliar justice', thereby bringing all law under 'central judicial supervision'.[3] This would become beneficial to Scots Law. Further, having four universities to England's two by 1707, Scotland was in a strong position to retain its unique education and legal systems.[4] Scotland also acquired financial security by its connection with England and thereby access to its eastern and western trading centres. Economic growth promoted intellectual expansion, which became known as the Scottish Enlightenment, the cultural values of which were 'tolerance, rationality and progressive improvement'.[5] The eighteenth century produced some of Scotland's most famous philosophers, economists, authors, architects and scientists. It was an Enlightenment enabled through the stability created by the Union of 1707 and whose legacy, it has been suggested, stretches to modern-day Scotland, influencing how Scots perceive themselves in twenty-first-century Britain.[6]

Since 1603, many 'uncouth' Scots had assimilated into English society, becoming absentee landlords, a trend which accelerated after the destruction of the Jacobite cause. On his journey through Scotland in 1772, English antiquary and social observer Thomas Pennant referred to the country as

'North Britain', inferring that Scotland was now subsumed into England.[7] Indeed, after the ruinous impact of the failed risings, many elite Scots began to assume North Britishness 'as a manifestation of the concentric loyalties which allowed Scots to capitalize on' opportunities down south, while also adopting 'an English political identity'.[8] At home, Scotland remained a largely rural, agricultural country.

Webster's census taken in 1755 reveals that more than half of the Scottish population lived north-west of the Highland line running from Stonehaven on the east coast to Dumbarton on the west.[9] Leneman's and Mitchison's research shows a birth rate 'lying in the 30s' per 1,000 population during the eighteenth century.[10] This relatively 'high pressure' birth rate would have placed an increased burden on farming communities, resulting in subdivision of farming tenancies leading to smaller and smaller plots. Combined with greater kelp and fishing production, the boom could only last so long. The potato famine crisis of the 1840s accelerated the need for agricultural improvements and emigration, while immigration from Ireland, where the famine also raged, to Scotland's south-west further exacerbated the situation.[11] The infamous Highland Clearances were the result of a combination of pressures on the land, resulting in internal migration to the south and the Scottish Diaspora, which was both forcibly and voluntarily enacted.

The west coast of Scotland, centred on Glasgow and the Clyde, experienced an economic boom in cotton, sugar and tobacco trade with America, due to advances in shipbuilding and its associated trades and rapid industrialization; while legal, medical and intellectual advances focussed around the capital at Edinburgh. Despite the Victorian romantic ideal of Scotland, of deer parks, mountains, lochs and turreted castles, the reality for many living in its urban centres was grim. This was largely due to population growth and internal Scottish migration. In 1801, the population of Glasgow was 341,000, which by 1851 had expanded to 938,000 and by 1911 had more than doubled to 2,191,000. At the same census points, Edinburgh's population grew from 224,000 to 422,000 to 843,000.[12]

Since the 1850s, economic expansion demanded a sharp increase in the size of the labour force, which led to high levels of internal migration from the Highlands to the Lowlands, and particularly to the Clyde region. Between 1851 and 1881, agricultural labour fell from 30 per cent to 19 per cent of the total workforce, with any significant employment in agriculture restricted to the Borders and Highlands.[13] The pressures placed on Glasgow by this population explosion and rapid, unplanned urbanization resulted in the worst slum living conditions experienced in Europe. By 1911, social commentator Cicely Hamilton described 'forty-seven per cent of the Scottish people' living in homes comprising one or two rooms, while 'south of the Tweed', in England, only 7 per cent lived in comparable slum conditions.[14] Most working-class housing was overcrowded with few shared facilities such as lavatories and water pumps. Middens – rubbish dumps – were situated in tenement back courts where children played and sanitation was poor. Infant mortality in Scotland increased from 118 deaths per thousand live births in 1855–9 to 130 in 1895–9.[15] And this despite Glasgow's claim to be Britain's 'second city of empire'.

The mid-late nineteenth century saw Scotland become 'the workshop of the world' with commercial output focussing on 'a highly specialized and intricately related mix of heavy industry products'.[16] Yet in government, Scotland continued to be governed from Westminster where Members of Parliament in the House of Commons did not always reflect the political affiliations of the Scottish people. While Scotland fuelled the British economy, its government was decidedly English. The feeling that Scottish interests were not properly represented in Parliament led to the home rule for Scotland movement, beginning in the late 1880s. Home rule was supported by many Liberal MPs and the labour movement, but not separation from the rest of the UK. Throughout the nineteenth century, the Scottish electorate returned mostly Liberal MPs to Westminster, but after the Great War in 1918, the growth of socialism due to disillusionment with the war saw the Labour Party take the lead as the Liberal Party disintegrated into warring factions. From the founding of the Scottish Parliamentary Labour Party in 1888 under Keir Hardie, to the Independent Labour Party formed in 1893, the Scottish labour movement grew until, by 1923, the number of Scottish Labour MPs returned to Westminster helped to form the nation's first Labour government.[17]

By 1913, Scotland's shipyards 'accounted for 756,876 launched tonnage', which exceeded the combined 'output of the German and American shipbuilding industries'.[18] Similarly, Dundee experienced rapid economic expansion in the jute industry, but the expansion only resulted in enriching the owners as low wages and slum living became the lot of the working classes. Glasgow dominated personal wealth-holding-at-death figures by 1881, yet that wealth was concentrated in the hands of only 5 per cent of the citizenry who accounted for 80 per cent of the city's wealth. While in Edinburgh, which also possessed pockets of slum dwellings, the main economic focus was cleaner service industries such as law, medicine and government, and the capital's private wealth held by 6 per cent of the population accounted for 63 per cent of the city's total wealth.[19] Urbanization was key to Scotland's success, but the majority of the country, particularly north of the Glasgow–Edinburgh corridor, remained rural into the early twentieth century. Although railways reached into the Highlands, they promoted tourism and markets in the south rather than an internal economy.

The 1920s and 1930s witnessed economic difficulties at all levels, with the working classes looking to trade unionism for representation and numerous

Scottish businessmen, recognizing the 'depressed condition of industry', attempting to intervene with calls for national economic planning. The outbreak of the Second World War in 1939 recreated a new wartime economy and boom, which extended into the 1950s. However, from the 1960s onwards, 'a general attrition of Scottish manufacturing' set in. Since the 1940s, ownership of Scottish manufactories had been in the hands of Scots, but from the 1980s, that changed to American and other overseas ownership. The concomitant effect has been the relaxing of hiring policies based on gender and religion, with many more women – single and married – employed in the new electrical and electronics industries. However, despite these advances, by the 1980s, 'Scotland was estimated to be the worst region in Britain for its disproportionate share of all low paid workers'.[20]

Throughout these changes in nationhood, politics, work and everyday life, two ubiquitous social problems have persisted: drink and crime, the latter being perceived by the nineteenth century as a 'social problem'.[21] Scottish men in particular had a reputation for hard drinking, which could lead to bar and street brawls.[22] Writing in 1903, Arthur Sherwell perceived the drink problem in Scotland as no better than it had been 'two generations ago' and quoted statistics stating that 'the consumption of spirits per head of the population' had been 1.85 gallons in 1901. Sherwell linked working-class expenditure on drink with poverty and crime using the recently published Criminal Statistics to support his argument. They showed that, despite only a 4 per cent rise in population between 1897 and 1901, there had been a 21 per cent rise in the number of people charged with crime, and in the specific offences of 'Drunkenness and Disorder', the increase was 12 per cent.

A late-century buoyant labour market had resulted in 'more money to spend on drink', and by 1900, 63.5 per cent of criminal charges 'were for offences directly connected with drinking'. Sherwell associated the drink problem with a growth in cases of insanity in which for every case of absolute insanity caused by alcohol, there were 'twenty in whom it injures the brain', and in others, it reduced their capacity to work.[23] Drink culture was admittedly a problem in Scotland, although it was also a problem in England, but the statistics supported an elite perception of working-class Scots as an intoxicated, aggressive, impoverished stratum of British society. The temperance movement which began in earnest in the mid-nineteenth century, and which was closely linked to the labour movement, effectively divided the respectable working class from the drinking working class. Respectable working families often signed a pledge, vowing to abstain from the demon drink, and Scotland's burgeoning Labour movement refused to accept drink advertisements in its party newspaper, *Forward*. Teetotalism and Labour politics went hand in hand by the late nineteenth century, with Labour's leader Keir Hardie professing pacificism, nationalism and teetotalism alongside socialism.[24]

However, drink provided an escape to hard-working men avoiding overcrowded homes crawling with children and women hard at domestic chores. By the early twentieth century, the new picture houses and dance halls also provided entertainment for young people as well as opportunities for courtship. And crime. Glasgow's razor gangs of the 1920s and 1930s were infamous. Turf wars often began in dance halls and spilled onto the streets where Glasgow's police struggled to contain the violence.[25]

Thus, a pervasive perception of Scots as an impoverished, drunken, violent people continued into the twentieth century. But that is a popular image often reached for when the Scots raise their collective voice. It speaks to a history, since 1707, of Scots considered from an English perspective. Yet the Scots retain their own education system and print their own bank notes; Scots Law is considered 'genius' by those it protects. Scotland's historical experience has been unique, although irrevocably entwined with England's for over a thousand years. Since 1707, the histories of two nations inhabiting a single, small island have been bound by government statute. At the beginning of the eighteenth century, Scotland was a sovereign nation. For almost three hundred years, it existed as a stateless nation before regaining some of its sovereignty through devolution in 1998. Throughout three centuries, the Scots have never ceased to agitate for nationalism and independence, their exceptionalism always front and centre.

****

It is against this background of Scottish political, economic and social history since 1707 that this book will examine fifteen violent crimes of incest, rape, infanticide, witchcraft, murder and serial killing. Crime is an important measure of a society's degree of civilization: high levels of crime produce perceptions of a barbarous and unruly society, while a nation with a low incidence of crime suggests a regulated, consenting and civilized people. However, criminal statistics only tell part of the story: if they show increasing incidences of crime, is that a real increase or is it the result of better policing? If statistics for a particular type of crime increase before decreasing, does that reflect intensified policing of that specific area of crime – a clean-up-the-streets campaign? Thus, understanding how society responds to crime complements the statistics. Equally, fluctuations in historical levels of crime and potential correlation with moments of political and societal stresses caused by war, famine and protest must be considered.

Societal attitudes can be found in newspaper reporting and memoirs, but it is rare to find a working-class memoir that describes crime and contemporary attitudes, whereas Scotland's criminal case records – the key archival source for this book – often do. First, once the evidence has been adduced, the judge's directions to the jury provide clear legal attitudes, those rooted in law but sometimes stepping beyond its confines to provide personal social comment. Second, the juries' verdicts offer insights into their attitudes towards the victim, accused and the crime before them; recommending a perpetrator of a capital crime to mercy may reflect reluctance to convict when the only sentence is state execution, or it may suggest sympathy for the accused's youth. Where a recommendation to mercy is absent, this might indicate the jury's utter condemnation of the accused and his or her crime. Lastly, the precognition statements – pretrial depositions – often provide brief opinions from eyewitnesses. Because prosecuted crime is mostly a working-class phenomenon, these snippets of working-class opinion are valuable in a judicial process otherwise conducted by the elites.

Except that of Madeleine Smith, the crimes discussed in this book were all committed by working-class individuals and prosecuted by members of the elite. This does not mean that middle- and upper-class individuals did not commit crimes, but there is evidence over the centuries discussed here that elite crime could be prosecuted differently in order to protect reputations.[26] Also, most of the crimes involve female victims of male perpetrators. Historians, criminologists, judicial officers and statisticians acknowledge that men commit most prosecuted, and often unprosecuted, violent crimes. That is not socially to construct all women as vulnerable to male predation, because after all the women in Chapters 2, 3, 7 and 10 are arguably 'dangerous actors' prosecuted for crimes ranging from witchcraft to child murder to poisoning and strangulation. In many ways, the stories of these individuals suggest women with a sense of their own agency. Yet once they entered the judicial system as alleged perpetrators of violence, they were at the mercy of an all-male judicial elite – voiceless and vulnerable individuals whose momentary agency had evaporated. Only Madeleine was acquitted and that is probably attributable to her middle-class status.

In the centuries under review, until the Sex Disqualification (Removal) Act in 1919, juries were all-male, and women did not appear on Scottish juries hearing sexual violence cases until 1921. It was assumed that the introduction of women jurors would bring a more sympathetic judgement to cases involving young children and girls, and that if women formed a majority on any jury, their influence and lack of juridical experience might result in poor verdicts.[27] Thus, criminal prosecutions aid our understanding of the pressures experienced by society and how they might be manifested through verdicts and sentencing; how attitudes towards killing – both interpersonal and judicial – develop across time and how public discourse discovered in newspapers and other commentaries might reflect elite and non-elite sensibilities, and our collective sense of becoming more civilized.

In 1939, Norbert Elias published *Über den Prozess der Zivilisation*, a book that in its use of 'process' in the title implies a linear improvement in civilization. Elias's book was untimely coincident with Europe's second experience of total war within twenty years – the Second World War – just as he argued for a theory of a reduction in violence producing a civilizing effect. Elias's theory outlined a seeming correlation between the reduction of interpersonal violence and the assumption of 'quieter' manners among the elite, which trickled down over the course of two centuries to the working class – a 'transformation … from a class of knights into a class of courtiers'.[28] As duels and recourse to interpersonal violence to resolve conflicts among elite men came under judicial control and the state constructed a monopoly on violence through the army, police force and capital punishment, Elias argued that elite men turned to the law to resolve conflicts.[29] Striving to dissociate themselves from non-elite behaviours as 'pressure from below' by the working classes imitating elite manners encroached, the upper classes adopted increasingly 'new models of conduct'.[30] This affected all social interaction from public violence to table manners. The question that plagues historians is: where is the evidence for the civilizing process?

Elias maintained that 'social transformation' is 'long-term … directional and structured'. However, his linearly improving approach leaves little allowance for short- or long-term reversals. For example, if medieval torture and other brutal judicial punishments and socially violent behaviours have been jettisoned in favour of non-capital punishments and a rejection of street brawling, then why is there a recurring debate on the merits of capital punishment and its continuance in countries such as the United States? Why have murder rates increased since the late twentieth century in Western societies? Why is knife crime, once the resort of pub brawls, increasing among urban young men? Elias emphasized that societies change over time and that tracing 'the interdependent long-term developments' constituting those changes will aid historians in their 'understanding of how social processes are interwoven' instead of seeking correlations of cause and effect.[31] Indeed, historians plot points on the timeline where change is identified before examining potential causes, of which there are most usually more than one. For example, as Eric Monkkonen discovered when analysing homicides perpetrated during street crime in New York during the nineteenth century, many deaths caused by knives that killed then would have been survivable by the late twentieth century. Advances in emergency response times and medical interventions appeared to reduce the number of homicides for a period (outside those victims who died immediately as a result of the assault), and Monkkonen posed the question: 'if violent men knew that medical intervention could thwart their attacks, might they have followed through more decisively, more often?'.[32] Arguably, the use of improved weaponry to produce the same fatal result is far from civilized behaviour.

Many have criticized Elias's work in the intervening decades, not least because of the theory's inability to accommodate minor or major reversals in improving trends. Elias's theory does not consider intra-country differences between rural and urban areas, where elite influences and state control may not have had a uniform impact. Rural areas, especially in Scotland's remote Highlands, may have experienced a time delay implementing intellectual and social changes emanating from London and Edinburgh, which will be examined in the witchcraft trial of Janet Horne (Chapter 2).

Further, Elias's theory appears not to examine gender-based violence. In the period under review, the state legislated for improved conduct towards women and girls, which is an indicator of expansion of elite and judicial responsibilities, but not necessarily of control over male behaviour, leading to a reduction in gendered violence. The rape of Margaret Paterson in 1830 (Chapter 6) and the trial for marital rape in 1989 (Chapter 15) bookend this period of legislation. Further, immigrant communities may not readily have assumed local *mores*. Equally, Scots may have assumed uncivilized and violent behaviour to be an indicator of foreignness as discussed in the trial of Oscar Slater (Chapter 9). Ultimately, the abolition of the death penalty may be seen as a supreme indicator of a state's and nation's level of civilization, a discussion that affects most of the trials investigated in this book. Thus, the historian must carefully analyse historical criminal cases, not necessarily looking for the amount of crime and its measurement, but instead questioning what crime tells us about society: have we become more civilized over time? If so, is that trend linear? If not, what societal challenges have caused momentary or long-term changes?[33]

A note on archival sources and Scots Law

If 'all law is the product of particular philosophical, religious and political views' and 'the very idea of crime is a social construct', then the law of a land is not immutable.[34] The common law, based on what society understands to be morally correct, and statute law, in which society has decided certain behaviours are criminal, are both subject to the changing attitudes of the society they serve. Thus, historians of crime must look to contemporaneous primary sources and legal commentaries in order to analyse and understand the crime, the criminal, the victim and the law in their own time.[35]

The key sources for this book are the criminal records of the High Court of Justiciary, which are 'an historical monument of the ideas of' the Scottish people and 'their manners and jurisprudence' from 1707 to 1989.[36] Through studying the precognition statements, which as Bill Knox comments contain invaluable details producing 'a much clearer picture of the social backgrounds' of those involved in the criminal-legal process, and judicial papers, it has been possible to recreate the circumstances of the fifteen cases explored in this book.[37] These have been augmented by the use of newspaper reports and other contemporaneous writings such as memoirs. Additionally, criminal statistics have been carefully used to explore contemporary crime trends.

Scots Law contains principals and details, which differ from English law. Notably precognitions are taken by the Procurator Fiscal, a public law officer, as near in time as possible once a crime is reported to him.[38] The Procurator Fiscal then reports his findings to Crown Counsel, often with a recommendation for the appropriate charge and court in which to prosecute. From the early nineteenth century, once a working police force was created, the public reported crimes to the police, who in turn reported to the Procurator Fiscal, who initiated an investigation often using police resources to seek out evidence.

All the cases discussed in this book were tried at the High Court of Justiciary where the most serious crimes are prosecuted, either in Edinburgh or on circuit at key cities around the country, notably Glasgow, Dundee, Aberdeen, Perth, Stirling and Inverness. The Lord Advocate or the Advocate Depute prosecuted the panel – the accused – in the public interest before a jury of fifteen men, which latterly included women. The jury's deliberations are never revealed; neither is the jury's division divulged if not a unanimous verdict. It would be inadvisable to reveal the jury's division, particularly if on a majority of eight to seven and especially in capital cases. The jury's verdict has always remained unquestioned. Three verdicts are available to a Scottish jury: not guilty and not proven, both of which are an acquittal, and guilty. It should be noted that while not proven might reflect the indecision of the jury, it is more likely that this verdict reveals the Crown's deficiency in proving its case sufficiently for the jury to convict 'beyond reasonable doubt'.

When not charged under statute law, such as the Incest Act 1567, Scots Law is based on the common law and has traditionally been interpreted through the institutional writers: MacKenzie, Hume, Alison, Cockburn and, in the twentieth century, Gordon.[39] While Scots Law rests on the shoulders of these giants, in recent decades, social behaviours have changed unrecognizably from the society in which these men lived; and so, the law is mutable, an apposite point made in the final chapter. Further, in Scotland the panel may be tried simultaneously on multiple indictments. Not only does this prevent the introduction of further accusations in court, but it also requires defence counsel to exonerate his client on all counts in order to be acquitted.[40]

The Scottish trial has largely been seen as less performative than an English one, being more inquisitorial than adversarial. The evidence adduced is only that contained in the precognition statements and other reports gathered pretrial, such as doctors' reports and post-mortems. All evidence must be corroborated either by an eyewitness or by medical or other corroboration.

However, Lindsay Farmer notes the enduring fascination with 'the spectacle of crime and punishment' from the eighteenth century into the twentieth.[41] Once capital punishment moved inside from 1868 onwards, the public engaged with criminal prosecutions through often sensationalist news reportage. This becomes most clear from 1857 onwards in the trial of Madeleine Smith (Chapter 7). The newsreader could now concoct his or her own judgement 'and directly participate in the trial process' from their breakfast table. After the 1898 Criminal Evidence Act, the accused might too become 'an important participant' if he or she decided to give evidence.[42] Hearing the voice of the accused became a further fascination.

From the middle of the nineteenth century, the debate surrounding the abolition of the death penalty grew, and cases with a potential capital sentence frequently attracted public petitions calling for a reprieve or commutation of sentence. Thus, public sentiment became further insinuated into the political responses to violent crime. It has been argued that until the mid-twentieth century, it was 'the politicians and their civil servants who would be tempted towards liberality', while the judiciary 'could be trusted to understand the sentiments and anxieties of society'. As the Parliamentary vote on abolition drew closer, 'the balance was to be progressively reversed' with politicians seeking longer sentences, while the judiciary responded to new public opinion.[43]

The crimes discussed here involve real people, and sensitivity to their predicaments and reputations is necessary. This becomes increasingly important with the twentieth-century cases where relations, and indeed the protagonists, may still be alive. In particular, the final case discussed has been anonymized for these reasons. The historian must also be aware of bias, which may be especially emotive in prosecutions for rape (Chapters 6, 8, 11 and 12) and incest (Chapter 1). Historical evidence, not just criminal evidence, may be misinterpreted, leading to wrongful conclusions. Equally, historians may select sources to prove a preconceived argument rather than attend to the widest collection of evidence to inform their thinking. Further, creating causal explanations based on selective research is poor practice; all lines of debate should be pursued. And the historian must always ask: who is talking to us? What is the motivation of those voices recorded in the archives? 'Mistakes in biased history are motivated, not accidental', and care particularly when dealing with real people is essential.[44]

Because of the nature of the crimes discussed in this book, care has also been taken to include the more unsavoury details only where necessary for the reader to better understand a specific point. Otherwise, the salacious has been avoided. Equally, presentism is absent in this book. Presentism may reflect an interpretation of history in which the past 'is the yellow brick road leading to the present'. It may also be interpreted as 'the pressure exerted by the present on historians' construction of the past', thereby injecting modern ideas and values into the exploration of a past, which did not anticipate such societal changes.[45] Therefore, in this book the past is the past; the cases are discussed in the context of their own time.

Thus, the violent crimes described in each chapter have been selected not only to assist understanding of specific events in Scottish history but also to explore social behaviour and attitudes as well as societal and juridical responses in the modern period.

The fifteen chapters chronologically explore specific cases under a common, cohesive theme of interpersonal criminal violence. These cases may be the 'last' or the 'first' in their category such as the last witch-burning in Scotland in 1727 described in Chapter 2 or the first prosecution for marital rape in 1989 discussed in Chapter 15. Others pinpoint moments of societal challenges such as the Tron Riots in Chapter 4 and commercialized body-snatching in Chapter 5. The book explores the possible development of a more civilized and quieter society in terms of interpersonal violence across three centuries, beginning with four important trials for incest and rape, witchcraft, child murder and rioting. Thus, Chapters 1 through 4 set the scene, establishing notions of the role of law, morality and gendered crime in a society emerging from economic disaster after the failure of the Darien Scheme into the Scottish Enlightenment. There is a gap in the chronology during the eighteenth century, not because serious interpersonal violence did not occur, but because notable trials that speak to societal changes and challenges are less obvious from the court records. This is a period when Georgian society was preoccupied with two Jacobite uprisings and their repercussions on elite society, Continental wars, imperial expansion and the threat of exported revolutionary politics from Britain's nearest neighbour, France.

From Chapter 5 onwards, the selected cases study more granular developments in social attitudes towards violent crime, exploring aspects of increasing tolerance of difference; interclass tensions; the agency and emancipation of women; rape myths and rape scripts; masculinity, misogyny and patriarchy; and legal developments designed to punish individuals who continued to behave outside expected and changing norms.

Notes

1 T. M. Devine, *Scotland's Empire 1600–1815* (London, 2003), 49–56.

2 J. G. Kellas, *Modern Scotland* (London, 1980), 88; J. Smyth and A. McKinlay, 'Whigs, Tories and Scottish Legal Reform', *Crime, Histoire & Societies*, vol. 15, no. 1 (2011), 113.

3 B. P. Levack, *Witch-Hunting in Scotland: Law, Politics and Religion* (Abingdon, 2008), 159.
4 The universities of St Andrews, Aberdeen, Glasgow and Edinburgh, compared to England's Oxford and Cambridge universities. Durham became England's third university only in 1832.
5 B. P. Lenman, 'From the Union of 1707 to the Franchise Reform of 1832', in *The New Penguin History of Scotland from the earliest times to the present day*, ed. R. A. Houston and W. W. J. Knox (London, 2001), 278.
6 Lenman, 'From the Union of 1707', 266.
7 T. Pennant, *A Tour in Scotland and Voyages to the Hebrides, 1772* (Edinburgh, 2019), 35, 93, 131, 135, 155, 159, 182, 290, 310, 329, 335, 337, 355, 358, 362.
8 C. Kidd, 'North Britishness and the Nature of Eighteenth-Century British Patriotisms', *Historical Journal*, vol. 39, no. 2 (1996), 363.
9 County-by-county population tables, A. Webster, *An Account of the Number of People in Scotland in the Year One Thousand Seven Hundred and Fifty Five* (Edinburgh, 1755), 1–69.
10 L. Leneman and R. Mitchison, 'Scottish Illegitimacy Ratios in the Early Modern Period', *Economic History Review*, vol. 40, no. 1 (February 1987), 43–4, 48.
11 Devine, *Scotland's Empire*, 124; R. H. Campbell and T. M. Devine, 'The Rural Experience', in *People and Society in Scotland*, vol. II, 1830–1914, ed. W. H. Fraser and R. J. Morris (Edinburgh, 1990), 51.
12 Kellas, *Modern Scotland*, table 2.2, 14.
13 W. W. Knox, *Industrial Nation: Work, Culture and Society in Scotland, 1800–Present* (Edinburgh, 1999), 87.
14 C. Hamilton, *Modern Scotland* (London, 1937), 29.
15 T. C. Smout, *A Century of the Scottish People 1830–1950* (London, 1986), 50.
16 K. Burgess, 'Workshop of the World: Client Capitalism at its Zenith, 1830–1870', in *Scottish Capitalism: Class, State and Nation from before the Union to the Present*, ed. T. Dickson (London, 1980), 181–3.
17 Kellas, *Modern Scotland*, 124, 130, 139–41.
18 Knox, *Industrial Nation*, 132.
19 N. Morgan and R. Trainor, 'The Dominant Classes', in *People and Society in Scotland*, ed. Fraser and Morris, 114–15.
20 Knox, *Industrial Nation*, 226–7, 254, 258.
21 L. Farmer, 'Responding to the Problem of Crime: English Criminal Law and the Limits of Positivism', in *The Limits of Criminological Positivism: The Movement for Criminal Law Reform in the West, 1870–1940*, ed. M. Pifferi (Abingdon, 2021), chapter 8.
22 L. Abrams and E. Ewan, 'Interrogating Men and Masculinities in Scottish History', in *Nine Centuries of Man: Manhood and Masculinities in Scottish History*, ed. L. Abrams and E. Ewan (Edinburgh, 2018), 1.
23 A. Sherwell, *The Drink Peril in Scotland* (Edinburgh, 1903), 7–19.

24 Knox, *Industrial Nation*, 96, 168–9.
25 A. Davies, *City of Gangs: Glasgow and the Rise of the British Gangster* (London, 2014), 76–7.
26 L. Heren, *Sex and Violence in 1920s Scotland: incest, rape, lewd and libidinous practices, 1918–1930* (London, 2024), 28–31.
27 Heren, *Sex and Violence*, 193–5.
28 E. A. Johnson and E. H. Monkkonen, *The Civilization of Crime: Violence in Town and Country since the Middle Ages* (Illinois, 1996), 4.
29 J. Fletcher, *Violence and Civilization: an introduction to the work of Norbert Elias* (Cambridge, 1997), 35.
30 P. Spierenburg, *Violence & Punishment: civilizing the body through time* (Cambridge, 2013), 143.
31 Spierenburg, *Violence & Punishment*, 85.
32 E. Monkkonen, 'New Standards for Historical Homicide Research', *Crime, History and Societies*, vol. 5, no. 2 (2001), 18–19.
33 Johnson and Monkkonen, *Civilization of Crime*, 6.
34 L. Blom-Cooper and T. Morris, *With Malice Aforethought: A Study of the Crime and Punishment for Homicide* (Oxford, 2004), 31–2.
35 R. Shiels, 'Historic Defective Representation: the defence case for Oscar Slater', *Scots Law Times*, News (2025), 167.
36 H. Arnot, *A Collection and Abridgement of Celebrated Criminal Trials in Scotland from AD1536 to AD1784, with historical and critical remarks* (Edinburgh, 1785), n.32, xv.
37 W. W. Knox, '"The Attack of the Half-Formed Persons": the 1811–12 Tron Riot in Edinburgh Revisited', *Scottish Historical Review*, vol. 91, no. 232, part 2 (October 2012), 290.
38 R. Shiels, 'The Mid-Victorian Codification of the Practice of Public Prosecution', *Scottish Historical Review*, vol. 98, supplement 248 (October 2019), 426.
39 These institutional commentators are referred to within each chapter where chronologically appropriate.
40 A. M. Kilday, *Crime in Scotland 1660–1960: the Violent North?* (Abingdon, 2021), 60–1.
41 L. Farmer, 'Notable Trials and the Criminal Law in Scotland and England, 1750–1950', in *Law and Society in France and Great Britain, XII–XX Centuries*, ed. P. Chassaigne and J. P. Genet (December 2020), 149.
42 Farmer, 'Notable Trials', 160–1.
43 Blom-Cooper and Morris, *With Malice Aforethought*, 119.
44 C. Behan McCullagh, 'Bias in Historical Description, Interpretation and Explanation', *History and Theory*, vol. 39, no. 1 (February 2000), 40.
45 D. Armitage, 'The Impulse of the Present', *Historical Transactions*, blog post 26 July 2023. Available online: https://blog.royalhistsoc.org/2023/07/26/the-impulse-of-the-present/ (accessed February 2025).

1

John Martine 1709: Incest, relations and the law

Set just after the tumult of the Union of the Parliaments in 1707, this chapter explores the definitions of incest and rape in Scots Law and how an abused young woman could be prosecuted, alongside her uncle, for this capital crime by the elites of her own community. It emphasizes the differences between Scots and English law at a pivotal moment as the Scottish administration endeavoured to retain its uniqueness.

Context

While sixty-seven-year-old John Martine was in court in Perth in 1709 listening to the evidence given for and against him for the crime of incest with his sixteen-year-old niece Elspeth and awaiting the jury's verdict, another male accused from St Andrews, also standing trial for incest, was acquitted. Either one man was guilty and the other innocent of what they were accused, or there was something irregular going on with prosecutions for incest in Scotland two years after the 1707 Act of Union.

The crime of incest – sexual intercourse between two related people – had been a secular crime in Scotland since 1567; it was not a criminal indictment in England and Wales and would not become so until 1908. The Act simply states that:

> Quhatsumeuer person or personis thay be that abusis their body with sic personis in degre as Goddis word hes expreslie forbiddin in ony tyme cuming as is contenit in the xviij Cheptour of Leuiticus salbe puneist.[1]

By 1797, Baron David Hume, at the time Scotland's greatest legal authority, described incest as 'the crime of carnal knowledge between persons who are near of kin', and within the forbidden degrees.[2] The restrictions on which relations could have intimate sexual associations were defined by Leviticus chapter 18 in the Bible, which provides guidance on the prohibition of fathers and sons having sexual relations with their mothers, daughters and sisters, and a nephew having intercourse with his aunt on either his mother's or father's side of the family, but nothing concerning an uncle and niece either committing incest by consanguinity, as blood relations, or by affinity, related only through marriage. This particular relationship was not specifically prohibited by Leviticus and thus was not contained within the 1567 Act.[3] Yet by the early eighteenth century, if both parties were over the age of consent, then an uncle and niece, whether blood-related or not, could both be charged with incest and potentially convicted.

As Hume explained, in pre-Protestant times, 'the restraint was carried to a far greater length, than any reason of policy or morality required'. Thus 'Popery' had treated incest as a spiritual sin, capturing a wider range of relationships than the Reformation settlement in Scotland intended in its 1567 Act 'Anent them that committis incest'. However, while 'Popery' had punished incest 'with the weapons of spiritual censure', by making incest a statute law in Scotland, it removed incest prosecutions from the governance of the Reformation Presbyterian Kirk, placing incest within the jurisdiction of the secular courts. The Act was intended 'to abolish the very wide categories of relationships' that had been deemed incestuous in canon law, but the new statute also made incest a capital crime. Thus if convicted, death became the only possible punishment.[4]

However, having found the Act to contain 'imperfections', which might be interpreted as not capturing all aspects of incest that the courts were encountering or that societal leaders wished to address, in 1649 the Act was amended. The timing of this revised Act is pertinent. After nearly a decade of civil wars, the Covenantors in Scotland aimed to construct a more godly society, and part of that socio-ecclesiastical settlement was evidenced by the extension of the original Act to incorporate 114 individual relationships prohibited as incest in the revised 1649 Act. However, a decade later after the Restoration of Charles II to the throne, the Rescissory Act of 1661 rescinded all interregnum legislation.[5] By reverting to the 1567 narrower interpretation of incestuous relationships, arguably the Martines' case should not have been libelled since it was not specifically described and therefore was not a secularly prosecutable crime. Yet it appears that either the extended list of prohibited relationships from 1649 lingered in the minds of some or that those prosecuting held to a stricter interpretation of the original 1567 Act and intended to influence the court accordingly. Thus, John and Elspeth Martine appeared in Perth at the north circuit hearings of the High Court of Justiciary before Judge Gilbert Eliot.

Case

From the brief, extant court papers, both John and Elspeth Martine were libelled for incest equally, as well as adultery. However, it was recorded that John had had forcible intercourse with Elspeth on two, and possibly more, occasions. John had both 'times also throw [sic] her down violently by force and that she cryed [sic] both times and there was none in the house with them', which importantly meant there were no witnesses to corroborate either parties' version of events. John had also 'begat the child upon her', making his niece pregnant.[6] John Martine, a married blacksmith from Dundee, was the half-brother of Elspeth's father, making him her half-uncle. He was approximately fifty years older than Elspeth and had used his superior position to force her into having intercourse with him. Elspeth's dittay, or statement, describes briefly his use of force on several occasions, but either she did not offer the detail or likelier it was not asked because crucially she did not explain if she had struggled to fend off his advances.

James Erskine defended John using a literal interpretation of the 1567 Act and its absence of uncle–niece incest. Elphinstone, the Advocate Depute prosecuting for the Crown, countered that the Bible described 'copulation betwixt such degrees as are forbidden in God's word', which was a loose interpretation that could capture uncle–niece incest which, if proven, would be punished by pain of death.[7] Yet, Leviticus chapter 18 did not expressly describe uncle–niece sexual relations as incestuous. The catch-all interpretation was a construal of Leviticus 18 verse 6, which Brian Levack has argued might have been Elphinstone's intention. Verse 6 reads 'none shall come nere to anie of the kindred of his flesh to uncover (her) shame', which meant that no man should sexually approach *any* female relation, by consanguinity or affinity.[8] If this interpretation were successful, both John and Elspeth would be executed. Levack has also suggested that verse 14 might have served to incriminate Elspeth alone, since 'thou shalt not uncover the shame of thy fathers brother', which meant John.[9] This verse might also be read to imply that Elspeth had been the initiator of their sexual intimacy. However, Levack appears not to have considered the second part of verse 14: 'thou shalt not go into his wife, for she is thine ante'.[10] Unsurprisingly, verse 14, like all Old Testament verses, is written from a male perspective and 'the shame of thy fathers brother' infers assault of his wife who would also be the incestuous male perpetrator's aunt. Thus, it is unlikely that Elspeth could have been found guilty under Leviticus 14:18.

Both parties were libelled equally, and Elspeth's dittay confirmed sexual intercourse had indeed occurred, making them both culpable if the libel were proven. The Advocate Depute had argued that the relationship of uncle and niece was incestuous, whereas Erskine maintained that the Act did not describe this relationship and therefore incest was not relevant. However, only ninety years after their trial, Hume based his argument on legal tradition stating that nephew and aunt incest was a criminal offence and 'the prohibition of either' would 'imply the other', meaning that uncle–niece incest was also criminal, and whether full or half-blood or by affinity was irrelevant.[11] In Scots Law, the relational prohibitions were 'all regarded as symmetrical'.[12] Therefore, Elspeth's statement that her uncle forced her into sexual intercourse is the only extant detail of their trial that seems to have turned the case in her favour. As Levack has most convincingly argued, if their closeness of familial relationship was not considered to be within the degrees of incest, then John had raped Elspeth. Yet the common law crime of rape was hard to prove on the woman's statement alone; Elspeth's dittay confirmed the absence of witnesses, and no one had come to her aid when she cried out. Thus, if the court followed Erskine's defence that uncle–niece sexual intercourse was not incestuous, a charge of rape would have been unlikely to proceed because there was no evidence, just an accusation against an older man by his young niece and the matter of the pregnancy.[13]

Levack suggests that the court was 'determined to prosecute both John and Elspeth Martine'.[14] It is a plausible supposition based on the prosecution's determination to interpret uncle–niece incest as criminal. However, the records are ambiguous concerning Elspeth's predicament. If she were still pregnant, the death penalty would have been postponed until after the infant's birth, but if she were postpartum at the time of the trial, then by condemning Elspeth, if the baby had survived, the parish would be left with an orphaned infant to support.

By prosecuting for incest, the Advocate Depute and John's defence had highlighted the elasticity of the 1567 Act and its ongoing variable interpretation. A previous incest prosecution in April 1640, before the 1649 revisions to the original Act, involved an uncle, James Strang, and his brother's daughter. Strang was convicted and beheaded for uncle–niece incest. This case was reported by Scotland's earlier legal authority, Lord Advocate Sir George MacKenzie, but either Elphinstone was unaware of the precedent or the Martines' case papers failed to record this part of the proceedings.[15] Having considered the scant evidence adduced, the trial was adjourned giving the jury time to contemplate their own interpretation of the 1567 Act, the meaning of Leviticus chapter 18 and whether Elspeth's claim of physical as well as sexual violence was supported.

The next day, it became apparent that the jury believed Elspeth's statement that she had been forcibly and sexually assaulted because they returned a guilty verdict against John and acquitted Elspeth. The judges 'assoilzied the said Elspeth Martine and ordain her to be dismissed from the barr', while John was sentenced to be hanged 'betwixt two and four in the afternoon' on 8 June with all of his 'movable goods & gear to be escheat and inbrought to her Majesty'.[16] Apart from John's fate, it is unknown what became of Elspeth after the trial or her baby.

Themes and analysis

It is impossible to understand how much sexual violence was perpetrated against women in the early eighteenth century because statistical evidence for reports of sexual crime is unavailable. A simple count of prosecuted

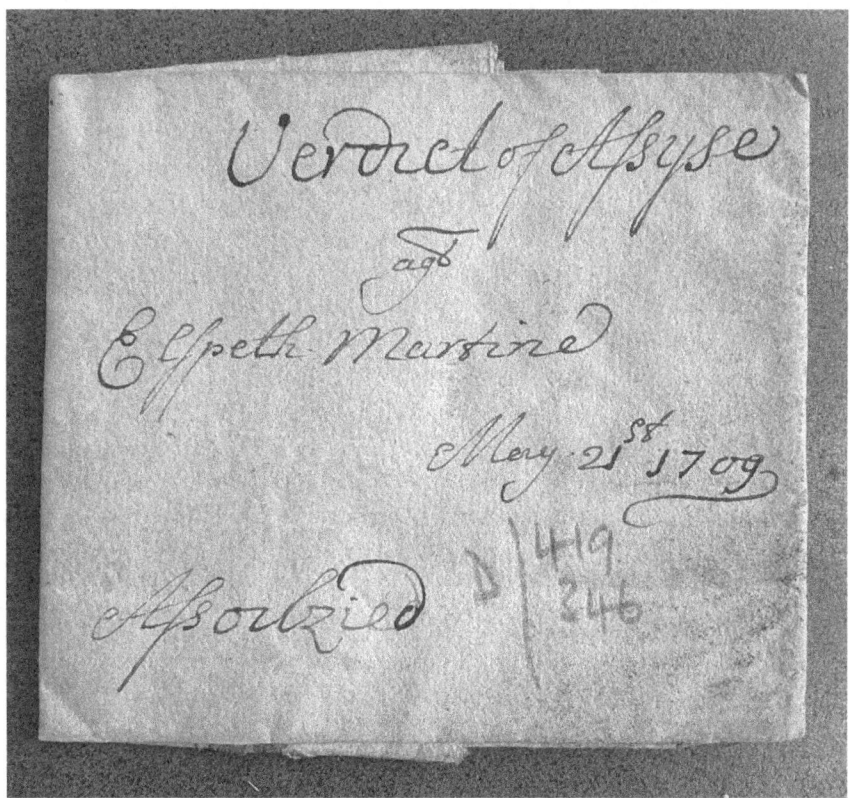

ILLUSTRATION 1.1 *Verdict of Assize, Elspeth Martine. Crown Copyright. National Records of Scotland, JC26/90.*

cases does not include the 'dark number' of assaults, which never became official and never went beyond the family's or local community's knowledge, if reported even to them. Reporting sexual assault demanded, and demands, considerable resilience and resourcefulness from the victim to recognize what had occurred as sexual violence, then to report it to someone who would listen before potentially reaching court where a jury might only return a not guilty or not proven verdict. Forensic medical analysis was impossible in this period and would be for another 150 years. Therefore, a successful conviction was unlikely on the female victim's testimony alone. When sexual assault prosecutions proceeded to court, they were largely his word against hers and a trial of character: did she look and behave as though she had been sexually assaulted; did he look like a rapist? And were both their reputations impeccable or did they suggest respectively loose and violent behaviours?

Elspeth did not struggle, or at least those interviewing her did not ask whether she had tried to repel her uncle's advances; it is also possible that this question and its answer were asked but not recorded. When attempting to prove unlawful sexual intercourse – rape – where the victim was above the age of consent, proof of the woman's efforts to fight off her assailant was always recorded in nineteenth- and twentieth-century cases. Exploring notions of consent in eighteenth-century Britain, Katie Barclay argues that 'legal treatises advised that female silence' and lack of 'active physical, and particularly vocal, resistance' could be construed as consent in some circumstances.[17] Elspeth was sixteen and therefore above the contemporary age of consent, yet the case papers do not include evidence of her struggling, although they do record her crying out for help, but no one heard. In later incest cases, generally the precognoscers did not ask younger victims whether they had attempted to fend off their attacker, presumably because the act of incest was sufficiently heinous and bringing a libel against a close relation was no easy emotional or legal task. Evidence contained in later incest cases suggests that the added detail of the girl's struggles was not required because she would be unlikely to resist a father, uncle or grandfather due to familial deference and shock at the assault by a 'loving' relation.[18] Did no one ask whether Elspeth had struggled against her uncle because they understood her deference to his superior position?

John's defence that uncle–niece intercourse was not incest might have won them both an acquittal, but the introduction of Elspeth's testimony of forcible sexual violence committed against her and the physical evidence of her pregnancy turned the case in her favour. Juries' deliberations were, and are, never disclosed, so it is impossible to know whether any one of the fifteen male jurors impugned her character and statement, or indeed John's, during their debate. What can be known is that they returned a guilty verdict 'by plurality', that is, by majority; unanimity was, and is, not required in Scots

Law.[19] The jury's verdict strongly indicates that they believed Elspeth to have been unconsenting to intercourse with her uncle, despite there being no recorded evidence of her struggling to evade his advances. Compared with research conducted on incest cases between 1860 and 1930, this verdict is neither surprising nor expected. In this later period, fathers and stepfathers, the latter having no blood relation to their stepdaughter victims, appear to have been treated on the merit of the evidence only, without any inference from the verdicts that direct blood incest might be viewed as more reprehensible or more provable than stepfather incest. Similarly, uncle–niece incest cases, some with half-blood relations, were treated alike.[20] In 1709 and extending into the twentieth century, Scots Law treated incest by consanguinity and affinity equally. Therefore, John's half-uncle's remove from Elspeth could not be argued as any mitigation.

Thus, it is reasonable to assume that the element of forcible violence was pivotal to John's conviction and Elspeth's acquittal, because up until the admission of Elspeth's dittay, the argument had revolved around interpretations of Leviticus chapter 18 alone. Levack suggests that the authorities were determined to prosecute and that incest was the only indictment on which they might convict both parties, because a rape charge solely against John would be virtually impossible to prove. As Edward Cox commented 150 years later, 'actual rape is so nearly impossible that it should be accepted only on the most conclusive evidence'. Cox alluded to a struggling woman being impossible to penetrate and therefore a woman who did not struggle had consented.[21] But incest was the only libel available to the Martines' prosecutors, if indeed they were determined to convict both, because John and Elspeth were known by their community to be blood-related. Elspeth's dittay confirmed: 'she knows John Martine also pannell to be her fathers half brother'.[22] Further, neither of them had rejected the accusation of sexual relations. Only Elspeth's testimony of physically violent coercion shifted the blame for their crime solely onto John. Whether the jury believed Elspeth's testimony on its merit alone or whether they possessed knowledge of John's previous character and behaviour, perhaps a capacity for brutality, which further influenced their decision cannot be known. A majority of the jury understood Elspeth to have been forcibly coerced into sexual intercourse with her uncle for which the only punishment could be death.[23]

Arguably, it was unusual for a jury to believe the testimony of a young woman above that of an older, married, established man, so does this trial suggest that female agency in the early eighteenth century might have been greater than historians have hitherto believed? No. It is a single case on which such a grand assumption cannot be hung. However, it is evidence that early eighteenth-century male Scottish juries were not so closed-minded towards female victims of sexual violence that they were all cast as alluring vixens complicit to some degree in their own assault. Elspeth's case also provides evidence of male juries' openness to notions of female non-consent. The court papers suggest that Elspeth had not struggled and equally in 1709 that evidence of struggling was not necessary to 'prove' a victim's non-consent to intercourse. It was a situation that would slowly reverse over the course of the following century, so that by 1858, in a rape case *R v. Sweenie*, one judge could maintain that evidence of violence against the victim was essential to a rape charge, and that no physical injuries implied no resistance, thereby confirming consent. In the same case, Scotland's Lord President countered that where no resistance was offered, no violence would be necessary, yet rape may have occurred.[24] The Lord President's attitude indicated that the victim's blind panic at being sexually assaulted could mean she gave no resistance. This is not a return to the situation in Elspeth's trial in 1709, but it appears that between the early eighteenth century and the mid nineteenth century, judicial and juridical attitudes towards female victims of sexual violence had hardened during the height of Scotland's Enlightenment.

In 1709, Scotland was only two years into its union with England and nearly half a century away from the Cromwellian jurisdiction that had witnessed Scots and English law at their closest. Before the Restoration, the Kirk session was viewed as a 'responsible local body' which acted as an 'intermediate judiciary' between local authorities and the central judicial administration.[25] However, after the Glorious Revolution, in 1690 the Presbyterian Kirk had been confirmed as the established church of Scotland operating alongside the episcopalian church. In 1707, the Kirk had been one of the Scottish institutions whose autonomy was protected by the Act of Union, along with Scottish education and Scots Law. As Alasdair Raffe has argued, the Presbyterian 'kirk-sessions may have had a moral authority' that did not interest the episcopalian church to the same degree, and as Christopher Smout has explained, the Presbyterians intended to use their power 'to lead Scotland back to a narrower path of morality' than they had experienced before the Restoration.[26] This would suggest that Presbyterian Kirk leaders might have viewed the Martines' case as a moral investigation.

Mitchison's and Leneman's research on sexual relations from 1660 to 1780 reveals that the Presbyterian Kirk was concerned with stability in marriage and may have regarded incestuous relationships and concomitant intra-familial rivalries as hugely disruptive, with the potential to tear families apart.[27] Yet despite the Kirk's interest in creating a godly society and with both rape and incest attracting a large degree of moral condemnation, the Kirk was legally prevented from adjudicating on either crime. A libel on a lesser sexual assault charge might have fallen within the purlieu of the ecclesiastical courts, but incest was statute law and rape was common law. Both could only be prosecuted in the High Court of Justiciary.

Thus, the Martines' incest trial appears fortuitously to have occurred at a pivotal moment in Scottish history when the secularization of Scottish society, which may not yet have been apparent at the community level, was becoming increasingly so at a judicial-national level and in urban areas. Smout quotes the 'lamentation' of the General Assembly of the Kirk at people promenading the streets of Edinburgh and walking the shore at Leith on the Sabbath, evidence that the strictures of the Puritan Kirk were waning in some areas of society. By arguing that John's assault on Elspeth had not been incestuous, his defence had relied on an earlier, pre-Puritan Presbyterian interpretation of Leviticus. Had Erskine anticipated that this gradual loosening of the morals of Scottish society would help the Perth jury to reframe John's behaviour more leniently?

An 'Act for the Queen's most gracious general and free Pardon', passed in 1708, extended a 'pardon of all crimes to all subjects' until 19 April 1709.[28] The Martines' trial took place on 20 and 21 May 1709, although their alleged incest may have occurred before the April cut-off date. The legislation offered a general pardon for a wide range of acts of violence against the state and among the population as well as financial crimes, but crucially, two crimes pertinent to this trial were excepted: neither rape nor incest was pardoned. The planned invasion of Britain by both Scottish and English Jacobite supporters of James VIII to restore the Stuart monarchy had failed in March 1708, and the Act had been intended to restore the peace without further reprisals. However, by actively exempting incest in the 1708 Act, the legislators had clearly had Scotland in mind since incest was not an indictable crime in England.

John's and Elspeth's crime was not captured by the general pardon, although for over 300 individuals already tried that morning, the Act had resulted in their acquittal. Their crimes ranged from adultery and fornication to witchcraft and theft, and their being on the lists for the court session indicates an intention to prosecute. The publication of the general pardon changed the fate of these 300 individuals. Levack has argued that this was the beginning of 'the *de facto* decriminalisation' of lesser sexual libels in the secular courts, and he offers strong evidence of other similar moral crimes attracting either acquittal or milder sentences than 'the kirk sessions customarily assigned' in the period after the queen's general pardon.[29] However, the Martines' case combined with another incest case heard the same day, that of John Laing from St Andrews, probably does not indicate 'that the secular courts were becoming more lenient in dealing with incest' as Levack suggests.[30] Instances of both male and female parties being found guilty of incest even when there was clear evidence of physical violence by the male continued into the 1920s. However, the debate about the relevancy of incest between relations by affinity saw at least two cases in 1920s Scotland convicted but then assoilzied and dismissed without incarceration. These case papers provide evidence of the judges' adherence to the law alongside acceptance of relaxing moral attitudes in the 1920s towards sex between non-blood relations.[31] In Laing's 1709 acquittal, the evidence may simply have not convinced the jury of his guilt, whereas Elspeth's dittay of violence contributed to her uncle's conviction. Probably more important than a potential change in legal attitudes towards minor sexual crimes such as fornication and adultery is the timing of the queen's general pardon.

Conclusion

The Laing and Martines' incest trials of 20 May 1709 provide insights into the legal interpretation of Biblical law at the start of the eighteenth century and suggest that while the debate continued, the division of ecclesiastical power from secular authority was incomplete. However, Queen Anne's 1708 general pardon was a clear indication that the future of judicial power was definitely secular and that it applied to all of the newly UK of Great Britain. Granting a general amnesty to assuage any vestige of Jacobitism also suggested that the notion of one kingdom united by a single polity emanating from London was open to all. The 1708 Act may be viewed as a consensus-building gesture. Scotland had endured the embarrassment and physical suffering brought about by the failure of the Darien Scheme and subsequent bankruptcy. Jacobitism would continue to divide areas of the country. The Act of Union of 1707, in part, had resolved many of those problems. Free of those encumbrances, Scotland emerged as a leader of the eighteenth-century Enlightenment.

After the Union, with ecclesiastical restraints loosened on secular life, the Martines' trial coincides with the beginning of a long period of cultural and academic flourishing in Scotland, which Smout describes as comparable 'in brilliance with any other such intellectual constellation in a small country' elsewhere in Europe.[32] Six of the crimes against the 300 listed at Perth were based on scripture, and Levack argues that the general pardons given proved 'these scriptural injunctions ... to be irrelevant'.[33] Whether their irrelevance can be proved on the basis of six cases remains debatable, but by acquitting over 300 individuals charged with a range of non-dangerous crimes through the queen's amnesty suggests some enthusiasm for a new and efficient judiciary focussed on trying the crimes that mattered at the High Court of Justiciary.

Set against the late seventeenth-century political and religious upheavals, the parliamentary unification of both kingdoms and war in the Low Countries, the Martines' trial for incest was not the tipping point that changed ecclesiastical and judicial attitudes. But it marks a moment in history when Scotland was accommodating itself to its new political identity and legal arrangements before settling into over a century of intellectual ascendancy.

Notes

1. Incest Act 1567.
2. Baron D. Hume, *Commentaries on the Law of Scotland, respecting the description and punishment of crimes*, vol. 2 (Edinburgh, 1797), 289.
3. Hume, *Commentaries*, 291; G. H. Gordon, *The Criminal Law of Scotland*, 2nd edition (Edinburgh, 1978), 35–2, 897.
4. Hume, *Commentaries*, 288–9; Gordon, *Criminal Law*, 35-01, 896.
5. I. F. Grant, 'Law of Incest in Scotland', *Juridical Review*, vol. 26 (1914), 447.
6. JC26/90.
7. JC11/1, 85.
8. *King James Holy Bible*, Leviticus 18:6.
9. B. P. Levack, 'The Prosecution of Sexual Crimes in Early Eighteenth-Century Scotland', *Scottish Historical Review*, vol. 89, no. 228 (October, 2010), 187.
10. Leviticus 18, verse 14.
11. Hume, *Commentaries*, 293.
12. Gordon, *Criminal Law*, 35-03, 897.
13. The court papers do not state whether Elspeth was pregnant during the trial or had already given birth.
14. Levack, 'Prosecution of Sexual Crimes', 188.
15. G. MacKenzie, *The Laws and Customs of Scotland, In Matters Criminal: Wherein is to be seen how the Civil Law, and the Laws and Customs of other Nations do agree with, and supply ours* (Edinburgh, 1678), 81–2.
16. JC11/1, 85–7.
17. K. Barclay, 'From Rape to Marriage: questions of consent in eighteenth-century Britain', in *Interpreting Sexual Violence, 1660–1800*, ed. A. Greenfield (London, 2015), 39.
18. Dimorphism between male assailant and female victim was rarely commented upon in late nineteenth- and early twentieth-century prosecutions for either incest or rape; L. Heren, *Sex and Violence in 1920s Scotland: Incest, Rape, Lewd and Libidinous Practices, 1918–1930* (London, 2023), 175.
19. JC11/1, 86.
20. However, blood father incest in 1920s Scotland may have been more robustly prosecuted since there are more cases of consanguineous incest than incest by step/affinity; Heren, *Sex and Violence*, 64.
21. E. W. Cox, *Principles of Punishment* (London, 1877), 81–4.
22. JC26/90.
23. MacKenzie, *Laws and Customs*, 82.
24. *R v. Sweenie* (1858), 8 Cox CC 223.

25 L. M. Smith, 'Sackcloth for the Sinner or Punishment for the Crime? Church and the Secular Courts in Cromwellian Scotland', *New Perspectives on the Politics and Culture of Early Modern Scotland*, ed. J. Dwyer, R. A. Mason and A. Murdoch (Edinburgh, 1982), 130.

26 A. Raffe, 'Scotland restored and reshaped: Politics and Religion, c.1660–1712', *The Oxford Handbook of Modern Scottish History*, ed. T. M. Devine and J. Wormald (Oxford, 2014), 264; T. C. Smout, *A History of the Scottish People 1560–1830* (London, 1972), 213.

27 R. Mitchison and L. Leneman, *Girls in Trouble: sexuality and social control in rural Scotland 1660–1780* (Edinburgh, 1998), 42.

28 7 Ann c.22, 'An Act for the Queen's most gracious general free Pardon', *The Statutes of the Realm, printed by command of his majesty King George the third, in pursuance of an address of the House of Commons of Great Britain*, vol. 9, chapter XXII, 95–101.

29 Levack, 'Prosecution of Sexual Crimes', 184–5. This claim requires more comprehensive examination of the High Court of Justiciary (HCJ) case papers from 1708 to 1868 before it can be totally supported.

30 Levack, 'Prosecution of Sexual Crimes', 189.

31 Heren, *Sex and Violence*, 78.

32 Smout, *History of the Scottish People*, 451.

33 Levack, 'Prosecution of Sexual Crimes', 190. Levack lists Leviticus 18:6–18 for incest; Exodus 22:18 for witchcraft; Exodus 20:14, Leviticus 18:20 and Deuteronomy 5:18 for adultery; and Jeremiah 13:27 and Corinthians 6:18 for fornication, among others.

2

Janet Horne 1727: Widow, misogyny, marginality and witch

Being the last woman to burn for witchcraft in Scotland is a terrible appellation, but Janet Horne's case reveals the disparity of the application of the law where vestiges of superstition existed and the long arm of the law was too short to save a vulnerable old woman.

Context

Witchcraft, like infanticide, has predominantly been a 'crime' reserved for allegation against women, especially old, widowed, poor, senile and otherwise unprotected women. However, the 'witch' had rarely committed any violence or other crime. Instead, an accusation of witchcraft can be seen as a violent injustice committed against the accused.

Janet Horne was the last witch to be burned in Scotland in 1727, just nine years before the repeal of the Witchcraft Act of 1563. Timing is everything in history, and Janet's death is unfortunate, but the details of her crime and putative prosecution reveal much about Scottish society in the early eighteenth century. The role of women in a community and the types of crime they committed; societal, judicial and juridical attitudes towards women who stepped outside the accepted norms for female behaviour; proximity to the rule of law; the use of torture to extract judicial testimony; developments in rational thinking and the role of religion are all encapsulated in one terribly distressing old woman's last weeks.

During the great witch hunts in Scotland, and across Europe, from the mid-1500s, many married women and some men were caught up in group prosecutions as one 'witch' named another and another, often under torture, until a whirlwind of panic had spread around the community and frequently extended to neighbouring villages and towns. Thus, it is estimated that between 1560 and 1707, some 3,000 to 4,500 individuals perished in Scotland.[1] A handful of sporadic, isolated cases thereafter, including Janet's, can be added to that figure.

Witchcraft became a statutory crime in Scotland in 1563, and the substance of Scotland's Act 'Anentis Witchraftis' both differed from and agreed with a similar one passed in England in the same year. Julian Goodare's forensic examination of both documents concludes that the 'textual autonomy' of the Scottish Act suggests it was drafted before the English one. However, the 'differences seem more marked than the similarities', because the English Act allowed for 'carefully graded punishments', whereas the Scottish Act went straight to death penalty for all offences.[2] Before 1563, witchcraft was mostly based on superstitious belief in devils and faeries, who might be tempted by offerings of milk or oatmeal. Further, as Christopher Smout describes, many old women must have had 'a small knowledge of herbal cures and a good line in invective'.[3] Did a widowed woman find it useful to her continued survival to be considered a witch, or did the community perceive her as such within their own definition of witch-like behaviours? Before 1563, behaving like a witch and being prosecuted for witchcraft was not necessarily a natural progression. However, thereafter, the 'practice of specific acts of witchcraft' such as interactions with the Devil, rather than the 'thought-crime of being a witch' became a statutory crime punishable by death. The Scottish Act had not been able to define what a witch was, but everyone could recognize the mischief created by a witch.[4]

Five stages have been identified that carried a woman from the discovery of witchcraft behaviours to prosecution. First, 'an unsanctioned and deviant act' had to be recognized as an instance of witchcraft and a suspect identified. Second, the witch's neighbours needed to demand justice; the Kirk session would investigate and imprison the accused awaiting possible trial. Third, court officers decided if a criminal trial would be necessary on the evidence provided, and if they proceeded, the trial became the fourth stage. The last part of the process was sentencing. Goodare has identified several areas where 'dark history' may account for more accusations: namely those instances where an accused witch's family argued successfully against a prosecution or when a court officer rejected a plea because of insufficient evidence. Further, acquittal adds to the whole number of prosecutions but not executions.[5]

As with incest cases, the Kirk session was not authorized to prosecute a statutory crime, and therefore, an accusation of witchcraft after 1563 could only be prosecuted in the secular courts. After 1590, most witch trials were authorized by the Privy Council – the executive of the Scottish government – as a 'commission of justiciary', and Goodare's research reveals that after 1610, 'autonomous local trials' were rare.[6] The system required local lairds to request a commission from the Privy Council, which would examine the evidence. If the evidence passed scrutiny, then a commission would be awarded, and the local authority could proceed to prosecute. Essentially, any subsequent trial and verdict were a foregone conclusion because the evidence had already passed the examination of the Privy Council. Therefore, if anyone were to be acquitted, it would occur during consultation at the Privy Council level rather than locally. The Privy Council was aware of the potential for bias: those who had interrogated the witch were the same men who had applied to Edinburgh for a commission and who would then conduct the trial.[7] Thus, although rare, the Privy Council might require the prosecution to be conducted in Edinburgh under the guidance of the Justice-Depute. Here acquittals reached 30 per cent rather than 4 per cent if prosecuted locally. Goodare argues that the Kirk session, which identified the witches, cooperated with the Privy Council's issuing prosecution commissions because they shared the same goal to 'purge the land of ungodliness'.[8]

The involvement of Scotland's elites in witchcraft prosecutions indicates a broad belief spectrum ranging from the superstitious and belief in the Devil to full acceptance of demonic pacts, metamorphosis of witches into various animals and the ability to fly and cause harm to others by cursing. However, after the last great witch-hunt panic of 1661-2, there was an intellectual change; belief in the Devil and witchcraft continued, but acceptance of fantastical claims of transformation and flying on broomsticks declined. Sir George MacKenzie, Scotland's greatest contemporary legal mind, was pivotal to this change among Scottish lawyers whose rational thinking extended to other elites. MacKenzie recognized that 'oft-times women who understand not the nature of what they are accused of and many mistake their own fears and apprehensions for Witch Craft'. He acknowledged that imprisonment and fear, and torture caused such 'distraction' provoking confession under duress, and he had first-hand experience of an accused old woman in such extremis in prison that she had confessed because she knew that if acquitted, she would be hounded and starved; burning was a release from that terrifying future. MacKenzie knew that 'Divines' could not accept the transformation of people into beasts nor passing through walls or closed doors, and he dismissed these things as 'ridiculous ... which hath no truth nor existence but in their Fancy'. However, MacKenzie did not reject the notion of a pact with the Devil, although he insisted on evidence before any of these poor wretches were tried and potentially executed.[9] As Brian Levack has argued, 'judicial scepticism' about the existence of witches and insistence from central government to follow 'due process' contributed to 'an overall pattern of decline' after 1662's last great witch-hunt panic.

However, the number of trials heard at the central courts in Edinburgh increased as trust in the ability of local commissions to conduct fair trials declined. The concomitant was an increase in acquittals because the evidence provided proved insufficient to convict. Once the High Court of Justiciary was established in 1672 in Edinburgh with its system of circuit courts, centralized and uniform law could be delivered throughout the country so that between 1671 and 1709 only two women were convicted and sentenced to execution by circuit judges.[10] Goodare argues that a further development in the judicial process in 1708 when the Privy Council was abolished allowed some local courts to act autonomously without recourse to Edinburgh.[11] However, as standards of evidential proof became more rigorous, it became apparent to juries, and more quickly to judges, that accusations of witchcraft did not hold water.[12]

There was a geographical aspect to the witch hunts. The Highlands and Islands did not suffer the same intensity of witch hunts experienced elsewhere in Scotland because learned conceptions of the Devil and malefice were less effectively communicated to the populace, and the Kirk was less involved. Historians recognize a 'weak voice' against witchcraft in Scotland more generally in the early seventeenth century and locate the densest concentration of prosecutions in counties closest to Edinburgh's courts and importantly the Kirk's General Assembly.[13] However, the decline in the use of torture after 1662 and its abolition by statute in 1708 further reduced the number of witchcraft prosecutions in Scotland. In England, torture had always been prohibited under common law and disallowed as a 'method of proof', although in practice it had occurred throughout the country.[14] Thus, at the pivotal moment in Scotland's and England's second economic and political union, the need to pass statute law to prohibit torture was perceived by some as condemnatory to Scotland's self-identity. Goodare states that 'waking', a form of extrajudicial sleep deprivation used by Scottish investigators to extract confessions, was 'never rejected by the courts'.[15] It was a neat circumvention of the 1708 prohibition on torture, since lack of sleep and its consequent psychosis was invisible, yet productive of irrational confessions. Between 1662 and 1708, the use of torture was reserved to the criminal courts in Edinburgh, because the legal authorities deemed torture still to be useful but only when conducted by 'the proper authority'. The last witchcraft trial prosecuted at the High Court of Justiciary took place in 1709. Detailed research on post-1708 witchcraft cases reveals that torture continued to be applied by some local authorities into the first decades of the eighteenth century.[16]

Thus in 1727, despite being accused by those in her own community, Janet might have expected not to be tortured into confessing, and she would have anticipated a fair trial by an Edinburgh justice on circuit to Inverness, her nearest city for the visiting assize.

Case

The first-hand written evidence for Janet's case is threadbare. The Dornoch presbytery minutes for 1727, which might provide details of Janet's preliminary interrogation before the Kirk ministers, no longer exist. Extant volumes run from 1707 to 1719 and then recommence in 1732. Nothing can be read into this crucial absence for Janet's case. However, others in succeeding decades wrote about her, and it is largely on their hearsay interpretation that understanding of what actually occurred is based. Arguably, oral testimony has always been susceptible to human embellishment, but in an age when it was relied upon to convey local news, the most contemporaneous account of Janet's demise may well be the closest to accurate.

Captain Edmund Burt was the first Englishman in the Dornoch region to record Janet's story. Posted to Scotland in 1727 as the Receiver General and Collector of Rents for the unsold Forfeited Estates, Burt had the unenviable task of wresting rent from people who had recently risen against the British monarchy in the Jacobite Rebellion of 1715. His letters to 'a friend' in London are sprinkled with miserly observations on the Scots working people he met. Thus, his comments on those adhering to witch belief in the north of Scotland were framed as a comparison to 'People of any tolerable Sense and Education in England'. In this context, he retells the story of Janet and her daughter, brought before a judge who was not as 'clear-sighted' as his English counterparts. The judge was the Depute-Sheriff, whom he did not name, and Burt believed the trial to have been conducted in a court.[17] Apparently, Janet's daughter managed to escape, but Janet was burned to death in a 'Pitch-Barrel'. He found the maxim incomprehensible that witches must exist because laws had been written to condemn them. If that were true, then poets writing about phoenixes would imply that phoenixes were real. He indicated that both Janet and her daughter had been tortured, at least by withholding food and water, which had led to their confession simply to relieve their suffering. He could not fathom why witchcraft was not seen in cities, whereas rural areas appeared to be 'Nurseries for Witchcraft'. Burt hoped that witchcraft laws would be annulled so that no 'ignorant Magistrate or Jury' could condemn a woman for something of which she 'never had the Power to be Guilty'. Ultimately, any witchcraft trial had to be 'proved by honest Witnesses' because Burt was incredulous that anyone could testify to a neighbour flying on a broomstick, squeezing through a keyhole or transforming themselves into a cat.[18]

Burt published his accounts of his time in the north of Scotland in 1754, by which time perhaps his recollections had hardened against the Scots, particularly after a further Jacobite Rebellion in 1745. The phrasing of his account suggests he was not an eyewitness to Janet's death, although he was in the area at the time. His retelling is mainly concerned with disparaging the Scots including their elites, among them the Depute-Sheriff and other judicial officers whom he criticized. Burt's rather pejorative account is counterbalanced by another English perspective on the case.

The next chronologically known account is that of Englishman Thomas Pennant, who toured Scotland in the late 1760s. His account of his journey in 1769 begins in Edinburgh where he passed 'a deep and wide hollow beneath Calton Hill', which had formerly been the place of execution of 'those imaginary criminals, witches and sorcerers in less enlightened times'. Like Burt, Pennant also reveals his incredulity at superstitious beliefs, but by noting the redundant site of former executions in the seat of the Scottish Enlightenment, Pennant compliments the capital's intelligentsia on its now enlightened attitudes. Two months later, Pennant arrived in Dornoch in Sutherland and records riding past a small croft near the sea – Thane's Croft – nearby where Janet, an 'unhappy creature', succumbed as the 'last of these frantic executions in the north of Scotland'. His recounting of another execution in 1696 in Paisley contains much fuller detail, suggesting knowledge of this better-known Scottish case had travelled south of the border, whereas Janet's case was a local affair only encountered when physically visiting the region. Writing only forty years after Janet's execution, Pennant recognized that witch beliefs were 'almost obsolete superstitions', which could not be used to denigrate Scotland because as recently as 1751 a ghastly witch trial and execution had taken place in Tring, in the home counties of London.[19] Pennant sojourned in the Dornoch area for a few days unlike Burt's longer posting to the region, yet Pennant's perception of the local people was one of greater enlightenment than Burt had believed them capable. Burt had, after all, accused legal officers of harbouring superstitious beliefs.

Both Burt's and Pennant's publications were intended for an upper-class British readership, which in their first editions were published just fifteen years apart. They provided contradictory assumptions about superstition in the north of Scotland, whereas thirty years after Pennant, very spare details were offered in the *Statistical Account of Scotland*. This version of events takes up just eight lines of print. The first Presbyterian minister to the parish of Loth in Sutherland, incumbent between 1717 and 1730, Mr Robert Robertson, is likely to have ministered to Janet or been part of her initial interrogation. 'It was from this parish, that the last unhappy woman that suffered for witchcraft' was executed in Dornoch.[20] This sentence injects ambiguity into Janet's history. It is most likely that hailing from the parish of Loth, Janet underwent preliminary questioning here, and although there is historical doubt about the legality of her prosecution, if a proper trial was conducted by the Depute-Sheriff, then Janet would have been removed to Dornoch for trial, which would make better sense of her execution there.

By 1884, Scottish antiquary Charles Sharpe had revisited Janet's story providing details of the Sheriff-Depute, Captain David Ross who passed sentence, and of Janet 'having ridden upon her own daughter' who she had transformed into a pony. The daughter was supposedly left lame by the horseshoes used to shod her. This is the 'young' woman of indeterminate age – her mother's age is unknown, but Janet is always assumed to have been 'old' – who fled her prison. Sharpe described 'weather proving very severe' and Janet warming herself beside the fire that would ultimately kill her.[21] As Cowan and Henderson remark, Janet would have been strangled first and therefore unconscious, if not already dead, when she was placed in the barrel of pitch.[22] The embellishment of time and retelling is apparent in Sharpe's version of Janet's execution. Sharpe's tale is packed with narrative detail that would have appealed to a Victorian audience keen to indulge in the 'romance' of the Highlands.

Sharpe had placed Janet's case in 1722, a mistake which was repeated in 1923 in a paper written by W.N. Neill. He described Janet as 'an insane old woman' accused of 'bewitching pigs and poultry' as well as transforming her daughter. She was 'wirreit at a stake and brint in assis', a quote in the vernacular for which he provided no source. Further, he recounted 'a stinging rebuke' delivered by the King's Advocate to the Sheriff-Depute of Caithness only four years beforehand (1718 or 1723 depending on which date is used for Janet's execution) for attempting to conduct a witchcraft trial without recourse to Edinburgh, the proper process for prosecuting a witch. Despite relying on the wrong year and displaying a dismissive attitude towards her, Neill provides a useful summary of Janet's death:

> If the minister of Loth considered himself aggrieved by a crazy old woman with a semi-paralysed daughter, and the matter was threshed out before a superstitious sheriff, the rope and stake at Dornoch were foregone conclusions.[23]

Themes and analysis

Janet's case appears to have been an isolated incident. There were no preceding or succeeding cases tried in the region, which might have suggested a late witch panic in its initial stages. Further, there is no factual evidence to support or counter descriptions of Janet as 'old' or 'insane', although this has been the assumption since Burt's 1754 account. It is probable that Janet was an older woman in her community and was likely marginalized.[24] Goodare states that 'in the small, enclosed communities of pre-industrial Scotland', everyone was keen to maintain the 'respect of their neighbours'. If Janet had been a quarrelsome woman, probably widowed and therefore unprotected, it would have been easier for her neighbours to accuse her of witchcraft if she transgressed their accepted norms of behaviour for an older woman. Ashlyn Cudney's research on Bute's witch panics in the late seventeenth century confirms that 'poor neighbourliness' might be construed as a motive for witchcraft, along with being quarrelsome and a gossip.[25] This confirms Christine Larner's earlier research on Scottish women accused of witchcraft. Larner describes individuals who refused to be subservient or deferential, possessed of the 'Scottish female quality of smeddum': spirited, hot-tempered with an 'angry tongue'. However, Larner acknowledges that not all those accused were quarrelsome, while difficult women who lived in the 'danger zones for witch accusation and prosecution' were not all accused.[26] This suggests either the individual's characteristics and circumstances or those of the locality coalesced to produce an accusation leading to prosecution. Larner suggests further that the counter-Reformation religious settlement of the Scottish Kirk required women to be responsible for their own souls for the first time, rather than being the responsibility of their husbands. Yet the Kirk remained 'strongly patriarchal', creating a conflict for some women between this newfound moral independence and overbearing male discipline.[27]

It is unknown if Janet fitted this description or who accused her first or if she was indicted after a succession of accusations over a period of time. However, in a small community like Loth where women formed mutually supportive peer groups, Janet was most likely accused by her female neighbours in the first instance. Goodare argues that the 'process of suspicion and labelling' of a witch suggests that by the time the accusation stuck, the accused was an older woman who had built up 'a reputation for witchcraft'.[28] This might include cursing or possessing healing and midwifery skills, the last of which could go badly wrong for the practitioner without any mal-intent. If the later accounts contain any truth, Janet appears to have been a widow, caring for and perhaps supported by her lame daughter, and there is mention also of a disabled son. The brief descriptions of the family suggest poverty, marginality and rejection by their community, the reasons for which are lost. However, from other witchcraft case evidence, the Hornes may have been 'othered' by their neighbours, constructed as a ready scapegoat for any ills that befell their community. Neill's misogyny simply illustrates centuries-old denigration of lonely old women, which Janet may have experienced since her widowhood.

There is no extant confession from Janet. However, the witchcraft caseload indicates that torture was involved to some extent in every instance. If Janet confessed to the minister in Loth, fear alone may have driven her statement, although physically non-injurious methods may have been employed. Pricking a witch to find an insensitive place on her body that was supposedly the

Devil's mark had mostly disappeared in the seventeenth century after the last great panic in 1661–2. Pricking had been a despicable method of extracting a confession. If the woman did not confess in order to avoid the intimate search of her body seeking the Devil's mark, she would be subjected to a horrific ordeal because 'flesh sell't to the Devil is no like common flesh'.[29] A long thin needle, some three inches long, would be inserted into the woman's body searching out places of insensitivity, with particular focus on her back, shoulder or thigh. If she did not feel it or could not locate it, the place on her body became evidence of a witch's mark.[30] Goodare's research reveals that many women confessed that the 'mark' was in their 'privy parts', thus evading an invasive search but also advancing the elite notion connecting female sexuality and the Devil.[31] However, 'waking' had been used before torture was abolished and as a method of extracting a confession that left no physical marks, its continued use in the remote north is possible. Arguably, because waking was an invisible torture, it was not considered illegal, and the Justice-Depute in Edinburgh was unlikely to have rejected a confession extracted in this way.[32]

However, there is no record of a representation from Dornoch to the courts in Edinburgh for a commission to hear the case locally or in the capital, although a request may have been made. Burt stated that Janet's and her daughter's trial was held in a court overseen by the 'Deputy-Sheriff'.[33] As the closest account to the date of the trial, this strongly indicates the women underwent a prosecution conducted by a law officer. In a pamphlet written to promote tourism in Dornoch, it is suggested that Captain David Ross acted 'against orders', indicating that he got on with the trial without informing or receiving instructions from Edinburgh.[34] This would concur with Goodare's comments on post-Privy Council abuses of local autonomy because if the High Court of Justiciary had received case papers regarding Janet's and her daughter's crime, based on any superstitious witness statements provided, the case would have been unlikely to proceed.

Writing twenty years after Janet's trial, the legal commentator, David Hume, had observed that 'weakness, fear, melancholy' in combination with ignorance, were 'the true sources of SUPERSTITION' [sic] and that 'superstition is favourable to priestly power', insinuating that ministers might use local adherence to superstitious beliefs for their own purposes. If 'enthusiasm' were added to the mix, such as that of 'the *levellers* and other fanatics in ENGLAND, and the *covenanters* in SCOTLAND' [sic], then 'the most cruel disorders in human society' might be produced. If 'superstition is an enemy to civil liberty' and 'enthusiasm a friend to it', then Janet and her daughter were caught in a socio-religious trap.[35] In a period when the Scottish Kirk was slow to relinquish its theological attachment to the Devil, the involvement of Loth's minister could have provided the element of superstition, fuelled by the enthusiasm of his congregation and their belief in witchcraft and its connection with the Devil. Cudney's research on 1660s Bute indicates that 'sermons were a form of mass communication' for Reformed ministers and a means of 'direct imposition of learned demonology' to their congregations and during witch interrogations.[36]

In the seat of Scotland's Enlightenment, rational thinking was likelier to be encountered. In his *Enquiries*, Hume had refuted the possibility of miracles, which he considered witchcraft to be. Any testimony purporting to support witchcraft could never 'amount to a probability, much less to a proof'.[37] If the testimony could 'establish a miracle', then the testimony itself was a miracle.[38] In Scots Law, if a properly legitimate trial were to take place, corroboration of evidence was essential; therefore, more than one person would have had to accuse the Hornes with credible evidence. These precognitions, if ever taken, do not exist. It is possible the Hornes never received a properly constituted trial, even with Captain Ross presiding, using whatever 'evidence' they had managed to force the women to confess.

Proximity to the seat of law and the role of religious leadership are key issues here. Dornoch is 200 miles from Edinburgh by today's roads. Levack argues that the expense of transporting witnesses to the High Court of Justiciary resulted in a preference to hold trials locally if permitted by Edinburgh.[39] This consideration may have extended even to the cost of sending a messenger to convey precognitions to the capital for scrutiny. In 1727, with no direct route through the mountains, it would have been quite an expedition to seek the judicial fairness of the centralized courts. In Edinburgh, it was more probable that a jury would acquit an accused witch. With corroboration essential to a prosecution, a precognition statement extorted under torture, visible or otherwise, could not have been plausibly corroborated by a witch's accusers: it was a supernatural crime committed in an increasingly sceptical society. The witnesses would be discredited and their testimony ridiculed. For nearly two centuries, witchcraft accusations under statute law had been easy to make and hard for the accused to disprove, but the obverse was now equally true in the new world of enlightened thinking.[40] In Scotland's centre of business, politics, law and medicine, rational thinking in 1727 would probably have given a representation from Dornoch short shrift.[41]

The *Statistical Account* provides no character detail concerning Loth's first Presbyterian minister, Robert Robertson. By 1727, he had been incumbent for a decade. Did his authority and personal flavour of Presbyterianism influence his congregation? As Smout quotes, 'whenever Presbytery was dominant witches became prominent'.[42] Or did Robertson spend a decade battling against local superstition, hoping to instil a forward-thinking brand of Presbyterianism in his flock who resisted him? In either case, the Depute-Sheriff appears to have conducted some form of trial, which indicates that among the local elite, belief in witchcraft was retained.

Keith Thomas argues 'categorically that no convincing correlation' can be made linking incidents of witchcraft prosecutions to socio-economic pressures or outbreaks of plague.[43] However, the *Statistical Account* in 1793 noted that Loth's population had not increased since the beginning of the century due to a lack of manufactures, fisheries and improvements in agriculture.[44] It appears to have been a stagnating community. Dornoch is described as having increased its population during the previous thirty years, which was attributed to the endeavours of the local women producing whisky and flax, and the *Statistical Account* describes a safe harbour allowing ships of 500 tonnes to berth.[45] Seventy years earlier, Burt had described Dornoch's quay with 'seldom more than two or three ships, and those of no great Burden' [sic], and sheep and goats grazing the herbs and grasses outside the town, before briefly noting the poverty of the lairds' tenants.[46] Despite later small improvements, Dornoch was plainly not a prosperous town, but whether an acute event such as a poor harvest followed by a harsh winter provoked the community to blame Janet remains speculative. However, in a community short on resources, if Janet's family required charitable help, the embarrassment and guilt at having nothing to share may have prompted accusations against the Horne women.

For earlier witchcraft panics in the first half of the seventeenth century that coincided with straitened economic circumstances, Jenny Wormald has argued that 'the beginnings of poor-relief ... undermined the obligation to give personal help'.[47] Unable to give an impoverished old woman anything to sustain herself could provoke a curse as she left empty-handed. If an accident or illness then befell the family or its livestock, an easy connection might be made and culpability apportioned. Loth's long-term struggles for survival may have contributed to the Hornes' rejection by their community, but it takes an extra degree of hostility to escalate from denying handouts to the poor to accusations of witchcraft and consequent execution.

Could Janet or her daughter have upset their neighbours in some other way? Goodare suggests that accusations of witchcraft contained 'connotations of uncontrolled sexuality'.[48] Janet was probably too old to solicit her neighbours' husbands, and the few accounts do not mention sexual intercourse with the Devil, which was a customary confession – often already implicit in the process – made by accused women under duress. However, her daughter may have attracted attention from their neighbours' sons, and as a younger woman disabled in some manner, she might have provoked offence.[49] A hint of impropriety would have attracted discipline from their female neighbours before coming to the notice of a minister who Goodare cites as often taking the initiative in prosecutions.[50] Misogynistic accusations concerning female sexuality and deviant behaviour would have cemented the Horne women's fate. However, incarceration either in Loth or in Dornoch, if the women were transported there for trial, was lapse. The daughter was acknowledged as lame yet managed to escape.

Conclusion

So, what does Janet's ordeal tell us about early eighteenth-century communal, societal and judicial violence against unprotected women? First, an accusation of witchcraft was an act of violence committed against the accused and recognized as such by the judiciary, because by 1727 a move towards incredulity in witchcraft and other superstitious practices was well underway among the educated elite. In the late sixteenth century, witchcraft had been viewed as a 'disease of the body politic' to be extirpated.[51] However, over a century later, among the general population, continuing superstitious adherence has been found to have been 'silenced, not convinced'.[52] This might explain why Janet was accused, but not why the local elites proceeded

ILLUSTRATION 2.1 *Stone commemorating Janet Horne's place of execution.*
© *Peter Wild, Historylinks Museum, Dornoch.*

with her trial. By making torture illegal in 1708, extorting a confession from Janet would have compounded the High Court of Justiciary's reasons to reject any representation from Dornoch. Among sensible individuals whose logical and rational approach to life could not countenance belief in witchcraft, any precognitions containing details of the Devil, intercourse with him and transformation of daughters into donkeys were ludicrous. Thus, Janet's demise suggests a pocket of superstition in the Dornoch area supported by a few local elites. Cowan and Henderson argue that belief in witches 'confers reality upon witches' and that belief in witchcraft continued to exist under the surface of rationalism.[53] Whether the minister can be included among the credulous is unknown, but the Depute-Sheriff, Captain David Ross, a man entrusted to uphold judicial fairness, certainly can be.

However, once convicted by whatever tortuous and judicial process, Janet's execution was the ultimate violence committed against her. It can only be hoped that Janet was strangled prior to being burned, but any public execution was a voyeuristic spectacle. Goodare argues that an execution was a participatory event attended by those who had accused the victim, through which they might witness the performative power of the state to exterminate the deadliest 'enemies of society', an argument that a century later continued to be debated as state executions were taken indoors to be conducted behind prison walls.[54] Janet was never a dangerous member of her community, and it is an extrapolation too far of the extant accounts to suggest that her death was an elite response to recent Jacobite agitation. However, as the last execution for witchcraft in Scotland, Janet's death may have caused the Scottish elite collective reputational damage. At the end of the seventeenth century, MacKenzie had already decried Scottish witchcraft trials – what would the English think?

Despite great advances in rational, scientific and enlightened thinking in the decades prior to Janet's death, clearly the Enlightenment centred on Edinburgh had not reached Inverness-shire in a meaningful way. One legal commentator wrote just three years after Janet's shameful execution that witchcraft was real.[55] Finally, in 1736, conducting legal witchcraft prosecutions ceased. The Act repealing the Witchcraft Act of 1563 elicited laughter in the House of Commons when it was introduced, a sign of its reception among Westminster's elite, yet the Act did not completely exclude notions of witchery. Instead, the repeal allowed for fining and imprisonment of individuals purporting to have magical powers.[56] Was this a sop to the lingering adherents to witchcraft beliefs? Probably not. Instead, it indicates that continuing to hold superstitious beliefs or claiming to have magical powers pointed 'to evidence of insanity'.[57]

It is unlikely that Dornoch's Depute-Sheriff could have continued in office if he had been insane. Instead, it appears that Janet's trial and execution were a reversal of the trend in the 1670s as prosecutions were becoming more centralized. Levack identifies three options: to lynch a witch, to give up on a prosecution or to request a commission from the High Court of Justiciary.[58] No one gave up on prosecuting Janet, nor did they send to Edinburgh for permission to proceed locally or to conduct a trial in the capital, although as an unprotected, undefended and isolated woman, they did lynch her.

Notes

1. T. C. Smout, *A History of the Scottish People 1560–1830* (London, 1985), 185.
2. J. Goodare, 'The Scottish Witchcraft Act', *Church History*, vol. 74, no. 1 (March, 2005), 50–1.
3. Smout, *History of the Scottish People*, 185.
4. Goodare, 'Witchcraft Act', 54, 51.
5. J. Goodare, 'Witch-hunting and the Scottish state', in *The Scottish Witch-hunt in context*, ed. J. Goodare (Manchester, 2002), 123–4.
6. Goodare, 'Witch-hunting', 130.
7. B. P. Levack, 'The Decline and End of Scottish Witch-hunting', in *The Scottish Witch-hunt in context*, ed. J. Goodare (Manchester, 2002), 171.
8. Goodare, 'Witch-hunting', 131–4.
9. G. MacKenzie, *The Laws and Customes of Scotland in Matters Criminal: Wherein is to be seen how the Civil Law, and the Laws and Customs of other Nations do agree with, and supply ours* (Edinburgh, 1678), 42–7.
10. Levack, 'Decline', 169–73; other witches were executed after trial at the High Court of Justiciary (HCJ) in Edinburgh.
11. Goodare, 'Witch-hunting', 142.
12. B. P. Levack, *Witch-Hunting in Scotland: Law, Politics and Religion* (London, 2008), 141, 143.
13. Smout, *History of the Scottish People*, 189–90; Levack, *Witch-Hunting*, 132.
14. D. Friedman, 'Torture and the Common Law', *European Human Rights Law Review*, no. 2 (2006), 184.
15. J. Goodare, 'Women and the Witch-hunt in Scotland', *Social History*, vol. 23, no. 3 (October, 1998), 302.
16. Levack, 'Decline', 174–5.
17. Depute-Sheriff and Sheriff-Depute are used interchangeably in the archives for this case and have been quoted as per the originals.
18. E. Burt, *Letters from a Gentleman in the North of Scotland to His Friend in London* (Edinburgh, 1876), facsimile of 1754 first edition, 240–6.
19. T. Pennant, *A Tour in Scotland, 1769*, 2nd edition (London, 1772), 57, 154–5.

20 J. Sinclair, *The Statistical Accounts of Scotland, 1791–1845*, vol. VI (Edinburgh, 1793), 321.
21 C. K. Sharpe, *A Historical Account of the Belief in Witchcraft in Scotland* (London, 1884), 199–200.
22 E. J. Cowan and L. Henderson, 'The Last of the witches? The survival of Scottish witch belief', in *The Scottish Witch-hunt in context*, ed. J. Goodare (Manchester, 2002), 206.
23 W. N. Neill, 'The Last Execution for Witchcraft in Scotland, 1722', *Scottish Historical Review*, vol. 20, no. 79 (April, 1923), 218, 221.
24 Janet has also been described as a lady's maid having returned from overseas service, married and then been widowed with a daughter; Anonymous, *Town Jail Craft Centre: a brief history* (Dornoch, 1974), 14.
25 A. Cudney, 'Social Control and Disciplinary Bias: Bute, 1642–1702', unpublished doctoral thesis, University of Edinburgh (2025), 224–5.
26 C. Larner, *Enemies of God: the witch-hunt in Scotland* (Baltimore, 1981), 97–8.
27 Larner, *Enemies of God*, 101–2.
28 Goodare, 'Women and the witch-hunt', 297–301.
29 J. Buchan, *Witch Wood* (London, 1927), reprinted (Edinburgh, 2021), 216. Buchan imagines the condition of the alleged witch after suffering the pricker's ordeal. Buchan's novel is based on research conducted for his biography of James Graham, 1st Marquess of Montrose.
30 W. N. Neill, 'The Professional Pricker and hist Test for Witchcraft', *Scottish Historical Review*, vol. 19, no. 75 (April, 1922), 208.
31 Goodare, 'Women and the witch-hunt', 302.
32 Goodare, 'Women and the witch-hunt', 302.
33 Burt, *Letters*, 246.
34 Anonymous, *Town Jail Craft Centre*, 15–16.
35 D. Hume, *Essays, moral, political and literary*, ed. E. F. Miller (Indianapolis, 1989), 74–8.
36 Cudney, 'Social Control', 250.
37 D. Hume, *Enquiries concerning human understanding and concerning the Principles of Morals*, ed. L. A. Selby-Bigge (Oxford, 1902), Part II, section 10.
38 Hume, *Enquiries*, Part I, section 10.
39 Levack, *Witch-hunting*, 152.
40 K. Thomas, *Religion and the Decline of Magic* (London, 1971), 688–9.
41 Thomas, *Religion*, 693.
42 W. Stephen, *History of the Scottish Church* (Edinburgh, 1896), 282, in Smout, *A History of the Scottish People*, 189.
43 Thomas, *Religion*, 697.
44 Sinclair, *Statistical Accounts*, 318.
45 Sinclair, *Statistical Accounts*, vol. viii, 1–6.

46 Burt, *Letters*, 239, 254.
47 J. Wormald, *Court, Kirk and Community: Scotland 1470–1625* (London, 1981), 169.
48 Goodare, 'Women and the witch-hunt', 299.
49 Disability may also have caused ostracism as a sign of a family's shame or God's lack of favour.
50 Goodare, 'Women and the witch-hunt', 300.
51 Smout, *History of the Scottish People*, 186.
52 Thomas, *Religion*, 693.
53 Cowan and Henderson, 'Survival', 217.
54 Goodare, 'Witch-hunting', 140.
55 W. Forbes, *Institutes of the Laws of Scotland* (Edinburgh, 1730), 32, in Levack, *Witch-hunting*, 133.
56 https://www.parliament.uk/about/living-heritage/transformingsociety/private-lives/religion/overview/witchcraft/ (accessed June 2024).
57 Thomas, *Religion*, 694.
58 Levack, 'Decline', 180.

3

Barbara Malcolm 1808: Mother, 'monster' and murderer

Barbara Malcolm is known as the last woman to hang in Scotland for infanticide, just a year before the law relented its severest punishment for this crime. Yet Barbara's child was no longer an infant, and she died by poisoning. This case explores developments in social and moral attitudes towards women, their reproductive rights and the cult of maternity across the eighteenth century.

Context

Scotland's 'Act anent the Murthering of Children' became law on 19 July 1690. It was enacted to protect 'innocent Infants' from mothers who might conceal the birth, 'whereby the Child might be easily stifled, or being left exposed in the Condition it comes to the World'. Thus, if the child were found dead or 'amissing', the mother was held accountable for its murder, until and unless she could prove otherwise.[1] The timing of this new Act reflected changing attitudes towards the law and religious influence in Scotland as well as a rise in infanticide cases in the previous decade.[2] Scotland's legal commentator Baron Hume declared infanticide 'of all murders the most frequent' and identified 1680 and 1681 as years with particularly high caseloads. However, to remove the need for juries to proceed 'on such presumptions as are not very desirable to be trusted', such as an infant victim displaying no physical harm or no body at all, the Act flipped the traditional presumption of innocence on its head.[3] Unlike all other criminal charges in Scots and English law, in a case of infanticide, the accused now became guilty until proven innocent; the accused being an unprotected, single mother with very limited resources to defend her case for which the sentence, if convicted, was death.

However, despite the burden of proof now resting on the mother who might only be able to produce circumstantial evidence, it was equally difficult for the prosecution to provide conclusive evidence of infanticide.[4] In their ethnographical study of parental homicide, Daly and Wilson argue that in the early modern period, because an infanticide left no 'aggrieved party' to pursue legal action, the authorities were disinclined to prosecute cases without 'insistent suitors'. There were no kin to be recompensed for the child's death, and potentially the perpetrator's relations had no interest in reporting the killer.[5] Further, medical examination of the woman would not necessarily confirm recent birth, and autopsies, if an infant cadaver could be found, were also not always irrefutable evidence.

For a mother to commit the crime of murdering her own child, particularly a newborn or very young child, situates her in an extremely emotional state. Further, such crimes elicit emotive responses – condemnatory and sympathetic – from society and the judiciary. In her extensive research into British infanticide and child murder across the past four centuries, Anne-Marie Kilday has described this particular species of murder as 'a close cousin of witchcraft'.[6] That is because, like witchcraft, infanticide is committed mostly by women and therefore it is accused women who have historically appeared before all-male juries, while the prosecution of infanticide can be seen as male control of female bodies and reproduction.[7] Traditionally, men have produced the legislation determining whether a desperate woman, fearful of the social opprobrium stacked against her for giving birth to an illegitimate child and unable to cope emotionally or financially, is guilty of the murder of her own infant. Since the seventeenth century, infanticide was viewed as the antithesis of 'normal maternal or feminine behaviour' and 'the negation of womanhood'.[8] One contemporary commentator moralized that 'ranked at the head of the animal creation and endowed with superior reason and intelligence', only 'a monster of the species, rarely to be met with amongst civilized beings' could kill her own child.[9] However, the nineteenth-century burgeoning 'cult of maternity' identified by Kilday and others was a middle-class phenomenon which precluded working-class mothers who, having to work, existed outside the 'patriarchal structures' endured by middle-class women. Working-class women who did not, and often could not, conform to this normative middle-class expectation were considered 'bad mothers' whose behaviour threatened the welfare of the nation.[10] More recently, women who commit infanticide have often been considered mentally unwell and treated with sympathy.

In the seventeenth and eighteenth centuries, there were three aspects to an infanticide accusation. First, concealment of pregnancy suggested criminal denial of a woman's condition and therefore indicated murder if no baby was forthcoming. Second, enduring labour and birth without midwife or similar assistance compounded a concealed pregnancy; the mother clearly did not invite witnesses to the birth, suggesting she intended to do away with the baby unobserved. Third, if stillborn, there was no one to confirm the baby's status on delivery, and if born alive yet had immediately died, the mother could not defend either circumstance.[11] It was assumed that no right-minded woman would conceal her pregnancy for nine months or the birth of her baby – alive or stillborn – from the wider community. Therefore, an unmarried woman's only motive for non-disclosure of pregnancy and birth had to be to conceal a murder. To commit infanticide was considered aberrant behaviour that contravened societally accepted norms for expectant mothers and women in general. However, there are several key reasons why a young woman might have felt pressured into such an extreme measure.

First, the stigma of illegitimacy hung over both the mother and her child. Having given birth outside wedlock, the woman signalled to her community that she had enjoyed illicit sex, thus diminishing her marriageability and status within her community. The reputational damage of sex before marriage also affected the illegitimate child, who would have carried that disgrace with him or her for life. Katie Barclay's study of Scottish illegitimacy suggests rates remained higher than in England and Ireland or in Europe.[12] These estimates pertain to known live births, which occlude the number of illegitimate pregnancies which resulted in stillbirths or infanticides. As contemporary commentator, Lord Kines wrote in the eighteenth century, where single parenthood and illegitimacy were not a disgrace, infanticide was rare.[13] Christopher Smout agrees that Lowland rural areas of Scotland experienced high levels of illegitimacy in the nineteenth century, but that unmarried mothers were better tolerated because the 'social restraints' here were looser than elsewhere, such as in the northern and western isles. Smout argues that sexual morality was 'largely a function of the authority relationship between parents and children' and where parents had more control over their teenage offspring, illegitimacy was lower because stricter supervision of daughters prevented prenuptial relationships. Whereas, in regions where the connection to parents was stretched, such as farming districts which relied on the bothy system to accommodate labourers living away from home, illegitimacy rates were higher.[14] Further, where grandparents might be persuaded to care for an illegitimate child while their daughter travelled for work, or where employment existed that might tolerate a young woman with an illegitimate child to support, infanticide was less prevalent.[15] Thus, rates of illegitimacy and potential concomitant infanticide appear to have been geographically determined, influenced by the degree of moral supervision and sexual opportunity in different types of communities. So, where familial support networks and supportive employers did not exist, pregnant women were faced with unemployment once their pregnancy was discovered and looming poverty once they had a second mouth to feed.

The late eighteenth century witnessed a migration from Scotland's rural areas to its expanding urban centres. This was the ultimate dislocation for many young people entering employment away from home, living among strangers and fearful for their futures if they lost their position. Many young women from both rural and urban areas entered domestic service where they were at risk of sexual assault from male servants and male members of the household, before even considering a consensual relationship with a young man. Since most domestic servants were of childbearing age, this cohort also became the most accused of infanticide.[16] Living in close proximity to other female domestic servants, all supervised by the housekeeper, Margaret Arnot argues that 'secret disposal' of an unwanted or stillborn baby was more difficult in cities compared to rural areas. The countryside provided hedgerows and woodland, whereas the household privy was really the only unobserved space where a female domestic servant could guarantee being alone.[17] However, contemporary evidence suggests the opposite, that female servants sharing garret beds might not notice or recognize their friend's pregnancy. The early nineteenth-century legal commentator, Archibald Alison, recalled an Aberdeen case in 1823 in which the woman's two bed-mates did not notice when she 'rose, was delivered, and returned to bed, without any of them being conscious of what had occurred'.[18]

However, Arnot argues that sexual knowledge gained in a rural family home where bed- and room-sharing with parents would have provided opportunity to witness intercourse was lost to urban domestic servants as well as knowledge of contraceptive practices generationally handed down. Equally, some girls may not even have understood what was happening to their bodies if menstruation ceased, having grown up in a 'stifling moral climate' in which women's bodies were not discussed.[19] For some young women, genuine ignorance about their condition may have existed, but for others, as Kenneth Polk recognizes, there was an 'exceptional capacity' for denial among women caught up in illegitimate pregnancy and considering infanticide.[20] Once pregnancy was discovered, a servant would be instantly dismissed, making concealment of pregnancy 'a rational strategy' when facing poverty on the streets of a potentially unfriendly city.[21]

Daly and Wilson suggest that the Industrial Revolution increased 'incentives for infanticide' because young women pursuing new urban opportunities were isolated from their families, and if they fell prey to pregnancy, it would preclude them from employment. They suggest that a young mother might evaluate her worth against her child's and decide that, with many years of potential motherhood before her, she might kill this baby to preserve her situation until a permanent partner could support her. This is a psychological analysis of the motivations for infanticide, whereas social historians consider the lived experience of the individual, faced with shame, penury and loneliness and the impact that may have on their decision-making, and more recently the potential for post-partum mental illness to provoke infanticide.[22]

Kilday's research reveals that despite the obstacles in the way of a successful conviction, guilty verdicts increased in the early part of the eighteenth century, possibly as an initial response to the new legislation. However, after 1750, guilty verdicts decreased in Scotland due to the introduction of a judicial escape route: the panel might petition for life-long banishment, thus avoiding the death penalty. A sentence of doom was reserved only for the most vicious infanticides.[23] This compares favourably to research conducted for England and Wales where Pieter Spierenburg argues that infanticide 'came to be viewed more leniently towards 1800' and Clive Emsley adds that from 1750 to 1900, all-male juries treated infanticides more moderately than the 'strict implementation of the law would have allowed'.[24] Among the wider public generally, infanticide was regarded 'as less heinous than murder of an adult', indicating that judicial opinion had some catching-up to do with societal attitudes.[25]

Greater medical knowledge acquired during the eighteenth century created a philosophical debate about the point at which a foetus should be considered 'alive', which was most pertinent in cases of abortion.[26] The ambiguous status of victims of infanticide is most apparent in the legal papers referring to foetuses and young children using the neutral pronoun 'it' rather than she or he. This may indicate societal reticence to accept a newborn possessing full 'human individuality' or reluctance by a mother to accept the reality of her child's existence; the use of neutral pronouns also suggests parents emotionally distancing themselves until the child had reached what could be considered a safe age.[27] However, for unmarried women, 'quickening' – detection of the foetus moving in the womb – was a good indication of pregnancy and potentially the beginning of a maternal relationship with her unborn child. Thus, not relishing in the pregnancy was another signal of aberrant female behaviour, and if it culminated in infanticide, the accused might be called a 'monster' and unnatural.[28]

Understanding of emotional disturbance and postpartum psychoses was over a century away when both England and Scotland considered revising their respective statutes on child murder. In 1803, Lord Ellenborough's revisions to England's original 1624 law shifted the burden of proof from the accused back to the prosecution, bringing a charge of infanticide into line with all other criminal charges. Ellenborough's reforms were a response to 'concerns about rising levels of illegitimacy' and pressure on the poor rates 'aggravated by the French Wars'.[29] With the prosecution now actually having to prove infanticide, the number of acquittals increased further. In Scotland, reforms to its 1690 Act took until 1809 to conclude. Kilday argues that these revisions were 'more modern' than those enacted in England. First, the Scots created a separate crime of concealment of pregnancy, which allowed for the distinction between intentional infanticide – murder – and a mother who had acted criminally but not intentionally. Thus, women who had wilfully killed their child would be indicted under a murder charge, and mothers who had accidentally smothered a child or deserted it would receive a sentence of two years imprisonment, the same as south of the border. The Scots had created 'a more flexible and nuanced approach', but as the nineteenth century progressed, if charged under homicide, the need to establish intent, or at best qualify its meaning, in court was hotly debated, and insanity pleas in mitigation became more prevalent.[30]

At the beginning of the nineteenth century, clearly societal and judicial attitudes towards women who committed infanticide were changing. However, the reasons for infanticide had not. An incestuous conception, an adulterous conception or a deformity at birth might lead a woman to kill her child, but the greater number of infanticides occurred amongst unwed, usually deserted young women, often domestic servants, fearful for their child's and their own future if discovered. Deciding whether to murder her newborn or to struggle unsupported required the mother to evaluate the merit of her life compared to that of her child. So why did Barbara Malcolm, an unmarried servant almost two years into motherhood, allegedly murder her illegitimate eighteen-month-old daughter just before Christmas in 1807?

Case

At some point in 1806 after her baby's baptism on 4 July, Barbara Malcolm had been deserted by the baby's father, John Sutherland, a private in the Inverness-shire Militia. The baby christened Margaret Sutherland was approximately a month old.[31] Until Margaret's birth, Barbara had been a servant in the New Town of Edinburgh and having taken time to convalesce, she had put her infant daughter out to nurse while taking a position to wet-nurse another woman's baby. Her new employer, Mrs Hamilton, lived on the south side of the city. Her job paid her £3 per quarter from which she paid the family who cared for Margaret £2 per quarter.[32] Presumably, Barbara used the difference to support herself and perhaps save for their future. Barbara's desire to baptize her baby, to pay for its welfare and to give it the father's surname does not suggest a young mother without hope of a future as a family. Indeed, naming of the father on an illegitimate child's birth certificate has been shown to indicate intent to marry.³³ Barbara had not concealed her pregnancy, and although it is not known whether she received assistance at the birth, she had not concealed the baby's existence from its father, the local minister, her new mistress or those who foster-cared for the girl. Thus, when charged, Barbara's case did not meet the criteria of the extant 1690 Act on infanticide, and so she was charged with murder.

Before June 1807, her mistress reduced Barbara's wages to £1 because she had successfully wet-nursed and weaned the child. Barbara remained in Mrs Hamilton's employment, but evidently her reduced finances made life difficult, and Barbara visited Musselburgh twice in June 1807, when Margaret was about a year old, to ask for support from Sutherland. He refused. The news reports of Barbara's subsequent trial do not provide details of how she existed or how she supported her daughter between June and early December 1807, but they offer a description of a woman who changed from being 'very mild' to one who 'did not appear to be the same person'. It is unclear whether this meant a change from mild to hot-tempered, or mild to desperate and depressed.

On Sunday, 6 December, Barbara visited Margaret at her foster-parents' home in Lady Lawson's Wynd where she found her suffering from 'a sore mouth from the cold'. Adam Gordon, the husband of Margaret's wet-nurse, was at home. The very next day, Monday, Barbara visited an apothecary in the Grassmarket and, according to her later declaration, bought oil of vitriol and then returned to Gordon's house on Tuesday morning to administer it to Margaret where she found Gordon and his wife Margaret McKay with her daughter. On this visit, Barbara was accompanied by Mrs Hamilton's child who she passed to Gordon while taking her own child on her knee and giving her the oil of vitriol to drink. McKay had gone on an errand and did not see what happened.

From evidence Gordon gave later, he said he had walked about the room with Mrs Hamilton's child and had paid 'little attention' to Barbara and her daughter until he heard the child 'scream out violently'. He asked what was the matter, and Barbara replied that she had given the child 'some raw sugar'. Gordon disbelieved her and insisted to know what she had administered to the child, so Barbara offered him 'a piece of sugar' and said that it was 'only a part of what she had given' to Margaret. It is unclear whether Gordon tasted the sugar for himself. Then McKay returned, and Barbara gave her money to go out again for honey to soothe the child. While McKay was gone, Barbara left, taking Mrs Hamilton's daughter with her, leaving her own child 'in great agony'. Around two o'clock, Gordon sent for a doctor who administered some medicine, but Margaret was dead by six o'clock that evening. Gordon was dissatisfied with the sugar and set out with some neighbours to find Barbara. When they confronted her, she 'still insisted it was nothing but sugar'. Barbara was later apprehended by the police and taken to the watchhouse, where she told the officers she had given her child 'sugar of lead'.[34] On 9 December, she was transferred to Edinburgh prison and on Thursday, 10 December, Barbara gave a declaration to Procurator Fiscal William Scot, Sheriff James Annan and John Auld, the Sheriff of Leith Walk.[35]

Barbara's declaration corroborates Gordon's version until the point at which Barbara left with her employer's child. She told the Procurator Fiscal that around two o'clock Gordon appeared at Mrs Hamilton's house to inform her of Margaret's decline, and she accompanied him back to Lady Lawson's Wynd to see for herself. As she entered his home, she discovered 'a number of people in the house, and she herself was handed over to the police'. She told the Procurator Fiscal that there 'was no poison in the sugar, nor was there any arsenic' as far as she knew, and no one had 'advised her to perpetrate the deed of which she is truly penitent'. Barbara could not write, which is noted at the bottom of her declaration. As usual in Scots Law, she had not given a confession to the prison warden or police but had emitted her declaration under the scrutiny of legal officers. Her trial was set for 5 January 1808.

In the meantime, the Procurator Fiscal obtained precognition statements from Gordon's family; the apothecary Thomas Alexander, who was also a surgeon; James Tait, another surgeon; John Abercrombie, fellow of and William Farquharson, president of the Royal College of Surgeons of Edinburgh. Alexander's report is dated 8 December, the night Margaret died, while the other medical reports are dated 10 December 1807, the same day Barbara gave her declaration. Alexander, the apothecary, performed the autopsy the night of Margaret's death, and then under 'Warrant from the Authority of the Sheriff of Edinburgh', the surgeons examined Margaret's remains to confirm the apothecary's findings. His autopsy revealed that Margaret's intestines appeared to have been 'dissolved by some corroding liquor' and some of her bowel appeared to be burned. Examining her body, they found the skin down the side of her throat 'hard and black as if seared by a hot iron' due to vomit, which had also corroded her clothes where it came into contact with them. They tested the substance on Margaret's clothes by applying the material to their tongues, which convinced them that it was 'some very strong mineral acid', probably 'sulphuric acid, commonly called oil of vitriol'.[36] Thus, the charge against Barbara was murder, 'wickedly and barbarously' perpetrated by poison against her daughter, of which she was 'guilty actor, or art and part of the aforesaid crime'.

In court, defended by two advocates, Barbara maintained her innocence and pleaded not guilty. The jury of fifteen comprised a writer (lawyer's clerk), a hatter, a jeweller, a woollen draper, six merchants, a painter, a candlemaker, a baker, a coppersmith and a bookseller, all from Edinburgh and Leith. The prosecution witnesses gave their evidence first, followed by four witnesses

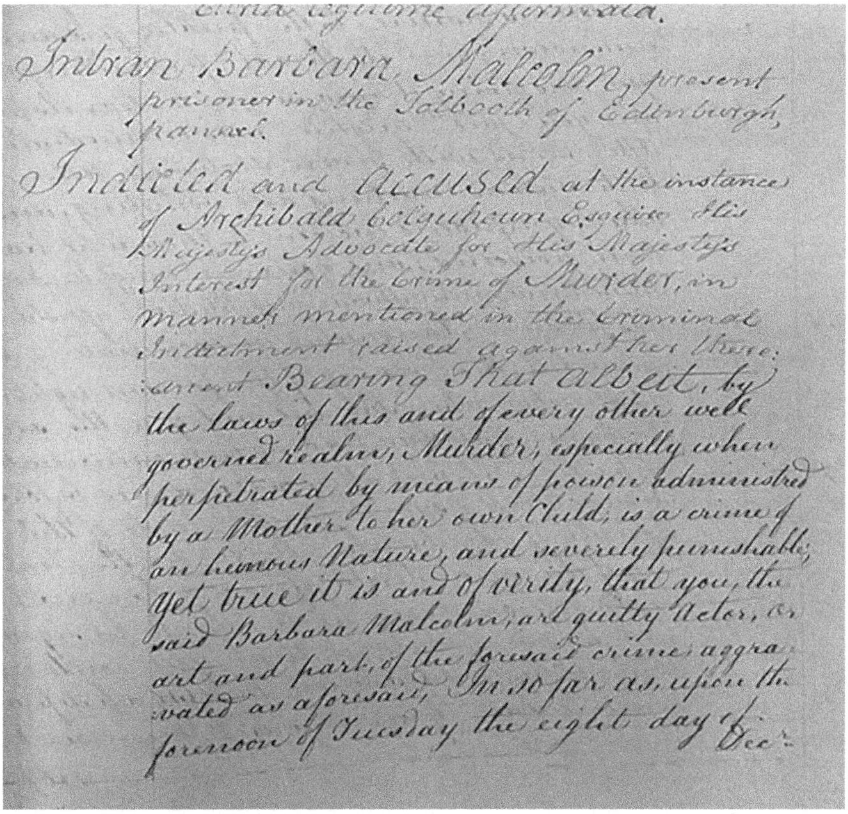
Intran Barbara Malcolm, present prisoner in the Tolbooth of Edinburgh, pannel.

Indicted and Accused at the instance of Archibald Colquhoun Esquire His Majesty's Advocate for His Majesty's Interest for the Crime of Murder, in manner mentioned in the Criminal Indictment raised against her thereanent Bearing That albeit, by the laws of this and of every other well governed realm, Murder, especially when perpetrated by means of poison administred by a Mother to her own Child, is a crime of an heinous Nature, and severely punishable; yet true it is and of verity, that you, the said Barbara Malcolm, are guilty Actor, or art and part, of the foresaid crime aggravated as aforesaid, In so far as, upon the forenoon of Tuesday the eight day of Decr.

ILLUSTRATION 3.1 *Indictment for Barbara Malcolm, 5 January 1808. Crown Copyright. National Records of Scotland, JC4/4, p. 115.*

in exculpation who included Mrs Hamilton, Barbara's employer, who is likely to have given a good character for Barbara; the three others may have been friends, similarly vouching for her.[37] The Minute Book does not record the finer detail of who said what, although for the prosecution witnesses this would have adhered to the content of their precognition statements; nor does it record whether Barbara's intent to murder was discussed or established. However, the trial was noteworthy for its length. One journalist reported that 'the examination of witnesses lasted till pretty late in the afternoon' after which the jury retired to the Robing Room. They did not deliberate for long before returning a unanimously guilty verdict.[38] According to one account, the Lord Justice-Clerk passed the sentence of doom, before delivering 'one of the most able, eloquent and impressive speeches' heard 'on a similar occasion', the contents of which have been lost.[39] Barbara was hanged on the afternoon of Wednesday, 10 February, and her body was given to the University of

Edinburgh to be anatomized. Any possessions she had were to be escheat to the Crown.[40]

Themes and analysis

Interestingly, the charge as 'art and part' confirms that Barbara's crime was not considered under the 1690 Act. Margaret's murder was not viewed as a form of infanticide or child murder, despite the case appearing two years before the Scottish revisions to that Act.[41] Alison confirms that 'no person can be guilty of the statutory offence [1690] except as actor, the charge of art and part being inconsistent with the nature of the crime'.[42] Thus, the Edinburgh authorities libelled this case as 'murder, especially when perpetrated by means of poison', and the insertion of 'art and part', while indicating no allowance for prosecution under the 1690 Act, may have offered a slim possibility of another accused or accomplice being found.[43]

Barbara's crime was not infanticide in the sense covered by the 1690 Act; she had killed an older and acknowledged child, and the choice of poisoning could be construed as 'irrefutably cold, calculating, and cruel'.[44] Her employer knew of Margaret's existence; the Gordons and the child's father knew. Barbara concealed nothing. In fact, her behaviour suggests she cared for Margaret and was concerned for her upkeep and wellbeing, visiting her when informed she was unwell. She had not done away with Margaret at birth fearing for her future caring for a 'bastard child'.[45] Giving the child its father's surname suggests that Barbara had hoped for a life with Sutherland, but when that plan failed, she had proved resourceful. While she had breast milk to offer, she found employment with a household who appear not to have considered her predicament an obstacle to having an unmarried mother wet-nurse their own daughter. Farming out Margaret to the Gordons made financial sense until something better came along. It has been argued that the reduction in her wages, which would have put her in a quarterly deficit to the Gordons, may have contributed to Barbara's decision to murder Margaret. Further, 'the unsympathetic attitude of parish officials' towards mothers of illegitimate offspring may have precipitated Barbara's decision.[46] Research conducted by Reid et al. confirms that welfare in Scotland was geographically highly variable and that everywhere, the parochial authorities 'were encouraged to restrict the relief' given to unmarried mothers, instead requiring their families to support them.[47] Thus, lack of financial support may well have contributed to Margaret's demise, but what if Barbara genuinely believed she had administered sugar for her child's sore throat? What if the medical evidence provided by eminent physicians of the Royal College of Surgeons had been considered so unassailable that the legal authorities and jury could not see that Barbara had no motive to murder her daughter?

Thomas Alexander, the apothecary who sold Barbara the oil of vitriol, conducted the autopsy on Margaret's body with Doctor James Tait on the same evening she died, 8 December 1807, at the Gordons' home. There is a clear conflict of interest in his dual capacity as apothecary and autopsy surgeon. Further, his report to the Procurator Fiscal identified extensive corrosion of Margaret's intestines, her skin and clothes. Without stating what had caused the damage, the autopsy had established she had died by some sort of corrosive poison before any other evidence had been precognosced. There was only one eyewitness, Adam Gordon, whose evidence was not precognosced until 10 December. Two days after the apothecary's autopsy when the Royal College of Surgeons' physicians inspected the contents of Margaret's stomach and viewed her body still at the Gordon's home, their opinion that 'some very strong mineral acid' – sulphuric acid or oil of vitriol – had been administered to the child confirmed the cause of these injuries and death.[48] The medical experts had concluded murder by poisoning, which inherently 'implied intention'.[49] Gordon's evidence, emitted two days after the apothecary's, was subsumed by the medical evidence, which corroborated the latter. As the only eyewitness who had self-admittedly not had his eyes on Barbara at the precise moment she tended to her child and whose statement did not confirm whether he tasted the sugar Barbara offered to him, Gordon's testimony was circumstantial. His wife, who had been out of the house returning to find Margaret in agony, only repeated the evidence as provided by her husband. Thus, the medical authority of the surgeons' evidence, which should have been used to corroborate Gordon's eyewitness account of the scene since he had reported the alleged murder, appears instead to have led the pretrial investigation. It is possible the authority of the medics occluded any mistake the apothecary may have made in selling the wrong substance to Barbara.

Further, Barbara's mental state, which would have informed her intent and motive, was not considered once the autopsy evidence had been reported. Since killing one's child was increasingly viewed as unstable behaviour, it might have occurred to the doctors and lawyers that Barbara's experiences since Margaret's birth had led her to a desperate and irrational act. Roger Smith's work on insanity and responsibility in criminal trials suggests that in the late eighteenth and early nineteenth centuries, 'the emergence of a forensic medical specialism' could be used to link 'infanticide and lunacy', which might persuade a jury to acquit even though a child had been murdered by its mother.[50] Smith argues that as courts relied more heavily on expert medical opinion, 'the medical language of individual internal disorder emptied the violent act of external social meaning', thus once considered insane, the woman's voice and her suffering, and potential motives, disappeared from the evidence.[51] Barbara's voice is not heard in court, but her declaration emitted two days after her daughter's death does not materially diverge from Gordon's, largely corroborating his testimony. It is written by a legal professional in the presence of three elite men, and it is possible the legal process removed the recording of any emotional detail or hint of mental instability in her declaration. Also, neither on the day of the incident nor once in court did Barbara present as insane in the visibly erratic and raving sense.

Archibald Alison's contemporary legal commentary on infanticidal working-class mothers states:

> It is a principle of law, that mere appearances of violence on the child's body are not *per se* sufficient, unless some circumstances of evidence exist to indicate that the violence was knowingly and intentionally committed, or they are of such a kind as themselves to indicate intentional murder.[52]

Yet, despite what the use of poison indicated, Barbara had no motive. She was informed of Margaret's condition during her Sunday visit, bought a 'remedy' on Monday and returned on Tuesday to give the 'medicine' to her child. She took Margaret on her knee, a maternal act of reassurance, to administer the medicine, and clearly, she had not anticipated Margaret's screams, or she might have attempted to smother them in some way, or at least to have removed Margaret from the house before poisoning her. Despite the weight of evidence against her, Barbara did not waiver in court and adhered to her not guilty plea. In the conversation at the house recounted in Gordon's testimony, at the watchhouse and the following day whatever words she spoke to describe the substance she had administered to her child, they were finally emitted in her declaration as 'oil of vitriol', a statement dated the same day as that of the senior surgeons who first confirmed oil of vitriol as the murder weapon.[53] Further, Gordon's statement does not suggest that Barbara presented as agitated, considering she was about to murder her child in plain sight. Asking McKay to go for honey when the 'sugar' did not appear to have worked is not the action of a murderous mother. Leaving so quickly after Margaret's first agonizing symptoms might be explained by her need to return her employer's daughter to their home; she may not have had any other choice. However, leaving when already aware of her child's distress may also indicate coldness and indifference.

The court papers do not include any discussion of a possible special defence of insanity being entered before her trial; therefore, it is probable that Barbara was not considered insane. The president and a fellow of the Royal College of Surgeons confirmed that Margaret's death had been occasioned by 'a strong sulphuric acid, commonly called oil of vitriol', and the apothecary's detailed description of blackened corrosion and charred intestines confirmed the terrible nature of the young child's death.[54] Thus, if this ghastly murder had not been perpetrated by an insane woman, the jury had only one other motive to consider, that it had been committed by a cold, callous, selfish 'monster'. It was a social construction of the infanticidal mother that had endured since before the 1690 Act which had proved societally difficult to shift despite impending, compassionate changes in the law.

Mrs Hamilton and the other exculpatory witnesses were reported to have given Barbara a good character as a 'sober, mild and attentive servant'.[55] It is notable that Barbara's employer did not attempt to distance herself from such a heinous crime. She may not have known where Barbara took her daughter on their walks out together, but she knew Barbara had born a child; otherwise, she would not have sought employment as a wet-nurse. Despite comments from prosecution witnesses that Barbara's demeanour had altered since June 1807, Mrs Hamilton had not removed her daughter from Barbara's care. It is unclear how Barbara had changed since Sutherland's rejection, but her continuing employment suggests she had not become violent, cruel or unkind to Mrs Hamilton's daughter, nor insane.

It can only be presumed that the other exculpatory witnesses offered supportive evidence of Barbara's character, trustworthiness and of a woman who they considered unlikely to murder her own child. The news reports of the trial do not describe Barbara's demeanour in court, but her insistence on her innocence suggests a woman of resilience, unwilling to show remorse for a crime she believed she had not committed. If she had demurred to the court, there is a remote possibility that the jury might have acquitted her. By displaying a more combative and unwomanly, 'unnatural' attitude to an all-male jury, this would undoubtedly have worked against her, when the expectation was deference and repentance.

Except for her financial circumstances, Barbara had no reason to kill Margaret. Given her resourcefulness at maintaining both their well-being for eighteen months without assistance from Sutherland, arguably she might have been successful yet again at remedying her situation. Daly and Wilson have identified a lack of paternal support leading to 'isolation and poverty', which may result in infanticide, and Reid et al. confirm that in this period, illegitimate children were nearly twice as likely to die before their first birthday compared with infants born to married parents.[56] Daly's and Wilson's theory that a young woman's 'residual reproductive value' may inform her behaviour towards an illegitimate, burdensome child might have influenced Barbara.[57] She may have decided that Margaret had to be sacrificed to secure her own future, but again, killing her in plain sight does not make sense for a sane woman anticipating a future life.

Conclusion

In 1809, the law on infanticide in Scotland was revised. Increasing understanding of postpartum mental instability might have benefited Barbara, but her crime was committed two years too early. No one had considered her mental state. No one had considered a chemical mistake by the apothecary. She had not given the impression of an unloving mother, so vicious and vindictive towards her soldier lover to destroy their child. The evidence does not suggest a woman fixated on her child as the source of all her woes. The revisions in 1809 sought to prosecute the concealment of pregnancy that had led to a child's unintentional death as separate from the wilful murder of a child. Kilday's research suggests that 'mental health testimonies' were used more readily after 1809 in infanticide cases, compared to homicide cases, to 'qualify intent', thereby providing mitigation of sentence and avoidance of execution.[58] Barbara is unlikely to have benefited from this development since the medical evidence and choice of poison had 'proved' her intent to murder; the forensic medical experts had failed to consider insanity or accident. Gordon's testimony, taken after the medical experts were precognosced, may have been influenced by their 'superior' authority. His precognition indicates his disbelief in Barbara's offer of 'raw sugar' as well as his readiness to 'monster' her as a murderous mother. Whether Gordon was 'prompted' by those precognoscing him will never be known.

Kilday identifies a trend towards low conviction rates in England in the eighteenth century and successful petitioning by Scottish women for banishment in lieu of a trial.[59] Alison recognized that there had been 'many inhuman convictions' and was satisfied by the 1820s that 'the law stands on a comparative lenient footing'.[60] A trial that put the onus on an unprotected woman to prove her innocence and the far-from-conclusive evidence used to prosecute had persuaded juries not to convict when the only sentence could be doom. Banishment circumvented both trial and sentence. The revisions in 1809 of the harsh statute enacted in 1690 reflected a changing attitude towards women, girls and children – vulnerable innocents whose circumstances were not necessarily of their own making, and therefore, punishments needed to match the act and its motives. Research for England and Wales, and Scotland suggests a declining trend both in indictments for infanticide and convictions.[61] So that by 1886, Harriet Cooper only suffered a sentence of three months' imprisonment for killing her 'living male child' by covering 'his mouth and nostrils with the clothes of the bed'.[62] By the end of the nineteenth century, this child-victim was given his correct pronoun, and the mother was dealt with lightly. Since juries continued to be all-male, this development towards leniency and compassion can also be interpreted as patriarchal condescension, supported by the new medical thinking on 'the social and biological function' of women and the 'strength and weakness of femaleness'.[63]

Barclay argues that 'material conditions' determined 'not just how children were cared for', but how much 'they were cared about'.[64] This is very true of Barbara's case. She cared about Margaret evidenced by their first eighteen months together, but her circumstances meant she could not care for her herself. Emsley confirms that, despite homicide being 'one of the best-reported crimes', infanticide was 'notoriously under-reported', likely because the perpetrators were young, unsupported women who attracted some sympathy.[65] Barbara's crime might have gone unreported by the Gordons, but presumably the terrible nature of Margaret's death affected them greatly, and they felt Barbara, the only person they could accuse, should face justice. However, the early intervention by the apothecary meant that his evidence closed any lacuna in which a consideration of insanity or a test of motive could be conducted. Speculatively, it must be considered possible that the apothecary realized his mistake and callously covered his tracks in a period when working-class women, and families like the Gordons, lacked agency.

Barbara's class, her 'unnatural' behaviour as a mother and the panel facing a juridical patriarchy contributed to her guilt. Barbara's behaviour on the scaffold suggests her continued belief in her innocence. She was described as 'very penitent and resigned' and being so feeble that she required the help of two men to reach the place of execution.[66] That sounds more like a woman who had hoped for justice, but whose pleas had been trumped by medical jurisprudence.[67]

Notes

1 Act anent the Murthering of Children, 1690, 1 Wm & Mary, c20, s2.
2 The modern definition of infanticide is the murder of a newborn child up to the age of two years; neonaticide is the killing of an infant within the first twenty-four hours of life.
3 D. Hume, *Commentaries on the Law of Scotland, respecting trial for crimes*, vol. 1 (Edinburgh, 1797), 462–3.
4 Alison cites a case of premature birth in Inverness in 1815 in which the panel confessed to having concealed her pregnancy. The Bench considered the case untenable because premature parturition where the baby was stillborn was 'entitled to an acquittal'; A. Alison, *Principles of the Criminal Law of Scotland* (Edinburgh, 1832), 155.
5 M. Daly and M. Wilson, *Homicide* (New Jersey, 2010), 62.

6   A. M. Kilday, *Women and Violent Crime in Enlightenment Scotland* (Woodridge, 2015), 63.
7   Rarely men are co-accused with the mother of the victim.
8   A. M. Kilday, 'Desperate Measures or Cruel Intentions?: Infanticide in Britain since 1600', in *Histories of Crimes: Britain 1600–2000*, ed. A. M. Kilday and D. Nash (Basingstoke, 2010), 66; C. Emsley, *Crime and Society in England 1750–1900* (Harlow, 2010), 104; R. Smith, *Trial by Medicine: Insanity and Responsibility in Victorian Trials* (Edinburgh, 1981), 144.
9   Anonymous, *An Account of the Crime, Trial, and Behaviour of Barbara Malcolm*, John Johnson Collection: An Archive of Printed Ephemera, Crime, Allegro ID: 20080125/16:54:19¢kg.
10 A. M. Kilday, '"Angels of the House" or "Angel-Makers"?: Problematizing Murderous Mothers in the Nineteenth Century', in *Beyond Deviant Damsels: re-evaluating female criminality in the nineteenth Century*, ed. D. Nash and A. M. Kilday (Oxford, 2023), 70.
11 R. Mitchison and L. Leneman, *Girls in Trouble: sexuality and social control in rural Scotland 1660–1780* (Edinburgh, 1998), 110.
12 K. Barclay, 'Love, Care and the Illegitimate Child in Eighteenth-Century Scotland', *Royal Historical Society Transactions*, 6th series, vol. 29 (2019), 115.
13 Kines quoted via W. E. Hartpole Lecky, *History of European Morals* (New York, 1869), vol. II, 27, via R. Sauer, 'Infanticide and Abortion in Nineteenth-Century Britain', *Population Studies*, vol. 32, no. 1 (March, 1978), 84–5.
14 T. C. Smout, 'Aspects of Sexual Behaviour in Nineteenth Century Scotland', in *Social Class in Scotland: Past and Present*, ed. A. A. MacLaren (Edinburgh, 1976), 80.
15 A. Blaikie, 'Scottish Illegitimacy: Social Adjustment or Moral Economy?', *Journal of Interdisciplinary History*, vol. 20, no. 2 (Autumn, 1998), 230, 233.
16 Kilday, 'Desperate Measures', 69.
17 M. L. Arnot, 'Understanding Women committing newborn child murder in Victorian England, in *Everyday Violence in Britain, 1850–1950: Gender and Class*, ed. S. D'Cruze (Harlow, 2000), 56.
18 Alison, *Principles*, 161.
19 Arnot, 'Understanding Women', 60.
20 K. Polk, *When Men Kill: Scenarios of Masculine Violence* (Cambridge, 1994), 144.
21 Arnot, 'Understanding Women', 59.
22 Daly and Wilson, *Homicide*, 62, 64, 65, 67.
23 A. M. Kilday, *Crime in Scotland 1660–1960: the Violent North?* (Abingdon, 2021), 33–4.
24 P. Spierenburg, 'Long-Term Trends in Homicide: Theoretical Reflections and Dutch Evidence, Fifteenth to Twentieth Centuries', *The Civilization*

of Crime: Violence in Town and Country since the Middle Ages, ed. E. A. Johnson and E. H. Monkkonen (Chicago, 1996), 65; Emsley, *Crime and Society*, 104.
25. Sauer, 'Infanticide and Abortion', 82–3.
26. Sauer, 'Infanticide and Abortion', 84. See Hume, 'Killing of a child *in utero*', for contemporary explanation; Hume, *Commentaries*, vol. 1, 274.
27. Arnot, 'Understanding Women', 61–2.
28. Kilday, *Women and Violent Crime*, 61.
29. Emsley, *Crime and Society*, 105.
30. Kilday, *Violent North?*, 34.
31. JC26/1808/27.
32. *Caledonian Mercury*, 7 January 1808, vol. 3, no. 13421.
33. A. Reid, R. Davies, E. Garrett and A. Blaikie, 'Vulnerability among illegitimate children in Nineteenth century Scotland', *Annales de demographie Historique*, no. 1 (2006), 103.
34. *Scots Magazine & Edinburgh Literary Miscellany*, 70 (January, 1808), 74.
35. *Caledonian Mercury*, 3.
36. JC26/1808/27.
37. JC4/4.
38. *The Edinburgh Annual Register*, London, vol. 1 (January, 1808), 4.
39. *Scots Magazine*, 74.
40. JC4/4.
41. Kilday, 'Angels of the House', 75
42. Alison, *Principles*, 158.
43. JC26/1808/27.
44. Kilday, 'Angels of the House', 79.
45. *Edinburgh Annual Register*, 4.
46. Kilday, 'Angels of the House', 76.
47. Reid et al., 'Vulnerability', 108.
48. JC26/1807/27.
49. Smith, *Trial by Medicine*, 147.
50. Smith, *Trial by Medicine*, 148.
51. Smith, *Trial by Medicine*, 149.
52. Alison, *Principles*, 159.
53. Sugar of lead is lead acetate, which has a sweet taste and has been used throughout history as a sweetener and in the nineteenth century as a medicine; C. Emsley, *The Elements of Murder: A History of Poison* (Oxford, 2005), 269, 314. Oil of vitriol was used in industrial processes from the eighteenth century, and it is likely that Barbara would have known its poisonous propensity because servants used it to clean kitchen utensils; Kilday, 'Angels of the House', 77. Did Barbara have both in her pockets, one as a medicine, the other to clean her mistress's home?

54 JC26/1808/27.
55 *Caledonian Mercury*, 7 January 1808.
56 Reid et al., 'Vulnerability', 89.
57 Daly and Wilson, *Homicide*, 52, 62.
58 Kilday, *Violent North?*, 34.
59 Kilday, *Women and Violent Crime*, 62.
60 Alison, *Principles*, 153.
61 Kilday, *Violent North?*, 46; Kilday notes the difficulty after 1809 in differentiating infanticide murder cases from other murders making statistical analysis burdensome, 34. S. D'Cruze and L. A. Jackson, *Women, Crime and Justice in England since 1660* (Basingstoke, 2009), 80. Statistics for infanticide in Scotland 1978–1993 indicate forty-three deaths per million population annually of babies under one year, a figure which is comparable with England and Wales in the same period of 45/million; M. N. Marks and R. Kumar, 'Infanticide in Scotland', *Medicine, Science and the Law*, vol. 36, no. 4 (October, 1996), abstract.
62 JC26/1886/266.
63 Smith, *Trial by Medicine*, 144.
64 Barclay, 'Love, Care and the Illegitimate Child', 125.
65 Emsley, *Crime and Society*, 48.
66 *Scots Magazine*, 156.
67 Further research on the impact of Scottish medical jurisprudence on criminal trials is much needed as a comparative to work conducted for England and Wales.

4

Tron Rioters 1811–12: Protest, murder and class conflict

Apprentices letting off steam was not uncommon at the turn of the eighteenth century and rarely resulted in their execution, but in early 1812, new social pressures were emerging in the Scottish capital that forced the elites into an unusually severe reaction to what had otherwise been a customary Hogmanay celebration.

Context

Before the introduction of universal suffrage, there were limited options for the lower classes to influence economic and social policies; everything from the price of bread to what they perceived as unnecessary intervention in their daily lives was outside their control.[1] Therefore, collective protest was a last resort to draw attention to their discontent. Generally, if the people's protests were heard and acted upon by the authorities, life returned to normal, but if not, then further protests could be expected.[2] The impetus for protest and riots usually formed around three issues: food, its availability and price; work, its practices, wages and opportunity, and less often radical politics.

It has been claimed that there was 'no tradition of political debate' after the 1650s in Scotland, and it is arguable whether the two key political conflicts of the eighteenth century could be framed as 'debate'.[3] The 1715 and 1745 Jacobite risings, which had aimed to return the Stuart monarchy to the British throne as well as restore Scottish home rule, among other things, were met with belligerent reprisals by the British establishment, resulting in extreme long-term after-effects. By the time of the French Revolution in 1789 and its aftermath into the 1790s, there was the beginning of a 'political awakening' in Scotland, which reached its peak between 1792 and 1794, when political divisions between radicals and the traditional ruling class were manifested. On the one hand the Tories, who considered that agitation for reform was tantamount to revolution, believed that 'the national support' they had previously enjoyed in times of crisis would continue. At the other end of the spectrum, the lower classes 'based their hopes on universal suffrage and annual Parliaments', which were supported by the Whigs alongside their 'detestation of judicial cruelties'.[4]

The response to the French Revolution during the early 1790s alarmed the authorities in Scotland and the rest of Britain. The King's Birthday riots of June 1792 had been especially volatile in Edinburgh. This was a premeditated and well-organized riot, with placards advertising the event in the preceding days. As Hamish Fraser notes, the impetus for the riot remains unclear, but the level of violence and planning was alarming. The riot had been political, aimed at the Lord Advocate Robert Dundas.[5] Chris Whatley agrees that despite contemporary comment, the event has disappeared into a historical 'black hole', possibly because historians have viewed it as insignificant or because it smeared the 'comfortable image of Scottish society' with a stain of violence. The King's Birthday celebrations in 1796 were similarly uproarious, but both outrages appear to have been traditional events of 'senseless orgy of fire and fury' in which the 'mob' assaulted the authorities and for which few were brought to justice. Whatley argues that these 'carnivalesque' events were a means of 'maintaining social control' – a safety valve which blew briefly before normality resumed.[6] Contemporary Whig commentator, Henry Cockburn, provides a similar view that there were 'few proper Jacobins' in Scotland in the 1790s, and their campaign for 'internal reform' fizzled out once the 'folly' and 'essential absurdity' of the French Revolution had become apparent.[7] So that by the first decade of the nineteenth century, political activism had largely disappeared from Scottish society.

Other riots pre-1811 were largely food and employment protests. As Anne-Marie Kilday argues, by their nature these were local protests, sparked by local issues, and where it was collectivized violence, this was enacted in the interests of specific groups to promote change.[8] Thus, weavers struck work as a body to seek higher wages in a cost-of-living crisis in August 1787, and a riot ensued. The riot reached its zenith on 3 September when Glasgow's Lord Provost and his magistrates attempted to persuade the rioters not to enter the city. Stone-throwing and a confrontation with troops called out to defuse the situation resulted in the reading of the Riot Act, rifles being fired and eight dead weavers. One weaver, James Granger, who was successfully apprehended some months later and convicted of mobbing and rioting, was sentenced to public flogging in Edinburgh, not his home city due to fears of public reprisals from potential supporters. The judges in Granger's case were divided on the 'degrading and undignified' nature of the punishment against those who supported the visible deterrent. The latter won. Thus, already at the end of the eighteenth century, even when confronted with widespread unrest, the elites might feel disquiet at a 'cruel and humiliating' punishment.[9]

Similar combination protests occurred in the environs of Glasgow in 1812 when the cotton spinners went on strike after their appeal to the Lord Provost for fixed prices on their finished cloth was rejected because of an intervention by the manufacturers. Their strike involved 40,000 men, and 'seditious or treasonable designs' were anticipated. After illegally entering their homes searching for incriminating documents, the strike leaders were charged under the Combination Acts of 1799 and 1800 and sentenced to eighteen months' imprisonment.[10] Again, the punishment for what were politically constructed charges appears to have been lenient when capital punishment was the possible alternative.

In the early 1800s, Scotland did not have a 'bloody code' like England; thus, Scots Law, with only thirty indictments for which the possible sentence, if convicted, would be execution, compared to England's 270 hanging offences, was definitely less sanguinary.[11] Throughout the eighteenth century in Scotland, those convicted of rioting were rarely hanged, with the judiciary transmuting capital punishment into imprisonment or transportation, and an occasional public flogging as a deterrent to remind the population of the authority of the law.[12] This leniency towards the convicted may have encouraged juries to return guilty verdicts in the knowledge that the culprit was less likely to hang. It is a 'chicken and egg' argument: did sentencing trends provoke juridical verdicts, or vice versa? Either way, execution for political riots and striking was less frequent than is generally perceived to have been the case. Additionally, although attitudes towards a protected period of childhood were not necessarily extended to the children of the lower classes in the same way that their middle-class peers enjoyed, Peter King argues for the 'rapidly declining incidence of juvenile executions' in England.[13] With fewer indictments in Scotland carrying a possible capital sentence, it must be assumed that a similar trend was experienced north of the border for involvement in serious insurrections.

Historians agree that food – prices and scarcity – was a key cause of urban riots. Fraser argues that meal – grain – riots reflected an imbalance in the 'moral economy', whereby the right to food at an affordable price was used to legitimize the mob's protest.[14] These events were not criminally motivated; they occurred in daylight and aimed to attract the authorities' attention to resolve the situation.[15] In Edinburgh, a grain fund was established so that the city magistrates could intervene in market prices to alleviate the suffering of the poor and prevent food riots.[16] But even in periods of the most severe dearth from 1795 to 1801, only twenty meal riots occurred in Scotland.[17] Evidently, the Scottish populace needed to be down to their last loaf before they took to the streets, which was unusual because the properly hungry do not rebel.[18] Unlike in England, the Scottish authorities lacked a militia to call upon to enact force; instead the 'public peace depended on mutual tolerance', formed through 'a complex web of patronage and deference relations'.[19] After 1790 when 'Volunteers' units were established in major urban centres, they were not always called out for fear they might side with the rioters.[20]

However, the symbiotic relationship of 'paternalism and dependence' had become increasingly strained as Scotland urbanized in the late eighteenth and early nineteenth centuries. By the 1801 census, 83 per cent of Scotland's population living in urban centres of over 5,000 inhabitants were located in the Lowland belt.[21] Glasgow and Edinburgh experienced the greatest growth as rural–urban migration was increasingly attracted by the new manufacturing and industrial opportunities. In a small city with close perimeters, newcomers packed into Edinburgh's medieval town alongside existing residents of all classes. Here, the titled, lawyers, government officials, the middle classes and the lower orders lived side by side. Differentiation of accommodation by class was minimal with families of different social status inhabiting a single building, separated by floor rather than segregated by district. This arrangement was noteworthy to English visitors to the capital.[22]

However, increasing wealth in the seat of Scottish administration led to the development of Edinburgh's New Town, a construction site since the 1760s, providing housing for the wealthy away from the overcrowded medieval centre. In 1811, the New Town's Charlotte Square remained a construction site as this section of the city expanded ever further north and west away from the teeming Old Town.[23] The new wide Georgian squares surrounded by elegant buildings with expanses of glass frontages screamed conspicuous wealth. In detaching themselves from the lower orders, the middle and upper classes fractured the old paternal consensus. No longer rubbing shoulders every day in the Old Town, the social fabric of Edinburgh had separated, creating two distinct districts of the haves and haves-not. The wealth and possessions of the elites had always been visible to the lower classes, but as more individuals moved away from the old centre, any instance of discontent among the less privileged was no longer readily obvious to the elites until matters reached a boiling point. Bill Knox argues that these residential social divisions were exacerbated by the development of consumerism, making the fashionable Princes Street 'an exclusive shopping thoroughfare for the well-to-do'.[24] Princes Street became a geographical and social status line rarely crossed.

Thus, rioting mobs had distinct reasons for their actions: socio-political and economic impetuses might create imbalances in the accepted *status quo*, which in turn spawned violent protest. At the turn of the nineteenth century, elite tolerance of a 'rumbustious people's' occasional outbursts appears to have held steady.[25] Unless the catalyst for rioting was something the elites had not yet experienced to any degree.

What if a traditional New Year's Eve revelry turned into a thieving spree, aggravated by violence, perpetrated by a newly disgruntled social cohort during which the better off were roughed up and robbed, and one policeman died?

Case

Heralding the new century on 1 January 1801, celebrations were anticipated to express 'national respect and exultation' and the union of England, Scotland and Ireland in the 'mutual happiness of the British Empire'.[26] By 2 January 1809, in the private correspondence newspaper pages, one Edinburgh citizen complained that on New Year's morning the capital's streets were thronged with people 'the worse of liquor'; one man was found dead in Westport, and an investigation was underway. Elsewhere in the city, 'a great number' had been committed to the City Guard.[27] This was nothing unusual for Hogmanay celebrations in Edinburgh, making the absence of reports for the intervening years unremarkable. It was traditional even after the elites had begun to move to the New Town for them to return to the Tron Church in the Old Town to see in the New Year gathered around the clock tower.[28]

However, at some point between the last hour of 31 December 1811 and the early hours of 1 January 1812, according to the Procurator Fiscal, Alexander Ponton, 'a number of riotous and disorderly persons' had paraded around the city's streets, 'committing the most outrageous acts of violence against the peaceable inhabitants, knocking them down, robbing them of their watches money' and 'sometime cruelly maltreating them'. Ponton identified Hugh McIntosh, Neil Sutherland, John Tasker and William Swan as the perpetrators of this outrage. Ponton petitioned the 'Bailies of Edinburgh' to grant a warrant for the men's apprehension.[29] Ponton's petition was made on 7 January, a week after the Hogmanay unrest. Yet, already on 2 January 1812, the 'official' version of events was in the public domain, contrasting the usual 'innocent festivities' with what had actually occurred this year.

From approximately 11.00 pm, 'a gang of ferocious banditti' had rampaged the capital's central streets armed with bludgeons and had 'wantonly abused almost every person who had the misfortune to fall in their way'. Some gentlemen who were assaulted fought back. One was noted to have been 'kicked on the head, and in the breast and stomach'; another had similarly resisted the robbing of his watch. The violence was immediately blamed on a gang of 'idle apprentices' who had 'lurked in stairs and closes' awaiting the signal to pounce on passersby. By 5.00 am, the city's magistrates had managed

ILLUSTRATION 4.1 *Grassmarket, Old Edinburgh.* © *Getty Images.*

to apprehend some of the culprits 'on the spot'. The following day, policeman Dugald Campbell was dead of injuries sustained on the night, and a few days later, James Campbell, a clerk at Leith, also died of his injuries. A reward of 100 guineas was offered 'upon conviction' for anyone willing to give evidence that would lead to the apprehension of other perpetrators and a further 100 guineas for anyone with information concerning the attack on Dugald Campbell. The riot was 'unexampled in Edinburgh' and 'a thing so new in the metropolis' that the magistrates were putting all their efforts into the discovery of the 'boys and young lads' who had run amok. A specific request was made to those in charge of apprentices to detect the guilty among them, and jewellers were alerted to look out for stolen goods being fenced for sale. It was only twenty-four hours after the uproar and already 'a sub-committee' had been formed to repeal the existing police act and introduce another 'containing a powerful system of police' to prevent another similar occurrence.[30]

Between 1 January and early March 1812, numerous individuals gave precognition statements testifying to what they had experienced, observed and couldn't be quite sure about. James Stewart had met Neil Sutherland, one of the key perpetrators of the violence, and returned to his lodgings with him where Sutherland produced a 'small watch the colour of gold' and had asked him to store it in his chest. Sutherland returned that afternoon with McIntosh and Swan to retrieve the trunk. Peter Maiden had been chased into a house on Blair Street by a 'thief gang' armed with sticks, but when out on the street, he had not seen anyone 'that he was the least acquainted with'. William Swan gave evidence that he had 'heard' Sutherland and McIntosh talking about a watch, but he had not actually seen it exchange hands, and he had also heard them discussing 'a great deal of disturbances and a great deal of mischief'. Hugh MacDonald, who was unable to give his age, had been apprenticed as a shoemaker, then spent two years at sea before returning to Edinburgh. He had left the city after the mobbing for fear of 'being put to sea again'. He was acquainted with Hugh McIntosh, his cousin, and he knew 'Neil Sutherland a little'.[31] These intricacies of the evidence were much streamlined by the time the first trial took place on 2 March 1812, and by then, some of the witnesses who had participated had turned King's evidence.

On Monday, 2 March 1812, John Skelton, apprentice gunsmith, was on trial for committing several robberies in the High Street. When giving evidence against him, George Edmonston was clear that the assault had taken place on Fleshmarket. The inconsistency caused the Solicitor General to waive this part of the charge against Skelton. A stoneware merchant gave evidence that he had been attacked by between 'forty and fifty lads' all appearing to be under the age of twenty. A divinity student had been assaulted by 'three dozen' youths, and being recognized as 'a country lad' had saved him when he had no money to offer. Apprentice Walter Alexander had met Skelton and brought some sticks, but he did not understand why they were needed, although there was some talk about 'lifting gentlemen's hats'. Kenneth McKenzie, an apprentice confectioner, declared he did not know Skelton and was unsure whether he had held a stick; having been precognosced three times, it was on the second instance that he had been informed of the name of the man who had helped him to throw an orange box at the policeman. However, McKenzie was sure the talk about lifting hats had occurred about 'a month, three weeks earlier'. Another placed Skelton in the middle of the mob wielding a stick, but only once. John Chisholm, a policeman, had witnessed Skelton with a stick crying out to attack the police; another policeman had helped him take Skelton into custody.

The inconclusive evidence against Skelton was balanced by his former employer's character statement: he had always behaved 'soberly, honestly and to his perfect satisfaction'. Once the exculpatory evidence had been heard, the Solicitor General apologized to the jury for the delay in bringing Skelton to trial due to 'the number of outrages' committed on New Year's Eve. He concluded that the prosecution 'had completely made his case' against the prisoner. However, counsel for the defence, Mr Gordon, remarked that there was 'a clear line of distinction between a person being engaged in the boisterous and riotous mirth to which the last night of the year has, by immemorial custom, been devoted' and another of involvement in 'a systematic plan' to plunder and rob. He concluded that it 'were better ten guilty persons should escape than that one innocent person should suffer'. The jury was out overnight after which they returned a unanimously guilty verdict with a recommendation to leniency due to Skelton's previous good character. The judge said that 'their humane recommendation would be transmitted to the Prince Regent'; he pronounced doom, and Skelton's execution was scheduled for 15 April 1812.[32]

On 11 March 1812, the bigger trial of Hugh McDonald, Hugh McIntosh, Neil Sutherland, George Napier, John Grotto and James Johnston took place. They were indicted on eleven separate charges, the most serious of which was the murder of Dugald Campbell, the policeman. The remaining ten charges all involved 'knocking down' and robbing various individuals. Evidence given by Mr Newbigging, surgeon at the Royal Infirmary, was key. He testified that Campbell could not have been saved due to the nature of the injuries sustained. James Gilchrist had been near the Tron Church at the time of the assault on Campbell, and although he had witnessed youths hitting him on the ground, he had seen neither Sutherland nor McIntosh among them. John Tasker had turned King's evidence and now confirmed that a group of young men, including the accused, used to meet three times per week at the bottom of Niddry Street where they discussed picking quarrels and striking people, but never stealing. Tasker told the court that Sutherland had declared he was 'going on board a man of war' and would not be with them at New Year, but McIntosh had persuaded him to stay to 'give the police a licking'. Tasker named other groups involved and how they had been instructed to deliver anything taken that night to McIntosh. The Niddry Street party along with the Canongate and Grassmarket groups all had distinctive whistles to signal to other gang members of the approach of a suitable person to target.

John Swan gave similar evidence, revealing Dugald Campbell's nickname of 'Royal Arch' and that he 'was very hard upon the boys'. Clearly, Campbell was reviled by the local youths. Swan had seen a man 'much smashed' by the Stamp Office Close and also admitted he had given a watch he had stolen to McIntosh. William Swan confirmed the evidence he had given in precognition that Sutherland and McIntosh had visited him at home to stow their trunk of stolen goods. Again, the exculpatory evidence described reliable and diligent young men. Only one witness testified to an alibi for McIntosh who had been at work 'the whole evening', but he could not name any of the other lads in the workshop who might corroborate that. After the judge's summing-up, the jury departed at 4.00 am, instructed to deliver their verdict by 2.00 pm the following day. Outside, the Royal Edinburgh Volunteers and the city's night patrol contained the agitation from the crowds awaiting the verdict.[33]

On Saturday afternoon, the jury returned: Sutherland, McDonald and McIntosh had all been found guilty of two charges of robbery, and McIntosh had been convicted of being 'art and part guilty of the murder of Dugald Campbell'. All three were scheduled for execution at the place of Campbell's death on 22 April. The Lord Justice-Clerk remarked on the youth of the prisoners and their accomplices whose evidence had helped to convict them. Some of them were only fifteen years old, and the judge hoped they would learn from the 'sad and melancholy scene' they were now witnessing and in future 'refrain from that idle and dissipated life'.[34] George Napier pleaded guilty only to the tenth charge of robbing Peter Bruce, while John Grotto pleaded guilty only to robbing John Buchan Brodie. Both were sentenced to transportation for fourteen years.[35] Sixteen-year-olds Robert Gunn and Alexander MacDonald had their cases abandoned by the Crown, which has been attributed to their involvement with the couple who fenced stolen goods for the Niddry Street gang. The couple were known resetters, taking in and selling on stolen property; they volunteered for life-long banishment, taking the teenagers with them. Cases against others collapsed due to the Crown's insufficient confidence in them to continue.[36] In May 1812, Skelton's sentence was remitted; the evidence against him had been declared circumstantial.

Of the three who hanged, none of them was over twenty years. MacDonald appeared to the reporter witnessing the execution as 'above 18 years of age', stout and fair. Sutherland was slender with black hair, and McIntosh was 'neatly made'.[37] Sutherland and McIntosh were probably only fifteen or sixteen years old.[38] As they were led to the gibbet at Stamp Office Close, they were accompanied by ministers and over 1000 militia, Volunteers, police and the city 'patrole'. Eyewitness reports noted that Sutherland gave the signal to the executioner when they were ready, and many in the crowd solemnly removed their hats at the crucial moment.[39]

In total, sixty-eight panels were charged with numerous counts of robbery and violence. Four had been condemned to hang, three of whom did; two were transported for life and a further two for fourteen years.[40]

Themes and analysis

Besides the obvious criminality perpetrated during Hogmanay 1811, a celebration that got out of hand in a way that previous festivities had not, analysis of the case of the Tron Riot reveals several facets of early nineteenth-century Edinburgh society. Knox poses a crucial question: 'what if the riot lay outside the existing nomenclature of social relations?'[41] Lower class protests had usually concentrated around an issue: food, wages, shortages. None of those impetuses fuelled the Tron Riot. Neither the High Court of Justiciary case papers nor the newspaper reports mention these catalysts. However, Knox's close reading of the reportage and its use of language indicates a key cause of the riot: 'a band of idle apprentice boys' and 'a gang of ferocious banditti'.[42] Those accused were mostly young men, many under sixteen years of age. All those who were hanged were apprentices. The case papers do not provide evidence of idleness, because it appears they were employed at the time of the riot. Yet, the elites had identified them as a blameworthy cohort capable of robbery and violence; bored young men with nothing else to do except form street gangs and assault innocent passersby.

Michael Flinn's research calculates that in the 1790s, in the Eastern Lowlands, the only region commensurate with Edinburgh, 45.2 per cent of the population was aged under twenty years and 61.86 per cent aged under thirty years. For the same region in 1801 and 1811, the ratio of men to women was 84.7 and 84.00, respectively. The differences between Edinburgh's youthful population and the Western Lowlands which encompassed Glasgow were negligible; here, percentages of those under twenty and thirty years were 46.12 and 62.15, respectively.[43] Clearly, a preponderantly youthful population agitating for recognition and position had not caused this particular event. Neither had relative poverty since the ringleaders indicted of the most serious crimes were all in employment. Idleness in both meanings cannot account for this riotous behaviour.

What if Hogmanay 1811 had been little different to previous celebrations? Skelton's defence counsel and others recalled 'boisterous and riotous mirth' in previous years; in 1809 someone had died. The one element of Hogmanay 1811 that appears different from earlier festivities is the premeditated nature of the venture, organized apparently by MacDonald, Sutherland and McIntosh. John Kidd's evidence identifies the Niddry Street gang who coordinated with the Canongate and Grassmarket gangs to maximize their robbing. Tasker recalled the plans having taken three weeks to formulate. However, Knox argues convincingly that 'the dispersed nature of the attacks and large numbers involved' does not correlate with testimonies, which described the men lurking in stairs and closes.[44] Thus, the premeditated nature of the event is well evidenced, but the number of precognitions and court reports that recount 'running up and down' in open streets and criss-crossing bridges does not support the 'lurking' element of accounts. Instead, that suggests an elite giving voice to their private fears of stepping foot in the increasingly unfamiliar dark wynds of the Old Town.

Peter King's study of juvenile delinquency in eighteenth- and early nineteenth-century rural and urban settings highlights this key fear of youth violence. His survey of crime and demographic data for England from 1780 to 1840 explores the impacts of rapid urbanization; changes in apprenticeship and other living-in service employment; changing attitudes by victims of interpersonal crime towards prosecution and changes to criminal justice administration. His research investigates whether the move from jury to summary justice had an impact on perceptions of crime and whether elite attitudes towards the poor and their children created fearful perceptions of the lower classes.[45] In each area of investigation, King identifies perceptions that are generally not supported by the crime statistics, and where they are supported for one region or city in England, another bucks the trend. Thus, more localized factors need to be explored to explain what happened in Edinburgh: why so few panels were sentenced and why the judiciary responded so harshly to those who were convicted.

First, the sheer numbers alleged to have been involved in the worst of the violence caused problems for the authorities. Not only did individuals who had committed their alleged crimes in cramped dark corners of the Old Town have to be identified, but they had to be located too. It is unclear when the key perpetrators were arrested, but by 7 January, the Procurator Fiscal had already identified some. His petition outlining the main charges against them was based on evidence pieced together from victims and probably added to by those who had perpetrated less serious offences that night.[46] Precognition statements from victims and witnesses are usually taken within a few days of a crime, but clearly, the case being built by the Procurator Fiscal had not been easy to collate and corroboration – key to Scots Law – was not abundant since most victims had not witnessed another's assault. To corroborate the testimonies against the key panels, the Procurator Fiscal had to negotiate with some of the perpetrators to persuade them to turn King's evidence.

The Procurator Fiscal had returned to James Stewart several times during January seeking corroboration of other evidence in process of collection, culminating in Stewart's final evidence written down on 30 January 1812. Similarly, William Swan was compeared again on 30 January, providing evidence of his knowledge of the trunks containing the stolen goods. George Napier, who was prosecuted, was precognosced on 4 and 5 February, giving similar statements both times.[47] Arguably, building a criminal prosecution on the evidence of King's witnesses was an unfair tactic, but the efforts of the Procurator Fiscal and the boxes of precognitions collected indicate the judicial system was hard at work throughout January into February to produce a case that was indeed fair. The delay in apprehending Sutherland, McIntosh and MacDonald suggests further that the police had not received clear instructions from Ponton on who to arrest and where to find them. In fact, it was alleged that there were worse participants still at large than those now in custody.[48]

Second, the delay between the riot and the trial allowed the print media to insinuate its influence. By 2 January, already the elites were being fed column-inches of strongly worded accusations against idle apprentices, the lack of discipline in their families and general society, so that by the time of the first trial in March, the Solicitor General felt it necessary to explain to the court how the delay had occurred and to confirm that the moment precognitions investigating Skelton's involvement had been taken, 'the present indictment was served in the course of two days after'.[49] It is unclear whether the Solicitor General's explanation was a response to accusations of a slow judiciary or whether he had made one of the first attempts to instruct the jury to disregard whatever they had heard in the press before attending court. However, by the time Skelton stood trial, the jury could not have failed to have been exposed to numerous news accounts and opinion pieces. Given the property qualifications necessary to be eligible for jury service in this period, it is reasonable to assume that those deliberating on this trial were all middle class or above. Thus, it is probable they too were outraged at the degree of violence used against innocent revellers and had no sympathy for the accused.

However, Kilday's research on aggravated robbery prosecuted at the High Court of Justiciary during the nineteenth century reveals that by the 1800s 'all robbery activity was carried out on foot' and usually after dark, and that of indictments prosecuted at the High Court of Justiciary, some 83 per cent involved 'knives, razors, pistols or cudgels'. These Scottish 'footpads' often operated in gangs, and because their means of transport was slow, they tended to beat their victims unconscious to avoid identification and apprehension. Kilday argues that Scottish violent property theft was 'more daring and damaging' than that committed south of the border, although she recognizes that only the most violent crimes were heard at the High Court. She questions whether Scots in this period might be 'more tolerant of acts of robbery' when the violence used was lower grade, but where real aggression had been employed, they dealt with panels more harshly. It might explain why the handful of panels convicted in 1812 were sentenced to death and transportation, whereas others among the accused cohort were acquitted. Further, Kilday argues that robbery in Scotland was often premediated in planning but was opportunistic in selecting victims.[50] This also applies to 1812, when several witnesses testified to the organization between the Niddry, Canongate and Grassmarket gangs; this indicates premeditation, but without knowing who the victims might be until the night.

Knowing that gangs of potential footpads walked the streets of Edinburgh, sufficiently organized to perpetrate crime at will, was hugely alarming to Edinburgh's elites. By identifying idle apprentices as the culprits, the media implied a generalized but recognizable cohort of young men largely to be found in the Old Town who were capable of committing the most feared crime: violent robbery. King argues that this type of crime created fear across all social strata. Among those with the most to lose, the fear was the most heightened; they perceived robbery as a crime for dark Winter evenings. Thus, 1812's Hogmanay riot fits neatly into the collective fears of the newly removed residents of the Old Town rubbing shoulders with their former neighbours. King concludes that street crime was 'over-represented in the media' and that this form of 'underdog crime' fuelled moral panics. Not only did scaremongering sell newspapers, but it convinced the already converted that crime levels were escalating and the lower classes were to blame. King maintains that 'public alarm ... generated support for repressive changes at various levels of the criminal justice system'.[51] In Edinburgh in 1812, that began with the severity of the sentences handed to the handful of panels executed and transported.

Imposing the death sentence on three young men aged under twenty years appears extreme in the modern world, yet it was also considered harsh by judicial contemporaries. It has been argued that by 1812 'age played an important role in tempering' the Scottish judiciary's responses to violent crime perpetrated by minors, although the qualification for being a minor remained fluid. Writing at the end of the eighteenth century, David Hume considered an individual's minority to commence at fourteen years of age, but he was less clear on minority's upper age limit.[52] This places MacDonald, Sutherland and McIntosh firmly within the sphere of minority. However, Hume also considered that maturity varied by individual and therefore each person's ability to know right from wrong – their 'dole' – informed their competence to stand trial.[53] It was unnecessary to establish dole, or evil intent, because killing was 'manifestly wrong' and that 'persons having the use of reason' would not commit murder.⁵⁴ However, Hume argued that it was unsafe to assume dole for a perpetrator not yet fully developed, although both he and his successor Archibald Alison believed minors were often capable of dole.⁵⁵ It was not unheard of for minors to be executed, but increasing sensitivities towards children, who might be saved from a life of crime, meant that a sentence of doom was frequently commuted to transportation, particularly if the panel could prove their extreme youth or looked very young.⁵⁶

Clearly, the Solicitor General, David Monypenny, acting for the Crown had convinced the jury that MacDonald, Sutherland and McIntosh were culpable of their crimes, while the Lord Justice-Clerk, Lord Boyle, had accepted their dole irrespective of their ages. Both Monypenny and Boyle had only been elevated to their respective roles in 1811, Monypenny taking Boyle's role after the latter's promotion to the bench.⁵⁷ Both men were in their forties in 1812, with large estates and destined for future titles.⁵⁸ They were upper-class members of the Establishment rather than middle-class advocates with their eye on their futures. Boyle and Monypenny had risen through the judicial ranks under the influence of George MacKenzie's late seventeenth-century commentaries. They were old-school lawyers brought up on Hume's 'eminently gentle' justice of the 1790s.⁵⁹ As Hume's successor in judicial commentary, Archibald Alison's preference was to commute a sentence of doom to transportation for younger offenders. Compared to Hogmanay 1809 when a man had died and riotous behaviour had left the streets strewn with rubbish, 1811 appears little different. So, what had MacDonald, Sutherland and McIntosh done that was so serious they deserved to hang, and in McIntosh's case, to be anatomized?

Ralston and Knox argue convincingly that the residential demarcation produced by the development of the New Town divorced Edinburgh's citizens from each other by class. No longer familiar with the lower orders, the elites were appalled by their behaviour this Hogmanay and reacted with severe punishment, because riot was 'increasingly being interpreted … as an attack on private property'.⁶⁰ And that private property had been hard earned by the new middle class, whereas the old establishment elites understood that a 'complex web of patronage' and hierarchical deference formed the social fabric of this 'citadel of Toryism'.⁶¹ While the old arrangement of patronage and tolerance survived, collective violence, even gang violence, could be acceptable, making expenditure on an improved and expanded police force unwarranted.⁶² However, the new Edinburgh middle class had yet to find an official outlet for their voice. Petitioning for a new police act only the day after the riot via the middle-class press was the middle-class voice clamouring for recognition. Was the upper-class elite more sensitive to the needs of the middle classes than cognizant of the plight of the working classes?

Conclusion

A Georgian housing boom and concomitant social anxieties feel insufficient to explain such juridical harshness when the judiciary was self-avowedly lenient towards juvenile offenders, particularly in a period when Scots society and law were transitioning through other civilizing developments.[63] However, if the pressure felt by the old elite from the new and more numerous middle class was perceived to be more important, then an example needed to be made: to the lower orders that patrician tolerance was no longer the order of the day, and to the middle classes that 'we hear you'.

Undoubtedly, some of the participants of the Tron Riot were just youths letting off steam, while others such as the members of the gangs had organized themselves with criminal intent. Also, policeman Dugald Campbell was disliked, but it is doubtful whether those who assaulted him – and there were many – had intended to murder him. If they had, his injuries would surely have been immediately fatal.

There were two outcomes of the Tron Riot. First, a revised Edinburgh Police Act was introduced by Act of Parliament in June 1812. It provided for enhanced powers among the Burgh Commissioners as well as increased numbers of police. Significantly, the capital and its newly widened boundaries were divided into wards. Wards one to twelve dealt with areas of the Old Town; thus, ward one comprised the Grassmarket, ward two included part of High Street, Lawnmarket to the 'back of the tenements on the north side of the Cowgate', while wards three and four further divided the streets, the latter including Niddry Street.[64] It is not a coincidence that the new wards were small, allowing for intense policing of working-class areas. Second, previously disapproved of by the Church of Scotland as evangelical-moderate, the Sunday School Movement expanded, providing 'moral and spiritual teaching' and literacy to working-class children.[65]

These developments must be set against widening industrial protest among the working class. The events of 1820 in the west of Scotland, known as the Scottish Rebellion, were ostensibly protests for improved wages and nascent hopes of working-class suffrage.[66] The insurrection that occurred in 1820 had a long tail that connected the Jacobinism of the 1790s to the working classes' lukewarm reception of early eighteenth-century industrial capitalism and subsequent craft combination and protest.[67] However, while the working class fought for the preservation of their way of life and working practices, the burgeoning middle class agitated for recognition and representation. Fraser suggests that 'successful middle-class pressure' to abolish income tax forced the government to introduce greater taxation on consumables such as salt, beer, tobacco and candles – all working-class staples.[68] By protecting themselves against income tax on their increased revenues, the middle class had spread the responsibility to those less able to subsume the increased costs of household items. Catriona MacDonald maintains that the middle class 'posed the biggest threat to established interests'.[69] While Kilday adds that 'urban businessmen' were unconvinced that the existing law adequately protected their interests.[70] Thus, during the first three decades of the nineteenth century, the middle classes petitioned increasingly for electoral reform and enfranchisement, which they won in the Scottish Reform Act of 1832. Notably, the expanded property qualification for the vote included small landowners and many of Edinburgh's smarter shopkeepers. Perhaps, among those newly enfranchised traders were some of the rascal apprentices who had rioted on Hogmanay 1811.

The Tron Riot was indeed a pivotal moment in Scottish history as Ralston states. It exposed the inconsistencies in the Scottish Enlightenment and highlighted class divisions. But arguably, the Tron Riot was more a moment of significance for the middle class than it was for those who had rioted. The riot did indeed lie 'outside the existing nomenclature' because there was a new middle-class voice in town.

Notes

1 A. M. Kilday, *Crime in Scotland 1660–1960: the Violent North?* (Abingdon, 2021), 166.
2 C. Whatley, 'An Uninflammable People', in *The Manufacture of Scottish History*, ed. I. Donnachie and C. Whatley (Edinburgh, 1992), 67.
3 W. H. Fraser, 'Patterns of Protest', in *People and Society in Scotland*, vol. 1, 1760–1830, ed. T. M. Devine and R. Mitchison (Edinburgh, 1988), 284.
4 H. W. Meikle, *Scotland and the French Revolution* (New York, 1969), 215.
5 Fraser, 'Patterns of Protest', 283.
6 Whatley, 'Uninflammable People', 66–7; K. J. Logue, *Popular Disturbances in Scotland, 1780–1815* (Edinburgh, 1979), 133.
7 H. Cockburn, *Memorials of his Time* (Edinburgh, 1856), 82–3.
8 Kilday, *Violent North*, 154–5.
9 Logue, *Popular Disturbances*, 156–7, 159.
10 Meikle, *French Revolution*, 218–19.
11 W. W. Knox, '"The Attack of the Half-Formed Persons": the 1811–12 Tron Riot in Edinburgh Revisited', *Scottish Historical Review* 91, no. 232, part 2 (October, 2012), 304; J. Smyth and A. McKinlay, 'Whigs, Tories and Scottish Legal Reform, c.1785-1832', *Crime, Histoire & Societes* 15, no. 1 (2011), 112.
12 Kilday, *Violent North*, 159.

13 P. King, 'The Rise of Juvenile Delinquency in England 1780–1840: Changing Patterns of Perception and Prosecution', *Past and Present* 160, no. 1 (August, 1998), 152, 158.
14 Fraser, 'Patterns of Protest', 273; A. M. Kilday, 'Hell-Raising and Hair-Razing: Violent Robbery in Nineteenth-Century Scotland', *Scottish Historical Review* XCII.2, no. 235 (October, 2013), 166.
15 Fraser, 'Patterns of Protest', 272.
16 Whatley, 'Uninflammable People', 66.
17 Logue, *Popular Disturbances*, 44–5.
18 Fraser, 'Patterns of Protest', 272.
19 Fraser, 'Patterns of Protest', 274; Kilday, 'Hell-Raising', 269.
20 Fraser, 'Patterns of Protest', 275.
21 M. W. Flinn, ed., *Scottish Population History, from the seventeenth century to the 1930s* (Cambridge, 1976), 315.
22 T. C. Smout, *A History of the Scottish People 1560–1830* (London, 1985), 346.
23 F. B. Singh, *Scandal and Survival in Nineteenth-Century Scotland: The Life of Jane Cumming* (Woodbridge, 2020), 99.
24 Knox, 'Half-Formed Persons', 300. Princes Street today continues to be a differential line between the New and Old Towns of Edinburgh.
25 Whatley, 'Uninflammable People', 51.
26 *Caledonian Mercury*, 1 January 1801, 3.
27 *Caledonian Mercury*, 2 January 1809, 3.
28 A. G. Ralston, 'The Tron Riot of 1812', *History Today* 30, no. 5 (May, 1980), 41.
29 AD14/12/101.
30 *Edinburgh Annual Register*, vol. 5, II (1812), 1–3.
31 AD14/12/101.
32 *Caledonian Mercury*, 5 March 1812.
33 *Caledonian Mercury*, 21 March 1812.
34 *Caledonian Mercury*, 23 March 1812.
35 JC8/9.
36 Logue, *Popular Disturbances*, 189.
37 *Caledonian Mercury*, 23 April 1812.
38 Knox, 'Half-Formed Persons', 304.
39 *Caledonian Mercury*, 23 April 1812.
40 Knox, 'Half-Formed Persons', 305.
41 Knox, 'Half-Formed Persons', 288.
42 *Edinburgh Annual Register*, vol. 5, 1812, 1; *Scots Magazine and Edinburgh Literary Miscellany*, vol. 74, January, 1812, 74.
43 Flinn, *Scottish Population*, 263, table 4.4.4, and 317, table 5.2.1.

44 Knox, 'Half-Formed Persons', 299.
45 P. King, 'The Rise of Juvenile Delinquency in England 1780–1840: Changing Patterns of Perception and Prosecution', *Past and Present* 160, no. 1 (August, 1998), 118.
46 AD14/12/101 Petition, Alexander Ponton, Procurator Fiscal against McIntosh, Sutherland, Tasker & Swan.
47 AD14/12/101.
48 Knox, 'Half-Formed Persons', 299.
49 *Caledonian Mercury*, 5 March 1812.
50 Kilday, 'Hell-raising', 262–7.
51 P. King, 'Moral panics and violent street crime 1750–2000: a comparative perspective', in *Comparative Histories of Crime*, ed. B. Godfrey, C. Emsley and G Dunstall (Cullompton, 2003), 54, 63–4, 69.
52 C. McDiarmid, *Childhood and Crime* (Dundee, 2007), 105, 113.
53 McDiarmid, *Childhood*, 108–9.
54 L. Farmer, *Criminal Law, Tradition and Legal Order: Crime and the Genius of Scots Law 1747 to the Present* (Cambridge, 2005), 150.
55 McDiarmid, *Childhood*, 112.
56 Scotland's first census was conducted in 1801 when the Tron Riot panels would have been young children; compulsory registration of births did not begin until 1855.
57 David Boyle, *Dictionary Of National Biography*, https://www.oxford dnb.com/search?q=Boyle%2C+David%2C+Lord+Shewalton+%281 772%E2%80%931853%29 (accessed July 2024). David Monypenny took the judicial title of Lord Pitmilly on elevation to the bench in 1813, https://www.electricscotland.com/history/nation/monypenny.htm (accessed July 2024).
58 David Boyle was the grandson of John Boyle, 2nd Earl of Glasgow, whose estate he inherited after his uncle, 3rd Earl of Glasgow died without issue; *Dictionary of National Biography*, vol. 6, 109–10.
59 D. Hume, *Commentaries on the Law of Scotland respecting Trial for Crimes*, vol. 1 (Edinburgh, 1800), 11.
60 Knox, 'Half-Formed Persons', 307.
61 Meikle, *French Revolution*, 229.
62 Kilday, 'Hell-Raising', 269.
63 Knox, 'Half-Formed Persons', 304.
64 *An Act for altering and amending an Act of the forty-fifth year of His present Majesty, for regulating the Police of the City of Edinburgh, and the adjoining districts, and for other purposes relating thereto*, 52 George III c. clxxii.
65 Knox, 'Half-Formed Persons', 309; Ralston, 'Tron Riot', 45. The Weavers' Strike in 1787 had also ended with the introduction of Sunday schools to 'improve' the working class.

66 S. Kavanagh, '"The Most Loyal of Towns": Greenock and the Radical War of 1820', in *1820: Scottish Rebellion, essays on a nineteenth-century insurrection*, ed. G. Carruthers, K. T. Gallagher, C. Lamont and G. Smith (Edinburgh, 2022), 100.

67 Whatley, 'Uninflammable People', 71.

68 Fraser, 'Patterns of Protest', 285.

69 C. MacDonald, '"The ebbing of the old shallow tide'": The civil context of the Radical War', in *1820*, ed. Carruthers et al. (Edinburgh, 1820), 2.

70 Kilday, 'Hell-Raising', 269.

5

Burke and Hare 1828: Multiple murder, vulnerability and the law

Medical advances and thirst for anatomical knowledge in the early nineteenth century spawned a new commercial enterprise – body-snatching – which linked to heated debates in Parliament on the deterrent effect of capital sentencing for murder, and resulted in changes to the law on sourcing medical cadavers, which did little to protect society's unprotected poor.

Context

Both Barbara Malcolm (1808) and Hugh McIntosh (1812) suffered the emotional stress of knowing their bodies would undergo the post-execution punishment of anatomization. In the eighteenth and early nineteenth centuries when religious belief remained strong, what happened to one's body post-death was important both to the individual and their family. If resurrection truly meant living for eternity in one's terrestrial body, it was important for it to remain intact. And if resurrection was not understood quite so literally, then the possibility of one's soul lingering after death and the shame of dissection had to be considered. Thus, being sentenced to execution plus suffering one's body to be dissected by anatomy students, often conducted in a surgeon's public theatre, was a psychological punishment that affected the individual as well as their family.

Anatomical dissection was nothing new in the early nineteenth century. In 1505, Edinburgh's town council had allowed the 'Incorporation of Surgeons and

Barbers' annually the body of one condemned man for dissection. However, a single cadaver was never going to be enough, and in 1694 the grant of bodies was extended to include those who had died 'in the correction-house'; foundlings who had died between being weaned and entering school, so children up to seven years old; infants who had died at birth or were abandoned and suicides. Still the available number of corpses was insufficient, and the consequent amount of opportunistic body-snatching led to riots in 1725 and 1742 in Edinburgh.[1] Yet for Edinburgh, as the centre of the Enlightenment and medical science, to maintain its global pre-eminence, even more newly dead bodies were required for an ever-increasing number of student surgeons to practise on. It has been estimated that between 1720 and the 1790s, the number of medical students taught in Edinburgh increased from fifty-seven to approximately 300, increasing to 400 students by the 1820s.[2] Similarly, in London, student numbers increased from 300 to almost 1,000 over the same period.[3] For the best anatomy lecturers to maintain their position, they needed to provide the freshest bodies to represent as closely as possible those of their students' future patients. In turn, this attracted more students, earning individual lecturers more money, which consequently increased demand for more cadavers. In 1827 in Edinburgh, Burke and Hare figured out how to fill that gap in the market without the need to do anything so grubby, or potentially criminal, as snatching bodies from relatively fresh graves.

The Murder Act 1751 purposely included a clause that added dissection to capital convictions, specifically for murderers tried at the Middlesex Assize from where the bodies of executed felons would be conveyed to the Company of Surgeons' premises in London. Elsewhere around the country, the wording for the disposal and dissection of the bodies of capital felons read:

> and in case such conviction and execution shall happen to be in any other county or other place in Great Britain, then the judge or justice of assize, or other proper judge, shall award the sentence to be put in execution the next day but one after such conviction.[4]

The Murder Act was the government's response to satiate the medical schools' increasing need for bodies for surgeons and their students to learn from, as well as a response to a perceived increase in murder.

In the early eighteenth century, body snatchers had supplied newly dead bodies by removing them from graves. Known as the Resurrectionists, their numbers comprised opportunistic, often professional, body thieves as well as medical students and sometimes their professors.[5] Exhumation was the most popular method of supplying the medical schools as well as stealing or swapping bodies from their coffins before burial. Again, the poor suffered the most since they were unable to afford elaborate, deep tombs or attendants to guard the grave until the body had putrefied sufficiently to be beyond value to an anatomist.[6] In 1725, the premises of Professor Alexander Monro, *primus*, Edinburgh's pre-eminent anatomist at the time, were attacked by the mob.[7] Generally, the authorities took little notice of body-snatching because it was predominantly perpetrated against the 'friendless and the poverty-stricken'.[8] Also, it was not yet a crime. After death, ownership of the deceased's body passed to their next of kin or executor of their estate. Once buried, unless the grave clothes or other accoutrements were stolen from the body, there was no crime.[9] In 1788, that situation changed when a judge ruled that it was a misdemeanour to remove a dead body from a cemetery because it was '*contra bonos mores*' – against good morals – further framing the Resurrectionists as 'more desperate and degraded'.[10] Cadavers were also sourced from Ireland, from where a regular traffic in bodies between Dublin and Edinburgh and other cities continued, but still numbers were insufficient.

As well as increasing the supply of dead bodies to the anatomy schools, the introduction of the Murder Act fulfilled other pressing societal issues. The expansion of the press provided greater publicity for executions, thereby promoting greater attendance. This led to 'plebeian frustration' with crowds behaving rowdily, especially if they disagreed with the punishment – what has been called 'chronic execution disorders' – and often they were not necessarily cowed by the deterrent enormity of the execution spectacle.[11] Not only introduced to increase the number of cadavers for anatomy schools, the Murder Act with its particular clause on dissection as an aggravated sentence was also intended to differentiate between types of capital crime. With so many indictments potentially attracting execution, differentiating between an 'ordinary' capital crime and murder was essential in a period of perceived increases in violent crime.

Bill Knox's work on eighteenth-century homicide largely correlates with research conducted by Anne-Marie Kilday that the homicide rate across the century remained 'fairly static' with a 'plateau lasting fifty years' from the 1720s before an increase from 1780, which increased again through the 'murderous decade of the 1790s' until the end of the century. In the 1750s when the Murder Act was introduced, the homicide rate in Scotland had fluctuated between 0.37 and 0.32 per 100,000 population.[12] The closest statistically comparable figures for England have been compiled by Lawrence Stone who calculates that for Essex in 1780 the homicide rate fell from 4.3 between 1700 and 1750 to 2.8 per 100,000 population by 1800.[13] Scotland and Edinburgh were not evidently more violent than elsewhere in Great Britain, but elite perceptions superseded statistical facts. The proliferation of publications detailing criminal cases in the mid-eighteenth century has been identified as a catalyst for increased fear of violent crime.[14] Thus, by introducing dissection as an aggravated punishment for murder, the judiciary was able to separate the most serious indictment from all others attracting a capital sentence, as well as adding an enhanced deterrent. However, by transforming the ultimate crime into a conduit to dissection, the judiciary inadvertently linked anatomists to execution in the minds of those most likely to suffer both, either as a felon or as the family of one.[15]

For a few years, the Act appears to have reduced the amount of public violence on execution days as well as sustaining the anatomy schools' demand for fresh bodies.[16] However, the moral stance of many politicians and judges continued a lively debate into the first decades of the next century as the requirement for and sourcing of bodies grew. One argument to increase the supply of cadavers focused on adding the aggravation of dissection to all capital sentences. However, this reduced the seriousness of murder and removed the deterrence of anatomization by equating its punishment with other capital indictments.[17] The surgeons argued against all use of dissection as a criminal punishment because it tarnished their reputation.[18] Instead they suggested plundering the workhouses and hospitals, which would place the burden of dissection on the friendless poor and other vulnerables, who, making the by-now customary connection between crime and dissection, protested that they were being treated like common criminals.[19] In the meantime, the reliance on bodies from Ireland and more local body-snatchers increased. It has been estimated that one of Edinburgh's leading private anatomists, Dr Robert Knox, required approximately 170 bodies per year to satisfy his expanding practice.[20] Knox's anatomy school was not the only one in operation in Edinburgh, and yet the number of felons executed for murder in Scotland from 1752 until May 1828 was 97, not all of whom were sentenced to anatomization.[21] The shortage of cadavers worsened in 1826 when the Royal Commissioners supported the medical fraternity's request to make 'practical anatomy' a key component of medical degrees with students dissecting one or more corpses during their studies, because 'the proper acquisition of medical knowledge' was essential before any surgeon could take a knife to a 'sentient body'. 'Confidence and skill' could only be attained by practising on the dead.[22]

William Burke and William Hare set to work in December 1827 with a plan that was the ultimate commodification of the human corpse.

Case

Burke and Hare lured, murdered and sold the bodies of sixteen individuals between December 1827 and 1 November 1828 to Dr Robert Knox, surgeon-anatomist in Edinburgh. They were not the first private individuals to 'produce' bodies for dissection. In 1752, Helen Torrence and Jean Waldie had been executed for the murder of an eight or nine-year-old boy whose guardian they seduced with drink while they suffocated the child. Having produced an unmutilated body – suffocation being the easiest method to achieve a blemish-free cadaver – they were paid two shillings and ten pence for his body by Edinburgh anatomists.[23] Thus, seventy years later when Burke and Hare struck upon the same commercial enterprise, they were not the first, but they were 'the most notorious wholesalers', and their discovery and Burke's execution stopped the trade in murdered bodies for sale to anatomy schools.[24]

Burke's and Hare's victim selection kept their activities hidden for almost a year. All their victims were either old, alone, disabled in some way and partial to drink. Burke and Hare got all of them, except one, drunk before suffocating them; twelve of their victims were unprotected, elderly women. Most of the victims had been lodgers at Burke's and Hare's West Port, Edinburgh address or had been lured back there, having been identified as potential victims on the streets. The West Port area was in Edinburgh's Old Town, near Grassmarket surrounded by narrow wynds, high tenements and the city's poorer residents. Burke's lodging house where he lived with his unmarried partner, Helen M'Dougal, comprised a single large room. The Burkes already had lodgers – Anne Gray, her husband and their son – who were Helen's relations.[25] Hare and his wife Margaret lived at Tanner's Close in the West Port. Burke, Hare and Hare's wife were all Irish immigrants; Helen was a native Scot.

None of their victims was of high social status, and no one in their personal networks was either aware of their absence or possessed sufficient agency to pursue a report to the police to investigate their disappearance. In general, the victims were 'nobodies' – the ultimate vulnerable and therefore perfect victim. However, two of the victims stand out.

James Wilson was an eighteen-year-old who roamed the Old Town. He was known as 'Daft Jamie', being a 'natural', mentally impaired. He hurt no one and lived by running errands for local people and was cared for by his sister and her daughter. As a 'familiar figure' in the Old Town, his disappearance was noted but unexplained. It was not until Mary or Madgy Docherty's murder that the connection to Jamie's disappearance was made. By this time, the evidence of Jamie's death had been anatomized. Knox's theatre assistants later testified they had been unable to confirm they had recognized Jamie when his body was brought in, although one of them had identified him by misshapen toes but had not informed the police.[26]

The murder which broke the supply chain to Knox's anatomy school was that of Madgy Docherty. The tale of Madgy's murder is best told in Burke's words through the declarations he made to George Tait, Esquire, Sheriff-Substitute of Edinburgh, the first of which was written on 3 November 1828. Burke explained his arrival in Scotland from Ireland ten years ago, when he was twenty-six years old. He was a shoemaker who had lived in the West

Port area for about a year, the last two months in his current lodgings with Helen M'Dougal, his unmarried 'wife' of ten years. Burke went into some detail about who got up first on the morning of Thursday, 30 October 1828, before he described a man who arrived requiring shoe repairs. The man paced their room and discussed a box which he returned with and began to unrope. After the man left, also leaving behind his box, Burke went to investigate and discovered a body lying on the floor covered in straw. He could not tell if it was a man or a woman. The man returned, there was an altercation, and the man agreed to return to collect the box. He did not return until Saturday by which time Burke said he had removed the box but, inexplicably, left the body where it was. On Saturday morning, Burke went out shopping and met an Irish woman, Mary (Madgy) Docherty. Burke told her that his mother's name was also Docherty, and she came from the same part of Ireland, so they might be related. Having made a personal connection, he offered to give Madgy breakfast at his home. There, Helen, Gray and Anne Gray spent the day with her by the fire, Madgy smoking her pipe, and they drank a dram because it was Halloween.

About 3.00 pm on Saturday, Burke believed Madgy had gone out begging as Hare's wife arrived to visit their neighbour John Cannoway. After cleaning the house, Helen and Anne Gray went to the Cannoways, leaving Burke with the body, about which he had told no one, and no one seems to have become suspicious despite the cleaning activities during the afternoon. By 10.00 pm, the man returned with a porter to collect the body and the box, paying Burke two guineas for his trouble. The man proposed to take the body to 'Surgeon's Square to dispose of it to' anyone who would take it. Burke suggested David Paterson, a surgeon's assistant; he did not divulge how he knew him. They duly took the body to Paterson who paid 'a number of pounds' and gave Burke two pounds ten shillings. Returning home, Burke was told that a dead body had been found in his house, and a policeman was looking for him. Burke located the policeman who searched his house and, finding no body there, took him to the police office. There Burke viewed the body of a dead woman, which he believed 'was the body below the bed but it had no likeness to Mary Docherty' and then he confirmed that the man who brought the body and then returned with the porter was William Hare, but there was no way anyone could have seen him enter his house or leave with the box. He then told the police that Madgy had not been in his house at all on Friday night, only returning at 10.00 am on Saturday. He did not know what had become of Madgy, but to obscure the smell of the dead body, he had 'sprinkled some whisky' about the house. The police produced Madgy's dark gown which he did not recognize, but he recognized his own pillowcase and a bloodied sheet which he explained was from his wife's nose after he had struck her, which Gray and Anne Gray had witnessed.

Burke gave a further declaration on 10 November because having had his initial declaration read to him, he realized it was 'incorrect in several particulars'. Burke had been confused; Madgy had gone out begging on Friday not Saturday, and the floor was washed also on Friday not Saturday. Then Hare arrived, and they sat together with Helen and Anne Gray drinking whisky. He went for more drink, and on his return, Madgy had reappeared. Burke and Hare had a fight, and Madgy became intoxicated; then she disappeared. They found her lying drunk in the straw by the bed, with vomit not blood coming from her mouth. Her body was warm, but she was 'insensible and was not breathing'. They confirmed she was dead. The men stripped the body, and then one of them, Burke did not recall who, suggested selling the body to the surgeons. At the police office, Burke confessed that 'no violence was done to the woman when she was in life', but it had been very difficult to get her body into the tea chest which is how she came by the cuts and bruises.

On 29 November, Burke was compeared a third time when he confessed to helping to pack a young man's body into a chest at Hare's stable, but he denied being involved in taking the body to Surgeon's Square to Knox's premises. In fact, he did 'not know of such things being done'. He had effectively confessed to being involved in Daft Jamie's murder.[27]

In court, Burke was defended by a number of illustrious advocates, among them Lord Moncreiff and Henry Cockburn, the Whig campaigner. Burke pleaded not guilty. His defence was that the three murders with which he was charged were unconnected and that by combining his trial with another panel's – Helen, who was not indicted for two of the same murders – the 'accumulation of offences' was 'inconsistent with right principle'. The same advocate used the same argument to defend Helen M'Dougal who was accused of only one murder. Having debated the relevancy of the charges, the Lord Justice-Clerk and Lords Commissioners of Justiciary decided to charge both panels with one murder and Burke with the remaining two. Again, both panels pleaded not guilty. The jury empanelled comprised shopkeepers, merchants and tradesmen. Among the witnesses were James and Anne Gray; John McCulloch, the porter; David Paterson, Knox's assistant and William Hare, who had turned King's evidence.

In court, Hare denied identifying Madgy's body or having ever received money directly for producing bodies. His version of Friday evening at Burke's house intersected with Burke's story in some places, but ultimately the evidence described how Madgy had attempted to escape the house. She had gone into the passageway and screeched for help, but Helen had brought her back inside where Burke smothered her. Hare denied having been involved in the actual murder. Margaret Hare also gave evidence, and largely she corroborated Hare's version of events. In his address to the jury, the Lord Advocate told them that it was his duty 'to afford all the protection which the

ILLUSTRATION 5.1 *Frontispiece,* Trial of William Burke and Helen M'Dougal: Before the High Court of Justiciary, Edinburgh, on Wednesday, December 24, 1828, for the murder of Margery Campbell, or Docherty *(Edinburgh, 1829).*

law can give to the community against the perpetration of such crimes'. He declared that he was unable to 'allow any collateral considerations, connected with the promotion of science, to influence' him.[28] The Lord Advocate was likely referring to the defence counsel line-up of Whigs, who were currently campaigning for more cadavers sourced from outside the penal estate. However, by rejecting the needs of scientific advancement, the Lord Advocate had turned his back on the benefit that using the bodies of the deceased, friendless and poor would afford to the elites who could pay for surgeons to operate on them while alive.

The jury found Helen M'Dougal's case not proven, while Burke, who had been tried on the third charge only of the murder of Madgy Docherty, was found guilty. His involvement in the other fifteen murders was not declared in court, but Madgy's murder was enough to condemn him to execution and, ironically, dissection.[29]

Themes and analysis

From the first two declarations given by Burke, either he did not realize the game was up or he believed that he was cleverer than the police and that they would neither link him to Docherty's death nor connect her murder to the other unexplained missing persons; with no body as evidence, the police had been unable to link each event. Or Burke was simply a desperate criminal scrabbling at excuses to evade prosecution?

Sixteen murders place Burke and Hare among Britain's most effective multiple murderers. However, they are not classified as serial killers. Historians and criminologists continue to debate the qualifications for serial killing, but essentially a serial killer must kill more than two, possibly three individuals; there must be no previous relationship between killer and victim; the murders are committed at different times with no direct connection; there is a cooling-off period between attacks; they are committed in different locations, and importantly the murders are not perpetrated for material gain.[30] Burke and Hare fit most of the criteria except for the material gain element. However, when their series is considered as a whole, it is evident that their motive was clear with the first murder, but the concept of a business venture had not yet dawned. Their first victim, Donald the pensioner, died a natural death at Hare's home, and having died owing rent, his body was sold to the anatomists, while his coffin was filled with 'tanners' bark' to replicate the weight of a body during burial.[31] From there the series of murders escalated, but each was an individual, opportunistic crime linked by motive and *modus operandi* – intoxication followed by suffocation and overlaying whereby one of them compressed the chest of the victim with their body weight – but their crimes still do not qualify for serial killing. The period between murders was not to allow their heightened emotional connection to the event to dissipate before 'needing' to murder again, which is a component more frequently found in sexual serial killing. Also, they committed the murders at home involving their partners as accessories to clean up the murder scene and to transport the bodies to Surgeon's Square. There was nothing lascivious nor sexual about their activities, and the court papers provide no evidence that they derived enjoyment or emotional release from the murders. Instead, Burke and Hare are multiple murderers whose crimes fascinated society *after* the event, not *during* their period of killing.[32] Further, only the marginalized needed to fear becoming their next victim.

In a highly mobile and transitory population with newcomers arriving all the time, knowing one's neighbours and keeping track of their whereabouts was becoming increasingly difficult as the number of lodgers staying with the Hares and Burkes attests. If anyone went missing, unless they were related or had lived in the area for a long time and were thus locally recognized, they were unlikely to be missed. The account of Donald's death does not describe any relations mourning at his burial, although they were a consideration to Hare if anyone decided to claim Donald's last pension payment.[33] Being old and uncared for, his death was unremarkable to anyone. Next was Joseph, another lodger in Hare's house. He was suffering from fever and reluctant to allow word to spread that there was contagion in their home Hare and Burke suffocated him and sold his body.[34] Abigail Simpson, who lived in Gilmerton on the outskirts of Edinburgh, had come into the city to receive her pension from an elderly sponsor. Afterwards, she had spent some of her money on alcohol and then bumped into Hare who enticed her home to continue drinking. She was described as 'old and weakly' and impaired by her 'potations'. Her body was sold for £10; she went unmissed.[35] Lisa Rosner places 'an Englishman, a native of Cheshire' as their next victim. He appears to have been a travelling salesman who stayed at Tanner's Close and was probably unwell with jaundice. A long way from home, again his death was unremarked because no one knew him.[36] He was followed by an old woman, lured to the house by Margaret Hare where she was plied with drink and smothered with bedding; her body also sold for £10 to Dr Knox, and again no one noticed.[37] Mary Paterson was a woman of 'doubtful character' in the Old Town who had been detained in the police office overnight with Janet Brown, before being released. They found themselves drinking with Burke and then returned to his brother, Constantine's home. Brown managed to get away from them at least once, having suspected foul play, but by the time she returned to the house to find Paterson, she was told Paterson had 'gone away with a packman to Glasgow'. At first, Brown did not believe the story but was dissuaded from further pursuing the matter. As a late nineteenth-century commentator on the murders noted, the women were 'of a class whose relationship with the authorities was not of the most pleasant description'.[38] Paterson's disappearance went unreported because she was socially disenfranchised from using the municipal law enforcement services.

Of the other victims, Effy was an old cinder raker who sold odd scraps of leather to Burke for his shoemaking; her body earned Burke and Hare £10. The recently widowed Mrs Hostler, who washed laundry, was intoxicated and smothered by them, adding £8 to their coffers. Margaret Haldane was described as an old 'drunken, worthless vagrant'. After her came an Irish woman and her grandson who had walked from Glasgow; then Ann M'Dougal who was a cousin to Helen M'Dougal's first husband.[39] Ann was an unusually younger victim whose death was followed by Daft Jamie's and finally Madgy Docherty who had travelled from Ireland in search of her son who was employed in seasonal work in southern Scotland. Docherty did not know his whereabouts and readily accepted the offer of a drink and breakfast from a man who purported to possess relations in her home town. Everyone who was murdered had few close relations to miss them; they were a long way from home and might disappear without trace; they were marginalized, vulnerable and probably regarded the police as an instrument of elite discipline used against them, not by them.[40]

In his study of vulnerable populations of the late twentieth century, David Wilson places responsibility for victimization not with the killers, but with the society in which the murders occur. The social, economic and cultural framework in which multiple (and serial) killing arises permits the murders to happen.[41] This could also be argued for early nineteenth-century Edinburgh, especially in the areas surrounding the Grassmarket where the riots of 1811–12 and associated criminality had occurred in the capital's narrow, dark wynds. Being friendless, homeless, poor, alcohol-dependent and dislocated from a familiar network maximized the chances of victimization and the opportunity for those intent on crime. Further, the poverty and precarity experienced by the likes of Burke and Hare and the Resurrectionists fuelled their innovation to become opportunistic criminals who had identified an unsavoury way to support themselves. Being female added another layer of danger to life as a 'vulnerable' in late Enlightenment Edinburgh. In a society where a male protector – husband, father or brother – was necessary for a woman to be properly visible, all of Burke's and Hare's victims lacked male protection.

While some of the victims were Irish, such as Docherty, which may have contributed to their 'friendless' existence in Edinburgh where the migrant Irish were 'othered' as addicted to drink, impoverished and criminal, the ethnicity of Burke and Hare does not appear to have greatly exercised the public. Significantly, they were named as lower-class perpetrators in the newspapers, among whom it has been argued that criminal behaviour was 'normative'.[42] As the 'most culturally valued resource for broadcasting information', the nineteenth-century media played a pivotal role in disseminating the details of the Burke and Hare trial and circulating all manner of printed materials to assuage the reading public's ghastly fascination with the macabre.[43] Yet, the reportage appears to have remained contained to the facts of Burke's and Hare's exploits rather than focusing pejoratively on their ethnicity.

Between the trial that commenced on 24 December 1828 and as late as 31 January 1829, after Burke's execution, *The Times* continued to report on his early life in County Tyrone, Ireland, his journey to Scotland and even his inner turmoil having murdered his first victim – 'the screams of distress and despair, the agonizing groans' could not be banished from his mind. Both men's backgrounds are detailed in several editions of *The Times*, but that of 5 January 1829 is probably the most informative of the journalist's editorial approach. Moving from a column on Burke's background, intelligence, religious faith and employment in Ireland and arrival in Scotland, it continues with an editorial reprinted from the *Caledonian Mercury*, which blatantly asks how 'a common Irish labourer of the very lowest class' could learn the apparent skill with which he and Hare murdered their victims without being taught by someone of greater skill and intellect. The reporter was also appalled that Hare was only in gaol for his 'personal protection' despite Hare being Burke's 'master in the art of murder'.[44] The report had travelled from Edinburgh to London, thereby informing many thousands of aghast middle- and upper-class

Times readers that the unthinkable had happened: two low-class Irishmen had managed expertly to despatch sixteen bodies producing perfect specimens for anatomizing and without any formal education, let alone university medical tuition. However, the author was again less interested in their Irishness and more exercised over the police and legal authorities' ability to deal with the situation. The 'credit and honour' of the country had meant that further investigation into the extent of their activities and others similar had been 'quashed', but the author reckoned that by silencing further investigation, 'a matter of such terrific magnitude' would lead to 'fancy horrors still more appalling than even the dreadful reality'.[45] He had wedged open the door to a moral panic, thus creating a sense of vulnerability among the wider population, particularly the elites.[46]

Philip Jenkins's research on twentieth-century moral panics reveals that media reporting concurrent with a series of violent murders creates more panic than post-event reporting.[47] However, rather than their 'celebrity' being short-lived because they had been apprehended and the opportunity for reporting was curtailed, instead Burke's and Hare's notoriety has endured. There are two possible reasons. First, while handling freshly killed bodies was less repulsive than the fascination of snatching newly dead bodies, although the criminality of the former far outweighed resurrectionism, no one except the grieving family was hurt by body-snatchers. Whereas now that people might be murdered for the anatomists, anyone could become a victim. Yet, the elites were protected, would be missed and did not lodge in houses for the itinerant or frequent drinking dens. Peter King identifies a second reason that the authorities did not view moral panics as being 'in their material, social or political interests'. Commerce may be affected; respect for the police may be eroded, and failure to control violent street crime damages the authorities' power.[48] As *The Times* journalist intimated, Edinburgh's city authorities had lost control of the situation and, realizing the challenge to their reputation, had squashed further investigation so that the extent of the problem was not made public. Whether Burke's and Hare's activities had an impact on the commerce of the city, they did affect the city's reputation.

Moral panics are rarely correlated with the likelihood of victimization; they are more concerned with the moral outrage that such criminal activity has been conducted in an otherwise civilized society, which is what occurred in Edinburgh in 1828–9. Before the sentence was pronounced, Lord Meadowbank summed up Burke's crime relating 'that in the whole history of the country – I may say in the history of civilized society – nothing has ever been exhibited that is in any respect parallel to this case'.[49] The prosecution of Burke's crimes (and Hare's if he had stood trial) coincided with developments in medical science, a concomitant demand for specimens on which to practise and Scottish intellectual, judicial and moral prestige. The arguments posed by prosecuting and defence counsel are illustrative of the judicial and political divisions apparent in Edinburgh society in the early nineteenth century and ultimately reveal sides in the ongoing debate regarding execution for murder and the aggravated punishment of anatomization.

Defending Helen M'Dougal, Henry Cockburn, a Whig, questioned the judicial morality of allowing the Hares to turn King's evidence. He considered that accepting their testimony as credible was 'sporting with men's lives' because their evidence could not be 'received in the same manner as the evidence of an honest person'. They were both accessories to murder, and yet the law had made Hare 'an admissible witness'. Cockburn queried whether 'the cold-blooded spectator' to murder was as culpable as the 'phrenzied actor' [sic]. When questioned in the witness box, despite both Hares confessing to involvement in other murders, Hare had sought 'shelter in his privilege'. Cockburn asked how the jury could believe the testimony of a man who was guilty of one murder but wanted to exonerate himself 'from blame by impeaching another who was not probably so guilty'; to do so might lead to returning a guilty verdict on doubtful evidence.[50]

There is no doubt that once discovered, Burke and Hare would have stood trial for murder. However, the only murder at which they could both be placed definitively was Madgy's, which also included both their wives. As well as Docherty's murder, those of Margaret Paterson and Daft Jamie were the other two indictments, but linkage between all three was circumstantial. Defence advocate for Helen M'Dougal, Mr Robertson, clarified this point in court: the jury could not be expected to separate the evidence presented so that they would not 'borrow evidence from one action in order to convict upon another'. The Lord Advocate defended his decision to indict Helen on all three charges and prosecute her simultaneously with Burke. She would 'derive some advantage from it' because if he tried Burke first, adducing all the evidence against him on all three charges, Helen's subsequent trial would have been prejudiced by news reporting, and the jury could not have judged her in 'an unprejudiced state'. The ensuing legal debate resulted in the Lord Advocate removing the charges relating to Paterson and Jamie from the indictment in return for prosecuting Burke and his wife simultaneously for the single murder of Madgy Docherty.[51] Thus, the same evidence would be used without time elapsing between trials, which might prejudice whoever was prosecuted second because of news reporting in the meantime.

Arguably, when deciding the indictment, the Lord Advocate might have anticipated defence counsel's argument; first, that Hare's evidence would be challenged as inadmissible and second that the evidence for the murders not only did not link them as perpetrated by the same individuals with the same intent, but that the evidence produced in precognition did not place both panels at all three murders. However, by eventually proceeding on Docherty's murder alone – the case with the strongest evidence – prosecution stood the greatest chance of proving its case. Cockburn and Robertson had not only contested the morality of the law in its ability to conduct a fair trial but also its diligence. It is an interesting case to have chosen to make their point amidst a moral panic influencing elite society. However, in pronouncing sentence, the Lord Justice-Clerk brought the debate on murder, anatomizing and degrees of criminality attracting the death penalty full circle: 'to satisfy the violated laws' of the country, ought Burke's body to 'be exhibited in chains, to bleach in the winds' as deterrence against others committing similar crimes? Considering the offence against 'the public eye' that particular spectacle would create, he decided therefore on the 'more lenient execution' involving public dissection.[52]

Despite two centuries of continuing notoriety, the contemporary moral panic provoked by Burke's trial proved short-lived, although Burke's and Hare's criminality, disseminated through extensive national reporting of the trial, contributed to, and arguably resulted in, the Anatomy Act of 1832. Anatomization had become a battle of wills between Whigs and Tories. The ongoing debate between those in support of extending dissection to all capital crimes and those wishing to remove it from murder verdicts and transfer the burden to the impoverished deceased in hospitals and workhouses was finally resolved through legislation. By May 1829, months after Burke's execution and dissection, Tory MP Sir Robert Inglis made the case for repeal of the Murder Act clause, which had connected execution to dissection. His intervention was not on the grounds of separating dissection from the ultimate crime as argued by the anatomists, but simply an expedient to pass the bill proposing the Anatomy Act in the House of Commons. It had become a straight 'choice between criminals and the friendless', most of whom were lower-class.[53] In future, bodies would be sourced from hospitals and workhouses. And there was a further development, probably beneficial to a wider stratum of working-class society, that execution only be sentenced against murderers, thus removing the punishment from all other previously capital crimes. King concludes that this was the end of England's Bloody Code.[54] Sentences were commuted from execution to transportation and imprisonment. Although in Scots Law, nowhere near the number of indictments had attracted capital punishment as in England, 'Burkophobia' had provided 'the short-term catalyst' ending penal anatomization for the entire country.[55]

Conclusion

Burke's trial did not completely stop dissection murders, but Kaufman has shown that 1832's Anatomy Act had a detrimental impact on the prices paid for bodies: pre-1832, an adult cadaver would earn £16 to £22, while post-1832, prices dropped to £5 and then £3.[56] Once the Act had been implemented, the larger hospitals and Poor Law institutions claimed a 'monopoly on the supply of bodies' in Scotland.[57] Philp concludes that by creating funeratories in Scotland post-1832, where bodies to be buried at public expense were collected and from where relations could claim their deceased, led to workhouses becoming 'places for the trafficking of bodies' because poor house officers could circumvent the funeratory and sell directly to the anatomy school customer.[58]

Burke's and Hare's murderous venture in Edinburgh changed the landscape of capital punishment for the whole of Great Britain, for the greater good, by the removal of post-execution dissection. However, by putting a poor man's business out of business, the Anatomy Act had simultaneously led to further exploitation of the unfortunate poor and had done nothing to improve the day-to-day experience of vulnerables living in Scotland's urban centres. Given the catalysts leading to Burke's trial – Docherty's murder and subsequent sensationalist reporting – Philp's conclusion that the Anatomy Act was not introduced 'on ethical grounds to protect the earthly remains of the poor' but to 'protect the liberty and income' of the anatomy schools is undeniable.[59] Apart from the few rational elites who donated their bodies for dissection, the poor remained attached to their deceased relations, and the connection between criminality and dissection would take longer to sever in most minds.

At the conclusion of Burke's trial, in condemning him to post-execution dissection, the Lord Justice-Clerk hoped his skeleton would be preserved so that 'posterity may keep in remembrance your atrocious crimes'.[60] He got part of his wish because Burke's skeleton is still exhibited at the University of Edinburgh, not as a deterrent against murder, but to remind society of how far we have come.

Notes

1 N. M. Goodman, 'The Supply of Bodies for Dissection: A Historical Review', *British Medical Journal* 2, no. 4381 (December, 1944), 807.
2 Goodman, 'Supply of Bodies', 807.
3 In England, Henry VIII had allowed four bodies for dissection to London anatomists; J. Philp, 'Bodies and bureaucracy: The demise of the body snatcher in 19th century Britain', *Anatomical Record* 305, no. 4 (April, 2022), 828–9.
4 An act for better preventing the horrid crime of murder, 1751: 25 Geo II, c37. In Scotland, the carrying out of an execution was never as immediate as the Act stated as was the case in England.
5 Goodman, 'Supply of Bodies', 807.
6 Goodman, 'Supply of Bodies', 808.

7 *Primus*, to distinguish him from his son and grandson christened with the same name, known as *secundus* and *tertius*.
8 C. W. Burr, 'Burke and Hare and the Psychology of Murder', *Annals of Medical History* 1, no. 1 (April, 1917), 76.
9 Goodman, 'Supply of Bodies', 810.
10 Goodman, 'Supply of Bodies', 807.
11 C. Emsley, *Crime and Society in England, 1750–1900* (Harlow, 2010), 274; S. Devereux, *Execution, State and Society in England 1660–1900* (Cambridge, 2023), 146.
12 A. M. Kilday, *Women and Violent Crime in Enlightenment Scotland* (Woodbridge, 2015), 44; W. W. Knox, 'Homicide in Eighteenth-Century Scotland: Numbers and Theories', *Scottish Historical Review* XCIV, no. 238 (April, 2015), 56–7.
13 L. Stone, 'Interpersonal Violence in English society, 1300–1980', *Past and Present* 101 (November, 1983), 28–9. Devereux uses Old Bailey trials only to argue that there was a decline in murder between 1720 and 1800; however, by using prosecuted murder only, his figures do not include homicides in which no perpetrator was discovered or tried; Devereux, *Execution*, figure 5.1, 143, 151.
14 Devereux, *Execution*, 147.
15 Philp, 'Bodies and Bureaucracy', 828.
16 Devereux, *Execution*, 161.
17 P. King, *Punishing the Criminal Corpse 1700–1840: Aggravated Forms of the Death Penalty in England* (London, 2017), 155.
18 King, *Criminal Corpse*, 153.
19 King, *Criminal Corpse*, 159.
20 Philp, 'Bodies and Bureaucracy', 832.
21 A. F. Young, *The Encyclopaedia of Scottish Executions 1750–1963* (Orpington, 1998), 161–2.
22 Anon, *Evidence, Oral and Documentary, Taken and Received By The Commissioners Appointed by His Majesty George IV. July 23d, 1826; And Re-appointed by His Majesty William IV., October 12th 1830; For Visiting The Universities of Scotland. Volume I, University of Edinburgh. Presented to both Houses of Parliament by Command of his Majesty* (London, 1837), 508 quoted in Kaufman, 'Transfer of Bodies', FN2, 234.
23 Burr, 'Burke and Hare', 75.
24 Burr, 'Burke and Hare', 75.
25 L. Rosner, *The Anatomy Murders: Being The True and Spectacular History of Edinburgh's notorious Burke and Hare and of the man of science who abetted them in the commission of their most heinous crimes* (Pennsylvania, 2010), 15.
26 Rosner, *Anatomy Murders*, 190–2.
27 JC26/1828/469.

28 *Trial of William Burke and Helen M'Dougal: before the High Court of Justiciary, on Wednesday December 24, 1828, for the murder of Margery Campbell, or Docherty* (Edinburgh, 1829), 87–95, 105–11, 111–17.
29 JC8/23.
30 S. Egger, 'A Working Definition of erial murder and the reduction of linkage blindness', *Journal of Police Science and Administration* 12, no. 3 (1986), abstract; K. D. Haggerty, 'Modern Serial Killers', *Crime Media Culture* 5, no. 2 (2009), 169.
31 G. MacGregor, *The History of Burke and Hare and the Resurrectionist Times* (Glasgow, 1884), 54.
32 Jack the Ripper's series began in 1888, some sixty years later. He is arguably the first recognized serial killer of the modern era.
33 MacGregor, *The History*, 54.
34 Rosner, *Anatomy Murders*, 53.
35 MacGregor, *The History*, 59–61.
36 Rosner, *Anatomy Murders*, 79.
37 Rosner, *Anatomy Murders*, 79–80.
38 MacGregor, *The History*, 63–8.
39 MacGregor, *The History*, 69–70, 74–5, 79–80, 82–3.
40 W. W. Knox and A. McKinlay, 'Crime, Protest and Policing in Nineteenth-Century Scotland', in *A History of Everyday Life in Scotland 1800–1900*, ed. T. Griffiths and G. Morton (Edinburgh, 2011), 216.
41 D. Wilson, 'Late Capitalism, Vulnerable Populations and Violent Predatory Crime', in *New Directions in Criminological Theory*, ed. S. Hall and S. Winlow (London, 2012), 221, 216–37.
42 D. Barrie, 'Naming and Shaming: Trial by Media in Nineteenth Century Scotland', *Journal of British Studies* 54, no. 2 (April, 2015), 368.
43 Barrie, 'Naming and Shaming', 376.
44 'The West-Port Murders', *The Times*, 5 January 1829, 3.
45 'The West-Port Murders', *The Times*, 5 January 1829, 3.
46 The day before Burke's trial, *The Times* again re-reported a Scottish murder, which was 'as great a sensation of horror and indignation as the West Port murders'. A party of Irish on board a boat travelling from Lochgilphead to Glasgow had poisoned and killed one man and attempted to murder another; the culprits were linked to similar crimes in Edinburgh earlier in the Autumn. The tone of the report suggests further moral panic that even on a passenger boat, no one was safe; *The Times*, 23 December 1828, 3.
47 P. Jenkins, *Intimate Enemies: Moral Panics in Contemporary Great Britain* (New York, 1992), 55–6.
48 P. King, 'Moral Panics and Violent Street Crime 1750–2000: a comparative perspective', *Comparative Histories of Crime*, ed. B. Godfrey, C. Emsley and G. Dunstall (Cullompton, 2003), 64.

49 'West-Port Murders, from the Edinburgh papers', *The Times*, 30 December 1828, 3.
50 'West-Port Murders, from the Edinburgh papers', *The Times*, 30 December 1828, 3.
51 'The Late Horrible Murders in Edinburgh to obtain subjects for dissection', *The Times*, 29 December 1828, 3.
52 'West-Port Murders, from the Edinburgh papers', *The Times*, 30 December 1828, 3.
53 King, *Criminal Corpse*, 157.
54 King, *Criminal Corpse*, 166.
55 King, *Criminal Corpse*, 167.
56 Kaufman, 'Transfer of Bodies', 230.
57 Kaufman, 'Transfer of Bodies', 229.
58 Philp, 'Bodies and Bureaucracy', 234.
59 Philp, 'Bodies and Bureaucracy', 235.
60 'West-Port Murders, from the Edinburgh Papers', *The Times*, 30 December 1828, 3.

6

Dobie and Thomson 1830: Misogyny, female agency and rape

Rape-homicide is historically and statistically a rare crime, but this particular case evidences not only the dynamics of a fatal rape but also reveals the deep-seated misogyny of certain types of men that permitted them to commit this crime. It also explores wider societal attitudes to victims of rape.

Context

During the nineteenth century in Scotland, Anne-Marie Kilday's research reveals there was an upward trend in rape-only indictments between 1805 and 1897, although as she emphasizes, rape convictions proved to be a woefully small proportion of the number of charges indicted.[1] For a crime that historians and criminologists acknowledge has been extremely hard for women to prosecute, the disparity between indictments and convictions across the nineteenth century, and beyond, begs several questions: does the nineteenth-century upward trend in indictments indicate a greater willingness of women to report a rape despite the difficulties they faced in proving a conviction? Or does it reflect a more sympathetic legal system more prepared to prosecute? And, does the low conviction rate reflect a juridical response that remained unconvinced by the quality of evidence presented? Or sceptical of the woman complainer before them? These are difficult questions for historians to explore with any degree of statistical proof. However, when a rape ends in murder, the rape remains open to juridical scrutiny, whereas there is no denying the evidence of a woman's sexually violated dead body. In this instance, what must be proved is: was she raped and by whom; who killed her and was it the same person or persons who committed both crimes?

Between 1800 and 1900, there were ten trials for rape-murder at the High Court of Justiciary and circuit courts in Scotland, indicting thirteen men. Rape-murder is indeed a rare crime to be prosecuted. It is even rarer for the panel to be found guilty of both charges, because of those thirteen accuseds, all of whom would have hanged if convicted on both counts, only five were executed. The others, having been found guilty of only one part of the charge, or not proven on one or both charges, were sentenced to transportation for life, imprisoned for twenty years or assoilzied and dismissed from the bar.[2] Proving a rape-murder was clearly as difficult as succeeding with a rape-only prosecution. The definition of rape and the evidence required to prove a rape charge, as well as exploring societal attitudes towards women who reported sexual violence, are pivotal to understanding why convicting those accused of rape-murder was so challenging.

The definition of murder has not varied over centuries: it is 'the greatest crime known in the law' and is perpetrated through 'a deliberate intention to kill, or to inflict a minor injury of such a kind as indicates an utter recklessness as to the life of the sufferer, whether he live or die'.[3] However, the actions required by the alleged perpetrator of rape have changed over time. Essentially, rape is the 'forcible carnal knowledge of a woman's person against her will'.[4] While proof of penetration has always been a requirement, proof of emission has not. In England, the Offences Against the Person Act 1828 changed the law on the requirement for proof of emission.[5] However in Scotland, common law prevailed without statute law. Although Baron David Hume had stated in his 1797 *Commentaries* that penetration only would be sufficient for a charge of rape, it was not until 1821 that Scottish judges adjudicating on the case of William Montgomerie concluded that 'complete penetration, without emission' was sufficient to justify a rape charge.[6] Partial penetration, which was allowed in England, was insufficient for a rape charge in Scotland, and in both jurisdictions, 'against her will' had to be proven. If the complainer could not prove that she had struggled 'with all her might', called out for help or lacked visible external injuries as proof of resistance, then consent was implied. That a woman might be terrified and not resist, and therefore was less likely to incur external injuries, did not occur to the judiciary until *HMA v. Sweenie* in 1858 when Scotland's Lord President declared that 'force essential for the crime of rape is relative to the resistance offered, and where there is not resistance to overcome, it is not necessary to prove force'.[7] However, despite Hume's and Alison's clarifications of the position of Scots Law on these matters, such notions of emission, resistance and proof of non-consent proved tenacious, while the woman's previous character remained a competent subject of investigation.[8] Thus, the victim's community were able to give evidence for and against her based on her previous relationships, potential illegitimate pregnancies and whether or not she was considered 'available' by those who knew her.

However, key to a rape victim's corroborative evidence was the story as told to family and associates which, even though *de recenti* – hearsay – was admissible in court.[9] Their version of the assault was considered corroborative of her own precognition, although practice dictated she had to report the crime as soon as possible to stand a chance of being believed, despite Scots Law not requiring such speed.[10] Not reporting immediately allowed the insinuation of a 'mere seduction' and her complaint to the Procurator Fiscal to be viewed as a 'malicious accusation' and cautious juries might return a not proven verdict.[11] Further, the language she employed to describe the assault could affect the veracity of her claim: if she used euphemism to describe the attack, this could be understood to show innocence of previous sexual activity and reticence to reveal what a respectable woman knew inherently to be immoral; obversely, it might contribute to rejection of her claim because evading the correct terminology might imply prior experience if combined with unfavourable 'character' evidence. The choice of vocabulary compounded a difficult situation if the Procurator Fiscal could not understand the nature of the assault; he would be unable to obtain instructions from Crown Counsel to indict correctly, and Crown Counsel might decide not to prosecute at all. Kim Stevenson's research on Victorian news reports of rape found that 'the desexualization of intimate language', to make discourse on sexual violence respectable, was used in the courtroom and repeated in news reports and would have been disseminated among the readership.[12] Basically, the complainer had to follow a 'rape script' of demure conduct and language; provide evidence of resistance and calling for assistance, and the report had to be most timely.

Credible and corroborated evidence to satisfy an elite male judiciary had to be supported by the physical evidence apparent on her body, even though medical forensic ability in the nineteenth century was unable to do anything more than determine bruises, ruptures and detection of mammalian semen. Thus, sexual assaults were, and are, the only criminal indictments for which the living complainer must not only provide the customary victim's testimony but must also offer up her body for forensic medical scrutiny if she stands a chance of proving her complaint.

In 1830, the sentence for a murder conviction was execution; rape also attracted a capital sentence. Because of the severity of the law, in a rape prosecution especially, it became 'indispensable to look minutely' at the complainer's evidence because to convict on a false accusation for a crime so difficult to prove, and if believed, for the defendant to disprove, might conclude with the death of an innocent man. Alison adhered to the notion that rape bore 'so close an affinity to voluntary connexion', that a woman desiring to preserve her 'character' might resort to revenge or extortion. Thus, her statement 'in regard to the *violence* used' [emphasis in original] had to be corroborated by physical evidence; her disclosure of the crime to relations and the legal authorities, and her complaint had to be evaluated against her 'previous character for modesty and correct demeanour'.[13] Deviation from that 'script' might result in the panel's acquittal if indeed the case had actually satisfied the Procurator Fiscal and Lord Advocate sufficiently to reach court.

Thus, the status and safety of women in early nineteenth-century society are revealed through the legal process. Not only were women not heard and might not be believed because of an inherent 'weakness' of their sex, but they were also physically unsafe from the advances and potential violence of men. Domestic servants could be raped by men in their employer's household without recourse to the law; women suffered abuse, often silently, from husbands. No woman or girl was completely safe or could rely on the judiciary treating her complaint as credible and herself as innocent of any collusion in the crime she alleged to be committed against her. The hurdles were high and numerous for a woman in the early nineteenth century to succeed with a rape prosecution and win a conviction. If she had died of her injuries between rape and reporting the crime, then the probability of either would have fallen dramatically.

Case

Margaret Paterson, aged approximately thirty-five years in 1830, died before she could be precognosced, but she did tell her father and some neighbours some of the details of her sexual assault and other aspects of the ordeal to which she alluded. Her mother's testimony stated that two men had 'used every kind of freedom with' her and that they had forced her corset stick into her private parts; Margaret did not tell even her mother what other injuries they had perpetrated on her or what other materials they had thrust into her vagina and anus.[14] She had been tossed out of a cart late in the evening on Saturday, 17 April 1830, and left by the roadside where some residents of Gilmerton had found her. At no point before her death did she actually say she had been raped, although her mother testified that it was only 'delicacy on her part', which had prevented her daughter from divulging the truth. And Margaret only named the two men once she had learned their names from those who had initially cared for her before conveying her to her parents' home in nearby Dalkeith. But Margaret had indeed been vilely treated by

David Dobie and John Thomson, the former a twenty-eight-year-old married father of two and the latter a single man of twenty-two years.

Margaret had spent the day in Edinburgh. She had been a servant and was now a lace seller who travelled the country peddling her stock; she smoked which was not unusual for anyone in 1830, and she enjoyed a dram of whisky. Some witnesses, including her father, alleged that she was addicted to drink. On Saturday afternoon, Margaret decided to leave Edinburgh and travel to her parents' home in Dalkeith, south of the city. She asked a carter whom she knew to meet her at a cross-roads, but their rendezvous failed, and she fell in with two men, both driving their own carts home to Gilmerton. William Ramage, the porter at Campbell's Close, had enjoyed a gill of whisky that morning with her and another around 6.00 pm, which Margaret paid for. The manager at Bridgend Coal Depot near Libberton confirmed he had seen her when she was 'not materially the worse of liquor', and he described her black bonnet and green 'tartan mantle' shawl. James Thomson, a servant, saw her around 8.00 pm 'quite able to walk'; also, he saw Dobie and Thomson talking at the door of Pentland's public house. Others' evidence confirmed Dobie's and Thomson's presence at Pentland's as well as their recognized employment as carters. The publican's wife recounted Margaret's enquiry about carts going to Dalkeith and stated that Margaret 'hardly tasted the last gill' of whisky before leaving with Dobie and Thomson, both of whom appeared 'perfectly sober' and Margaret 'not at all the worse of drink'. Her husband, Colin Pentland, stated that Margaret was an 'entire stranger to the men'.

Dobie's and Thomson's horses and carts arrived back in Gilmerton without their drivers, where William Dingwall, a tacksman, took charge of the animals. Dingwall found 'a small bundle' in Thomson's cart and later challenged him that he had had a woman there. Dingwall said Thomson alluded to a woman, and he remained unaware of who she was until Sunday morning when he heard that a woman had been found and carried to Bamberry's house. She was in a 'very bad' state. Bamberry had found her near the garden dyke at the back of William Gillon's property. She had been lying in water and smelled of drink, which Bamberry took to be the reason why she could not walk. She complained of a 'pain in her belly' but he did not observe any signs of a struggle in the vicinity, which he believed he would have done, even when he returned on Monday to investigate. There had been no rain in the interval to muddy the site. On Sunday, both Thomson and Dobie had returned to Gilmerton. Dobie was reported to be complaining of a headache, while Thomson had made some allusion to the stable hands of having been with a woman in his cart.

By now, the women had gathered to assist Margaret. Grace Proudfoot was with Dingwall when Dobie laughed and told him he knew nothing about a woman; Dingwall declared that he was 'a rogue'. Ann Bamberry found blood on Margaret's gown and heard Margaret wail that 'her bowels were gone'.

There was blood on the chair where she had been sitting, but Ann stated that Margaret 'never hinted' at who had hurt her. Ann did not ask Margaret about it, even after she had heard that Thomson had abused her. Thomson and Dobie were named as the perpetrators by those gathered in the Bamberrys' home, after which Margaret was able to call them by their names. Between Sunday's discovery and some time on Monday, 19 April, Ann Bamberry and Violet Gillan made an application to Margaret's father to accept her home, but he refused on the grounds of her drinking. However, on Tuesday, the Gillans accompanied Margaret home in their cart during which time apparently she divulged none of the details of her abuse, although they recalled Margaret saying she needed to see Dr Morrison and that 'they will suffer for me yet'; she also said she 'had been ill used and murdered' by the men she had met at the public house.[15]

Her father, William Paterson's precognition describes her stay in his home and how she mentioned Thomson's name frequently, but not Dobie. She explained that when they were 'ill using her they were cutting her with sharp instruments', but she had said nothing about them having 'their will of her'. She told her father about a tin money box and two pawn tickets which had vanished, but Margaret was unable to say whether she had dropped them or they had been stolen.[16] Dr Morrison attended her on Wednesday, 21 April. He found Margaret in bed, complaining of lower abdomen pain with her petticoat covered with 'feculent matter' discharged from her anus. In front of him, Margaret passed a stone, and then another, and on examination, Morrison found her rectum 'much lacerated' with 'mortification' already set in. He found 'slight abrasions' to the opening of her vagina which at first he considered to be venereal lesions but then concluded otherwise. Her pulse was 'weak and sinking'. On Wednesday evening, he sent her some wine laced with laudanum for her pain – there was little other remedy available to him – and on Thursday, when Morrison was accompanied by Dr James Renton, he understood she had suffered a 'restless night'. Further examination discovered 'gritty' substances in her vagina which proved to be coal dust of about an 'ounce in weight' and more 'angular stone'; there were knots of hay inside her also. She had begun to vomit but was able to tell him some of what had happened. She gave the doctor greater detail than anyone else, and when asked if the men had wanted to have connection with her, she replied in the affirmative but also told him that they had been unsuccessful. Margaret retained 'full use of her faculties' until her death around 3.00 pm on Thursday, 22 April 1830.

Morrison's first statement is dated 7 May, in which he gave the above evidence as well as stating that he had known Margaret for thirty years, commenting that until recently she had borne 'the character of a common prostitute' but was now 'partially reclaimed'. He noted that 'the dilation of the parts which her mode of life had occasioned' and the injuries to her vagina were not the cause of death, but the 'injuries in the rectum' had been. He denied that a detailed newspaper report had emanated from him, and that, in his opinion, the men who had done this to her had committed this crime because they had been 'irritated by her refusal to allow them to have connection with her'. Dr Renton's precognition was corroborative, although less detailed.[17]

Thus, by the time of her death, Margaret had made some declaration of the assault she had endured, and those caring for her had contributed corroborating evidence of events from when they had found her in the dyke. She had maintained her reticence to divulge all the details of her ordeal and had denied being raped to her doctor, although her mother believed her daughter's words had implied Dobie and Thomson had raped her. The declarations emitted by Dobie and Thomson tell a different story, especially when supported by their gossip to other prisoners once apprehended and incarcerated in Edinburgh's Tolbooth.

In their initial declarations, taken on the night of 22 April, both men gave elaborate versions of a similar story that involved who had paid for the drinks at Pentland's public house, which route they had taken home and whose cart had gone before the other. Thomson described how Margaret, trying to exit his cart near Gilmerton, had woken him, but she was too drunk to manage alone, so he had helped her. His horse had gone on ahead of him, and Margaret had told him she was visiting a sister nearby. He had met Dingwall and his stable hand and told them that a woman had lain down by the wall and was drunk. On Sunday, he had been informed that Bamberry had found her, and he denied to the Procurator Fiscal having used 'any liberties of any kind' with her. On 29 April when interrogated again, Thomson added that he had not told anyone, including Dobie, that he had had connection with a woman in his cart and also that he had found a handkerchief in his cart among the hay on Sunday. He did not recognize Margaret's green shawl.

Dobie's declaration given on 22 April follows a similar vein. However, he gave a second and third declaration on 29 April and 13 May, respectively. In the second declaration, Dobie described Thomson 'having to do' with the woman in his cart who made no resistance and who he thought was 'dead drunk'. He did not consider helping her, nor did he have anything to do with her, and he did nothing to encourage or prevent Thomson. His opinion of Margaret was that she could 'not have been a very decent woman' because she had been in the company of strange men at Pentland's. Dobie explained that Thomson had told him he had had sex with her two or three times, and on Sunday, in the presence of the stable men, he had joked with Thomson about his exploits. He denied all knowledge of anything having been inserted into Margaret's person.

By 13 May, Dobie had more to divulge. By now he had boasted to fellow inmates about his exploits. James Wilson reported Dobie had told him that he and Thomson had intended to make Margaret's 'two holes meet' and that between them they had injured her so that she would no longer 'hold wind or water'. Wilson confirmed the details of the corset stick and other materials and reported that Dobie had said the two men had discussed their behaviour before forcing Margaret into the cart. Other prisoners corroborated some or all of these details. Thus, by 13 May, Dobie was keen to tell the Procurator Fiscal that he had seen Thomson with his breeches unbuttoned, positioned above the woman in his cart whose petticoats were up and her legs exposed. He could not be sure whether Margaret's hands were by her side or if she had resisted. At home, his wife had accused him of having had sex with someone while out on Saturday night which he had denied. Also, in Dobie's third declaration, he had suggested to the sheriff's officer that so far, he had not told the 'whole truth', and he was eager to be considered as King's evidence to assist the prosecution's case. His offer was denied.[18]

On 1 May 1830, *The North Briton* newspaper published a full account of Margaret's ordeal in Latin to protect the sensitivities of its readers, except of course those elite men, and a few women, with a classical education fluent in ancient languages, whose breakfast digestion presumably could take it. The newspaper's non-Latin report largely followed the details emitted by the various witnesses and expressed great sympathy for the victim. Margaret was described as 'remarkably neat and clean in her person' and was 'strapping' and 'handsome'. The men who had perpetrated the crime were 'monsters' and for a country which 'fancied moral superiority of its people' over those of other kingdoms, this was a disgrace incomparable to Burke's and Hare's recent crime and was 'more inhuman and more diabolical' than anything in living memory. The author described how Dobie was 'the spokesman' who had shifted the blame to Thomson, both of whom displayed not 'the remotest conception that there was any guilt or criminality' in their actions. The newspaper suggested that if both men had been identified by Margaret on the Wednesday before her death, the case would have been stronger. It reported that when asked which of them had behaved the worst, she had replied 'they were both alike'.[19]

The day after Margaret's death, Dr Morrison was commanded to write to the Procurator Fiscal with a further medical report, the details of which confirmed extensive, horrific injuries to her rectum and lower intestine. He repeated Margaret's answer when asked who had committed these injuries: 'two carters with whom she had been previously acquainted' and who she had asked for a ride back to Gilmerton. They had 'forcibly abused her by thrusting up into the bowel the foreign substances' he had found there pre- and postmortem.

From all the evidence gathered across seventy-one precognitions, the Procurator Fiscal was able to present a case, albeit one without any eyewitnesses to corroborate Margaret's story, but one with ample witnesses to events once she had been discovered lying in the dyke. The indictment against both men was 'rape and assault with intent to ravish as also murder; also robbery'. Throughout their declarations, they had adhered to the same plea. On 12 July 1830 in the High Court of Justiciary at Edinburgh, once again, both men pleaded not guilty on every charge.[20]

Reporting a week after the trial, the *Sheffield Independent* wrote that 'the Scotch courts exercise the wise discretion' to hear such cases behind closed doors, thus no particulars of the trial had leaked out until reporting was permitted post-trial.[21] And even then, having passed sentence, the Lord Justice-Clerk advised all those present in the strongest terms not to publish the details of the evidence; they were permitted only to print the courtroom

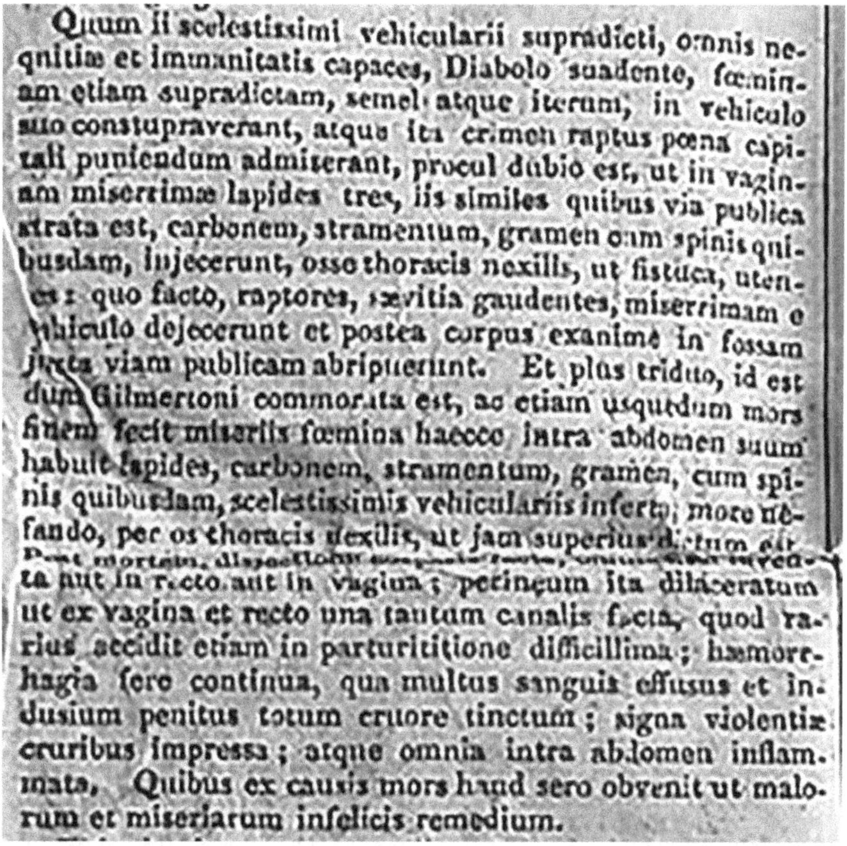

ILLUSTRATION 6.1 *Latin extract describing Margaret Paterson's ordeal.* The North Briton, *1 May 1830.*

scene and verdict. Thus, the interested public who may have read *The North Briton*'s article some two months earlier learned that the jury had only retired for a few minutes before returning a verdict of unanimously guilty on the charge of murder as actors or art and part; guilty of robbery and assault, but rape was not proven.[22] The sentence could only be execution with the aggravation of dissection. They were hanged on 18 August 1830 and anatomized in November.[23] News of the trial was circulated by the national and British press so that anyone interested learned that even 'the utmost stretch' of the judges' imagination could not have anticipated such a case, and all within 'three miles of the metropolis of this most civilized country'.[24]

Themes and analysis

The two key charges against Dobie and Thomson were rape and murder. Margaret had demurred to confirm penetration, or it had not occurred, but she had certainly died of her injuries for which someone must be held culpable. From the nature of her injuries and absence of her testimony of rape, an indictment of assault, at best indecent assault, might have been expected. However, the Lord Advocate preferred the highest charge of rape, presumably because the logical conclusion was that any man sexually assaulting a woman would rape her before perpetrating any other monstrosity on her person. However, the evidence for either man's participation in rape or murder was circumstantial: no one had seen all three people together after they left Pentland's, so no one knew what had occurred between them. But the number of precognitions taken was apparently sufficiently corroborative for the Lord Advocate to prosecute. If it could be proved that she had been raped, and Margaret herself had described how Dobie and Thomson had thrust her corset stick into her, then if they were the rapists, they also had to be the murderers. If rape could not be proven, the link between the corset stick, her injuries and death meant murder alone might be proven.

However, many of the seventy-one precognitions were revisited by the Procurator Fiscal which suggests that having taken the key individuals' testimonies, it had become apparent that minute details required clarification. It was also clear that the delay between the assault, Margaret's discovery and the official report to the Procurator Fiscal the evening after her death had allowed the residents of Gilmerton and Dalkeith to share information. Now the Procurator Fiscal had to determine what was first-hand testimony and what was *de recenti* evidence; whether it was hearsay testimony of Margaret's words or something the community's gossiping had created. Thus, it became important to know the point at which Margaret had learned the names of her assailants: before, during or after the attack. All the testimonies covering this detail reported that she had learned the men's names at Bamberry's house and only thereafter had used them to identify the men. Between being turfed out of the cart and her death, Margaret had seen neither man to attach their names to. But clearly, the Procurator Fiscal had accepted the wealth of testimony from her rescuers to apprehend and charge Dobie and Thomson.

In addition, the testimony of their cellmates supported the villagers' precognitions. Archibald Allison had shared the day room with Thomson in prison and had heard him say that he had had connection with Margaret but not whether she had consented.[25] John Kelly had spent time with Thomson in the 'airing ground' exercising where Thomson had confessed after receiving his indictment that 'it was a damned good thing that all that Dobie could say was that Thomson had had connection with the woman', because he had kicked her and 'jerked her' with the corset stick around her anus. He said she was comatose with alcohol, but the pain had made her 'roar out'. James Wilson's testimony contained the most horrific description of events as told to him by Dobie.[26] Evidently, both men had participated in the sexualized mutilation of Margaret, and Dobie's tone, recounted by Wilson, suggests bragging about their exploits. Research into male group behaviour suggests that sexually aggressive men conflate the concept of 'power with the concept of sex'.[27] Thus, rape becomes the ultimate power over a woman and recounting the details of one's behaviour buys masculine capital. None of the prisoners is listed as witnesses in court, and it is possible their testimony was orchestrated by the Procurator Fiscal, placing them with Dobie and Thomson to extract a confession. However, it is more probable that the confessions were idle inmate gossip, which served to clarify for the Procurator Fiscal that he had the right men.

The Procurator Fiscal also took detailed evidence on Margaret's degree of intoxication. Both panels assessed her as 'dead drunk' and unable to walk unaided, which served to mitigate their behaviour by impugning Margaret's reputation. Others at Pentland's had seen her drinking, but not incapacitated. At Gilmerton, those who assisted her could smell drink, and it appears several people made an assumption that she could not walk because she was drunk. The Gilmerton group did not know of her reputation as 'much given to liquor'; therefore, their evidence was not prejudiced. However, her father's evidence was damning of her alcohol consumption; he also mentioned that she had borne an illegitimate child several years ago and was of no fixed abode. He had refused to receive her because of her drinking.[28] *The North Briton* skimmed over Margaret's history with alcohol before declaring that she had told her story 'so minutely' to her doctors that 'her naturalness and consistent account' had impressed 'their minds with a conviction that she could not have been intoxicated at the time'.[29] In his defence, Dobie told the sheriff's officer he 'knew nothing about it, I was drunk'.[30]

In Scots and English law, mere drunkenness was insufficient to mitigate culpability unless the panel could be proven as insane, however temporarily, through inebriation.[31] Despite stating that they had both fallen asleep on their carts, neither man was insane from drink. In fact, *The North Briton* had printed a description of a group of Gilmerton carters treating 'this matter lightly' thinking, erroneously, that because two of their number were 'waur o' drink', they would not be held responsible; it had been a 'drunken frolic'.[32] Margaret's situation is more problematical. There was, and is, no law concerning the contribution of a victim to their own victimization through intoxication. However, in the nineteenth century, the insinuation that a woman had placed herself in a compromising position through being inebriated could influence the jury's judgement of her credibility and reliability. In Margaret's case, this would have meant the credibility of her recall of events prior to death.

Fiske and Rai identify further issues that may provoke rape: that men are 'entitled' to sex and if refused will rape, since refusal is 'an assertion of her will' over his, which challenges male authority.[33] Margaret said she had denied Thomson's advances, although she did not describe how she had tried to fend him off. Also, that provocative dress or being unaccompanied or in an 'inappropriate locale' suggests the woman is 'asking for it'; she has demeaned herself and the man may commit rape because of her perceived lowered status.[34] Margaret's attire was not questioned, but being alone in a public house on the outskirts of Edinburgh, leaving with two strangers was questionable, possibly irresponsible, behaviour in nineteenth-century society. Margaret's additional reputational issues of an illegitimate pregnancy, previous although unevidenced prostitution and vagrancy would, arguably, have counted against a complaint of rape, but Margaret had died *because* of rape, which was an exceptional crime. Her physical presence in court could not be evaluated for 'character', and sympathy for the manner of her death had already been expressed in the newspapers. It is probable that the jurors – all farmers and small businessmen – had read the published accounts.

Margaret's behaviour post-assault followed a typical 'rape script'. She had not divulged the details of her assault to anyone until she had been examined by a doctor, and those details expressed to her mother were clouded in ambiguity. Her unwillingness to tell her story in detail made her an 'ideal' rape victim, meek and feminine, too ashamed to tell all, although the carter community in Gilmerton had a reputation that suggests they were not a sensitive bunch, as commented in *The North Briton*.[35] Thus, her post-rape behaviour and death had constructed Margaret as a respectable working-class woman, although arguably, if this had been a straightforward rape, she may not quite have qualified in nineteenth-century eyes.

Everything pointed towards Margaret having put herself in the way of sexual assault. Her consent to sexual intercourse could not be established from the evidence submitted. Dobie's various declarations about the position of her hands and whether she had resisted Thomson's advances were unhelpful either to prove non-consent or her willingness to participate. However, their prison confessions described how they had both held her down.[36] That indicated non-consent. And, if the connection between rape followed by post-rape mutilation was obvious to the jury, then no sane woman would consent to that brutality.

The requirement to report a sexual assault quickly as proof of credibility probably did not apply in Margaret's case. Clearly, she was incapacitated by her injuries, but one of the villagers might have acted on her behalf. After his first attendance on her, Dr Morrison wrote a letter on Wednesday, 21 April, to Scott Moncrieff, advocate at Dalkeith employed by the Duke of Buccleuch, who incidentally also paid Margaret's father's pension. The precognition of Angus McLeod, sheriff's officer, describes his visit to Moncrieff to gather information to communicate to the Procurator Fiscal on Wednesday, only to learn that Moncrieff had already written to him. McLeod visited Margaret on Thursday morning but was unable to learn anything more from her. Thus, the crime perpetrated against Margaret was only officially reported on Wednesday, 21 April, four days after her assault.

The verdict of guilty on all charges except rape appears, at this distance, the only response the jury could have returned. A callous interpretation might suggest that being raped no longer mattered because Margaret had died, but the jury did not declare Dobie and Thomson not guilty of the rape charge; they considered the charge not proven. Arguably, this is an example of Scots Law at its best, and the verdict of not proven is most properly used. Their verdict does not necessarily suggest juridical indecision, but that the quality of the evidence did not, beyond all reasonable doubt, confirm rape had been perpetrated on Margaret. The Procurator Fiscal's minute interest in Margaret's tin box, its contents and her garments supported the charge of robbery; the physical injuries testified by two doctors confirmed assault, and Margaret's death was an absolute for murder. The weight of evidence pointing to Dobie and Thomson, although essentially circumstantial, was credible and corroborated and indicated their involvement and no one else's. The sentence pronounced on them was commensurate with their crimes in this period. But why had they done something so monstrous to another human being?

Neither Dobie nor Thomson explained their motive, and the case records contain no contemporary comment on what provoked such a shocking act. However, their behaviour suggests toxic masculinity and hyper-misogyny. Fisk and Rai identify a 'metarelational' need to belong in a competitively male group and suggest that this need can provoke gang rapes; the 'consubstantial assimilation' of raping together cements a brotherhood among the gang.[37] Dobie and Thomson – a gang of two – encouraged one another to rape, followed by joint participation in Margaret's mutilation. Dobie's account, given to his cell mate, clearly describes their simultaneous grasping of Margaret's genitals to tear her. Fiske and Rai further argue that 'dehumanization and moral disengagement' are also key factors in gang rapes in a way uncommon in single perpetrator rapes.[38] This modern research helps to understand the dynamics of what appears to have been a frenzied assault on Margaret by two men having reckless 'fun' at her fatal expense, but it does not explain why they sexually assaulted a woman of their own class.

Opportunity may have been a factor. Margaret was alone; she had been drinking with them and may not have been able to pay for her drinks; she was unprotected, therefore vulnerable and potentially they viewed her as 'available' because of these circumstances; the non-consensual sex was their 'payment' for buying her whisky. While none of this excuses their behaviour, in early nineteenth-century society it may go some way to explain it. Margaret was no one's wife; therefore, she commanded little power. She possessed a degree of independence that married women would not attain until the Married Women's Property Act (1870) when for the first time women could legally keep the money they earned and inherit property without it transferring automatically to their husbands.[39] However, Margaret had already attracted the opprobrium of her father and brother, who were ashamed of her because of her drinking.[40] Thus, male censorship of female conduct affected all women whether single and independent or married and legally controlled. Whether Margaret's status was an affront to Dobie and Thomson will never be known. It was not unusual for a working-class woman to exist without male protection, but to any man contemplating unlawful sex with a single woman, assaulting Margaret was unlikely to attract another man's indignation because she belonged to no one.

Further, without a man to speak for her, Margaret's voice lacked efficacy. If she had had the opportunity to accuse Dobie and Thomson, they could have replied that her word was as good as theirs, and without physical evidence of rape and her reticence to admit penetration, they may have been acquitted. Even if she had described in greater detail their assault, the balance of evidence may still have remained in their favour. Anna Clark cites a rape-murder from 1817 in which a twenty-year-old woman enjoying herself at a fair 'without proper protection' had been killed by a male fair-goer; he was acquitted. The message learned was that 'women who take their freedom for granted will be punished by rape'.[41] While Clark's feminist argument marks this case as the point after which all women came under patriarchal control, it also helps to explain how the audacity of a lone woman, who was happy to drink with two strangers and then request a cart-ride home, may have elicited a violent response from Dobie and Thomson. To believe that an independent woman 'deserves' to be raped is the ultimate expression of toxic masculinity, but in 1830s Edinburgh, it was nothing uncommon, and it must be seen in historical context. However, what was unusual was the aggravated element of the assault, which suggests hyper-misogyny. The frenzied nature of Dobie's and Thomson's joint attack points to the worthlessness of women in society – a disregard for their agency as citizens and for their existence as human beings.

Conclusion

Today, the definition of rape in the UK is the penetration of someone's vagina, anus or mouth by a penis without consent, or reasonable belief of consent.[42] The woman's character and previous sexual history evidence are no longer admissible in court, although it remains difficult for complainers of sexual violence to win a conviction. Aileen McColgan's research on the influence of sexual history evidence on juries' verdicts found that 94 per cent of defendants charged with raping a 'respectable' woman – one without a sexual history – were convicted, whereas only 48 per cent of those charged with raping a woman with a sexually active past were convicted. Socializing with her attacker before being raped meant that the legal process concentrated on 'her life style, background and actions before and after the incident'.[43] If she had survived, Margaret may have suffered the further indignity of not benefitting from 'the presumption of truthfulness', which alleged victims of other crimes enjoy.[44] But Margaret died, and thereafter the indignation expressed at the crime perpetrated against her entered the public domain.

Kilday argues that this case contributed to a pervasive view of Scotland as violent and may have contributed to a moral panic, following the Burke and Hare murders among others, that Scotland was a dangerous place. She asks whether selecting a few cases, perpetrated close in time, warrants 'labelling an entire nation as violent in perpetuity?'.[45] It certainly does not. However, while the newspaper coverage may have fed the prurient tastes of their readership, whether printed in broadsides or broadsheets, and whether in rhyme or Latin, the reportage also helped to raise wider awareness of the plight of working-class women in Britain's cities. Real sympathy for Margaret was expressed in *The North Briton* and other newspapers. Margaret's murder was a hyper-misogynistic crime, but its perpetration highlighted the plight of all women in British society if they encountered depraved, dangerous men who displayed untrammelled male authority. Her rape-murder was a turning point in the collective consciousness that is a development still in process into the twenty-first century and arguably will be into the next. The way in which Dobie and Thomson bragged about their behaviour in the days immediately after the assault and again in prison equates to today's social media sharing by men of their sexual abuse tales and deep-fake images of women they do not know.[46]

Notes

1 A. M. Kilday, *Crime in Scotland 1660–1960: the Violent North?* (Abingdon, 2021), 84–5.
2 JC26/1810/17; JC26/1830/346; JC26/1844/294; JC26/1849/85; JC26/1851/173; JC26/1855/33; JC26/1868/88; JC26/1890/112; JC26/1890/15 and JC26/1892/50.
3 A. Alison, *Principles of the Criminal Law of Scotland* (Edinburgh, 1832), 1.
4 Alison, *Principles*, 209.
5 Offences against the Person Act, 1828, XVIII, 9 Geo IV, c.31.
6 Baron D. Hume, *Commentaries on the Law of Scotland, respecting the description and punishment of crimes*, vol. 2 (1797), 2; Alison, *Principles*, 210.
7 *R v. Sweenie*, (1858), 8 Cox CC 223.
8 Alison, *Principles*, 215.
9 Alison, *Principles*, 217.
10 Hume, *Commentaries*, vol. 2, 34–5.
11 M. R. Block, "For the Repressing of the Most Wicked and felonious Rapes and Ravishments of Women': Rape Law in England, 1660–1800', in *Interpreting Sexual Violence, 1660–1800*, ed. A. Greenfield (Abingdon, 2016), 26–7.
12 K. Stevenson, 'Unearthing the Realities of Rape: utilising Victorian newspaper reportage to fill the contextual gaps', *Liverpool Law Review* 28 (2007), 413.
13 Alison, *Principles*, 220.
14 AD14/30/334 Jean Meldrum Paterson.
15 AD14/30/334.
16 AD14/30/334.
17 AD14/30/334.
18 JC26/1830/346.
19 *The North Briton*, 1 May 1830; the case papers do not reveal who informed the press.
20 JC4/20.
21 'The Gilmerton Murder', *Sheffield Independent*, 24 July 1830.

22 'The Trial of the Gilmerton Murderers', *The Morning Post*, 16 July 1830; JC4/20. The phrase 'the jury retired' may actually only mean they conferred briefly in the court room without having exited.
23 It remains unclear why the dissection was delayed, but possibly it may have been to maximize the number of medical students attending and to sell sufficient tickets.
24 'The Trial of the Gilmerton Murderers', *The Morning Post*, 16 July 1830.
25 For clarity, this is not the person of the same name (different surname spelling) who was sheriff at the time.
26 AD14/30/334.
27 A. P. Fiske and T. S. Rai, *Virtuous Violence* (Cambridge, 2015), 169.
28 AD14/30/334.
29 *The North Briton*, 1 May 1830.
30 JC26/1830/346.
31 Alison, *Principles*, 661; J. Glaister, *A Text-Book of Medical Jurisprudence and Toxicology* (Edinburgh, 1913), 587.
32 *The North Briton*, 5 May 1830.
33 Fiske and Rai, *Virtuous Violence*, 170.
34 Fiske and Rai, *Virtuous Violence*, 168.
35 *The North Briton*, 5 May 1830.
36 AD14/30/334.
37 Fiske and Rai, *Virtuous Violence*, 169.
38 Fiske and Rai, *Virtuous Violence*, 177.
39 Married Women's Property Act (1887), 33 and 34 Vict, c.93.
40 AD14/30/334.
41 A. Clark, *Women's Silence, Men's Violence: Sexual Assault in England, 1770–1845* (London, 1987), 110.
42 Sexual Offences (Scotland) Act 2009, section 1.
43 A. McColgan, 'Common Law and the Relevance of Sexual History Evidence', *Oxford Journal of Legal Studies* 16, no. 2 (1996), 278.
44 McColgan, 'Sexual History Evidence', 277.
45 Kilday, *Violent North*, 15–16.
46 The use of social media in the twenty-first century and AI-generated deep-fake images as digital forms of, often extreme, pornography is a frightening phenomenon discussed in L. Bates, *The New Age of Sexism: How the AI revolution is reinventing misogyny* (London, 2025), chapter 1.

7

Madeleine Smith 1857: Class, gender and sexual morality

When used to kill, poison is a murder weapon largely chosen by women. This was the product allegedly used by Madeleine Smith, a middle-class daughter, to poison her lover; a case which alarmed Glaswegian and wider British society and reveals not only fear of 'the murderess' in the home but also attitudes towards sexual experience and class expectations of propriety in unchaperoned young women.

Context

Poison is insidious and does not require force to administer, which is why historically it has been the woman's choice to despatch troublesome relations, employers and lovers. Poisons were, and some continue to be, widely available in society for industrial and domestic use. However, in the mid-nineteenth century, the key poison most people were aware of was arsenic. It was used in the manufacture of paints and dyes; thus, it hung in dining-room wallpapers and rubbed against the skin in dress fabrics. It was used as a cleaning product and rodent killer; thus, with long usage, it could seep into the skin or could accidentally be mistaken for baking powder or sugar and introduced into comestibles. Arsenic was pervasive in all aspects of life for everyone, from shepherds using it to delouse their flocks to young women dancing in 'arsenical gowns' in ballrooms; it floated in the air whether one lived in a squalid tenement or glittering Victorian townhouse. Everyone breathed it in.[1] However, as an accepted everyday product, increasing awareness of its dangers prompted the enactment of the Sale of Arsenic Regulation Act 1851, in response to a 'mid-century profusion' of malicious arsenic poisoning cases.[2] From 1851 onwards, anyone selling arsenic was legally obliged to record each sale in a written register noting the date and name of the purchaser, their address, occupation and its intended purpose. Further, vendors were required to mix arsenic with soot or indigo unless doing so would render the product unusable. Failure to comply with the terms of the Act attracted a fine of up to twenty pounds.[3] Mixing arsenic with soot or indigo was intended to reduce the number of accidental poisonings, but where arsenic was purchased for domestic use, such as cleaning solutions or in cosmetic products, a clean white powder was preferred.

Karen Merry's research into prosecutions for malicious poisoning in Scotland reveals that the 'rat excuse' was used in 66 per cent of prosecutions, where poisoning had allegedly occurred through accidental consumption. Notable was the number of cases that had occurred in rural areas, where Merry suggests arsenic poisoning may have been a means of 'settling grievances or profiting from the death of another' in remote areas where the risk of prosecution and punishment was 'patchy' due to the lack of toxicological medical knowledge.[4] However, of more acute concern to the wider population were the number of intentional poisonings in urban homes. James Whorton suggests that the mid-century increase coincided with the 'rise of the insurance industry'.[5] Husbands and unwanted children were despatched by arsenic, and other poisons, to claim insurance payouts, but possibly more insidious was the killing of employers by their live-in servants. While some of these latter murders were accidental, others were malicious, although the perpetrators seldom appear to have been convicted. Merry's research notes that 56 per cent of the cases studied were either acquitted or the case found not proven, which again she attributes to the unsophisticated state of medico-toxicological jurisprudence in this period. Tests for arsenic poisoning were contested by various scientists, and when the expert evidence was presented in court, it was so perplexing that jurors were unable to grasp the complexities.[6]

Christopher Hamlin questions how far medical experts were able to employ 'central norms of impartiality, emotional neutrality' in a world of nascent medical jurisprudence where the highest paid experts were engaged for the most high-profile cases; where non-standardized tests resulting in 'inconsistent conclusions' were then pulled apart by skilled barristers who led expert witnesses to reveal discrepancies in their argument and ultimately the 'insecure foundations of' the expert's testimony. Hamlin argues that 'rhetoric and reputation' were insufficient to replace 'rigour' because without the latter, 'the utility of expertise and the authority of science' were pointless.[7] However, much as nineteenth-century society experienced an increase in arsenic poisoning, there was also an increase in reliance on forensic medical experts in trials of this nature and a concomitant trust in the jury to decipher the expert testimony. Merry's data for the nineteenth century detailing the number of acquittals and not proven verdicts suggest that forensic experts were not as credible as they anticipated their scientific knowledge made them.

Potential murderers using tasteless, odourless arsenic to despatch employers and family members created fear in all strata of nineteenth-century society, which was further fuelled by sensationalist press reporting. From an attempt to kill King Louis XVIII with poisoned carrots to a 'diabolical attempt' by a servant to kill a family of ten by lacing their breakfast porridge with arsenic, the possibility of death by poison, intentional or accidental, had become a national fixation.[8] Merry's data for prosecutions for arsenic poisoning suggest servants were a significant threat to their employers, but interestingly from her data, spouses and blood relations were more so. There are sufficient cases of husbands and wives despatching each other, often to make way for a lover or to collect on insurance. Randolph Roth argues that 'stealth murder' of a spouse was motivated by abuse, the desire for a better life or a 'chance at love'. If a wife killed her husband, she gained sole ownership of any property, custody of the children and no fear of reputational damage through divorce or desertion.[9] Brothers and sisters also murdered their siblings, often for financial gain or in retaliation for other familial rankles.[10] The close proximity of family members and established trust between them may have delayed immediate suspicion.

Acknowledging that women generally were rarely involved in fatal violence in the nineteenth century, Anne-Marie Kilday's research on deviant women reveals that when murderous women did come to the public's attention, their behaviour was 'routinely sensationalised' by the press. By murdering male relations and lovers, the behaviour of these women 'inverted extant patriarchal norms'.[11] Sheila Sullivan argues that there was a 'change in the nature of the conversation' regarding criminality and women in the 1850s and suggests further that the advent of 'respectable criminal women' upended the 'conceptual universe of transgression'.[12] Whereas previously, working-class women had been perceived as potentially criminal, now there was a possible new source of criminality among middle-class women, a notion that exploited the concept of gendered spheres. The quiet, obedient sister or daughter could no longer be trusted, especially if she revealed wayward tendencies such as independence of mind, a desire to choose her own future husband or the need for independent financial means to live a life outside the constraints of male authority. Disaffected daughters became a particular concern.

Both outside and within the family home, middle-class daughters were controlled, even if the behaviour of their male relations was not intentionally restrictive. It was simply the way most elite households lived. David Roberts argues that the wives and daughters of elite men 'subordinated themselves totally' to male authority. During their youth, daughters were expected to be 'at home, tender, affectionate, attractive'.[13] As daughters reached their teenage years, the issue of sexual awareness and the search for a suitor, partly to legitimize premarital sexual experimentation, became pressing. Sex before marriage – or betrothal – transformed a virginal daughter of marriageable value into a problem to be disposed of. Christina Simmons argues that, among middle-class men and women, sexual continence 'had become the dominant cultural ideal'.[14] Despite experience to the contrary, given the large numbers of children born in middle-class Victorian households, women were constructed as passionless, possessing maternal instinct rather than sexual desire; by restraining their own sexual needs, women dampened men's 'unnatural obsession with sex'.[15] Victorian memoir and literature suggest that women were repressed by the men in their lives, and often also by their female elders.

The separate gendered spheres of domesticity for women, and work, business and outdoor leisure for men, were on the cusp of change in the 1850s. Any debate on 'The Sex Question' was a few decades in the future when the 'reconceptualisation of the everyday and intimate heterosexual interactions' between the sexes would be explored by pioneering couples such as Glasgow's Bella Pearce and her husband Charles.[16] In the meantime, reimagining a sexual life for herself – a dalliance, a flirtation, possibly intercourse – before marriage was a risk to all classes of women, but most particularly for a middle-class teenage girl. Because a middle-class girl had much further to fall than her working-class sister. Her behaviour risked her own and her family's reputation and future among their peers.

Case

Moving away from Enlightenment Edinburgh to Scotland's rapidly industrializing west coast, to sprawling, smoky mid-century Victorian Glasgow, with rising crime among the residuum increasingly considered beyond redemption, middle-class Madeleine Smith was in love. The object of her attentions was Jerseyman Pierre Emile L'Angelier, a man of limited financial means with a French name, French clothes and pejoratively described by his contemporaries as having a 'pretty' face and 'dainty hands'.[17] They had been in love enjoying a sexual relationship for two years, but in June 1857, Madeleine was on trial for murder, and Emile was dead, allegedly poisoned by her hand. The case was a sensation not just in her home city of Glasgow but in Edinburgh where the trial was conducted, across Scotland, throughout Britain and internationally. Madeleine's alleged crime of murder by arsenic poisoning was the least of it. Aged nineteen when their affair began, already on the marriage market in middle-class privileged Glasgow, she had had illicit sex, perhaps even initiated

ILLUSTRATION 7.1 *Frontispiece,* Trial of Miss Madeleine H. Smith: Before the High Court of Justiciary, Edinburgh, June 30 to July 9, 1857, for the alleged poisoning of M. Pierre Emile L'Angelier at Glasgow *(Edinburgh, 1857).*

it, with a man ten years her senior and her social inferior. Her transgression was beyond countenance.

The trial commenced on 30 June 1857 at Edinburgh's High Court of Justiciary. The judge was the Right Honourable Lord Justice-Clerk John Hope, assisted by Lords Handyside and Ivory. The Lord Advocate James Moncreiff and Solicitor General Edward Maitland along with Advocate Depute Donald Mackenzie formed the prosecution team, while Dean of the Faculty of Advocates, John Inglis, assisted by advocates George Young and Alexander Moncrieff mounted Madeleine's defence.[18] If holding the trial outside her native city had been intended to reduce the size of the crowds, the law officers were mistaken. From the first day, the public gallery was packed to capacity with queues waiting their chance outside, and that was before they even got to the salacious evidence.

The indictment against Madeleine was threefold. First, between 19 and 20 February 1857, she was charged with having 'wickedly and feloniously' administered a quantity of arsenic to L'Angelier in either cocoa or coffee, or some other 'food or drink to the prosecutor unknown'. Having enjoyed his drink, subsequently L'Angelier became unwell. The second charge was that between 22 and 23 February, at her family home in Blythswood Square, she had again offered L'Angelier cocoa or coffee, which he had drunk and again had suffered 'severe illness'. The third charge was that between 22 and 23 March 1857, Madeleine had repeated her alleged crime, and this time, the quantity of arsenic in L'Angelier's night-time beverage had killed him. By 31 March 1857, after a week of fretful tension since his death and two years since the start of their affair, now aged twenty-one, Madeleine was arrested and examined by Archibald Smith, Sheriff-Substitute of Lanarkshire.

In her declaration, Madeleine stated that she had been 'acquainted' with L'Angelier for two years, who had 'recently paid his addresses' to her and who she had met 'on a variety of occasions'. She had not seen L'Angelier for three weeks before his death and only learned of it on the afternoon of 23 March via her mother who had been informed by a Miss Perry, who knew L'Angelier. She admitted that on one occasion, L'Angelier had tapped at her bedroom window, and that he was 'in the habit of writing notes' to her. That was an understatement. If L'Angelier had responded to every letter she wrote to him, she would have had over 250 letters in her possession as he had in his. She admitted they had arranged to get married. September 1856 had been proposed as well as March 1857 when the first date came and went. They planned to take furnished lodgings, but his illness in early 1857 had prevented their elopement. On his visits to her window to drink cocoa, she confirmed she had prepared the drinks and had partaken of some herself. She also admitted to buying sixpence-worth quantities of arsenic in recent months at Murdoch's apothecary in Sauchiehall Street, Glasgow's fashionable shopping centre.

She had used the arsenic for facial cosmetic preparations. Another portion of arsenic purchased at Currie's was used in one go as a face wash. Her use of arsenic as a beauty product had been kept secret from her family and the servants, and when asked to sign the register at Murdoch's, she had lied telling him it was for 'a gardener to kill rats or destroy vermin' because she did not wish to appear vain. Next, the precognoscer asked about her relationship with William Minnoch who had proposed to her a month earlier. Minnoch was her father's business associate and his preferred suitor for his daughter. It now became urgent for her to break off relations with L'Angelier, so she wrote him a note to explain. At no point did she declare her sexual relations with L'Angelier, primarily because the indictment against her concerned his alleged recent murder by arsenic poisoning and was unconcerned with the sordid details of their lengthy affair.[19]

Thus, as the proceedings of the trial opened, a jury of fifteen farmers, merchants, traders and a clerk were empanelled. First called to give evidence was Mrs Ann Duthie Jenkins in whose house L'Angelier had lodged. She recounted his illness and calling for the doctor before his death. Between 30 June and 2 July, the first three days of the trial concentrated on the minutiae of arsenic purchases, L'Angelier's illness and death. Their letters had been mentioned in passing but had not so far proved material to the case. On the morning of Friday, 3 July, the fourth day of the trial, Dean of Faculty Inglis realized Madeleine was in serious trouble. The *Scotch Thistle* publication had threatened to print the contents of all the letters in time for Saturday morning's edition. Inglis recognized the damage this could do and argued that the letters were 'unfit for publication' and adjured the Lord Advocate only to introduce those essential to the case. Lord Justice-Clerk Hope ordered the immediate attendance in court of James Cunningham, the man supposedly responsible for the threat, during whose interrogation a legal procedural irregularity was discovered concerning the means by which Madeleine's letter to L'Angelier had been obtained and how they had been kept by the Procurator Fiscal. Eventually, the court ruled that they were admissible and would be read the following day. On Saturday, 4 July, Madeleine arrived in the dock and 'continued to exhibit that wonderful calm and self-possession' she had displayed all week. She appears not to have even blinked as the details of her affair and her sweet nothings to her lover were read out.[20]

Madeleine and Emile had lovers' names for one another. She called him her 'dear husband', and he called her Mimi. He had first seen her in a Glasgow park and had supposedly inveigled his way into her acquaintance, and from there the romance bloomed. Whether he was a social climber, adventurer, 'dazzled by wealth and position' he never had the chance to explain, but it has become one construction of his desire to court and marry Madeleine. Like her father who had risen in social rank from a mason-architect's son to an architect and businessman, L'Angelier may have hoped to advance from the son of a Jersey seed merchant now working as a clerk to something with more financial stability. Marriage to Madeleine could have been his passport to middle-class success.[21] They agreed to marry and supposedly entered into a Scottish irregular marriage, equally as binding as a church wedding, but privately professed. Their clandestine affair had been conducted in both Madeleine's family homes at 'Rowaleyn', their country residence outside the city and in their Blythswood Square apartments. Unchaperoned by any female relations or a maid, Madeleine had advanced from relatively benign intimacies, refusing to have sex before their marriage, to intercourse at Rowaleyn in late Spring 1856. Thereafter, most of their trysts were conducted outdoors at Rowaleyn, although Madeleine transgressed the ultimate societal prohibition when she invited L'Angelier into her family's private rooms, and finally into her bedroom at Blythswood Square. She had signalled to him by opening the curtains in the dining room to let him know she would open the front door.[22]

In their letters, not only had she expressed her love for Emile, but she had also revealed a position of deference to him despite their reverse social inequity. She paraded her gender-normative obedience, offering to be a 'dutiful wife'; it was her 'duty' to make him happy, and she promised to dress demurely. Equally, he asserted his male superiority after their first sexual encounter, evidenced by the responses in her letters promising not to flirt with the young men in her family's social circle. L'Angelier had asked her to tell her father about their relationship, but her conversation with her father had not gone well, and he had forbidden her to see L'Angelier again. She told Emile how much her father hated him. L'Angelier was unbowed and pressed further for recognition while also encouraging Madeleine's sexual participation. Once William Minnoch proposed marriage which her parents had virtually arranged, combined with Emile's persistent fault-finding, Madeleine's letters reveal a distinct cooling-off. She was fearful that his £50 annual salary was insufficient for them to live on if she set up home with him and criticized him for his dress. Their correspondence continued during his illness in February and March 1857, and while his letters to her were not kept, hers to him had been. On the day after his death, they were discovered in his desk by his employer.[23] Efforts by a friend, the chancellor to the French Consul at Glasgow, Auguste de Mean, to hand them to Madeleine's father failed, and they were passed to the Procurator Fiscal as evidence in support of the growing case against her. Once the letters had been adduced as evidence and were in the public domain, the 'Glasgow Poisoning Case' became a torrid story across the British press.

Admissible in court, the detail of her not bleeding after their first sexual encounter stunned the Lord Justice-Clerk who, in his summing-up, offered an excoriating description of Madeleine which ran counter to her defence counsel's attempts to paint her as an innocent in the seducing hands of a

Frenchman. Inglis emphasized L'Angelier's weakness as a foreigner by intimating he had committed suicide, after all he had a history of hypochondria and potion-taking. Prosecution counsel was applauded for his restraint in condemning Madeleine, but had not been deterred from pronouncing her a murderer using the content of the letters and an 'unbroken chain' of largely circumstantial evidence to build his case. From witnesses who had seen Madeleine purchase and use arsenic on dates before each of L'Angelier's vomiting episodes to those who knew of their affair and had facilitated it, their testimonies pointed only to one person who could have introduced arsenic into Emile's digestive system, and that was Madeleine. Throughout her trial, not a single family member appeared in the public gallery. On the ninth day, the jury retired for thirty minutes to debate their verdict. On the first charge, Madeleine was found, by a majority, not guilty. On the second charge, by a majority the case was found not proven. And on the last charge of murder, the evidence had not convinced the jury; their verdict was again not proven. Before Madeleine was assoilzied and dismissed, there was a moment when the jail matron reached to squeeze her hand as did her solicitor. The evidence heard in court had clearly so upset the judge's personal moral compass that he relieved the jury 'from similar duties for five years'.[24]

Themes and analysis

There are two key academic analyses of Madeleine's murder trial: Mary Hartman's, and Eleanor Gordon's and Gwyneth Nair's. Hartman's analysis relies heavily on three key assumptions. First, that Madeleine's education at boarding school in London had prepared her for the marriage market by teaching her 'cunning and stratagem'. Supposedly, this stood Madeleine in good stead for future deceits enacted against her parents and her fiancés Emile L'Angelier and William Minnoch, and by implication deception of her class and wider society.[25] Second, that Madeleine lied to Emile about having discussed marriage to him with her father. By not bringing their relationship to his knowledge, she could 'taste romantic adventure' before she was barred from such excitement by marriage.[26] In deceiving Emile, she also deceived her parents into believing she was a perfect example of Victorian filial obedience. However, Gordon and Nair argue more convincingly that Madeleine's letter of 28 November 1856 in which she told L'Angelier that her father hated him indicates that she had divulged at least some of the details of their romance because her father forbade her to see Emile again.[27] Third, Hartman argues that Madeleine had a disregard for social rules because she said so in some of her letters, but Hartman fails to consider whether this was performative for L'Angelier's benefit.[28]

Gordon and Nair suggest that Madeleine's avowals of 'obedience and submission' are evidence of familiar 'nineteenth-century discourse' portraying herself to L'Angelier as an 'angel of the house'. Whereas Hartman argues that the influence of nineteenth-century romantic literature on Madeleine produced deceitful character traits, Gordon and Nair, more plausibly, argue that the experiences of Madeleine's early life had not prepared her for conducting a love affair.[29] More likely, Madeleine was dreamily in love with someone to whom she was probably very attracted, but inherently knew he could not be hers. Aged nineteen when they met and twenty-one when she stood trial, Madeleine may not have been sufficiently mature or experienced in life beyond middle-class protections to acknowledge her teenage-girl fantasy. However, her calm composure in court suggests recognition of her plight on trial for murder. If convicted, she faced capital punishment. Here she was most likely obeying her defence counsel's instructions, not twitching a single facial muscle because to betray emotion might lead to conjecture about her guilt.

The letters between L'Angelier and Madeleine reveal emotional manipulation by both parties. L'Angelier's attempts to control Madeleine after they commenced a sexual relationship and her denigration of his apparel and insinuations about his poor finances suggest two people wrapped in desires beyond their individual control: Emile's increasing realization that he could not possess her and Madeleine's awareness that middle-class expectations would overrule her future. For the present, she could attend balls, go shopping and make tea-time visits, none of which, from the number of times these activities were mentioned by her, suggests teenage boredom toying with a love interest. Her attempts to retrieve her letters from L'Angelier once he threatened to disclose all to her father suggest teenage panic at being found out.

Thus, Madeleine possessed no clear motive for murdering Emile. Why kill him before the letters had been returned, since their continued presence in his lodgings would reveal her connection to him? Despatching L'Angelier before her father found out she had enjoyed pre-marital sex with a social inferior and before the retrieval of her letters suggests a hasty murder, not a slow death, which allegedly began in late February and took a month to complete. At any time during those four weeks, L'Angelier might have gained access to her father and divulged their affair to him. Further, if she anticipated her letters to L'Angelier could ever be introduced as evidence of her role in his death, then surely, this supposedly conniving young woman would have found some means by which to have them destroyed in the week-long interval between his death and her arrest? Rather, not destroying the letters suggests she did not expect to be charged with his murder since they did not include convincing evidence of murder. All they proved was their illicit and ill-advised affair. Madeleine did not anticipate their reputation-damaging impact. She had no idea the letters would become crucial evidence joining the dots from sex to cups of cocoa outside her bedroom window to murder.

In court, the prosecution case was grounded in just such an assumption that Madeleine's purchase of arsenic during the month prior to L'Angelier's death and their love letters provided an 'unbroken chain' of evidence – yes it was circumstantial, but in the absence of any other potential perpetrator, and the addition of the emotional turmoil produced by the fear of her father's response if discovered, the circumstances led only to Madeleine. Such extreme anxiety might have led another young woman to insanity, but an insanity defence was not attempted by defence counsel Inglis despite its usefulness to avoid the death penalty if convicted. In a period where judicial sympathies towards homicidal women were increasingly lenient in cases of infanticide and child-murder, it might be anticipated that if the evidence truly indicated culpability, a middle-class woman could have hoped for similar lenience by pleading insanity. However, either Inglis was convinced of Madeleine's innocence or the power of his legal expertise, or her behaviour at no point in the weeks prior to Emile's death or in the interval between death and apprehension supported a medical diagnosis of an insane mind. Instead, Inglis transferred the insinuation of mental instability to L'Angelier, suggesting he had committed suicide.

Inglis's attempts to frame Emile as suicidal were left unanswered by the jury's not proven verdict; not guilty would have suggested their agreement with his line of defence. However, there was no doubt that L'Angelier had been poisoned by arsenic, and the episodes of vomiting during Spring 1857 corresponded with the known symptoms. Dr Thomson had attended Emile during his illness and after his death was asked to view the body. Describing the cadaver in court, he said, 'the symptoms were such as might have been produced by an irritant poison'. Dr Stevens had assisted him with L'Angelier's postmortem. They discovered little abnormality with his external or internal appearances and excised his stomach, sealing it in a glass jar before delivering it to Dr Penny, Professor of Chemistry at the Andersonian University, Glasgow. Penny's examination of the contents revealed 'arsenious acid'. He conducted Marsh's test for arsenic which produced metallic arsenic, and he considered, like most other forensic experts at the time, 'unequivocally that the said white powder' was arsenic.[30] Marsh's test could 'isolate even minute quantities of arsenic' from everyday foodstuffs such as coffee and soup and was recognized as conclusive proof of the presence of arsenic.[31] Penny concluded that the arsenic had 'been taken by' or 'administered to' L'Angelier while living. Dr Christison corroborated Penny's evidence and arsenic as 'unequivocal proof' of Emile's death.[32] Having conducted Marsh's test, death by arsenic poisoning could not be refuted by any other forensic experts called to testify.

ILLUSTRATION 7.2 *Madeleine offers Emile a cup of chocolate from her bedroom window. Courtesy of University of Glasgow Archives & Special Collections, Wylie Collection, Bh12-g.5.*

However, none of the doctors was able to distinguish between suicidal and accidental digestion of arsenic, and since the expert witness testimonies were unambiguous as to the cause of death, Inglis introduced L'Angelier's 'French' characteristics to denigrate him as someone who might not only commit suicide but might also seduce a respectable and impressionable young woman. L'Angelier's ethnicity allowed Inglis to emphasize British superiority in terms of proper masculine behaviour towards women and absence of effeminacy. His depiction of L'Angelier as vain, temperamentally mercurial and dandily dressed was decidedly un-British and suggested a man capable of committing suicide if thwarted by his love interest. He did not go so far as to suggest that L'Angelier had attempted to fake his suicide, which had gone wrong, in order to further his social-adventuring antics. However, linking L'Angelier's French-ness via his Jersey background to seducing and social-climbing tendencies was unsuccessful. If the jury had agreed that L'Angelier was suicidally thwarted in love, they would have returned a not guilty verdict against Madeleine, but instead they decided the case was not proven. A decision revealing either that they were undecided on Madeleine's guilt or that the evidence had been insufficient to prove it.

The evidence was constructed as L'Angelier the seducer and Madeleine the seduced, which was hetero-normal for the nineteenth century. So, any hint that Madeleine had instigated their sexual relationship remained undiscussed. It was sufficiently damaging that she had participated in intercourse and that her letters described her enjoyment of sex. In his summing-up, Lord Justice-Clerk Hope had fairly instructed the jury to adhere to the facts of the evidence and separate 'suspicion from truth', but equally unfairly he had delivered 'a blistering attack' on Madeleine.[33] By injecting his personal, patriarchal and class-based bias against wayward young women, Hope had also summed up mid-century elite attitudes towards headstrong daughters.

Conclusion

The inconclusive verdict in this murder case reaches beyond the details of the evidence presented in 1857. For nearly two centuries, Madeleine's and Emile's love affair, its illicit and class and ethnicity transgressions have subsumed any logical step-by-step dissection of the case. Was Madeleine scheming and manipulative and murdered L'Angelier once she had been rumbled? One reading of her correspondence with him could infer that conclusion. Whether he committed suicide, accidentally or intentionally, will never be known. With both their reputations at stake – his as an example of Victorian masculinity and authority, hers as a coquettish flirt – did she possess a strong enough motive not only to defy her parents and social class in her sexual moral conduct, but to become a murderess to protect her elite interests? Emile may have been as big a fantasist as Madeleine. She indulged a romantic reverie that could never end well, and he hoped for social advancement by marriage to her, again a desire and end-game over which he had little control.

It is a case of huge emotional and social complexity; by comparison, exploration of the legal process is relatively simple. However, the importance of this case rests in the contemporary public gaze it attracted and the elite debates it opened concerning women's place in society. Exploration of this case provides a contextual understanding of mid-Victorian Scottish and British society. In the late 1850s, one young woman's alleged poisoning of her lover forced Victorian society to examine, although not change, its attitude towards women, daughters and female sexual desire. Madeleine's behaviour was too awkward to comply with socially acceptable norms. Gordon and Nair succinctly summarize the meaning of the Madeleine and Emile affair to Victorian society. It was wrapped up in 'gender relations, the meaning of masculinity and femininity, class, social order, national identity and human nature'.[34]

Notes

1. J. H. Whorton, *The Arsenic Century: how Victorian Britain was poisoned at home, work and play* (Oxford, 2011), ix–xi.
2. K. J. Merry, 'Murder by Poison in Scotland during the nineteenth and twentieth centuries', unpublished thesis, University of Glasgow, 2010, 31.
3. Sale of Arsenic Regulation Act (1851), 14 Vict, c.13.
4. Merry, 'Murder by Poison', 47.
5. Whorton, *Arsenic Century*, 27.
6. Merry, 'Murder by Poison', 47.
7. C. Hamlin, 'Scientific Method and Expert Witnessing: Victorian Perspectives on a Modern Problem', *Social Studies of Science* 16, no. 3 (August, 1986), 486, 492, 499, 504.
8. 'Attempt to Poison Louis XVII', *The Times*, 21 August 1804, 3; 'A most diabolical attempt to poison a whole family in the neighbourhood of Carlisle', *The Times*, 1 June 1809, 4.
9. R. Roth, 'Gender, Sex and Intimate-Partner Violence in Historical Perspective', in *Oxford Handbook of Gender, Sex and Crime*, ed. R. Gartner and B. McCarthy (Oxford, 2019), 185.
10. Merry, 'Murder by Poison', Appendix 1, 51–6.
11. A. M. Kilday, ' "The Life and Loves of a She Devil": the "Potton Poisoner" and the Premeditation of a Serially Deviant Woman', in *Beyond Deviant Damsels: re-evaluating female criminality in the nineteenth century*, ed. A-M. Kilday and D. Nash (Oxford, 2023), 104.
12. S. Sullivan, ' "What's the matter with Mary Jane?": Madeleine Smith, Legal Ambiguity, and the Gendered Aesthetic of Victorian Criminality', *Genders 1998–2013* (February, 2002), 4.
13. D. Roberts, 'The Paterfamilias of the Victorian Governing Classes', in *The Victorian Family*, ed. A. Wohl (New York, 1978), 63–4.
14. C. Simmons, 'Modern Sexuality and the Myth of Victorian Repression', in *Passion and Power: sexuality in history*, ed. K. Peiss and C. Simmons (Philadelphia, 1989), 159.
15. Simmons, 'Modern Sexuality', 159.
16. T. Cheadle, *Sexual Progressives: Reimagining Intimacy in Scotland, 1880–1914* (Manchester, 2020), 7, 43.
17. W. W. Knox, *Lives of Scottish Women: women and Scottish society, 1800–1980* (Edinburgh, 2006), 53.
18. JC26/1857/371/1.
19. JC26/1857/371/1.
20. *Trial of Miss Madeleine H. Smith before the High Court of Justicary, Edinburgh, June 30th to July 9th, 1857, for the alleged poisoning of M. Pierre Emile L'Angelier at Glasgow, special verbatim report with portraits and plans* (Edinburgh, 1857), 37, 44–5.

21 Knox, *Scottish Women*, 53–5.
22 E. Gordon and G. Nair, *Murder and Morality in Victorian Britain: the story of Madeleine Smith* (Manchester, 2009), 21.
23 Gordon and Nair, *Murder and Morality*, 42, 44–5, 49, 59, 46, 72, 66, 47.
24 *Trial*, 124.
25 M. S. Hartman, 'Murder for Respectability: the Case of Madeleine Smith', *Victorian Studies* 16, no. 4 (June, 1973), 385–6.
26 Hartman, 'Murder for Respectability', 392.
27 Gordon and Nair, *Murder and Morality*, 46.
28 Hartman, 'Murder for Respectability', 389.
29 Gordon and Nair, *Murder and Morality*, 44.
30 *Trial*, 15–18.
31 Whorton, *Arsenic Century*, 86.
32 *Trial*, 19–22.
33 Gordon and Nair, *Murder and Morality*, 141.
34 Gordon and Nair, *Murder and Morality*, 149–50.

8

Patrick Higgins 1895: Lodger, same-sex child abuse and syphilis

There are no circumstances in which child sexual abuse can ever be excusable, but social circumstances of poverty, close-living and fear of disclosure to near neighbours may explain how one young man could abuse a child over an extended period in the home of his landlord and work colleague. Also, this chapter briefly examines new statute law that was intended to protect minors from abuse.

Context

Men have exercised hegemony over society throughout history. It is a simple equation: men rule, and women and children obey.[1] But what happens when men do not act within the societal construction imposed on them by other men? Social historians Henry French and Mark Rothery have traced the evolution of masculinity over the past four centuries with 'anxious, patriarch, godly' men inhabiting the mid-seventeenth century; the 'foppish' man succeeding him; followed by 'polite or civil' then 'sincere, serious or evangelical' men, before the middle-classes took firm grasp of masculinity 'based around an ideology of domesticity' in the late nineteenth century.[2] Fellow masculinity historian, John Tosh, recognized the fluidity of masculinity and acceptability of other forms of 'maleness', identifying the 'innocen[ce] of the binary divide between gay and straight' in eighteenth-century London.[3] Clearly, being male has inhabited different identities across time, with society to a greater or lesser extent accepting of men who did not adhere to the norm. Thus, at times, adult male-on-male sex has been tolerated, and in certain societies, adult and adolescent same-sex relations have been promoted. For example, Athenian and Spartan pederasty was socially enacted as a 'practice of elite mentorship' of juveniles by adult men to develop 'skills as a warrior and defender of state interests'.[4] However, even as the eighteenth century witnessed 'a decisive break' in sexual restrictions moving towards secular regulation and an increased permissiveness, the rise of the moralizing middle-classes during the nineteenth century coincided with increasing intolerance of non-normative relationships.[5] Especially, toleration of sexual relations between adults and children became increasingly taboo towards the end of the century, and same-sex sexual abuse was regarded as particularly heinous.

Louise Jackson's research on child abuse in Victorian England found that of prosecutions heard at the Middlesex and Yorkshire courts, 100 per cent conviction rate was achieved in cases involving boy victims under the age of twelve, whereas for girls of similar age the conviction rate was 79 per cent.[6] This suggests that when reported and prosecuted, same-sex child abuse was regarded as more serious than abuse of young girls by adult men; perhaps more damaging to the boy's future than to a girl's because of the social construction of any same-sex relations as 'abnormal'. Yet Jackson's research also found that only 7 per cent of prosecutions involved boys, and she asks why was abuse of boys 'so frequently side-stepped and concealed?'[7] The answer is likely that because of the social construction of same-sex relations, same-sex abuse might reflect badly on the injured party and their family. In 1895, when Patrick Higgins assaulted the McKenzie family's youngest son, they too attempted to keep quiet about the abuse.

In 1885, the Criminal Law Amendment Act specifically addressed concerns regarding the sexual protection of women and girls, among other interpersonal issues. It was a response to W. T. Stead's article 'Maiden Tribute of Modern Babylon' published in the *Pall Mall Gazette* earlier that year. Stead was a passionate campaigner for the protection of young girls from the predatory activities of sex-traffickers. He demonstrated through a real-life concocted scenario just how easy it was to transport girls to Belgium for 'training' before returning them to London to work as prostitutes. The public furore resulting from his publication, which described the compass of the sex trade in young women, led to the raising of the age of consent for women and girls from thirteen to sixteen years old. While section 4 of the Criminal Law Amendment Act dealt with sexual violence against girls which was now a statutory offence, section 11 addressed non-consenting same-sex relations between men and between men and boys.

Section 11, which has become known as 'Labouchere's Amendment', was a late addition to the Act. It was rushed through Parliament on the night of 6

August 1885 before a 'thin House' of Commons keen to prorogue Parliament and get on with the business of a general election, in preference to debating the serious issue of personal freedoms between men and the protection of minor boys. On the night it was passed, Labouchere's Amendment was already recognized as being a 'totally different class of offence' from that intended by the Criminal Law Amendment Act.[8] This was statute law, different from the common law of sodomy in Scotland which was 'the unnatural connexion of a man with a man', and like rape of women, it required proof of penetration but not emission.[9] Until 1887, a conviction for sodomy in Scotland was a capital offence.[10] By the late nineteenth century, legal commentator Anderson stated that the common law offence was 'never tried now', presumably because the Criminal Law Amendment Act had taken precedence.[11] And probably because the Act allowed for more lenient punishment for homosexual acts by introducing a 'gross indecency' catch-all charge under which male same-sex sexual behaviour could be tried at the lower sheriff court where sentences were shorter. A guilty verdict under section 11 of the Act – 'Outrages on Decency' – was deemed a misdemeanour, a term translated in Scots Law as a more minor crime, attracting sentences up to two years' imprisonment 'with or without hard labour'.[12]

The psychology of homosexuality was a nascent discipline in the late nineteenth century. While London psychiatrist Bernard Hollander agreed with Freud that 'homosexuality was an intolerable act', he distinguished between 'true homosexuals [and] ... the adolescent who is curious only'.[13] A young man might indulge in same-sex activities, but he was not necessarily considered an inveterate 'invert' for life. However, certain homosexual men were not 'interested in homosexual relations between adults'; instead, they preferred 'the aesthetic and spiritual appeal' of adolescent boys.[14] These early psychologists did not correlate homosexuality specifically with paedophilia since it was acknowledged through Stead's work that adult men could be equally attracted to female children, which is also paedophilia. In fact, the word 'paedophilia' was not introduced to Britain until the wider acceptance of German psychiatrist Krafft-Ebing's work in the 1920s. Krafft-Ebing referred to men drawn to sexual relations with children not as morally degenerate but suffering from a 'psycho-sexual perversion', a 'morbid disposition', which he called *paedophilia erotica* [italics in original]. Krafft-Ebing distinguished between adult men attracted to adolescents who were '*pubertati proximi*' and who were opportunistic roués, and men attracted to 'sexually immature' boys whom he considered 'genuine' paedophiles.[15]

Mahood's and Littlewood's research on nineteenth-century Scottish delinquency identifies a gendered difference in societal approaches to sexual precocity in minors. Young girls were protected from 'too often and too early' sexual indulgence, whereas boys' sexual experience focussed on 'what one did with whom'. The different emphasis between 'street corner' boys and 'vicious' girls thus failed to protect male children and adolescents from predatory behaviour in the way the Criminal Law Amendment Act had been designed to protect female children.[16] Before 1885, in Scots Law a sexual act between an adult man and a male minor was often constructed as indecent assault and after 1885 as gross indecency, unless actual penetration could be proved and the victim was under fourteen years; in which case the common law indictment of sodomy was charged.

Thus, when a child complained of being abused, depending on the exact nature of the abuse and what evidence could be discovered by the child's testimony or medical examination, the courts were often reluctant to indict under the common law charge, preferring a quieter, less public lower court procedure, if they prosecuted at all.

Case

Six-year-old Thomas McKenzie lived in a house with a room and kitchen on the ground floor of a tenement in Paisley in 1894, with his mother, father, an older sister aged nine, a four-year-old brother and a sister who was two. Lodging with them was Patrick Higgins, a twenty-year-old carter. In such a cramped home, the sleeping arrangements were tight. Mrs Mary McKenzie and her husband, also a carter, shared a bed in the kitchen with the two youngest children, and Mary, the nine-year-old, slept on a 'chair bed' in the other room where Thomas shared the bed with Patrick Higgins. Mrs McKenzie said Thomas had been in good health since birth in 1888 until September 1894 when he had started to experience disturbed sleep, crying out 'ma ma' during the night. When she went to check on him, Mary McKenzie often found him 'crying bitterly' and lying at the foot of the bed which was not his usual place. Every time she checked on Thomas, Patrick appeared to be asleep. Occasionally, she found blood on Thomas's nightclothes, and she challenged Patrick about having struck her son. Patrick never made any response.

Thomas had changed by the end of September. He was pale and weak and complained of stomach pains. By October, he had swollen glands in his neck, throat and ears. He suffered head- and back-ache and complained of a painful bottom. Mary checked him and discovered what she thought were 'large piles'; he had been 'passing blood for about three weeks', and then a rash appeared on his body. On 1 December, Mary took Thomas to the doctor, who prescribed a lotion to 'paint' on Thomas's throat which she did for a week, but marble-sized lumps then appeared in Thomas's mouth, so they returned to Dr Richmond. On examining Thomas's mouth and bottom, Dr Richmond was 'horrified' and said that if Thomas had been an older boy, he would have suggested he had 'been misconducting himself'. Dr Richmond asked Mary who had been interfering with her son and had 'ruined him'.

At home that evening, Mary challenged Patrick again, but he simply rose from the dinner table and went to bed. So, on 26 December, Mary again visited Dr Richmond and reminded him that he had seen Patrick around March or April for 'stress'. Mary did not understand the doctor's response, but at his request, she attended again the same evening accompanied by her husband. The doctor appears to have explained his misgivings to Mr McKenzie because by the time they reached home, Mary was sufficiently well informed to say, 'Paddy, this is a terrible thing to do to my boy'. Patrick confessed and then offered to pay Thomas's medical expenses, even 'if it were for seven years'. Patrick left the McKenzie home that night, and by 31 December 1894, he had married. He continued to send two shillings weekly to the McKenzies.

When Mary asked her son for his account, Thomas told her that 'Paddy had "jagged" his bum', but he did not know what with because he had been forced onto his front. The boy feared that if he told his parents, he would get a 'leathering' or that Patrick would carry out his threat to kill him. Mary had wanted to inform the police, but Mr McKenzie refused because of 'shame'. It took until 11 April for Mary to inform the police after a quarrel with a neighbour. Mary had reported the upset and then divulged 'its origins chiefly in what had happened to her boy'. Only then did the police investigate.

It transpired that Mary had been washing Patrick's laundry from April to September when she had ceased to do so because the discharge on the sheets had become too much. She had advised him to go to the infirmary and believed he had attended as an outpatient. Detective Inspector James Watt confirmed that Mr and Mrs McKenzie had been 'not at all anxious to press the charge' and 'wished to avoid exposure for the boy's sake as well as their own'. His investigation revealed that Dr Richmond had diagnosed primary syphilis in Patrick in March 1894, and the house doctor at the infirmary had confirmed secondary syphilis by September. Patrick was arrested on 19 April 1895 and charged with indecent practices and communicating syphilis to Thomas. Patrick made no attempt to refute the charge but told Watt that he had been 'drunk at the time'. The police account described the McKenzies as 'respectable working people', and someone had noted on the last page of Thomas's precognition that he was 'a nice child & apparently truthful but shy'.[17]

During the investigation, Dr Richmond was questioned about his original diagnosis. He acknowledged his anxieties about Patrick's condition and confirmed that he had treated him for 'a chancre'. Despite making the connection between Thomas and their family lodger, Dr Richmond did not report his suspicions. He told the precognoscer that in his opinion, 'the disease could not be communicated to the boy by a man's penis' unless the skin was broken. He believed 'the mucus membrane' to have been 'the seat of absorption' of 'the poison from the chancre'. A more senior medic, Dr Graham, examined Patrick who confirmed the diagnosis of secondary syphilis and declared that if Patrick had children, they 'would probably be affected by syphilis'. In Graham's opinion the disease could have been 'communicated by contact without penetration'.

The original indictment against Patrick Higgins was 'lewd, abominable or indecent and libidinous behaviour' towards Thomas and communication of venereal disease. The common law charge of sodomy was not mentioned.[18] In correspondence, the Procurator Fiscal discussed with the Crown Agent whether the Sheriff ought to be persuaded to send the case to the High Court of Justiciary for sentencing 'in view of the aggravated nature of the case, and the permanent injury to the child's constitution'.[19] In the meantime, Patrick had agreed to plead guilty to an alternative charge if the words 'lewd, abominable' were removed. The Crown Agent directed the Procurator Fiscal to accept the plea 'as tendered' and leave it to the Sheriff's discretion whether to remit the case to the High Court of Justiciary for sentencing. Crown Counsel's preference was the latter given the grave nature of the case.[20] Appearing before Lord Wellwood, Higgins was sentenced to five years' penal servitude on a charge of indecent and libidinous behaviour.[21] Patrick Higgins had never been charged with any previous crime at police, sheriff or High Court.

Themes and analysis

Because Higgins had not appeared in court before on any charges, it is impossible to understand his sexual orientation: was he homosexual, or did he take a more fluid attitude towards sexual relations? His marriage only a few days after being ejected from the McKenzies' home suggests fluidity because there was no evidence precognosced that suggested involvement in Glasgow's 'homosexual subculture'.[22] Arguably, his behaviour may have stemmed from loneliness and the desire for comfort or pre-marital sexual need. These potential excuses were not evidenced during the investigation, although such emotional reasons for seeking same-sex intercourse with a minor were unlikely to have been confessed by a working-class panel involved in a masculine occupation living in a male-dominated environment. His excuse that he was drunk was not corroborated by Mrs McKenzie or Thomas. He would have had to have been intoxicated every night between September and early December 1894, and even if he had been, intoxication was no mitigation of culpability.[23] Also, Higgins was not recognized as a paedophile in the emerging understanding of that form of sexual attraction.

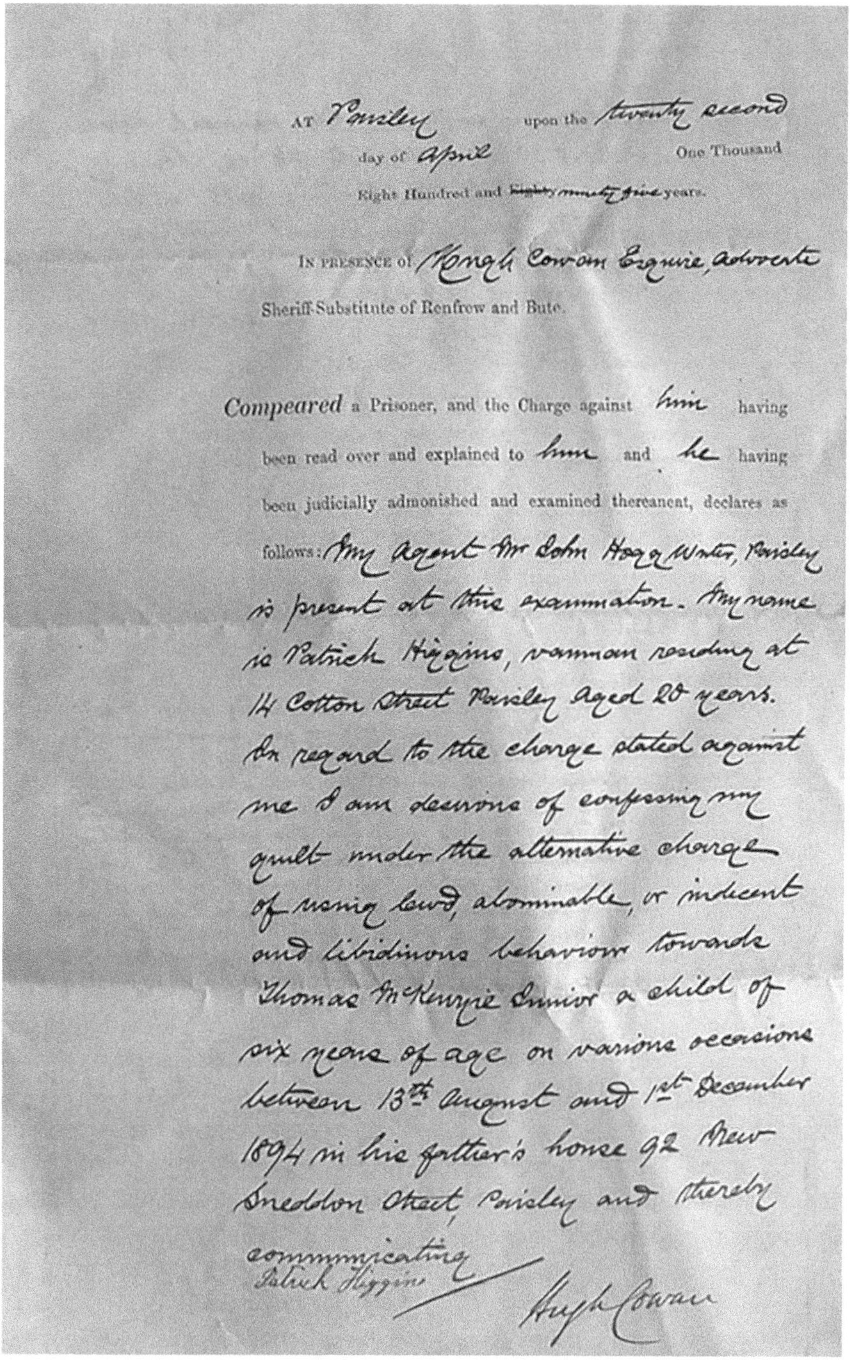

AT Paisley upon the twenty second day of April One Thousand Eight Hundred and ~~Eighty~~ ninety five years.

IN PRESENCE OF Hugh Cowan Esquire, advocate Sheriff-Substitute of Renfrew and Bute.

Compeared a Prisoner, and the Charge against him having been read over and explained to him and he having been judicially admonished and examined thereanent, declares as follows: My agent Mr John Hogg Writer, Paisley is present at this examination. My name is Patrick Higgins, vanman residing at 14 Cotton Street Paisley aged 20 years. In regard to the charge stated against me I am desirous of confessing my guilt under the alternative charge of using lewd, abominable, or indecent and libidinous behaviour towards Thomas McKenzie Junior a child of six years of age on various occasions between 13th August and 1st December 1894 in his father's house 92 New Sneddon Street, Paisley and thereby communicating

Patrick Higgins
Hugh Cowan

ILLUSTRATION 8.1 *Declaration of Patrick Higgins. Crown Copyright. National Records of Scotland, JC26/1895/35.*

By pleading guilty to the lower charge, Higgins avoided a jury trial and consequent reporting in the newspapers, although given the nature of his crime, it would have been sparingly reported because it would have been heard 'behind closed doors'. However, the McKenzies had not avoided the shame of their neighbours knowing their private matters, but they had been spared the ignominy of wider public awareness. Since Higgins's motive is not recorded in the archives, and there may never have been one he could identify even to himself, there are two key questions that underpin a better understanding of this case: why had the McKenzies felt the need to squeeze a lodger into their already-cramped living conditions? And how had Dr Richmond failed to connect Thomas's venereal disease with Higgins's obvious syphilis?

Mrs McKenzie reported that Higgins 'only paid us 10/ per week' for his bed and board, implying that she felt this was insufficient money for the service. Being a carter was an unskilled occupation subject to the vagaries of the market, which is possibly why Mrs McKenzie had taken a lodger, because her husband, like Higgins, was also a carter. It is probable that Mr McKenzie had taken in a fellow carter, half his age, as a favour and also to augment his household income. Their family home at 92 New Sneddon Street was on the ground floor of a tenement building, which notoriously had outdoor lavatories and limited indoor facilities, and the McKenzie household was unlikely to have been well-off with six mouths to feed.[24] The records contain no evidence of Mary McKenzie working or taking in piecemeal tasks. The median weekly wage for a carter in 1906 was between twenty and twenty-four shillings, although Mr McKenzie might have earned as little as fifteen and nineteen shillings.[25] Thus, the McKenzies were living on a maximum of four shillings per week per capita, which included the cost of their rent.

Jeffrey Meek's detailed examination of lodger and boarder practices in Govan, a district not far from Paisley, at the turn of the century reveals that 'the majority of female heads [of households] taking in lodgers were reacting to the limited options available for single or widowed women'.[26] Mary McKenzie was neither a single mother nor widowed, but she was married to a man who was unable to provide for his family without supplementary income. Meek's research also highlighted workplace relationships between lodgers and their head of household, which is apparent between McKenzie and Higgins in the same occupation.[27] This relationship might forge increased trust between occupants of a single house: connected by work and living space, McKenzie may not have considered Higgins a threat to the well-being of any member of his family; Higgins had too much to lose by violating that trust. It may also have been fear of shame among his peers at work that influenced McKenzie's decision not to report the abuse to the police. Thus, the McKenzies relied on Higgins's lodging fees to boost their household income, while Higgins would have struggled to find accommodation to rent on his individual wages.

It was an arrangement that suited all parties, and with no reputation for abusive behaviour, McKenzie had no reason not to offer Higgins a home. As a young, unmarried bachelor, the situation in the McKenzie household also offered Higgins a family. Sharing meals with Mary and the children when McKenzie was not yet home from work and a bed with their elder son, and his ready conversation with Mary suggest an easy, trusting familiarity with the McKenzies. They were not necessarily the only family in New Sneddon Street taking in a lodger, but in such an environment, neighbours knowing each other's business was hard to avoid.

How the McKenzies' neighbour discovered their predicament is unknown. Walls were thin, making private conversations far from secret. Equally, Mary would have hung out her weekly laundry where conversations between wives were customary. She may have divulged her concerns about Higgins's sheets or that her lodger had visited the doctor. His summary ejection from the household, after over a year lodging with the family, would not have gone unnoticed. Harry Cocks identifies a 'popular antipathy to homosexual behaviour' with reporting largely stemming from 'a local and familiar level'. His research reveals that in the 1840s in the early years of policing, resources and manpower were insufficient to deal with the number of reports of homosexual activity and therefore, private individuals bore the brunt of responsibility for initiating investigations. In turn, this invited the expansion of police surveillance from the public to the private sphere.[28] Thus, what occurred behind a family's front door had become a matter of public and police interest, even if the family did not acknowledge any criminality in their home; something they were unlikely to do if the shame of reporting and becoming the subject of local gossip was too much to bear. A family's reluctance to report to the police was understandable in these circumstances. Once reported, any subsequent investigation by police would have required intrusion into private family space and, for the working classes, the potential accusation of running a disorderly household, which was shame enough without further revelations about venereal disease in the home.

Both Thomas and Higgins were diagnosed with secondary syphilis, a sexually transmitted disease to which there are three stages. Dr Richmond reported that Thomas was likely to develop tertiary symptoms, but he could not predict when or where on his body these would appear. He was also of the opinion that 'the disease could not be communicated to the boy by a man's penis coming in contact with the skin, if the skin was unbroken'. He found 'a large condylomata' on Thomas's anus, a form of genital wart usually found on the penis.[29] The wart's discovery on Thomas's anus suggested anal sexual activity; hence, Dr Richmond's comment that if he had been older, he would have considered Thomas to have been 'misbehaving'. Dr Graham's examination of Higgins revealed recent 'syphilitic ulcers of the penis' with the continued presence of its 'secondary effects'. While Thomas was in poor health, having once been 'a robust boy', Higgins was described as 'active and vigorous'.[30] Key to understanding why Dr Richmond did not react to Thomas's first presentation with syphilitic symptoms by informing his mother or reporting to the police is the late nineteenth-century lack of understanding of the disease's means of transmission.

Syphilis could be hereditary, hence Dr Graham's comment on Higgins's future capacity to have a non-diseased family. It could also be acquired, but in the nineteenth century it was thought that venereal disease might be transmitted not necessarily through sexual intercourse but by contact with infected bed linens, bath towels or lavatory seats.[31] Karen Taylor argues that 'venereal disease may convey a very special message about the child's family', suggesting either incestuous sexual assault or poor family hygiene, and possible intimate 'touching and caressing' between infected siblings.[32] Thus, syphilitic infection might be attributed to poor living conditions, or a chaotic and disrupted household, in which the mother was often blamed for bad hygiene and lack of protection of her children from incestuous or extra-familial abuse.[33] The McKenzies were described by the police as 'respectable', which indicates that Mary kept a clean house and managed a well-behaved family. 'Respectable' in nineteenth-century police parlance suggests 'not known' to the police: not alcoholic and not violent or quarrelsome with neighbours. Further, Taylor argues that the medical profession was 'not scientifically and culturally prepared' to countenance the idea that minors contracted sexually transmitted diseases through sexual contact, particularly if the patient was 'too young to be considered sexually active and too old to be diagnosed' with congenital acquired disease.[34]

Thomas was too old only now to present with acquired venereal disease and too young to be legally sexually active, but like children of all ages, he was old enough to be sexually abused and to be expected to keep the abuse secret through fear of further violence. Even if Thomas had consented to Higgins's approaches, he did not have legal capacity to do so, which made Thomas a victim. Taylor's research emphasizes society's response to social taboos and the 'discomfort and anger' sexual abuse of minors evokes. Her research also reveals that 'Victorian adults exploited children sexually' more often than our perception of Victorian, and early twentieth-century, Britain might allow.[35]

Higgins's sentence of five years' penal servitude is the same as the sentence handed to a seventeen-year-old young man who was found guilty of sodomy with five boys aged twelve to sixteen in 1872.[36] But it is significantly shorter than a man, in 1879, found guilty of rape of a nine-year-old boy in a public place, who had another previous conviction for raping a young girl.[37] Brian Dempsey suggests that this man's sentence of fifteen years' penal servitude came at the behest of the Advocate Depute who restricted 'the pains of law to an arbitrary punishment', thus avoiding a capital sentence and thereby permitting the jury to return a unanimously guilty verdict – they would not be responsible for a man's death, only for his conviction.[38] Higgins's case falls in a peculiar period for same-sex child sexual abuse. The indictment against him, based on the absence of proof of penetration, permitted prosecution at a lower court where the post-Criminal Law Amendment Act catch-all charge of gross indecency might have earned Higgins a sentence of less than two years' imprisonment. Yet Crown Counsel was keen to remit him to the High Court of Justiciary for sentencing where the court's powers allowed for longer carceral punishments, presumably to take into consideration the aggravation of venereal disease. It is possible that another Crown Agent might have counselled differently, and Higgins would have been out within two years. But Higgins's case coincided with the Oscar Wilde sensation trial in 1895.

Cocks argues that Wilde's trial for gross indecency on multiple counts in April 1895 is not representative of the 'sodomite of the nineteenth century'.[39] Wilde was an upper-middle-class author and playwright of flamboyant personality who had seduced an aristocrat, Lord Alfred Douglas, who was sixteen years his junior. Their affair was relatively widely known among their peer group and, until Douglas's father discovered their liaison, also relatively well tolerated. However, in the last decade of the nineteenth century, societal toleration of homosexual behaviour had narrowed. Cocks points to the Lancaster sodomy trials in 1806 as the 'point of intolerability' when the law began to isolate and distance homosexuality from everyday society. The Lancaster trial found five men guilty of sodomy, all of whom were hanged from a group of twenty-four arrested.[40] Cocks's research provides statistics for England and Wales showing committals for sodomy ranging from ten in 1813 to seventy in 1850, decreasing to twenty by 1892; while Harvey shows that more than fifty men were hanged for sodomy in England between 1800 and 1835.[41] Yet in Scotland throughout the nineteenth century, only twenty cases of sodomy and attempted sodomy were prosecuted at the High Court of Justiciary, and no one convicted was hanged. These Scottish prosecutions involved either adult males, consenting and non-consenting, or relations between an adult male and multiple young boys. With more than one victim, a body of evidence against a single perpetrator meant that it was only a matter of time before an individual child or parent reported the crime, thereafter revealing the abuse against the other boys. These cases reveal a lower rate of prosecution and conviction per head of population in Scotland and possibly a greater degree of judicial toleration of homosexual behaviour in general.[42] However, Higgins's activities had been conducted in private with a single child. Without the neighbours' quarrel, it may never have appeared in the justiciary records.

As Thomas's case indicates, there was a propensity among parents to cover up what had happened, maintaining invisibility from the judiciary, allowing families to deal with the emotional damage as they thought fit. The McKenzies certainly wanted no fuss, which they stated was to protect Thomas and themselves.

Conclusion

Higgins was not a 'habitual' homosexual. A 'homosexual identity' was only just forming in the public consciousness and discourse. In fact, Higgins's behaviour may have been a short period of aberration before marriage; it was certainly his first reported crime and given his invitation to live with the McKenzies by a fellow carter, it is probable that his reputation was unsullied by rumours of previous activities. Neither was Higgins a paedophile, an adult whose sexual fascination with children – boys or girls – was about to become a psychiatric debate that remains ongoing.[43] Higgins was not a homosexual 'type' but an individual who had committed repeated same-sex child sexual abuse. As Cocks describes it, 'the perverse ... was "implanted" within normality, whereas before it was merely a deviation from the natural'. He adheres to Michel Foucault's thesis that throughout the eighteenth and nineteenth centuries, society was increasingly subjected to 'bio-power', the notion that the government collection of statistics – census, trade, work, wages, birth, death, reproduction – aimed to 'govern the entirety of natural processes within any population'.[44] Or, the government's analysis of statistical trends as social control. If the argument is followed to its conclusion, the collection of criminal statistics and therefore indictments for sodomy and related charges forged the creation of a homosexual 'other' within heterosexual society. Add to that Wilde's highly publicized trial due to his very public reputation, it would appear that everything changed south and north of the border. But prosecutions in Scotland did not increase towards the end of the century as had occurred in England.

Harvey suggests that as the notion of separate spheres of male and female work and leisure confined women to increasingly narrow social roles, 'an established code of manly behaviour and manly attitudes' developed, which in turn outlawed 'sexual ambivalence'. Thus, more intolerance was generated, not more homosexuality.[45] And where intolerance existed, subsequently a greater number of reports would occur, although not necessarily prosecutions and convictions, if those prosecuting did not adhere to the sexual prejudices of the reporting class.

It will never be known how Higgins contracted syphilis; it may have been with a heterosexual partner or even his prospective bride. Equally, why he injured Thomas in such an abhorrent way will never be understood. But his non-appearance in the criminal records before 1895 and after his release from jail in 1900 suggest that he had learned his lesson. Mary McKenzie's precognition as well as his own declaration to the Procurator Fiscal after arrest reveal Higgins's remorse for his acts. He knew what he had done was wrong but could provide no explanation. He injured Thomas physically and probably emotionally and destroyed his health. In 1895, syphilis was untreatable and would have affected Thomas for the rest of his life.

However, like Wilde who was not representative of the same-sex attracted man in nineteenth-century British society, Higgins was unrepresentative of the identity of the homosexual man that was emerging as he pleaded guilty in court.

Notes

1. The use of certain nineteenth-century contemporary terms describing homosexuality are used in this chapter; no authorial bias is inferred.
2. H. French and M. Rothery, 'Hegemonic Masculinities? Assessing Change and Processes of Change in Elite Masculinity, 1700–1900', in *What is Masculinity? Historical Dynamics from Antiquity to the Contemporary World*, ed. J. H. Arnold and S. Brady (Basingstoke, 2013), 139.
3. J. Tosh, 'The History of Masculinity: An Outdated Concept?', in *What is Masculinity?*, ed. J. H. Arnold and S. Brady (Basingstoke, 2013), 19.
4. T. K. Hubbard, 'Athenian Pederasty and the Construction of Masculinity', in *What is Masculinity?*, ed. J. H. Arnold and S. Brady (Basingstoke, 2013), 192.
5. F. Dabhiowala, 'Lust and Liberty', *Past and Present*, no. 207 (May, 2010), 90.
6. L. A. Jackson, *Child Sexual Abuse in Victorian England* (London, 2000), 102.
7. Jackson, *Child Sexual Abuse*, 100–1.
8. F. B. Smith, 'Labouchere's Amendment to the Criminal law Amendment Bill', *Historical Studies* 17, no. 67 (1978), 171.
9. A. Alison, *Principles of the criminal law of Scotland* (Edinburgh, 1832), 566.
10. M. Kirby, 'The Sodomy Offence: England's Least Lovely Criminal Law Export?', in *Human Rights, Sexual Orientation and Gender Identity in the Commonwealth*, ed. C. Lennox and M. Waites (London, 2013), 61; B. Dempsey, ' "By the law of this and every other well governed realm": investigating accusations of sodomy in nineteenth-century Scotland', *Juridical Review*, no. 2 (2006), 104.
11. A. M. Anderson, *The Criminal Law of Scotland* (Edinburgh, 1892), 93.
12. Smith, 'Labouchere's Amendment', 165; Dempsey, 'By the law of this realm', 105; Criminal Law Amendment Act 1885, 48 and 49 Vict. c.69, s.11.

13 B. Hollander, *Psychology of Misconduct, Vice and Crime* (London, 1922), 63, 142.
14 J. Tosh, 'Domesticity and Manliness in the Victorian Middle Class', in *Manful assertions: Masculinities in Britain since 1800*, ed. Roper and Tosh (London, 1991), 66.
15 R. von Krafft-Ebing, *Psychopathia sexualis: With Especial Reference to the Antipathic Sexual Instinct, a Medico-Forensic Study* (London, 1931), 555, 558.
16 L. Mahood and B. Littlewood, 'The "vicious" girl and the "street-corner" boy: sexuality and the gendered delinquent in the Scottish child-saving movement, 1850–1940', *Journal of the History of Sexuality* 4, no. 4 (April, 1994), 557.
17 AD14/95/31.
18 However, this case appears on National Records of Scotland (NRS) catalogue under sodomy.
19 JC26/1895/35 Letter Procurator Fiscal to Crown Agent 24 April 1895.
20 JC26/1895/35 Handwritten note on reverse of letter, 24 April 1895.
21 JC8/80.
22 Cook, *London Culture*, 39.
23 J. Glaister, *A Text-Book of Medical Jurisprudence and Toxicology* (Edinburgh, 1913), 587.
24 Mary McKenzie was twenty-nine in 1895 and had given birth to a child every two years for the past nine years; AD14/95/31.
25 Report of an Inquiry by the Board of Trade into the Earnings and Hours of Labour of Workpeople of the United Kingdom (1906), cmnd. 6556, 264.
26 J. Meek, 'Boarding and Lodging Practices in early twentieth-century Scotland', *Continuity and Change* 31, no. 1 (2016), 95.
27 Meek, 'Boarding and Lodging', 88.
28 H. G. Cocks, *Nameless Offences: homosexual desire in the 19th century* (London, 2010), 48, 20.
29 A. Sewell and J. Oxley, 'An Overview of benign and premalignant lesions of the foreskin', *Diagnostic Histopathology* 25, no. 10 (October, 2019), abstract, 370.
30 AD14/95/31 Medical Reports.
31 R. Davidson, *Illicit and Unnatural Practices: The Law, Sex and Society in Scotland since 1900* (Edinburgh, 2019), 38; M. C. Tod, 'Gonorrhoeal Vulvo-Vaginitis in Children', *British Journal of Venereal Diseases* (1927), 115.
32 K.J. Taylor, 'Venereal Disease in Nineteenth-Century Children', *Journal of Psychohistory* 12, part 4 (1985), 431.
33 A. Bingham and L. A. Jackson, 'Scandals and Silences: the British Press and child sexual abuse', *History and Policy* (August, 2015), www.historyandpolicy.org/policy-papers/rss_2.0 (accessed October 2024).
34 Taylor, 'Venereal Disease', 439.

35 Taylor, 'Venereal Disease', 459. Statistics for 1920s research on gonorrhoeal infection in Glasgow suggested that abuse played 'a comparatively small part in the spread of gonorrhoea in these young children', Tod, 'Gonorrhoeal Vulvo-Vaginitis', 113.
36 JC26/1872/116.
37 JC26/1879/121.
38 Dempsey, 'By the Law of this realm', 126; capital sentence not abolished until 1887.
39 Cocks, *Nameless Offences*, xvii.
40 Cocks, *Nameless Offences*, xiv.
41 Cocks, *Nameless Offences*, figure 8, 30; see also Cook, *London Culture*, table 1, 151 for London-only arrest and conviction statistics. A. D. Harvey, 'Prosecutions for Sodomy in England at the beginning of the nineteenth century', *Historical Journal* 21, no. 4 (December, 1978), 939.
42 Population of England and Wales 1800–1900 ranged from eight million to thirty million; https://www.visionofbritain.org.uk/unit/10061325/cube/TOT_POP (accessed October 2024). Population for Scotland in 1801 was 1,608,420 growing to 4,472,103 in 1901; *Scottish Population Statistics including Webster's Analysis of Population 1755*, ed. J. Gray (Edinburgh, 1952), xvii.
43 'Paedophile' was a relatively unknown term in Britain pre-1970s; A. Bingham, '"It Would Be Better for the Newspapers to Call a Spade a Spade": The British Press and Child Sexual Abuse, c. 1918–90', *History Workshop Journal* 88 (Autumn, 2019), 101.
44 Cocks, *Nameless Offences*, xx.
45 Harvey, 'Prosecutions for Sodomy', 946.

9

Oscar Slater 1909: Murderer, 'other' and justice

The brutal murder of a defenceless old woman has remained unsolved for over a century, yet in Edwardian Glasgow the obvious perpetrator had to be someone from the city's criminal underworld, a man living on the margins of society. This case explores what it meant to be 'other' in early twentieth-century Scotland and how a miscarriage of justice and one man's wrongful incarceration changed the law.

Context

If a British man committed a murder, how would he go about it, and who would be his victim? Would he choose brutality, bare fists, a cobbler's hammer, skull fractures; violence so excessive that the pulverized face of the victim was barely identifiable? Would a nearly eighty-three-year-old defenceless woman be his first choice of victim? And was this type of frenzied murder the kind of behaviour usually associated with a routine house-breaking? The prosecution of Oscar Slater in 1909 for the murder of Marion Gilchrist in her Glasgow apartment shortly before Christmas in 1908 has been called Scotland's greatest miscarriage of justice. It may be, but the Slater case also forced a change in Scots Law on the admissibility of character evidence in court and allowed for the creation of Scotland's Court of Criminal Appeal. But that occurred almost twenty years after Miss Gilchrist's murder. These were developments that happened in a post-Great War society, adjusting to near-universal suffrage and devastating economic slump. In pre-war 1908, committing an atrocious crime against a defenceless, wealthy old woman was a crime against the individual and against the established order. It was a crime that surely no British man would commit.

By the end of 1909, the year in which Oscar Slater's trial for murder was prosecuted, some 3,690 individuals had been charged with crimes against the person. These included murder, attempted murder, culpable homicide and all forms of assault. A separate category of individuals who had committed crimes against property with violence amounted to 2,106 people charged.[1] Among both these categories, a total of only eight men were indicted for murder in Scotland in 1909, of whom Oscar Slater was one. This figure was below the decennial average of ten cases per year.[2]

Of those eight people proceeded against for murder in 1909, five were called for trial, of whom one was found not guilty; another was acquitted not proven; one was found insane at the time of the offence, and Slater along with one other were the only two panels convicted and sentenced to death in 1909. Between 1900 and 1909, four years returned no capital sentences, and only 1904 exceeded 1909's count with three death sentences.[3] The statistics, therefore, do not reveal great fluctuations in violent criminality or capital sentencing; case numbers remained consistent across the decade, revealing neither an increase in murder nor a decrease. However, the statistics might also suggest that juries were turning away from guilty verdicts in crimes where the death penalty was the only sentencing option available to the judge.

As Anne-Marie Kilday points out, Scotland's 'notorious reputation for enacting tough justice' was largely a thing of the past by the mid-eighteenth century by when Scotland 'rarely deployed the ultimate sanction at all' and earned a new reputation for being 'innocent of the noose'.[4] The move away from public hanging continued until in 1868 this spectacle ceased. Thereafter, any judicial executions were conducted behind prison walls.[5] The transition from public to fewer private executions was prompted by socio-legal developments. Using public hanging to punish property and violent crimes was increasingly perceived as 'irrational' and had become unpopular with the public, whose boisterousness 'undermined the rule of law'. While public hanging had 'demonstrated the power of the crown' over individual citizens, prison hanging not only prevented public displays of rowdiness on execution days but also 'reclassified the offender as a deviant'.[6]

Vic Gatrell's research on eighteenth- and nineteenth-century criminality reveals that 'juries' self-confidence and independence' increased steadily in this period, their bias towards fellow 'farmers, tradesmen and publicans' revealed through their juridical verdicts.[7] With the expansion of the franchise in the Reform Act 1867, increasing numbers of working-class men became eligible to perform jury service.[8] Following Peter King's and Richard Ward's argument, which focuses on jury behaviour in eighteenth-century England, social-class similarity between the accused and jurors created greater sympathy towards those on trial. Their research has also revealed regional differences in jury behaviours, particularly those located on the peripheries, for example, Cornwall and Wales.[9] Common and statute law were universal across Scotland, thus regional differences in procedure and outcomes were unlikely, although detailed research similar to King's and Ward's has yet to be conducted for Scotland. However, given Scotland's established reputation for execution avoidance, it is not unreasonable to expect that by the first decade of the twentieth century, once more working-class male jurors were balloted for service, they expressed their repugnance at state execution through juridical independence and avoidance of guilty verdicts on cases attracting a capital sentence.

ILLUSTRATION 9.1 *Oscar Slater.* W. Roughead, The Trial of Oscar Slater *(Edinburgh, 1910).*

Scotland's ultimate working-class city – Glasgow – at Christmas 1908 was the 'second city of empire'. Glasgow's population at the 1911 census was 748,496 or 16 per cent of the Scottish total population.[10] The city and its surrounding towns accounted for 70 per cent of Scotland's urbanized population at the end of the nineteenth century and was 'the most urbanized country in the world' after England.[11] This influx of people had been driven by rapid industrial growth in the west of Scotland since the late nineteenth century; thus by 1913 the Clyde's shipyards accounted for 756,976 launched tons of shipping, or 33.4 per cent of the UK total, more than Germany's and America's shipbuilding industries' output combined.[12] By the early twentieth century, this dense concentration of hard-working people endured the worst housing in Europe, with 60 per cent of inhabitants living in single-end and two-roomed homes.[13] Conditions were squalid in many of Glasgow's districts where immigrants from Europe rubbed shoulders with those who had already arrived at the turn of the century from Scotland's Highlands and other rural areas. There was also the influx of Irish since the 1840s who had largely assimilated by the early twentieth century.

European immigrants to Glasgow were drawn from new sources: Italians, Lithuanians and Poles from Eastern Europe and Russians. Many of the last groups were also Jews fleeing the pogroms. Between 1901 and 1911, the number of Eastern European immigrants to Scotland increased, and by 1911, one-third of the new immigrant group had settled in Glasgow, of whom 9,000 were Jewish.[14] Their industrial and craft skills helped them to find employment in Clydeside's heavy engineering industries and to set up their own workshops.[15] William Kenefick's research on ethnic communities in twentieth-century Scotland reveals there was an 'established Jewish community' who had mostly entered the country before 1914. Both the existing Irish community and Eastern European immigrants congregated in the Gorbals, where it has been commented that a 'lack of inter-ethnic tensions was remarkable'. More widely in Glasgow, oral history testimonies have recounted low levels of antisemitism experienced by the Jewish community from either the Irish or native Scots. In fact, Kenefick's research further reveals that Glasgow's Protestant community hated Irish Catholics 'more than the Jews', and the lack of antipathy towards Jewish immigrants may be attributable to the Scots' concentrated hostility to the Irish – the Scots could be 'kinder' to the Jews than the Irish.[16]

While the immigrant Irish were viewed as filthy, indigent and lazy – possibly a legacy perception of the wretched state in which many of their ancestors had arrived in Scotland – Eastern European immigrants, whether Jewish or otherwise, could also attract 'animosity and negative stereotyping'.[17] Living in segregated 'ghettos' such as the Gorbals meant that if they stepped beyond societal boundaries, being immigrant and identifiably 'other' could pose problems. Being an immigrant in Glasgow, trying to make a new life, gambling a little, dealing in second-hand goods at the pawnbrokers and having a particular form of Eastern European or German-accented English could result in an individual being labelled as a foreign Jew, whatever that person's country of origin or professed faith.

Case

The charge against thirty-eight-year-old Oscar Slater was that on 21 December 1908, he did 'in Marion Gilchrist's house, at No. 15 Queen's Terrace, West Princes Street, Glasgow, assault the said Marion Gilchrist, and did beat her with a hammer or other blunt instrument, and fracture her skull, and did murder her'.[18] The indictment included no mention of the theft of a diamond brooch from her jewellery collection. It was now May 1909, and Oscar Slater,

ILLUSTRATION 9.2 *West Princes Street. W. Roughead,* The Trial of Oscar Slater *(Edinburgh, 1910).*

a German Jew, was on trial for his life for the murder of an elderly woman he claimed not to know. However, several witnesses had identified Slater as the culprit.

Marion Gilchrist led a reclusive life at Queen's Terrace where for thirty years she had rented her first-floor apartment. She was looked after by her maid Helen Lambie and received visits from a former servant Mrs Ferguson, the only person with whom she appears to have been intimate. Marion's collection of precious stones was kept among her clothes in the apartment, which was bolted by an unusually 'heavy bolt and two separate patent locks'. On the night in question, the Adams family who lived in the flat below heard 'a heavy fall'. Arthur Adams went to investigate, but Marion's door was closed, and he could not raise anyone, so he returned downstairs. On a second visit, he intercepted Helen Lambie returning from an errand. They entered the apartment together where Helen encountered a man who sauntered towards the front door as if he had been a visitor before dashing down to the street. Marion was found by Helen and Arthur lying on her back in the dining room amidst spattered blood. Her papers had been rifled, and only a single diamond brooch among those on display had been stolen.

The next day, the police put out Adams's and Lambie's description of the burglar: 'a man between twenty-five and thirty ... 5 feet 8 or 9 inches, slim build, dark hair' and clean shaven, a descriptor readily altered over time.[19] On 23 December, Glasgow's eminent forensic medical expert Professor Glaister and Dr Galt conducted a first inspection of the locus followed by a postmortem. As the police investigation progressed, various individuals stated they had seen a man fitting the description speeding away from the property. One witness called the police, informing them that a man resembling Slater had attempted to sell him a pawn ticket for a diamond brooch.[20] On Christmas day evening, the pawn ticket led the police to Slater's lodgings, which he had just departed. Now the chase was on, although Slater remained unaware of his predicament. He took a night train to Liverpool with his girlfriend. Travelling under the names of Mr and Mrs Otto Sando, two days later they embarked on the *Lusitania* bound for New York, where they were later intercepted by the police. Witnesses Adams and Lambie, along with another Barrowman, had accompanied the police to New York on a separate vessel. Each of the witnesses described Slater at his extradition hearing as 'exceedingly like' the man they had seen in Glasgow almost two weeks earlier. However, extradition proceedings proved unnecessary when Slater volunteered to return to Glasgow to stand trial and clear his name.[21]

Between Christmas 1908 and the murder trial which began on 3 May 1909, many newspaper column inches printed various details of the fateful night as well as the police investigation on both sides of the Atlantic. The nation followed the manhunt, arrest and return to Scotland, outraged at the affront

ILLUSTRATION 9.3 *Dining Room, 15 Queen's Terrace.* W. Roughead, The Trial of Oscar Slater *(Edinburgh, 1910).*

to an elderly, privileged woman. And the excitement did not abate as the first witness took the stand. On the first day of the trial, several witnesses 'spoke to having seen the prisoner hanging about' West Princes Street in the days before the murder, including Lambie who gave a full account of the night and her journey to New York to identify Slater.[22] On the second day, Professor Glaister considered that between '20 and 40 blows were inflicted on the victim in the fiercest fashion', probably by the hammer found among Slater's possessions. Crucially, Glaister could not confirm that the blood found on Slater's clothing was in fact human blood and therefore could not be certain that it belonged to Marion.[23]

On the third day, the evidence for the defence commenced. Slater did not appear on the stand, which was unusual. On day four, Mr McClure K.C. concluded the evidence for the defence and counsel delivered their addresses before the judge's, Lord Guthrie's summing-up. The same afternoon, the jury of fifteen men, among them a retired farmer, a teacher, a watchmaker, a traveller, a spirit merchant and an artist, all from Glasgow, except one juror from Leith, returned its verdict. McClure's lengthy address to the jury took up twenty-two and a half close-typed pages in the published record of the trial. He concluded by comparing Slater's case to that of Adolf Beck, a Norwegian tried for misdemeanours and fraud in England in 1907. As a case of mistaken identity of less severity, Beck had been found guilty and sentenced to penal servitude, but the judge at his trial considered there was 'something wrong about his conviction' and a Parliamentary inquiry quashed the verdict and sentence due to the wrongful identification of the suspect. That was for a non-capital case, so with so much at stake for Slater, McClure adjured the jury to 'lay aside all pre-possessions created by the newspapers' and to give Slater the 'benefit of the evidence which has been led'. He considered the evidence 'required an acquittal' and that if they found Slater guilty, then that 'irreparable wrong' would be their sole responsibility.[24]

Lord Guthrie's charge to the jury was not so lengthy. He commented on Slater's ill-gotten earnings, living on the proceeds of his female associate's prostitution, which would become a key component of the trial's future. Guthrie was shocked that 'a brutal offence of this kind' could be committed in 'a crowded part of a town alleged to be civilised' against an 'unoffending old lady'. He was disturbed that Marion's murder might go unpunished if the jury found that 'the whole matter is in the region of speculation or suspicion', in which case they could not convict. He explained that 'the Crown have undertaken to prove, not that he is possibly or probably the murderer, but that he *is* the murderer' [italics in original], and if they agreed with the Crown case, then they must convict. An hour and ten minutes later, the jury returned their verdict: guilty by a majority of nine to six.[25] For four days, Slater had remained silent, and now he spoke. 'I know nothing about the affair, absolutely nothing. I never heard the name.' He repeated these short sentences as Lord Guthrie reached for the black cap to impose the inevitable sentence of doom. Slater was scheduled for execution in twenty-one days' time.[26]

Themes and analysis

Almost from the moment sentence was pronounced, some commentators have viewed Slater's case as a miscarriage of justice. The case concluded on 6 May, yet by 13 May 1909, Lord Guthrie had been requested to write his trial report, stating that 'the whole community, legal and non-legal, would approve commutation of the sentence' because carrying out the capital punishment would 'outrage a body of public opinion'.[27] Lord Guthrie was responding not only to the Secretary for Scotland but also to a hastily raised public petition containing the signatures of 20,000 Glaswegians. Guthrie also considered that 'had the majority, instead of being 9 to 6, varied by one, that is to say,

Oscar Slater on trial in the High Court of Justiciary, Edinburgh
From a Photograph taken in Court

ILLUSTRATION 9.4 *On trial, High Court of Justiciary, Edinburgh.*
W. Roughead, The Trial of Oscar Slater *(Edinburgh, 1910).*

had it been 8 to 7', he presumed that 'a reprieve would follow'.[28] In fact, the jury division had been nine guilty, five not proven and one not guilty, a fact at the time unknown to the public.[29] Yet despite the weight of public and legal opinion, the Scottish Office waited until the night before Slater's scheduled execution to deliver its decision: the sentence had been 'respited "until further signification of His Majesty's pleasure" '. It was literally a last-minute stay of execution since during the day rumours had spread around Glasgow that a reprieve had been refused.[30] The Crown waited until 6 July 1909 to commute the sentence to penal servitude for life.[31]

The speed at which the petition was raised and the numbers involved suggest wide popular support for Oscar Slater and rejection of the sentence imposed, and possibly also disagreement with the jury's verdict – could Slater have been innocent? Widespread publication of the pretrial case from Slater's identification in New York, Lambie's and Barrowman's shared cabin on the Atlantic voyage which allowed them to align their evidence, and the provision of Slater's photograph to twelve witnesses about to identify their man from among a line-up of men who looked nothing like him, did not go unnoticed by the news-reading public.[32] Not only was the investigation blatantly unfair and biased, but as Lord Guthrie commented, the death penalty on a guilty verdict may have 'helped to drive some of the jury into the minority'; he suggested these jurors may have returned a guilty verdict if the punishment had been penal servitude.[33] However, the fact that five jurors found the Crown case not proven also speaks volumes about the circumstantial nature of the evidence adduced. The petition also suggests a grassroots blindness to Slater's German Jewish ethnicity. Admittedly, some among the petitioners were Eastern European immigrants themselves, but the mostly Glaswegian signatories wished to see Slater reprieved or acquitted.

Lord Guthrie's legal comments suggest cognizance that the law fraternity also struggled to support the unavoidable sentence for a murder conviction. However, despite his argument that with such a close jury division, 'it is certain that reprieve would follow', Guthrie confirmed his opinion that Slater was guilty. Not only did he believe that all the evidence, most of which was circumstantial, pointed to Slater's guilt, but that Slater's 'failure to go into the witness box ... I thought proved that the prisoner was the murderer'.[34] After the Criminal Evidence Act 1898, 'the accused became an important participant' in the trial, but for some reason, either Slater declined or his counsel advised against an appearance.[35] Whether Guthrie's comment was judicial bias against Slater personally or all panels, or anyone charged with brutal violence or ethnic minority panels, is impossible to determine from his case report, but it insinuates a less-than-fair consideration of Slater's courtroom performance.

Lord Guthrie had also alluded in his summing-up to Slater's undisclosed background: no one knew where he had been born, who his parents were, if he had been trained in a trade or skill, or 'if he ever did an honest day's work in his life'. This suggested, to Guthrie, that 'a man of that kind has not the presumption of innocence in his favour', which 'the ordinary man' could assume, and that 'the prisoner's sinister record may be capable of exhibiting a callous behaviour' after having committed murder.[36] What was that 'sinister record'? Guthrie had just determined that no one knew anything about Slater's background, except of course his existence on the proceeds of his associate's prostitution. Robert Shiels argues that 'Guthrie's unhappy instruction to the jury' stemmed from his 'displacement of the application of the presumption of previous good character where bad character was obvious from the evidence'.[37] Thus, Slater's way of life contributed to an assumption of guilt because he was the 'type' to commit such a brutal crime. And arguably, Guthrie's deep-seated Protestant faith had led him to an un-legal, overly moralistic assessment of Slater's character.[38]

However, Lord Guthrie's comments on Slater's appearance suggest judicial blindness to ethnicity. Guthrie instructed the jury that 'A Scotch man is apt to say, "Oh, he is a foreign-looking man"' because he argued the 'subtle differences' between ethnicities were indistinguishable to most Scots, and therefore the testimony of witnesses who spoke to seeing Slater leave the house and who identified him in the police line-up went 'for very little'.[39] However, even if the average Glaswegian was not equipped to distinguish one foreigner from another, the circumstantial identification evidence helped to convict Slater. Cassie Watson's research suggests that 'eyewitness testimony is reliable' if tested properly the first time, but in Slater's case, eyewitnesses had been given suggestive material – his photograph – prior to the identity parade.[40] Thus if a foreign 'type' existed in the psyche of those witnesses who attested to Slater as the perpetrator, then his 'coolness under pressure' as the witnesses endured 'sustained questioning' from defence counsel confirmed 'his character and capacity to perform the monstrous deeds' of which he was accused, despite the obvious unreliability of Lambie's and Barrowman's identification evidence.[41]

In addition to the problematic misidentification of Slater, the forensic medical evidence produced by Professor Glaister and Dr Galt concluded that blood had only been discovered on and around Marion's body lying in her dining room. Given the acknowledged spurting blood from the injuries to her temporal arteries inflicted repeatedly 'with almost lightning rapidity, ... a furious assault', defence counsel queried whether Glaister would have expected to find blood stains on the perpetrator's person. Glaister declined to confirm other than to say it depended 'on the angle and the force' of the blows.[42] Thus, Slater's clothing did not even condemn him.

Shiels states that the 'central elements of legal proof' at Slater's trial were 'commission and identification', neither of which had been irrefutably confirmed by prosecution counsel, but neither had Slater's counsel presented a conclusive defence.[43] No written notice of an alibi was submitted, and although one was adduced in exculpatory testimony, Slater's counsel could not absolutely prove it.[44] Any instructions to his counsel given by Slater which may have aided the preparation of his case are now lost, but as Shiels argues, whether it was a matter of 'presentation or preparation or both', defence counsel was professionally responsible for conducting a meaningful defence. Counsel could act independently and of 'his own discretion and judgement' but ultimately had to act irrespective of his own views.[45] Thus, Slater most likely received the best defence expected, particularly since this was a capital case and defence needed to be sure to accurately defend key evidential points.[46]

Slater's conviction provoked immediate public outcry, which resulted in a commutation of the capital sentence, but did not prove to be the remittance, indemnification or pardon suggested by the wording of the royal order given in July 1909.[47] Slater's life was saved, but what kind of life could he lead in Peterhead gaol? In 1912, Arthur Conan Doyle's intervention in the form of a lengthy pamphlet detailing the case and growing public concern about a miscarriage of justice led to an inquiry in 1914. Evidence brought by Detective

John Thomson Trench indicated that some witnesses had not been as truthful as expected and that police investigations into other possible suspects had not been fully considered.[48] However, the inquiry seems only to have ended in the 'discreditation, humiliation and persecution' of Trench and no release for Slater.[49] Throughout his incarceration, Slater wrote to his parents at home in Germany where the press also took up his case. A decade later, Dr Mamroth, a German legal agent, offered to represent Slater in another appeal attempt. His letter to Slater at Peterhead was returned with a curt note from the prison secretary: it was 'against the Commissioner's practice to permit law agents to have access to convicted prisoners'.[50]

However, Slater did not give up, and as Lindsay Farmer states, 'it is a measure of enduring public dissatisfaction with the verdict' that Parliament was presented with a special bill which finally allowed for an appeal to be heard in 1927. An appellate criminal court had been established in Scotland in 1926, but only to hear appeals for crimes prosecuted after October that year; this was an attempt to keep the flood waters of historical cases from being brought to appeal. Without the special bill enacted in 1927, Slater's case would not have qualified. There were three grounds for Slater's appeal: evidence beneficial to Slater had not been adduced; the Lord Advocate's address had misrepresented the evidence and put Slater's character on trial, and Lord Guthrie had further compounded the Lord Advocate's mistake by himself remarking on Slater's ill-gotten way of life.[51] Eventually, the five appeal judges determined that 'the appellant had not the benefit of ordinary presumption of innocence' because of Lord Guthrie's misdirection to the jury. In July 1928, Slater was finally released on a legal technicality and on licence for the rest of his life. He was awarded £6,000 in compensation and was handed the legal bill for his appeal case.[52]

Conclusion

No matter that the accused fitted the generic description of a 'foreigner' seen fleeing the crime scene at pace and had a spurious background that suggested he was a criminal type, for such a brutal murder, it was crucial to establish a motive. The disappearance of a single diamond brooch did not suggest a sufficient motive for such a frenzied attack on a defenceless old woman. Professor Glaister had testified that he believed Marion had stood up as the intruder entered her dining room because the physical evidence of the initial assault had indicated a frontal bludgeoning rather than from the rear as she sat.[53] So, if the intruder did not creep up behind Marion with intent to knock her unconscious so that he could freely burgle her apartment, was he known to her? Had she stood up to welcome him or to eject a man she did not wish to receive? Despite allegations that Slater, or someone looking like him, had been seen loitering in the vicinity for a few days prior to the attack, the crime scene does not suggest burglary. In fact, the brooch that was eventually found proved to be different from the one in Marion's possession. Instead, the crime scene and injuries inflicted on Marion suggest the actions of someone who detested her or the behaviour of a lunatic.

In the immediate aftermath of this horrendous murder, Glasgow, Scotland and the whole nation needed to identify a suitable perpetrator for such an inexplicable crime. It was inconceivable that a Scot or Briton would commit such unspeakable violence. Therefore, once the perpetrator's distinctive gait and 'foreign' appearance had been precognosced, clearly the police were only looking for a foreigner. When an individual who had lodged a pawn ticket for a diamond brooch proved also to look like Slater, a foreigner who lived off the earnings of a prostitute and who was then found to have gone to Liverpool docks, of course the case stacked up.

The violent murder of Marion Gilchrist says more about early twentieth-century British and Scottish society's need to accuse outside itself rather than to consider inwardly whether one of its own was capable of such brutality. The hurried and lengthy petition raised in support of Slater suggests strongly that antisemitic, anti-German sentiment was not widespread in Glasgow, nor was it institutionalized within the legal fraternity as evidenced by Lord Guthrie's instruction to the jury to consider whether they were able to distinguish one foreigner from another. However, it is possible that prejudice towards foreigners existed among Glasgow's police. Shiels suggests that the police's concerns with the expansion of crime in Glasgow may have induced them to arrest Slater, a man known to them with previous minor offences, an international reputation and supposedly on the run.[54] Farmer's research on the proliferation of police evidence in this period suggests that the police struggled to interpret everything they gathered. This may have led to omissions and misinterpretations as Trench indicated at the 1914 inquiry. It may also have overwhelmed the jury, since sixty witnesses for the prosecution appeared along with fifteen for the defence in Slater's four-day trial. To make sense of this quantity of detailed evidence, the jury had to rely on the interpretation of counsel and guidance from the bench. As Farmer concludes, the Lord Advocate's summing-up was 'riddled with inaccuracies and inconsistencies' and did not reflect the required 'professional norms regarding fairness and restraint' expected of any lawyer.[55]

Slater's case continues to appeal. Most authors on the subject attempt to answer the perennial question: who dunnit? Toughill has argued for the other suspects who the police rejected early on in their investigation, namely Marion's estranged nephews, in particular her 'mentally unbalanced' nephew

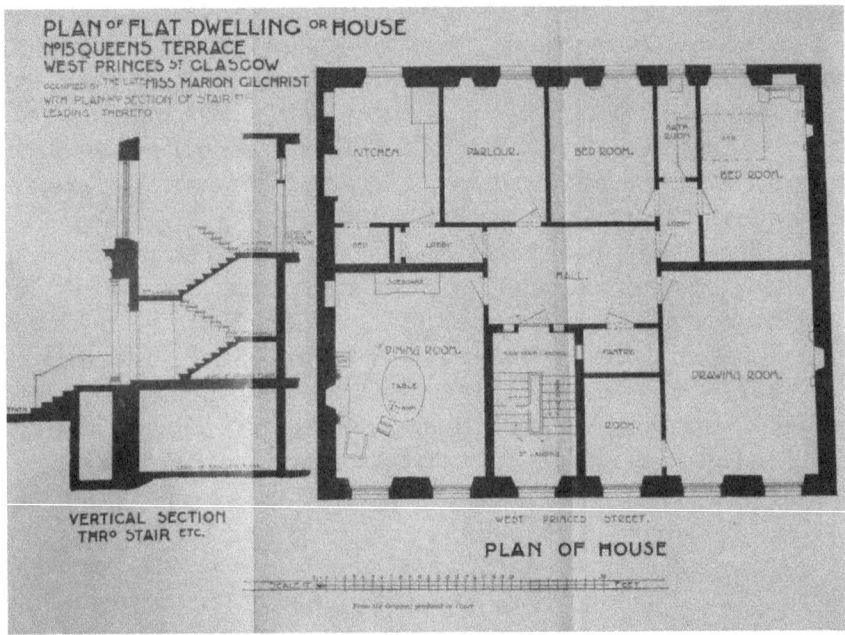

ILLUSTRATION 9.5 *Plan of Marion Gilchrist's home. W. Roughead,* The Trial of Oscar Slater *(Edinburgh, 1910).*

Wingate Birrell.[56] While, after 'long study of the circumstances surrounding the case', Whittington-Egan is 'very much persuaded' that Marion's murder was the work of 'a pair – or possibly a trio or quartet, a gang' – take your pick – of professional jewel thieves, who had 'planned fastidiously'.[57] However, the debate between Whittington-Egan and Toughill becomes irrelevant when writing over 100 years after the crime. Kilday's assessment is more credible. After dismissing the rest of the Birrell Gilchrist nephews, she suggests that George Gilchrist Birrell was the prime suspect, but the police did not pursue him because by the time evidence pointing to him had come to light, they were already hot on Slater's tail across the Atlantic.[58] Prejudice and 'fitting the bill' had superseded thorough detective work. However, the historian's purpose is not to solve historical 'cold cases' but to analyse so as to promote understanding of society, police and legal behaviours. And there is much to understand from Slater's experience.

Notes

1 Report on the Judicial Statistics of Scotland for the Year 1909: Statistics relating to Police Apprehensions, Criminal Proceedings, Prisons,

Reformatory and Industrial Schools, Criminal Lunatics etc. (1910), cmd 5417, Appendix B, 11.
2. Report on the Judicial Statistics (1910), Table IV, 17.
3. Report on the Judicial Statistics (1910), 8 and Table XII, 69. The Report counts two sentenced to death and 122 sentenced to penal servitude for 1909. It is unclear whether Oscar's case was counted under the capital sentence or penal servitude or may have been double counted after his sentence was commuted.
4. A. M. Kilday, *Crime in Scotland 1660–1960: the Violent North?* (Abingdon, 2021), 8.
5. The last public hanging in Scotland was of Dr Pritchard on Glasgow Green in 1865.
6. D. D. Gray, *Crime, Policing and Punishment in England, 1660–1914* (London, 2016), 288.
7. V. A. C. Gatrell, *The Hanging Tree: Execution and the English People, 1770–1868* (Oxford, 1996), 523–4.
8. Representation of the People Act 1867, a.k.a. Reform Act 1867, also Second Reform Act, 30 & 31 Vict., c.102.
9. P. King and R. Ward, 'Rethinking the Bloody Code in Eighteenth-Century Britain: Capital Punishment at the Centre and on the Periphery', *Past and Present* 228, no. 1 (August, 2015), 181–2.
10. www.visionofbritain.org.uk/census/ (accessed November 2024).
11. R. Rodger, 'Urbanisation in Twentieth Century Scotland', in *Scotland in the Twentieth Century*, ed. T. M. Devine and R. J. Finlay (Edinburgh, 1996), 124.
12. W. W. Knox, *Industrial Nation: work, culture and society in Scotland, 1800–present* (Edinburgh, 2009), 132; C. Harvie, *No Gods and Precious Few Heroes: Scotland since 1914* (Edinburgh, 1981), 4.
13. Knox, *Industrial Nation*, 192.
14. A. Taylor, ' "In Glasgow but not of it" "? Eastern European Jewish immigrants in a provincial Jewish community c.1890 to c.1945', *Continuity and Change* 28, no. 3 (2013), 452.
15. M. Flinn, *Scottish Population History, from the seventeenth century to the 1930s* (Cambridge, 1976), 456–8.
16. W. Kenefick, 'Comparing the Jewish and Irish Communities in Twentieth Century Scotland', *Jewish Culture and History* 9, no. 2–3 (2007), 60–5, 67.
17. Taylor, 'In Glasgow but not of it', 462.
18. HH15/20/1, Indictment of Oscar Slater.
19. In 1911, Oscar wrote that a photo taken of him seven days after the date of Marion's murder showed him with a full moustache, yet witnesses claimed the man fleeing her flat was clean shaven; HH15/20/2, letter Oscar to his parents, 10 January 1911.
20. W. Roughead, *Trial of Oscar Slater* (Edinburgh, 1910), xiii–xvi.
21. A. Conan Doyle, *The Case of Oscar Slater* (London, 1912), 22.

22 'The Glasgow Murder', *The Times*, 4 May 1909, 15.
23 'The Glasgow Murder', *The Times*, 5 May 1909, 4.
24 Roughead, *Oscar Slater*, 260–83. Beck's acquittal led to the Criminal Appeal Act, (1907), U.K., 7. Edw. VII, c.23 and the formation of England's appellate court.
25 HH16/109, 7.
26 Roughead, *Oscar Slater*, 296–7.
27 HH16/109, 7; 'The Glasgow Murder', *The Times*, 7 May 1909, 15.
28 HH16/109, 8.
29 Conan Doyle, *Oscar Slater*, 58. Knowing this level of detail of the jury division is unusual.
30 'The Glasgow Murder', *The Times*, 26 May 1909, 8.
31 HH15/20/1, 18.
32 A. M. Kilday, '"Circumstances of Unexplained Savagery": The Gilchrist Murder Case and Its Legacy, 1908–1927', in *Fair and Unfair Trials in the British Isles, 1800–1940: microhistories of Justice and Injustice*, ed. A. M. Kilday and D. Nash (London, 2020), 148–9.
33 HH16/109, 8.
34 HH16/109, 8, 5.
35 L. Farmer, 'Notable Trials and the Criminal Law in Scotland and England, 1750–1950', *Law and Society in France and Great Britain, XII–XX centuries*, ed. P. Chassaigne and J. P. Genet (Paris, 2003), 160.
36 Roughead, *Oscar Slater*, 286.
37 R. Shiels, 'Reassessing the Criminal Appeal of Oscar Slater', *Scots Law Times*, News (2024), 43.
38 Guthrie was legal adviser to the Church of Scotland from 1881 to 1900 and had published on John Knox and the Reformation in Scotland, *Encyclopaedia Britannica*, vol. 31 (1922), 330–1.
39 Roughead, *Oscar Slater*, 288.
40 C. Watson, 'The Trouble with Eyewitness Identification', *Legal History Miscellany* – https://legalhistorymiscellany.com/2024/09/27/the-trouble-with-eyewitness-identification/ (accessed 27 September 2024).
41 L. Farmer, 'Notable Trials', 162; L. Farmer, 'Arthur and Oscar (and Sherlock): The Reconstructive Trial and the "Hermeneutics of Suspicion"', *International Commentary on Evidence* 5, no. 1 (2007), 14.
42 Roughead, *Oscar Slater*, 144–5.
43 R. Shiels, 'Historic Defective Representation: the defence case for Oscar Slater', *Scots Law Times*, News (2025), 163.
44 Roughead, *Oscar Slater*, 268.
45 Shiels, 'Historic Defective Representation', 164.
46 Shiels, 'Historic Defective Representation', 166.

47 HH15/20/1, 18.
48 Farmer, 'Arthur and Oscar', 1.
49 Kilday, 'Unexplained Savagery', 161–3.
50 HH15/20/2, Letter Secretary to Dr Mamroth, Breslau, 7 October 2022.
51 Farmer, 'Arthur and Oscar', 3–4.
52 Kilday, 'Unexplained Savagery', 157–8.
53 Roughead, *Oscar Slater*, 145.
54 Shiels, 'Historic Defective Representation', 13.
55 Farmer, 'Arthur and Oscar', 11.
56 T. Toughill, *Oscar Slater: the mystery solved* (Edinburgh, 1993), 211–13.
57 R. Whittington-Egan, *The Oscar Slater Murder Story* (Glasgow, 2001), 305, 312.
58 Kilday, 'Unexplained Savagery', 171–2.

10

Susan Newell 1923: Murderess, evidence and insanity

Gossip, witch, scold are words that have been hurled at women who have stepped outside accepted norms for female behaviour across time and geography. As a woman known to smoke, drink and verbally abuse her husband, when Susan Newell was indicted for the murder of a young boy, there was little hope for her counsel's attempt at a diminished responsibility special defence. As the last woman to hang in Scotland, Susan's case explores attitudes towards nonconforming women in a period of interwar social readjustment.

Context

The antecedents to most individual's criminal behaviour are socio-economic, especially when that crime is apparently motiveless, spontaneous interpersonal violence. Whereas the responses of wider society and the judicial system to individual instances of violent crime are prompted by perceptions of ethnicity, faith and class. The elites are fearful of lower-class crime; the middle classes fear encroachment from below, and within the working class, the differentiation between respectable and non-respectable is often based on the fear of sliding down the class ladder to join the residuum at its foot. The last woman to hang in Scotland, Susan Newell's case illustrates all those fears and prejudices in interwar Clydeside.

Post-Great War Britain was a country undergoing a socio-economic rebalancing as the nation returned to a peace-time economy, but by mid-1920, any post-war boom had dissipated into economic collapse. Domestic and international markets had contracted with mass unemployment on the horizon.[1] A further result of the post-war economy was gender conflict. Often against their wishes, women had returned to home and kitchen sinks after years of relative freedom, contributing to the war effort. Gender antagonism within individual households was also an increasing issue. Susan Kingsley-Kent attributes 'the disorders of contemporary life' in this period to 'hostility in marriage' caused by 'women who sought to dominate their husbands or who struggled with them for power'.[2] Alongside a realignment of gender roles, a move towards 'companionate marriage' evolved in the 1920s, an idealistic arrangement in which husbands were encouraged to participate in housework, childcare and shared leisure and companionship – ideals promoted by a growing circulation of women's pictorial weekly magazines.[3] However, as Annemarie Hughes's research reveals, such benefits to marriage were rarely experienced by lower working-class couples, who 'tended to replicate the traditional normative family ideal as defined by their parents and peers'. Thus, men and women raised in chaotic households where drinking, domestic abuse and poverty were the norm, were generationally predisposed to repeat that learned behaviour when their time came to form partnerships.

Hughes's oral history research confirms that domestic violence was endemic in working-class areas and 'extremely visible', especially in Glasgow and was frequently fuelled by alcohol. Children would seek help from the nearest police office, often on Friday and Saturday nights, when fathers returned drunk from the pub and set about their mother, who might have challenged her husband about squandering his wages before handing over any housekeeping. Hughes argues that working-class 'gender conflict permeated the Clyde' in the interwar years, where the new 'domestic respectability' was rarely achievable by families existing in poverty, and where a 'good wife' who kept house and children clean and fed on short money without speaking out was a rarity. She concludes that men's expenditure of the 'family wage' on personal leisure pursuits – drink and gambling – created tensions and a 'struggle for resources' in the home.[4] Unable to make ends meet, even when a husband was in employment, many wives scolded their husbands, who frequently responded with physical violence.

Economic decline in the immediate post-war years led to widespread unemployment and stagnant wages. Scotland's unemployment rate never dropped below 10 per cent of the insured workforce during the 1920s and consistently exceeded the UK national average by several per cent. But not all families had an out-of-work husband, although even when in work, many families still could not afford their rent.[5] Rent restrictions triggered by Glasgow's rent strikes in 1915 had benefited the working classes during the conflict, but in the post-war period when those restrictions were lifted, private landlords who had been unable to finance housing improvements during the war were now eager to recoup their losses.[6] At the bottom end of the rental market, accommodation conditions worsened, and large families, and those who spent their money unwisely, were unable to afford healthy homes. In her Scottish journey, contemporary observer Cicely Hamilton noted the 'black reputation' of Clydeside's 'mean street dwellings' where 47 per cent of inhabitants in 1911 occupied homes of only one or two rooms.[7] For many, as Hamilton observed, overcrowding and shortage of good housing were exacerbated by Irish immigrants, particularly on Scotland's west coast around the Clyde. Hamilton estimated Clydeside's Irish population to be 'something like six hundred thousand' who were reportedly accused of being accountable for 'more than its due proportion of crime and offence'.[8] In the opinion of Regius Professor of Law at the University of Glasgow and social commentator A. D. Gibb, the 'stream of low-grade immigrants' from Ireland to Scotland's west coast were 'as a rule quite unprosperous' and possessed a 'monopoly' on 'pawnshops and the public-houses'. Gibb also attributed responsibility for 'Scottish slumdom' to the Irish.[9] In 1923, the Church of Scotland exacerbated an already hostile environment for Irish Catholics by publishing its report *Menace of the Irish Race to our Scottish Nationality* in which it aimed to address 'the alarm and anxiety' caused by the 'incursion into Scotland' of a large number of Catholic Irish immigrants. Their influx was considered 'formidable' in the west and threatened 'thorough permeation' in the east. The overall tone of the report denigrated the Irish individually and as a race.[10]

While these contemporary commentators did not directly attribute perceived increasing criminality – Irish or otherwise – with drink, a report commissioned in 1903 had. Arthur Sherwell's investigation confirmed that 'small crimes and offences' had increased since 1881 and that increases in the prison population were 'due to greatly increased numbers of casual irregular workers' who spent their money on drink. Of 179,821 individuals charged with criminal offences in 1900, approximately '63.5 per cent were for offences directly connected with drinking'. Sherwell was not arguing against improved wages. However, he correlated drunkenness with the 'creation and toleration of slum conditions', especially among the working classes who were attracted to 'the tippling houses' for entertainment and comfort away from overcrowded homes.[11] Contemporary psychologist Bernard Hollander recognized that alcohol consumption relaxed inhibitions, thereby promoting social intercourse, but if indulged excessively, self-control was 'progressively weakened until suspended' and often revealed 'concealed traits of character'. The insane and 'weak-minded' and those who had sustained head injuries were particularly susceptible to 'the evil influence of alcohol' in his opinion. Inebriety in anyone might provoke wife-beating, assaults on children and associates with 'drunkenness and immorality often go[ing] together especially in women' to whom intoxicants were 'positively disastrous'. 'Chronic alcoholism' and concomitant 'ungovernable passion' might even lead to 'violence and homicide'.[12]

Many historians have commented on the drink, violence and hyper-masculinity culture of post-war Clydeside, among whom Hughes's work on domestic abuse highlights the everyday nature of spousal violence.[13] It is acknowledged that most historical domestic abuse resulted in female casualties not male. As Murray Strauss comments, outside the home, the cultural taboo of hitting a woman prevails, but indoors, men may hit their wives. However, his research reveals that when women fight back, their higher proportion of 'acts of severe violence' may result from self-defence against a 'dangerous assailant'.[14] Thus, if in fear of her life, a wife may inflict worse injuries than a drunken husband accustomed to using his fists against a quarrelsome wife.

Grinding poverty among Scotland's working class, already dire when Oscar Slater stood trial for murder in 1909, had not improved in the intervening decade and a half. Post-war economic precarity, slum rented accommodation across much of the Clyde corridor and generationally learned abusive marital relations resulted in many households experiencing poor living conditions, often exacerbated by a pervasive drink culture. Despite Scotland's welfare officers endeavouring to encourage healthier living and the temperance movement's promotion of abstention from alcohol, drink provided men with an escape from overcrowded homes and supported a sense of male dominance: men could spend their wages how they wished, if they wished and wives were expected to maintain the family on what was left. Attempts to challenge a husband's masculine 'rights' might result in violence. But what if the wife had the drinking problem? What if she spent her employed husband's wages on alcohol, thereby reducing herself and children to such poverty that they rented a single room vacated by a disabled woman who was living in her kitchen subletting to a difficult family to eke out her own existence?

Case

On Wednesday, 18 September 1923, husband and wife John and Susan Newell stood trial at Glasgow's High Court of Justiciary for murder.[15] By the second day of the trial, John Newell had been acquitted. Lord Kinross, Patrick Balfour, the Advocate Depute, had withdrawn the charge against him, and Susan stood alone charged with the murder of thirteen-year-old newspaper boy John Johnston.[16] John Newell's special defence of alibi had been corroborated by several witnesses, few of whom knew him personally, but all could confirm his whereabouts in the days either side of the murder, and their collective evidence materially assisted his defence and ultimately proved his innocence. However, Susan had no alibi and all the evidence from the witnesses for the prosecution pointed at her, despite there being no eyewitnesses to the assault. Their collective evidence would prove Susan's guilt.

The charge was that on Wednesday, 20 June 1923, a boy named John Johnston had been murdered in the room occupied by Susan and John Newell.[17] Young John had been throttled so violently that he had sustained fractures to his neck, which were the likely cause of death.[18] He had been a well-loved local lad employed by a newspaper seller for whom he delivered newspapers to regular and speculative customers. He kept a portion of the proceeds for himself having repaid his employer. John was 'a humble boy widely known and generally popular', a Boy Scout and member of the Good Templars, who 'delivered newspapers with a smile and a cheery word'.[19] John's sunny nature had led him to Susan Newell's home at 2 Newlands Street, Coatbridge, where the Newells rented a single room from Mrs Annie Young, a disabled widow who lived in the kitchen adjacent to the room she had let to them three weeks earlier.

Annie Young confirmed that the couple rowed and that she had not seen John Newell at the property since a big commotion on 17 June. On the night of the murder, Mrs Young had asked a friend to inform Susan that she must quit the property by Saturday. Susan had already borrowed money from her, and she was fearful she would not receive her rent of 9/ at the end of the week; she was also afraid of further rows if Newell returned.[20] Having been informed she would have to clear out within a few days on top of having been recently left penniless by her husband with a young daughter to care for, John Johnston knocked at Susan's door with a newspaper to sell. Able to hear everything across the landing between the room and her kitchen, Mrs Young and her friends then heard three 'dumps' followed by the sound of Susan leaving the house. Mrs Young only observed her once she had crossed the road heading for the pub with a jug in her hand. On Susan's return, she collected her daughter Janet McLeod, the offspring of a previous marriage, who was playing in the street and went indoors. Shortly afterwards, Susan and Janet emerged, and Susan asked Mrs Young to keep an ear out for the police; if they visited, it was about a complaint she had made concerning her husband's assault of her little girl. Mother and daughter returned a few minutes later, before Susan left again, this time alone. When she returned in the early hours, Mrs Young could smell whisky and cigarette smoke through the door, a point Lord Kinross later emphasized in court.

During the night, Susan had attempted to lift some floorboards; her daughter thought it was to conceal the boy's dead body, which she had seen on the sofa. The next morning, Susan wrapped John's body in a blanket, placed it on top of Mrs Young's borrowed go-cart and headed towards Glasgow with her daughter sitting on top of the bundle. They accepted a lift for part of the journey from a lorry driver before setting down near a patch of vacant ground. Here, Susan was observed by a handful of women who called the police when they saw a foot protruding from the bundle. Susan was taken to the Eastern Police Office where she was cautioned 'that she might be charged with murder' to which she answered repeatedly that her husband had 'choked the life out of the boy with his hands', and she had not known what to do with the body. John's body was taken to the mortuary, where forensic experts, Professor Glaister and Dr Anderson, conducted a postmortem.

Since late on Wednesday night, John's father had searched all over Coatbridge for his son when he did not return home. By 1.00 am, he had reported John missing at the police office and gave a description. Later at work, a detective called for him to attend the Eastern Police Office in Glasgow where he identified his son. There had been a delay in identifying the body because as the chief constable of Coatbridge Burgh Police explained, word had been circulated that a much younger boy of about six years had been found. Only later was John's body identified as aged 'about 12 or 13'. The Procurator Fiscal's investigation encompassed interviews with Susan's neighbour and her friends, the women who witnessed her with the bundle on the vacant ground, the lorry driver and a number of witnesses who spoke to her husband's alibi including members of his family. No one gave precognition or court testimony for Susan, either as good character or in exculpation. Her daughter Janet provided two stories when precognosced, which were later used at trial to intimate that Susan had coached her.

John Newell's alibi started with his attendance at his brother's funeral on Tuesday, 19 June, after which he had returned to his wife, but there had been another row. He found a room in a lodging house where there was a discussion about a urinal, which made him remarkable to the lodging-house attendant. Throughout Wednesday, 20 June, Newell spent the day 'hanging about Glasgow'. He bought a 'quarter pound of liver' and suet at a butcher's before purchasing a 'pipe and lid' at a tobacconist's; both shop owners remembered him. By Thursday, he had taken a bus to Leith, and on Friday, he learned of John's murder when he read a newspaper in a pub. He went to the nearest police office where he informed them that he was Susan's husband but knew 'nothing of the crime'. The pay clerk at the British Tube Works where John worked confirmed seeing him on 19 June and had persuaded him not to leave his job to seek employment at the company's other factory in Birmingham. He advanced him 30/ as an inducement to stay. Susan had arrived at the Tube Works on Wednesday morning asking for John and seeking his 'lying-in money'; the pay clerk confirmed she had seemed desperate but did not hand over any money to her.[21] The trail of eyewitnesses confirmed Newell's story.

A note from the Advocate Depute to the Lord Advocate explained that 'to conduct the trial in his [John Newell's] absence would be difficult' for two reasons. On the one hand, it was 'conceivable that a jury might stretch a point in their natural disinclination to convict a woman' in a case with a capital sentence hanging over it and thus find her not guilty, and witnesses to the alibi might not give precognitions if the man was not also indicted. Doubt 'might be created', and the wrong person might be convicted. However, 'there was a certain awkwardness' in trying Newell on a capital charge if all the Crown evidence indicated he was not guilty; by prosecuting him, it might suggest the Crown was 'antecedently uncertain' who was the guilty party. The Advocate Depute advised that both should be prosecuted, thus allowing the evidence to the alibi to be adduced and the jury to decide whether the recollections of witnesses to the alibi were faulty as to 'precise timings'.[22]

Newell's alibi had been entered into the trial proceedings in good time, but as her defence counsel, Mr Gentles K.C., explained as the case opened, the special plea of insanity was only entered 'five or six days ago' because Susan had 'benefit of Poors' Counsel', and he had only recently received instructions to represent her. Lord Kinross for the prosecution made no objection since 'it would be improper to object in a case of the kind'; the Lord Justice-Clerk allowed the special plea.[23] Despite 'putting up a great fight' for Susan, Gentles was unable to persuade any of the medical experts, or the jury, of Susan's insanity at the time of the commission of the crime.[24] Forensic medical expert Professor Glaister admitted that women were 'more easily affected mentally than the average man' by 'great trials', particularly if 'in hard straits with regard to money'. He acknowledged that Susan had been left by her husband in a cruel situation. Susan had been found with only a penny on her person, a point Gentles used to explore the absence of motive for her assault on John. He argued that Susan could not have attacked young John to steal his money, because she had been arrested penniless. Thus, did this motiveless crime 'infer something as to her state of mind at the time?' Glaister thought that the 'inference would be problematical, so problematical that it would be valueless'.

Gentles tried again on points of 'absence of pre-meditation' and 'complete absence of rational motive', but Susan's demeanour when apprehended was unhelpful. She had been cool and clear-headed, and Glaister would not allow that 'acts of gross cruelty and callousness' might indicate madness. Glaister's colleague Dr Anderson concurred with his appraisal that Susan was neither insane now nor at the time of the crime, even though he admitted he had not examined her in June after her arrest. However, Anderson's further opinion did not assist Susan's case. He described her as a member 'of the tinker class' from a family of thirteen, brought up in neglect in Oban with little education. She was not of 'a particularly high moral type' and her class had 'a want of moral fibre'. It was sufficient information to provide an unfavourable, pejorative 'character' for Susan, which arguably made it unnecessary to accord her the usual court protection of inadmissibility of previous criminal charges, so as not to influence the jury. Susan had a record for breach of the peace, assault and prostitution between 1908 and 1911.[25]

Next, prison doctor, Dr Garrey presented his assessment of Susan during her time in gaol. He explained that the accused in every murder case was examined immediately for 'their mental condition', an assessment he had carried out for Susan on 22 June, and intermittently during the three months she had been in prison. Garrey did not rule out that Susan may have experienced 'some temporary maniacal frenzy' on the night of the murder, but he had not witnessed anything since to support that notion. He too described her as 'pretty low class'.

Lord Kinross's speech to the jury was relatively short for such a serious case. He told them that an alibi 'is one of the very best defences if it is a true alibi', and that under the Criminal Law of Scotland, a husband could not give evidence against his wife. If the case had indicted Susan only, Newell would have been disallowed from explaining his movements, and given Susan's allegations that he was the murderer, a jury might have believed her, which would have led to a separate prosecution against Newell. Kinross told them that John had 'met his death before the first occasion on which Mrs. Newell went out' and that it was 'indisputable' that John was dead when she left for the pub. She had hunted for her husband seeking money 'to get away'. There was no motive for the murder except to steal John's newspaper money, of which there had been only 9 d. No one had confirmed Susan's 'alienation of reason', which might support her insanity defence, because not all 'savage and brutal' crimes were committed by insane individuals or those insane at the time.

Mr Gentles's speech clung to the possibility that Susan had been 'in so abnormal a state of mind' that the jury might return a guilty verdict on a charge of culpable homicide. 'The whole responsibility for this woman's fate' rested with them, and without premeditation, not knowing who knocked at her door and 'no malice against the boy', nor motive, these were 'cardinally important factors'. The Crown had supplied no motive; attempting to hide the body of a thirteen-year-old in the few inches available beneath the floorboards suggested 'some abnormality'; travelling into Glasgow to dispose of the body rather than heading into the countryside also indicated 'an unbalanced, abnormal mind'. To Gentles, Susan had been 'temporarily unhinged'. However, the Lord Justice-Clerk disagreed.

Lord Alness told the jury that Susan's story read like a 'novelist wrote it'. He followed a logical cascade of argument: if John had been killed by some person, was Susan his assailant? If she were, was she sane at the time? And if she had been sane, 'what was the quality of her act'? Had it been murder or culpable homicide? He dealt with the absence of eyewitnesses because such crimes were rarely committed *coram populo* – murder was a private act – and the circumstantial testimonies from Mrs Young and her friends spoke 'as eloquently and as truly, if not more truly, than a human being', by which he meant they had not been eyewitnesses to the event. Susan's reason may have been 'dethroned', but there was no family history of insanity, and her actions post-assault indicated 'that her mind was not unbalanced'; she had been 'cool, collected, intelligent, balanced' throughout. The case weighed on 'the Accused to establish beyond reasonable probability of doubt that she was insane at the date of the crime', and the doctors had confirmed that she had not been. He told the jury, 'It would be very difficult to reach a conclusion' of culpable homicide on 'the proved facts', because diminished responsibility, a 'comparatively recent doctrine', 'must be applied with care', having only twice before been 'said from the Bench to a Jury'. As the jury retired at 2.30 pm, it was clear what the judge thought of the case. Thirty-five minutes later, they returned with a majority verdict: guilty on the capital charge, fourteen to one. A strong and unanimous recommendation to mercy was given. If no reprieve or commutation of sentence was forthcoming, Susan would hang on 10 October 1923, which she did with no public petition raised on her behalf and limited assistance from those in authority.

The case was concluded after three days on 20 September. On 25 September, a fatal coal mining accident took the lives of forty men at the Redding Pit near Falkirk. Rescue teams attended from across the north; a fire team attended from Susan's hometown of Coatbridge. The nation was transfixed by the disaster for several days as men emerged with chilling stories of entrapment, suffocation from 'black damp' and drowning.

Susan languished in gaol. She was thirty-three years old and had been born in a field in 1890. Her previous convictions for prostitution and assault included addiction to alcohol. Her first husband of more than ten years, McLeod, for whom there was no marriage certificate, had died in July 1922. Susan had a reputation for 'intemperate habits' and quarrelling and had met Newell the month of her husband's death, moving with him to Coatbridge in October 1922 where they married a month later. Eight months on, their quarrelling had become so extreme that Newell had left her penniless with her eight-year-old daughter.

On 28 September 1923, Mr John Lamb at the Scottish Office received a letter from Gerald Steel; they were clearly socially acquainted and Steel implored Lamb to look into Susan's 'antecedent character' because even in his post-trial appeal, Gentles was unable to 'urge more than gipsy blood & low morality & mentality, easily leading to frenzy'.[26] An undated, post-trial Home Office memo noted that 'where the Judge strongly opposes [mercy], the recommendation of the jury alone can have very little weight' and the Lord Justice-Clerk had strongly directed the jury to convict for murder. Thus, no 'statutory inquiry' was held because there was no reason to believe Susan

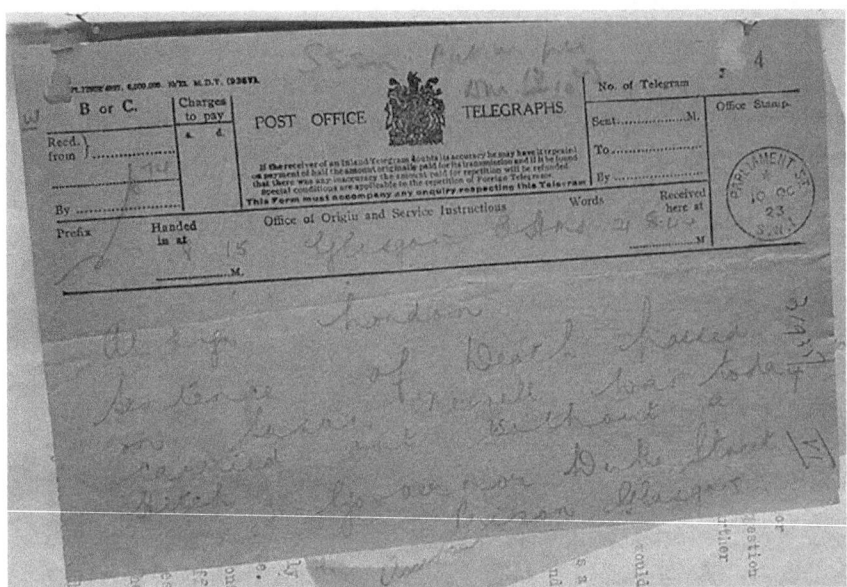

ILLUSTRATION 10.1 *Telegram confirming Susan Newell's execution, 10 October 1923. Crown Copyright. National Records of Scotland, HH16/180.*

had been insane under section 2 (4) of the Criminal Lunatics Act 1884. Being thirty-three years old, 'special disturbance owing to change of life' could not be considered, and simply being of the 'tinker class' with possible gypsy blood would 'not account for much either way'.[27] Writing to the Secretary for Scotland, Lord Novak, on 4 October, Lamb concluded that if Susan had been 'a man the sentence would undoubtedly be carried out' and queried whether sex 'in all the circumstances, should turn the scale'.[28]

On 9 October, Glasgow's city magistrates pleaded with the Scottish Office not to force them to hang a woman or at least to delay until a more extensive assessment of her mental state could be conducted.[29] That evening, Susan was informed she would hang in the morning. She cried for her daughter and swooned; no woman had hanged in Glasgow for seventy years, and Susan would be the last woman ever to hang in Scotland.[30] The following morning, Susan was attended by two Roman Catholic nuns and refused the hangman's cap: 'don't put that thing over my head'.[31]

Themes and analysis

There are two ways to analyse Susan's case: the evidence presented to the jury in court on which she was convicted and the societal evidence that pointed to a life of poverty, addiction and hopelessness, which culminated in murder and execution. The authorities investigating her case had the resources to explore Susan's background, but what they discovered could not be directly presented to the jury. Such evidence would have been prejudicial, thereby building an unfavourable 'character'. However, there were other means to admit such evidence before them.

There were no eyewitnesses to John's murder, although Susan's disposal of his body clearly indicated her involvement. However, the circumstantial evidence collected from those who observed her and her neighbour Mrs Young was, in the words of the Lord Justice-Clerk, 'sufficient, and is often more reliable than direct testimony'. Lord Alness also impressed upon the jury that Professor Glaister 'had unrivalled experience in such cases', thereby promoting Glaister's absolute opinion above the wavering answers provided by prison doctor Garrey when both were questioned on more theoretical aspects of insanity. As Lord Kinross built the Crown's case on circumstantial evidence, Gentles presented a defence constructed wholly around a theoretical situation, the possibility – not probability – of Susan's insanity in the moment of murdering John. The Crown had to prove guilt beyond reasonable doubt, whereas the defence was not required to prove Susan's innocence; Gentles only had to insert doubt into the jurors' minds and ask them to consider a situation in which the woman before them had temporarily lost her reason. In which case, they could return a guilty verdict on the lesser charge of culpable homicide. However, on that reduced indictment, Lord Alness warned them to be 'careful'. Previously, he explained, there had been 'two classes of prisoner': those completely responsible and those completely irresponsible. Now there was a third class: those who did not merit a description of insanity, but whose condition would reduce 'the quality of their act from murder to culpable homicide'.[32] The doctrine of diminished responsibility had a long history in Scots Law, but whether juries would support it depended on their opinion of the evidence presented and their personal position on mental illness.[33]

If the jury had known certain elements of Susan's life story, their deliberations might have been even shorter. In court they learned only that she drank and through Mrs Young's testimony that she smoked on the tenement stair. Both behaviours, if indulged by women, were frowned upon by the general public. When Mrs Young only recalled whisky and failed to mention cigarette smoke in her first answer, Lord Kinross prompted again, 'Was it a smell of tobacco?' He received the answer he had sought: Mrs Young had smelled tobacco smoke coming from Mrs Newell's room and the admission that she had bought cigarettes for Susan in the past. Whisky may have lowered Susan's inhibitions and impaired her judgement, allowing her to assault John, but smoking did not. All it achieved was further diminishment of

Susan's character, painting a picture of a loose woman, and by identifying her thus, it placed her in the tenement at the correct time.

Although there was much that Lord Kinross could not discuss in court, Professor Glaister and Dr Anderson were able to answer direct questions about their investigation into Susan's background. Lord Kinross asked Anderson, 'Did you find from what class in life Mrs Newell had come from?' Anderson confirmed Susan's poor upbringing and neglected schooling. Then Kinross added, 'Practically of the tinker class?', which Anderson also confirmed. Eventually it was agreed that Susan was not 'of a particularly high moral type either'. Mentioning that Susan came from Oban may have inferred some further delinquency to the jury.[34] None of Susan's previous convictions had any relevance to the case, and because he was not allowed to introduce this material as evidence in court, Kinross's questioning of Mrs Young and Dr Anderson on elements of Susan's way of life may have been an attempt to insinuate that her 'type' was likelier than most to commit unpremeditated, motiveless murder.

Questioning of both civilian and police witnesses also highlighted Susan's coolness when fetching whisky, when discovered with John's body and again in the police office when first questioned. Her cool, calm demeanour did not correspond with societal preconceptions of a murderess's behaviour in the immediate aftermath of the crime, whether by accident or due to temporary insanity. Susan had presented neither as confused nor erratic. Precognition evidence had described her as a rational individual at all stages before the trial. Thus, Lord Kinross confirmed that she did not 'fit' the perceived persona of a confused, bewildered, remorseful and insane woman. Gentles did not attempt to contradict this characterization in his counter-questioning; instead, he followed a line of argument exploring Susan's state of mind at the moment of the crime. However, he did not attempt to connect her drunkenness to a possible lack of responsibility, nor did he show that 'the accused was too drunk to form the intention of doing the act'. It was a difficult test for the jury to apply since a person's capacity for alcohol differs by individual; if *delirium tremens* were present, 'then the tests become the same as for insanity'.[35] Gentles may not have explored this contemporary argument because he did not wish to emphasize Susan's alcohol addiction. However, he pressed Dr Anderson on his understanding of the stresses prompted by misfortune and their 'bearing on the party's self-control and sanity for the time being'. Anderson queried whether such behaviour indicated 'insanity, or temper'. The Lord Justice-Clerk interjected at this point to emphasize Anderson's credentials to the jury and to denigrate Susan's class further: 'have you found them deficient in their appreciation of what is lawful compared with what is unlawful?'

From the news reports, it is unclear whether prosecution or defence counsel made the peremptory challenge to the randomly balloted women on the jury, but Lord Alness upheld the objection, making Susan's case one heard before an all-male jury.[36] Since the Sex Disqualification (Removal) Act 1919, women who qualified for the vote were also eligible as jurors. Research on English juries in the 1920s suggests that juries were predominantly 'male, middle-aged, middle-minded and middle-class' and 'judicial discretion under the 1919 Act' promoted single-sex male juries.[37] However, this was not the case in Scotland with minority female juries appearing in criminal cases, including murder charges, from 1921, suggesting that Susan's trial was unusual.[38] It is possible that either counsel simply did not like the look of the women balloted. However, arguably it was more likely that prosecution counsel objected to the female jurors selected because Lord Kinross knew already that the evidence would exonerate the male accused, leaving only Susan on the stand; there was a presumption that women jurors would sympathize with a woman in Susan's plight. Questioning Susan's eight-year-old daughter Janet could have gone either way: sympathy from women jurors witnessing the family's poverty, or disgust at Susan's supposed coaching of Janet to lie for her. Thus, the few personal details admissible in the Crown's case against Susan had been teased out, repeated and emphasized by prosecution counsel. Similarly, Mr Gentles had done his best, but he was working with very little in Susan's favour except a theoretical argument concerning the nature of temporary insanity and a reduction of the charge to culpable homicide.

Scant details about Susan's background were reported, with the press only giving her address and disclosing her maiden name McAllister and her place of domicile in Oban.[39] The Newells' address in Coatbridge may have denoted the family as poor to newsreaders and the jury, and her dual Irish-Scots maiden surname may have suggested 'tinker' to some long before Dr Anderson used the word in court. But jurors were under oath to consider the court's evidence alone. By all accounts, Susan had committed John's murder while in a passion of anger, confusion or inebriety. She had been described as quarrelsome, as someone who hit her husband and who liked to drink and smoke. She was not a 'good wife' by Scottish standards, and the admissible evidence had gone sufficiently far to denigrate her in the jury's eyes.

After her first husband died in hospital, Susan had met Newell within the month, moved in with him and married him by Autumn 1922. Hughes confirms that many women depended economically on marriage, which, given Susan's dependent young daughter and alcohol addiction, may have necessitated such a quick liaison.[40] Living away from her familial support network, with fines for prostitution on her Oban police record, without grandparents or other carers locally available to look after Janet, Susan was unable to work to support herself. She had descended into multi-dependency on a man, drink and tobacco. Suki Haider's research on early twentieth-century Dundee suggests that 'alcohol was central to prostitute culture'. Women picked up male clients in pubs where they might also take a drink to fortify themselves before the task ahead.[41] Susan had been employed for short periods as a domestic servant, but even as a young girl was 'given to drink and immoral habits'.[42] Louise Settle argues that while some girls descend into prostitution and drink voluntarily, 'it is equally true that innocence, inexperience, poverty, and lack of employment are responsible'.[43] Whether drunkenness leads to prostitution or vice versa, in most cases the two are symbiotic. With four married sisters living in Oban, Susan's singleton lifestyle suggests involuntary behaviour forced by want rather than choice. The sisters may have been unable to support their sibling, leaving her few options. Thus, Susan may have supplemented her income between servant jobs with prostitution, likely among fishermen on Oban's waterfront, before her reputation and drunken behaviour ruled out further domestic employment in respectable households. Susan moved south to Glasgow around late 1910 or early 1911, possibly to avoid tainting the reputation of her wider family.

Susan's alcohol addiction was clearly established as she entered her twenties. As the Procurator Fiscal's investigation confirmed, McLeod and Susan had been ejected from their home in Glasgow in 1917 'on account of her drunken habits'. They moved across the city to Maryhill, but again the neighbours confirmed Susan's 'intemperate habits and quarrelsome' nature. Once living with Newell, their first Coatbridge landlady repeated accusations of drunkenness and Susan taking 'sheets off the bed, pawned them, and spent the proceeds on drink', confirming she had been 'violent when in drink'.[44]

Conclusion

Clearly from a young age, Susan's life had spiralled downwards into petty crime and addiction. What could be adduced in court about her was a collection of bald facts; no one was called to give narrative testimony to her poor start in life. Equally, Susan had never received welfare support to help her out of her predicament. Condemning the 'moral miasma' of Britain's industrial cities of the 1920s, Beatrice Webb recognized that 'morbid alcoholism and sexuality, furtive larceny and unashamed mendacity' had poisoned the working classes; Webb gave the impression that she did not consider their behaviour necessarily their fault.[45]

Susan was guilty of murdering John Johnston, but the Lord Justice-Clerk showed little empathy in his direction to the jury: 'you are concerned not with mercy but with justice. ... Merciful considerations reside elsewhere'.[46] The jury had delivered their verdict of guilty as charged, confirming their rejection of any argument for temporary insanity, but they showed compassion by unanimously recommending Susan to mercy. In a report written a week later for the Home

Office, it was stated that Lord Alness was strongly opposed to mercy and did not consider Susan's 'gipsy blood' as a contributory factor. And since there was no reason to believe that Susan was insane, 'at any rate not of the tangible kind usually regarded as essential' as 'decided by the jury upon evidence', then there was no reason to commence a 'statutory inquiry'.[47] Robert Munro, Lord Alness, was not wrong in his actions; he was a man of his time, a son of the manse, fifty-five years old and part of the legal and political establishment throughout his adult life. Acting for the Crown, Lord Kinross had fulfilled his role as prosecutor working in the public interest. However, in a period which historians acknowledge displayed strong tendencies against capital punishment, especially when female panels were involved, Susan was hanged.

The Redding Road pit disaster did not occur until five days after Susan's sentence was pronounced, allowing sufficient time for a public petition to be raised. Her sentence was reported in the national press, but nothing further happened. No one attempted to appeal her sentence, and requests for a reprieve or stay of execution only came at the last minute. The City of Glasgow's senior magistrate wrote to the Secretary for Scotland, Lord Novak, on 8 October asking, 'is it too late my lord?'[48] On 9 October, telegrams were sent from Bushey in Hertfordshire to Lord Novak begging a reprieve for Susan and 'all other persons now under sentence of death'; another 'urgently crav[ing] for the reprieve of Mrs Newell'.[49]

The lack of empathy shown by the Scottish Office suggests that Susan's sex which might have been expected to count in her favour was negated by her drunken and quarrelsome behaviour. Her gypsy, potentially Irish background may also have been a contributory factor in a period acknowledged as hostile to the Irish or those of Irish descent in Scotland. Susan had transgressed gendered social norms during a period of gender conflict, and perhaps the singular fact adduced in court and reported in the newspapers which dissuaded Glaswegians from raising a petition was Susan's effrontery to appear at John Newell's works demanding money. It was a crime against masculinity, Glasgow's citizenry and a much-favoured little boy.

Susan's trial emphasizes the potential for a lack of societal sympathy when the judicial evidence outweighs the social. Mr Gentles, for her defence, had done his best for the last woman to hang in Scotland, but there was no saving Susan.

Notes

1 M. Pugh, *'We Danced All Night': A Social History of Britain between the Wars* (London, 2008), 16–17.

2   S. Kingsley-Kent, *Making Peace: The Reconstruction of Gender in Interwar Britain* (Chichester, 1993), 111.
3   Pugh, '*We Danced All Night*', 177–8.
4   A. Hughes, 'Working-Class Culture, Family Life and Domestic Violence on Clydeside, c.1918–1939: a view from below', *Scottish Tradition* 27 (2002), 60–76.
5   W. W. Knox, *Industrial Nation: Work, Culture and Society in Scotland, 1800–Present* (Edinburgh, 1999), 190.
6   L. Heren and G. Barclay, *Tanks on the Streets? The Battle of George Square, Glasgow 1919* (Barnsley, 2023), 48–9.
7   C. Hamilton, *Modern Scotland* (London, 1937), 27, 29.
8   Hamilton, *Modern Scotland*, 50–51. Irene Maver's figures suggest 10 per cent of the total population or 446,400 were Irish with 70 per cent of that number focussed in and around the industrial and urban centre of Glasgow; I. Maver, 'The Catholic Community', in *Scotland in the Twentieth Century*, ed. T. M. Devine and R. J. Finlay (Edinburgh, 1996), 271.
9   A. D. Gibb, *Scotland in Eclipse* (Edinburgh, 1930), 54–7.
10 Report of Committee to consider Overtures from the Presbytery of Glasgow and from the Synod of Glasgow and Ayr on "Irish Immigration" and the "Education (Scotland) Act, 1918", 29 May 1923, 750–6.
11 A. Sherwell, *The Drink Peril in Scotland* (Edinburgh 1903), 8, 16, 51.
12 B. Hollander, *The Psychology of Misconduct, Vice and Crime* (London, 1922), 50–64, 80.
13 Hughes, 'Working-Class Culture', 66.
14 M. Strauss, 'Victims and Aggressors in Marital Violence', *American Behavioural Scientist* 23, no. 5 (1980), 684, 691.
15 Newell was alternatively spelled Newall in some reportage.
16 Patrick Balfour, 2nd Baron Kinross; his title was hereditary rather than courtesy.
17 JC36/43.
18 Home Office Memo, HH16/180, 1.
19 'Amazing Scenes in Go-Cart Mystery', *Weekly Record*, 30 June 1923, 8.
20 Compare this nine shillings per week for a family to rent out a single room with Patrick Higgins's lodgings nearly 20 years earlier, which cost ten shillings per week, similarly with meals and laundry included.
21 JC36/43; AD15/23/71.
22 Note A.D. to Lord Advocate, pencilled date 31 July 1913; AD15/23/71.
23 JC36/43.
24 'Coatbridge Murder', *Glasgow Herald*, 20 June 1923.
25 Letter Chief Constable's Office to Under Secretary for Scotland, 30 September 1923, HH16/180.
26 Letter G Steel to Lamb, Scottish Office, 28 September 1923, HH16/180.
27 Home Office Memo, HH16/180.

28 Letter J Lamb to Lord Novak, 4 October 1923, HH16/180.
29 'The Go-Cart Murder', *Glasgow Herald*, 10 October 1923.
30 'No Reprieve!', *Glasgow Herald*, 9 October 1923.
31 'The Coatbridge Murder', *Glasgow Herald*, 11 October 1923.
32 JC36/43, 198.
33 Writing two decades later, Gibb also rejected the concept of diminished responsibility attributable to 'weakness of mind', calling the reduction of the charge from murder to culpable homicide 'a blot on our criminal law'; A. D. Gibb, *A Preface to Scots Law* (Edinburgh, 1944), 97.
34 JC36/43 134.
35 Gibb, *Preface*, 97.
36 'Go-Cart Crime', *Glasgow Herald*, 19 September 1923.
37 K. Crosby, 'Keeping Women off the Jury in 1920s England & Wales', *Legal Studies* (2017), 3.
38 For example, Higgins et al. AD15/21/128, JC14/36; Savage AD15/23/13, JC5/16.
39 'Boy Murdered', *Glasgow Herald*, 22 June 1923, 9; 'Boy's Death', *Glasgow Herald*, 23 June 1923, 9.
40 Hughes, 'Working-Class Culture', 60.
41 S. Haider, 'Female Petty Crime In Dundee, 1865–1925: Alcohol, Prostitution and Recidivism in a Scottish City', University of St Andrews, doctoral thesis (2013), 151.
42 HH16/180.
43 L. Settle, *Sex for Sale in Scotland: Prostitution in Edinburgh and Glasgow 1900–1939* (Edinburgh, 2016), 24.
44 HH16/180.
45 B. Webb, Passfield Papers, 6/84, draft of BBC talk, 21 January 1932, 'The Diseases of the Capitalist System', 5, as quoted in R. Overy, *The Morbid Age: Britain and the Crisis of Civilization, 1919–1939* (London, 2010), 70.
46 JC36/43, 202.
47 Home Office Memorandum, 27 September 1923, HH16/180.
48 Letter John Lyett to Lord Novak, 8 October 1923, HH16/180.
49 Telegrams Bushey to Home Office, 9 October 1923, HH16/180.

11

Robert Handley 1926: Lover, murderer and culpability

Rape-homicide is a rare crime, but what if the murder was accidental and the rape was actually consensual sex? Or if defence counsel could introduce a special defence of insanity, present the panel as sympathetic or persuade the jury to consider a reduction of the charge to culpable homicide? This case explores the possibilities available when the evidence was circumstantial and juries were increasingly reluctant to convict if the only available sentence was capital punishment.

Context

In Scotland, into the 1920s, it was usual for a rape case to be heard 'behind closed doors'; thus, the public and news journalists were not permitted to attend. Any details in the newspapers' court reports were brief, giving few specifics except the panel's name, the charge and location of the crime's commission, the verdict and, if guilty, the sentence. The reason for hearing sexual violence cases 'behind closed doors' was to protect the news readership from prurient detail when it was considered that the case evidence was of 'such a character that its publication is undesirable in the public interest'.[1] Although there was a provision in the Criminal Law Amendment Act, revised in 1922, permitting newspaper reporters to attend such cases, in practice, journalists' presence was in the gift of individual judges.[2] However, such reticence did not prevent perceptions taking hold that post-war society had become more violent and that young women were especially at risk of sexual violence.

Writing in 1920, war journalist and social commentator Philip Gibbs noted that 'The many murders of young women, the outrages upon little girls, the violent robberies that have happened since the demobilizing of the armies' had appalled upright citizens; it had become an epidemic 'after a period when there was less crime than usual'.[3] Commentators like Gibbs dealt in perceptions, not statistics. The five-year average in 1914 for individuals charged in Scotland for crimes against the person was 4,427; the report for 1925 totalled 2,642, with the highest post-war count of 3,201 occurring in 1921. The number of rape cases prosecuted had fluctuated from eighteen in 1914 to thirteen in 1925, with a high point of twenty-six in 1922. Thus, the reality was that serious offences, especially rape, had not increased after the war, although lesser sexual offences such as indecent assault and the indictment of lewd and libidinous practices had.[4] Thus, no matter how exceptional the reporting of serious sexual violence in the newspapers, the pervasive notion that society had become more violent in the post-war era persisted.

However, in this case, the 'Paisley Picnic's Tragic Ending' meant that the charge of murder was of more importance than the charge of rape. The accused, twenty-two-year-old Robert Handley, was indicted on both charges. Thus, this very rare case of rape-murder was heard in an open court. If found guilty of murder, Handley could only avoid capital punishment by a successful appeal to His Majesty for clemency and a reprieve.

Case

On 21 or in the early hours of 22 July 1926, Robert Handley attended a 'summer evening picnic arranged by a number of the younger members of the staff' of Dykebar Mental Hospital where Handley was an attendant and his victim, Euphemia Bryden, was a nurse.[5] The news reporter described Handley as 'a good looking young man in the early twenties, with clean-cut features'. He was well dressed for his court appearance and 'appeared calm and self-possessed' as he sat down in front of a jury of eight men and seven women. Among them were variously a drapery buyer, teacher, ladies' tailor and grocer; of the female jurors, only one was unmarried and a music teacher.[6] Lord Ormidale heard the case, and Handley was represented by Mr Craigie Aitchison K.C. He was charged with two indictments: that he had ravished Euphemia, injuring her sufficiently, that she had 'sustained severe injuries and shock that she died in consequence thereof'.[7] To secure a conviction, the Crown had only to prove guilt on one charge, but for his client to be acquitted, Aitchison would have to disprove all of the Crown's case, or at best call evidence that would convince the jury to return a guilty verdict on a reduced charge.

Giving evidence for the prosecution, Nurse Scouller described how they had arranged the picnic for Wednesday evening with nine nurses and eight male attendants who had been given special leave of absence until midnight. Handley and another attendant arrived slightly after the party had started at 8.30 pm bringing a bottle of whisky with them. Scouller was clear that neither of them 'were under the influence of drink', indicating that Handley was sober, and Lord Ormidale enquired about the size of the whisky bottle, which Scouller confirmed was 'a small bottle'. She added that Euphemia and Handley had 'been keeping company for some weeks' but had recently had 'a difference'. When Scouller last saw the two of them, they were 'walking arm in arm' as the whole party made its way back to the hospital. She considered Handley to be 'kindly and gentle in manner'. About 1.00 am, Handley entered Alexander M'Lean's room in the attendants' hostel. M'Lean saw blood on Handley's shirt front which he explained to M'Lean was from a nose bleed. Handley asked M'Lean for a loan of £1 which he was happy to give because previous loans had been repaid. Handley told M'Lean that Euphemia had 'gone into Barrhead' which seemed strange because M'Lean thought she was meant to be on duty the following morning, and it was now 2.15 am. Handley left, then returned to M'Lean's room five hours later to borrow a hat.

In court, M'Lean described how Handley had been working with a 'very bad suicidal patient' for a month, keeping long hours on duty from 6.30 am to 8.00 pm with few breaks. He confirmed he had heard Handley was drinking heavily because of the strain but had not witnessed it. Other witnesses confirmed that Handley had appeared to act normally the following morning as he went on duty. Louis McAuley gave evidence that he had warned Handley to stop drinking so heavily and had had to assist him to bed after a day at the races. Lord Ormidale interjected to ask if the witness had ever seen anything to suggest Handley 'was in any way mentally wrong'. McAuley replied, 'Nothing whatever'. Another witness confirmed that Handley had never displayed any 'violence or loss of temper' and that he was 'a good attendant'. Handley had been engaged as an attendant aged seventeen, which his defence counsel remarked upon, possibly hoping to characterize Handley as an exceptional young man.

Nurse Euphemia Bryden had last been seen alive at the 'white gates', the main entrance to the institution, but was found dead the following morning covered by her own coat in some bushes; her jumper had been used to cover her head, and one sleeve was 'still clinging at the wrist'. Euphemia's head and face were covered in blood, her hair matted with it, there were cuts to her forehead, and her 'nose was split'. She had suffered other bruises and cuts, and her 'clothing was much disarranged' and 'all blood-stained'. Nearby grass 'was saturated with blood', and a 'sharp stone was protruding slightly above the grass', sufficient to have caused a fracture to her skull. Forensic medical examination confirmed that Euphemia had been 'outraged' with 'unmistakable evidence that until then the girl was a virgin'.[8] The accused's clothing in his room was also bloodstained. The investigating officer of the Renfrewshire Constabulary quickly circulated a description of Handley across the entire country. Handley handed himself in at Ayr on Friday, 23 July.

In court, Handley pleaded not guilty and entered a special defence of insanity or to be 'in such a condition of mental abnormality as not to be fully responsible for his actions at the time of the crime'.[9] In correspondence between the Procurator Fiscal and the Solicitor General before the trial, it was suggested that the Advocate Depute had anticipated defence counsel would 'go for mental abnormality in the hope of reducing the charge to culpable homicide', a 'modern plea' which the Procurator Fiscal considered had 'not been made a special plea'. He also anticipated the defence might 'cite sadism'.[10] Handley had been examined while on remand in Greenock prison by Dr Thomas Tennent who considered that he displayed no signs of abnormality. He had cooperated freely, giving Dr Henderson the impression he was sane. Handley admitted he had been drinking but was never 'unfit for duty', although he confessed that he had always been 'of a sensitive disposition' and alcohol raised 'a sort of madness in him', prompting 'queer thoughts of a homicidal nature'. Dr Henderson testified that Handley was fit to plead because he had been 'unable to elicit any facts' to support him having been 'in a state of mental abnormality' at the time of the crime or since. In cross-examination, Mr Aitchison attempted to link the mental illness of two of his cousins to Handley to which Henderson replied, 'I do not think we know enough about collateral relationship and insanity', although he acknowledged hereditary mental illness from parents was a medically accepted diagnosis. Dr Henderson agreed with the prosecution that being an attendant from the age of seventeen was unusual, but he had never seen evidence of attendants becoming mentally ill because of their 'association with mental patients'. He attributed Handley's behaviour to 'sexual passion present in a strong degree and inflamed by drink'. Two further doctors confirmed the absence of long-term or temporary mental illness.[11]

Handley's defence began on the third day of the trial. Witnesses were brought who confirmed that Handley suffered 'fits of abstraction', 'deeper than day-dreaming', and Edinburgh University's lecturer in psychiatry, Dr M'Allister, refuted Henderson's opinion and stated that he believed a cousin with mental illness was an important factor to consider when diagnosing Handley; it was 'evidence of tainted stock'. He confirmed that 'when the act was committed he [Handley] was insane and irresponsible'. He added that he 'suspected the presence of sadistic tendencies' and that Handley may well have committed the crime even without the influence of alcohol. Another psychiatric expert attested that it was 'a short step from a homicidal thought to a homicidal obsession', escalating 'to homicidal impulse'. This witness considered Handley to be someone who could be 'insane from time to time'. When Lord Ormidale asked if Handley was fit to plead to a capital charge, this expert did not think he was.[12]

On the last day of the trial in his address to the jury, the Advocate Depute determined that the presence of the stone in the grass which was thought to have killed Euphemia could not have been known to Handley, thus making this case 'a fatal accident'. He criticized the defence for not suggesting that without the stone, this would have only been a prosecution for rape. On the special defence of insanity, the Advocate Depute did not feel that Handley had been 'fully insane'. However, if the jury considered that there had been mental disease, then they might return a verdict on culpable homicide, instead of murder. For the defence, Mr Aitchison explained for the last time that in Scots Law, 'no man could be responsible if he were not a sane man at the time the crime was committed'; if the jury considered Handley not to be insane but to have 'something wrong with him', then 'they were entitled to say he was guilty of culpable homicide' only. Aitchison considered Handley's acts as those 'of a madman' suffering from 'mental unsoundness'. Lord Ormidale explained further that according to the defence, the rape had not been the 'ultimate object' and that the defence wished the jury to understand Handley's behaviour to be sadistic, thus indicating insanity. The jury retired briefly and returned a verdict of unanimously guilty of rape and culpable homicide. Lord Ormidale expressed his opinion that it 'was a merciful view' before imposing a sentence of fifteen years' penal servitude.[13]

Themes and analysis

From the press reporting, it is apparent that the details of the rape were secondary compared to the facts of the murder. As the Advocate Depute suggested, if Euphemia had not been killed, probably, by hitting her head on the unfortunately placed stone in the grass, Handley would have only faced a rape charge, which would have attracted little press attention. However, the journalist also hinted at societal attitudes towards unchaperoned young women, and the evidence he heard in court had suggested the character of an innocent and virginal young woman. Handley was also portrayed favourably, with defence counsel asking the jury to consider Handley's mental state in connection with sadism, stress and alcohol. Similar to Margaret's rape-murder in 1830, this case allows examination of societal attitudes towards courtship and female victims of sexual crime, the 'character' of both the victim and the panel. But one hundred years on, aspects of diminished responsibility in Scots Law were considered: was Handley insane or under the influence of alcohol?

On the first day in court, Euphemia's mother was called to give evidence. She described Euphemia as 'a healthy girl of good character'. Mrs Bryden was noted as a widow whose 'husband was killed in the war'.[14] The inclusion of Euphemia's father's war service and sacrifice, alongside her own 'character', is interesting. It suggests that war service remained notable seven years post-Armistice, which the Advocate Depute used possibly to curry sympathy for the widow now also grieving her daughter. This might persuade the jury towards a verdict of murder, particularly when combined with the information that Euphemia was a virgin prior to the rape. Euphemia's good character was supported by her colleague, Nurse Scouller's comments. With Euphemia unable to give evidence herself, which would have given the jury an opportunity to appraise her appearance, painting a favourable character for the deceased was essential. The middle-class jury might consider a girl prepared to attend a party and leave unchaperoned in the company of a young man as non-compliant with accepted ideals of feminine behaviour; being unchaperoned could signal availability.[15] As Julia Laite comments, early twentieth-century society 'fetishized virginity' and a young woman who was not a virgin might be culpable, to a degree, in her own demise.[16] However, since working-class women were rarely chaperoned and Euphemia was unable to speak for herself, the Advocate Depute created the best innocent character for her.

Obversely, Handley was physically present for the jury and journalists to observe. The reporter provided a favourable description of a nervous young man in a decent suit trying his best to remain calm.[17] His defence would later describe an individual intermittently susceptible to insanity, yet Handley's appearance remained critical to the outcome of his case: a dishevelled, skulking man might have supported the 'type' attributed to a working-class rapist and drunkard, whereas a cleanly dressed, anxious young man who had supported himself in a difficult job since his teens painted a different picture. It suggested to the jury that they were judging a member of the respectable working class.

The jury comprised eight men, all of whom were employed in non-manual trades or owned their businesses, thus not working-class, while six of the female jurors were married, and the seventh was an unmarried teacher. To qualify for jury service in this period, the individual had to be a man over twenty-one or a woman over thirty years who also met a minimum property qualification.[18] As jurors, they were required to set aside class biases and judge their fellow men on the merits of the evidence presented in court. However, none of the evidence provided by witnesses and colleagues was eyewitness testimony. No one actually saw what transpired between Euphemia and Robert after they left the picnic, and it appears that much of the circumstantial evidence was contradictory. Some commented on Robert's drinking and his mental instability, while others did not think he was drinking too heavily or that his role was taking a toll on his mental health. Not even the medical experts agreed on Robert's mental state.

The evidence for rape was provided by a medical examination of Euphemia's body conducted by Professor John Glaister, the University of Glasgow's pre-eminent forensic physician. The court journalist noted that Glaister 'described the results of' blood tests but did not comment on any analysis of semen samples. In this period, forensic examination of blood could only confirm that it was mammalian, and analysis of semen was able to confirm that it belonged to a human, but not which one. Thus, proximity to the crime might be used to confirm that a semen sample was attributable to the panel: a 'it must be him' deduction. However, in 1926, the law stated that a charge of rape did not require emission of semen as proof of penetration; in fact, only partial penetration might support a rape charge and 'the usual signs of virginity' might not be interfered with. However, if other physical signs of rape were evident, the presence of semen was considered 'unequivocal evidence of their cause'.[19] In the 1920s, of all rape cases prosecuted in Scotland, only 31 per cent included a forensic medical report; the majority relied solely on the report supplied by the most immediate examination conducted by a general practitioner without laboratory tests.[20] Thus, evidence for rape was as reliable as could be expected, but this was primarily a murder case and finding significant quantities of blood on the body and on Handley's clothing suggested a single source – Euphemia – and a single perpetrator of both rape and murder.

Evidence of 'several abrasions' on Euphemia's throat was adduced, but there was no suggestion that she had been throttled pre- or post-rape. All the evidence indicated her death was caused by her head injuries. Despite prosecution counsel acknowledging the injury to Euphemia's skull most likely caused by the protruding stone in the grass, in common law, the 'thin skull rule' – or 'eggshell skull rule' – applied. No one in court suggested that Handley had purposely and premeditatively killed Euphemia by smashing her head against the stone, despite the charge of murder. Yet, irrespective of the condition of Euphemia's skull before her death, whether it was unnaturally fragile or not, and whether the stone actually caused her spontaneous death or whether blood loss as a result of the head wound had killed her, Handley remained criminally liable for her death – he took his victim as he found her.[21] Since no one questioned this common law argument in Handley's case, it appears that it was accepted by both counsel. Thus, to convince the jury of his guilt, the Crown now had to prove that Handley had been cognizant of his actions at the point Euphemia was raped and murdered.

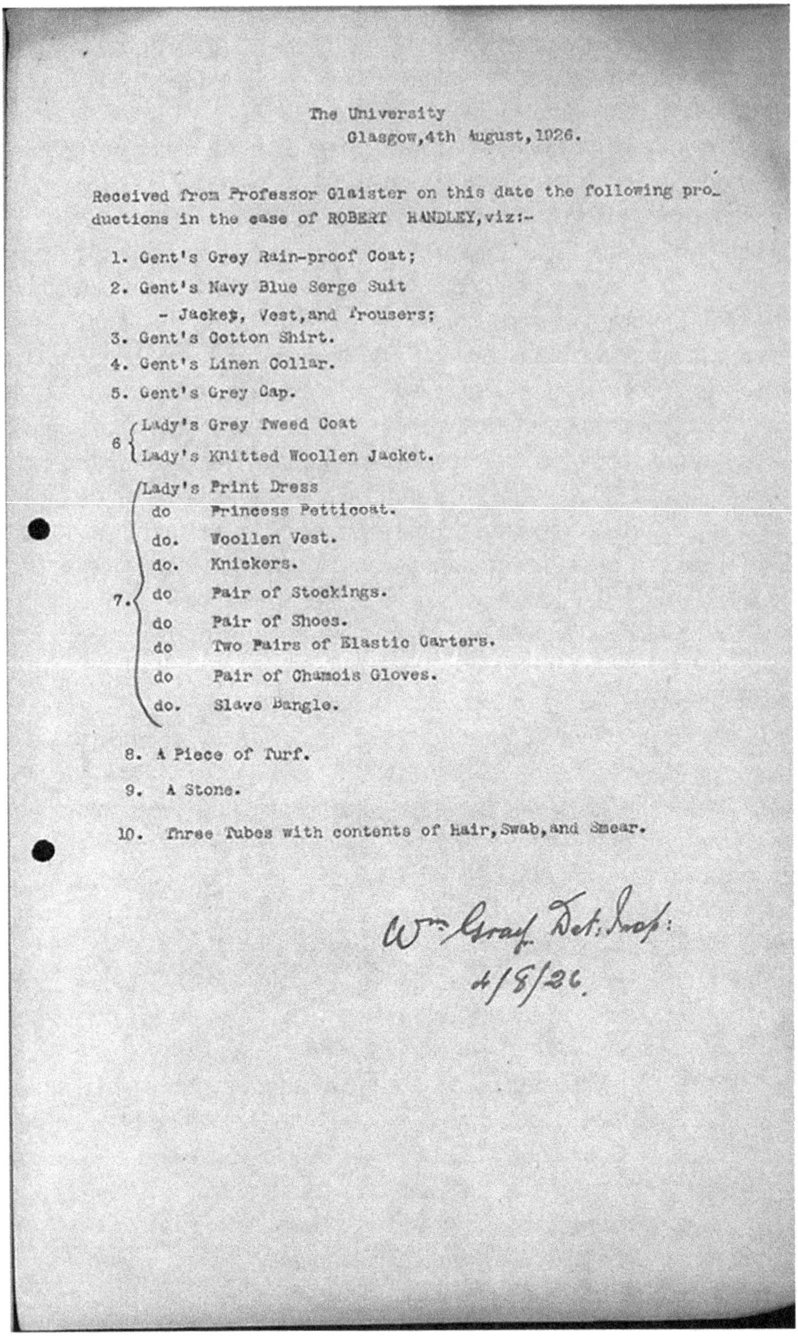

```
                                The University
                                Glasgow, 4th August, 1926.

Received from Professor Glaister on this date the following pro-
ductions in the case of ROBERT HANDLEY, viz:-

    1. Gent's Grey Rain-proof Coat;
    2. Gent's Navy Blue Serge Suit
        - Jacket, Vest, and Trousers;
    3. Gent's Cotton Shirt.
    4. Gent's Linen Collar.
    5. Gent's Grey Cap.
       ⎧ Lady's Grey Tweed Coat
    6 ⎨
       ⎩ Lady's Knitted Woollen Jacket.
       ⎧ Lady's Print Dress
       ⎪   do    Princess Petticoat.
       ⎪   do.   Woollen Vest.
       ⎪   do.   Knickers.
    7. ⎨  do    Pair of Stockings.
       ⎪   do    Pair of Shoes.
       ⎪   do    Two Pairs of Elastic Garters.
       ⎪   do    Pair of Chamois Gloves.
       ⎩   do.   Slave Bangle.

    8. A Piece of Turf.
    9. A Stone.
   10. Three Tubes with contents of Hair, Swab, and Smear.

                              W^m Gray Det. Insp:
                              4/8/26.
```

ILLUSTRATION 11.1 *List of Forensic Evidence Productions at the trial of Robert Handley. Courtesy of University of Glasgow Archives and Special Collections ref: FM/2B/19.*

Witnesses for both prosecution and defence testified to Handley having been drinking on the night of the crime, although Nurse Scouller did not think he had drunk sufficient to be intoxicated. Whereas his colleague MacAuley had 'advised Handley two or three weeks before the picnic to stop drinking' because he thought he was 'taking too much'.[22] Handley himself had admitted to his doctor he had been drinking more recently, although not sufficient to interfere with his work, yet he also confessed that 'drink seemed to raise a sort of madness', leading to 'queer thoughts of a homicidal nature'.[23] The common law was clear on the influence of alcohol on a panel's state of mind and his culpability in a crime: 'mere drunkenness cannot be pleaded as an excuse for crime', but 'if a state of mental unsoundness' resulted from inebriation, that could be argued as mitigation, the test being whether the panel could be proved to be insane or not.[24] If Handley had been inebriated at the time of Euphemia's death, that alone was not allowed in law since 'anomalous states of mind resulting from extrinsic causes' such as alcohol did not constitute insanity. However, in 1881, Lord Deas had allowed that 'if drink produced insanity for however short a time, and the man did certain things while insane that there was no reason to think he would do while sane, that was quite enough'. Other judges in the late nineteenth century also directed that intoxication was the individual's responsibility, but it might mean that the accused was 'not necessarily guilty of murder'.[25]

Psychiatrists of the period acknowledged that alcohol reduced 'social inhibitions', which might result in a man acting out his 'natural role of woman-hunter'.[26] However, in rape-only cases involving adult women during the 1920s heard at the High Court of Justiciary, the mitigation of inebriation was not attempted as a defence; Handley's case lies among this sample.[27] This suggests that the Scottish judiciary took a hard line on abuse of alcohol, not allowing inebriation as a special defence of insanity in rape trials. Thus, if Handley's history of alcohol use to dull the disquiet caused by his asylum job or potential excess on the night of the picnic were to be employed as mitigation, it was unlikely to be successful. Except in this instance, Handley was also on trial for his life, and the judge had to ensure the jury was given every opportunity to assess his state of mind at the time of commission of the alleged murder: was Handley suffering from diminished responsibility temporarily or long term? From a condition that would induce him to commit acts there was no reason to believe he would consider when sane?

Thus, the mitigating factor that might win Handley a reprieve would be the jury's understanding of his sanity on the night he was seen departing the picnic alone with Euphemia. If they believed the evidence for insanity posed by defence counsel, the jury had two options. First, to return a guilty verdict that might be accompanied by a recommendation to mercy, which would rely on the Crown's intervention to reduce a capital execution to indefinite incarceration at His Majesty's pleasure. Or second, a reduction in the indictment to culpable homicide, thus also avoiding the death penalty to be replaced by a sentence of imprisonment at the judge's discretion. This second option might also disguise the jury's reluctance to condemn a man to death even if they believed he had committed rape and murder.

Nurse Scouller's evidence for the prosecution stated that she had seen Handley drinking but not sufficiently to become inebriated and be senseless to his actions. Alexander M'Lean who chatted with Handley during the night did not notice anything 'strange about his manner', while the asylum's gardener said 'there was nothing to suggest any anxiety or nervousness about him' when he woke Handley the next morning. A further attendant who had consumed 'two half-glasses of special and two small bottles of beer' with Handley before sharing the cost of a 'half-bottle of whisky' confirmed to the judge that he had never witnessed anything mentally wrong with Handley.[28] Prosecution counsel had built a case of no mental abnormality either in general or caused temporarily by inebriation. Equally, the Crown had not established whether anyone considered Handley might behave so brutally in general.

For the defence, Mr Aitchison had clearly advised Handley to enter a plea of not guilty and a special defence of insanity at the time of the crime 'or in such a condition of mental abnormality as not to be fully responsible for his actions'.[29] To present Handley as sympathetic, first, Aitchison introduced evidence implying that Handley had suffered long-term mental disturbance as a result of his excessive drinking; he linked this to Handley also having commenced his role as an asylum attendant at a young age. When asked by Aitchison whether he had 'ever known of a boy of seventeen being taken on as an asylum attendant', the asylum's charge attendant gave the simple reply 'No'.[30] The implication was that carrying out such a stressful job had been affecting Handley's mental well-being for a long time. Aitchison might also be able to introduce a further element to the insanity defence: a suggestion of sadism that had already been anticipated in Crown pretrial correspondence. If Handley had raped Euphemia followed by murder, that indicated he was a sexually violent criminal, whereas if he had murdered her followed by rape, that was manifest evidence of mental abnormality. Handley's family's mental health had already been called into question by Aitchison and rejected by Dr Henderson, but Dr M'Allister had considered hereditary mental illness a possibility. Defence counsel had done the best he could to insinuate the idea into the minds of the jury.

Whether the stone had killed Euphemia or Handley had done so with intent, he was still on trial for murder. The special defence was one of diminished responsibility, and if successful, the jury could return a verdict on the lesser indictment of culpable homicide because the judiciary could not execute a man who was not responsible for his actions. Insanity was a common law concept in this period, 'described but not defined', thus leaving the plea to a jury's discretion and sense of justice.[31] If the special defence were unsuccessful, a guilty verdict for murder would indicate that the jury did not believe Handley was insane either long term or at the time of the crime. Logically, if guilty of murder, they might also convict on the rape charge because rape followed by murder looked like the latter was perpetrated to hide the former. Consequently, the jury would have been unlikely to recommend mercy. However, the legal concept of *mens rea* – intent to harm – plays a crucial role here. If Handley had murdered with intent, then he was blameworthy. Yet if he had murdered with intent but was proved to be insane, then his degree of blameworthiness would be reflected in the lesser charge of culpable homicide while still signalling the gravity of his crime.[32] In this instance, a conviction on the rape charge, while still pertinent to the trial, would become irrelevant to the sentence.

In a 1923 case of murder committed by a fifty-year-old pedlar under the influence of methylated spirits, the examining physician declared him 'fully responsible for his actions', despite exculpatory witnesses testifying to how badly alcohol affected him and one witness who had known him for thirty years testified that 'he was never right in the head' and had a 'queer appearance when sober'.[33] The Lord Justice-Clerk, Lord Alness, had directed the jury that 'there must be aberration or weakness of mind' and if this did not amount to insanity, then the panel's mind must 'be so affected that responsibility is diminished ... to partial responsibility'.[34] A jury of eleven men, again all tradesmen, and four women found him unanimously guilty after thirty-five minutes' deliberation. In this case, an itinerant older man, without a 'respectable' history of employment in service to the community, had cut a woman's throat with a razor, and in court his special defence of insanity had proved unsuccessful. There was no recommendation for mercy from the jury, nor a petition raised by Edinburgh's citizens for clemency: neither jury nor citizenry considered him worthy of reprieve.

However, in Handley's case, the jury's verdict of guilty of rape and culpable homicide, not murder, suggests two possible courses. The defence evidence had not proved that Handley was so inebriated at the time of the rape-murder that he was so insensible of his actions he had unwittingly raped and killed Euphemia. In fact, the uninhibiting effects of alcohol in regard to the rape charge may have counted very much against him as a young man wilfully displaying his masculinity through sexual violence. Thus, either Aitchison had managed to persuade the jury that Handley had been insane because of the stresses of his job, possibly combined with hereditary illness, or the jury had shown compassion by reducing the charge to culpable homicide. Were they reluctant to see the death penalty carried out against a young man?

Compassion in this area of Scots Law had been argued since Lord Deas' direction in *Dingwall* in 1867 in a case involving an unpremeditated attack by the panel on his wife with a knife while suffering a fit of *delirium tremens*. Deas had asked the jury to consider whether there had been 'extenuating circumstances' which would place Dingwall's actions at the culpable homicide end of the scale of murderous behaviour.[35] Earlier cases had displayed similar compassion for panels facing the death penalty who pleaded the special defence of insanity.[36] In the nineteenth century, the Scottish judiciary had asked jurors to consider where on the scale an individual's responsibility might be placed if they suffered mental illness or had been so drunk they had lost all reason. However, by the early twentieth century, there was increasing fear that a plea of diminished responsibility would 'lead to many murderers escaping their just desserts'. Later, this would be described as 'the danger that unverified hypotheses of individual psychiatrists might lead to abuse of the defence of diminished responsibility' as forensic medical research into psychiatric disorders expanded.[37]

The conflicting expert evidence concerning Handley's state of mind was left to the jury to decipher. Although Professor Glaister's forensic medical skills remained insufficiently advanced to determine whether the rape had been committed pre- or postmortem, the insinuation of sadism might have decided the jury. This was the only rape-murder case tried at the High Court of Justiciary since at least 1900, and probably since Margaret Paterson's rape-murder in 1830. Other rape-only cases of the 1920s suggest that the influence of alcohol was not considered a mitigating factor.[38] And the jury had unanimously agreed that Handley had raped Euphemia. But the murder charge put Handley's life in danger, and it would be on the jurors' consciences if they convicted him. He had no previous convictions of any kind and had remained in employment, in a caring role, for some years. Was he really such a threat to society that he should hang?

Conclusion

What was not considered at trial was the possibility that the incident had been a matter of over enthusiastic courtship sex which had ended in a fatal accident. Handley may not have intended to commit either crime. His irregular behaviour in the early hours of the morning may have been provoked by the derangement of fear. That this scenario was not proposed speaks volumes about judicial investigations and social attitudes towards working-class everyday sexual relations and criminality. Euphemia was dead, and there had been only one person with her at the time, making a guilty verdict for rape-only and acquittal for murder impossible. Consensual sex that had gone wrong when Euphemia's head hit the stone was not only inconceivable, it was also unprovable by medical science in this period.

However, the jury's verdict and request for clemency suggest, that in other respects, societal attitudes were changing. The medical opinions presented in court had been inconclusive and conflicting, which was insufficient grounds to condemn a man to death. If the jury had found Handley guilty of both charges but recommended him to mercy, there was the risk that the rape conviction would dissuade the Crown of his merit for a reprieve. Thus, the inconclusive medical evidence combined with Handley's social usefulness as an asylum attendant and his good reputation resulted in the jury's compassion. Yet among the jury's unanimous verdict, any division between those in favour of insanity and those simply wishing to avoid responsibility for judicial murder is occluded.

As the contemporary social commentators indicated, post-Great War society was fearful of perceived increases in violent crime, and juries remained uncertain of the new forensic medical opinions, while attitudes towards newly enfranchised female jurors supposed they might be harsher on drunk rapists in an attempt to clean up the streets. However, the jury was unanimous that Handley had not committed murder with intent, yet their compassion was not reflected in the judge's sentence of fifteen years' imprisonment with penal servitude. It had not been a brutal rape with attendant life-threatening injuries, except the injury to Euphemia's skull, and men in the 1920s had received shorter sentences for worse sexual violence. Buchan argues that in the nineteenth century, increasingly 'a finding of diminished responsibility' was considered as 'an expression of compassion', it was 'not only a just but a humane verdict'. But in the early twentieth century, as the concept 'crystallized', it muddied the established demarcation between 'responsibility and non-responsibility'.[39] In Susan Newell's case three years earlier, Lord Alness had similarly directed the jury. Later, Sir Gerald Gordon K.C., when Professor of Scots Law at the University of Edinburgh, considered the twentieth century showed 'an increasing distrust of the concept of diminished responsibility'. Not only might murderers escape hanging, but judicial fear of 'new-fangled notions with strange names' and psychiatrists explaining them might altogether destroy the doctrine of diminished responsibility.[40]

But the 1920s was a pivotal decade in Scottish society. Not only had an appellate court been established, but the support for capital punishment among newly enfranchised jurors and the general population was waning. In 1923, Susan Newell may not have benefited, but Handley's case suggests that where the individual's character was sympathetic, attitudes were warming. Post-war Scottish society was changing the social order from the bottom up.

Notes

1. *Scots Law Times*, 23 May 1908, 15.
2. M. A. Crowther and B. White, *On Soul and Conscience: the medical expert and crime, 150 years of forensic medicine in Glasgow* (Aberdeen, 1988), 51.
3. P. Gibbs, *Now it can be told* (London, 1920), facsimile edition 2015, 167.
4. Criminal Statistics: statistics relating to police apprehensions, criminal proceedings, and Reformatory and Industrial Schools, for the year 1925 (Edinburgh, 1928), 17, 20.
5. *Glasgow Herald*, 19 October 1926, 5.
6. JC13/137.
7. AD15/26/81.
8. AD15/26/81, medical report; 'Picnic Tragedy', *Glasgow Herald*, 20 October 1926, 7.
9. JC15/37.
10. AD15/26/81, Procurator Fiscal's report to Solicitor General, 18 October 1926. 'Abnormality' was a different approach to an insanity defence from Susan Newell's counsel where Mr Gentles had tried to prove temporary insanity in the moment of committing the crime due to external stresses, rather than an ongoing debilitation affecting Handley's behaviour.
11. *Glasgow Herald*, 20 October 1926, 7.
12. *Glasgow Herald*, 21 October 1926, 3.
13. *Glasgow Herald*, 22 October 1926, 7; JC13/137.
14. *Glasgow Herald*, 19 October 1926, 5.
15. S. S. M. Edwards, 'Provoking Her Own Demise: from common assault to homicide', in *Women, Violence and Social Control*, ed. J. Hanmer and M. Maynard (London, 1987), 153.
16. J. Laite, *The Disappearance of Lydia Harvey: A True Story of Sex, Crime and the Meaning of Justice* (London, 2022), 127.
17. *Glasgow Herald*, 19 October 1926, 5.
18. Representation of the People Act 1918, Parliamentary Archives, HL/PO/PU/1/1918/7&8G5c64.
19. J. Glaister, *A Text-Book of Medical Jurisprudence and Toxicology* (Edinburgh, 1915), 480, 486.
20. L. Heren, *Sex and Violence in 1920s Scotland: Incest, Rape, Lewd and Libidinous Practices, 1918–1930* (London, 2023), 178.
21. 'Eggshell skull rule', *Oxford Reference*, https://www.oxfordreference.com/display/10.1093/oi/authority.20110810104823582 (accessed February 2024).
22. *Glasgow Herald*, 19 October 1926, 3.
23. *Glasgow Herald*, 20 October 1926, 7.

24 R. S. Shiels, 'The uncertain medical origins of diminished responsibility', *Journal of Criminal Law* 76, no. 6 (2014), 467; Glaister, *Medical Jurisprudence*, 587.
25 A. M. Anderson, *The Criminal Law of Scotland* (Edinburgh, 1892), 4–5; Glaister, *Medical Jurisprudence*, 587.
26 B. Hollander, *The Psychology of Misconduct, Vice and Crime* (London, 1922), 129.
27 Heren, *Sex and Violence*, 147.
28 *Glasgow Herald*, 19 October 1926, 5.
29 JC15/37.
30 *Glasgow Herald*, 19 October 1926, 5.
31 T. B. Smith, *A Short Commentary on the Law of Scotland* (Edinburgh, 1962), 159; D. Buchan, 'Diminished Responsibility and the Scottish Law Tradition', LLB thesis, University of Glasgow (2022), 73.
32 Buchan, 'Diminished Responsibility', 18.
33 AD15/23/13.
34 JC36/41; *Edinburgh Evening News*, 21 May 1923. This case was tried by the same judge as that presiding at Susan Newell's trial.
35 Buchan, *Diminished Responsibility*, 54–5.
36 See *Sommerville* 1704.
37 G. H. Gordon, *The Criminal Law of Scotland*, 2nd edition (Edinburgh, 1978), para.11.18; Smith, *Short Commentary*, 160.
38 Heren, *Sex and Violence*, 27.
39 Buchan, *Diminished Responsibility*, 67.
40 G. H. Gordon, *The Criminal Law of Scotland*, 2nd edition (Edinburgh, 1978), para 11–18.

12

Thomas Lutton 1928: Stepfather, rapist and the law

Even before it was made illegal in statute law in 1567, incest has always carried a moral taboo, yet some perpetrators have gone to extraordinary lengths and convoluted legal arguments to avoid conviction. In this case, the panel's behaviour strongly suggests his cognizance of incest law, age of consent legislation and sentencing practices. This twentieth-century incest case also allows exploration of Scottish society's attitudes towards female minors: if they could summon the strength to report abuse, provide sufficiently compelling evidence to reach court, would a jury believe the word of teenage twins against that of their stepfather?

Context

Forty years after the Criminal Law Amendment Act 1885 – Parliament's response to the fear of the 'white slave' trafficking trade brought to the notice of the British public by journalist W. T. Stead – the position of women and girls in British society had not improved. Julia Laite describes 'white slavery' as 'a fear fashioned by crusading journalists and anti-vice campaigners', which effectively kept young women and girls in their traditional place in society, while ostensibly aiming to protect them.[1] There had been an increase in the number of prosecutions under the new statute in the years immediately succeeding the Act. However, as Laite explains, the number of convictions remained miserably low and the 'sheer magnitude of these offences', whether their number was officially or unofficially captured, reveals the 'quotidian nature of sexual assault and rape'.[2] By highlighting the 'white slave' traffic, Stead had diverted the focus of sexual abuse away from the domestic sphere and placed it beyond national boundaries; it had become an international concern of white English-speaking countries.[3] Yet, at the end of the nineteenth and beginning of the twentieth centuries, welfare officers had been primarily concerned with the amount of abuse occurring behind family front doors. They were unable to quantify it, but like those searching for white slave traffickers, they were alarmed by the evidence they discovered and the implications of wider abuse.

In 1925, the government formed a committee of lawyers and doctors to investigate and report on sexual offences in Scotland. They discovered that Glasgow, Edinburgh and Aberdeen were the main loci of sexual crimes; sexual offences were 'far more numerous than is generally supposed', and a medical witness to the report confirmed that 'mild' sexual offences which were not reported to the police were 'an extremely common thing'. He testified from personal experience that many parents declined to report sexual assaults because they were 'apt to shrink from the publicity' of an investigation and trial, while others regarded such occurrences as 'part of the normal risks of life'.[4] It appears that sexual assault was an everyday event for some – possibly many – girls and young women in Scottish cities at the turn of the century. Sexual abuse was endemic and largely beyond the powers of the police or welfare officers to prevent as Thomas Lutton's case proves.

The Criminal Law Amendment Act 1885, and its 1922 revisions, had maintained an important distinction dependent on the age of the victim: for girls twelve years and under, a conviction under the statute was a felony and attracted a sentence of penal servitude at the discretion of the judge, whereas for girls thirteen years and over, a guilty verdict was a misdemeanour, and sentencing should not exceed two years' imprisonment.[5] The committee recommended raising the age limit of section 4 of the Act to fourteen years, which would place more perpetrators of sexual violence against children within the parameters of a felony rather than a misdemeanour, thereby attracting a lengthier sentence if convicted. This change aligned more with the medical opinion that girls in Scotland rarely attained 'the age of puberty before the age of 14', and even if in some cases puberty had begun earlier, the change to the Act would provide girls with 'the maximum protection from sex experience'.[6]

Of the range of sexual assaults children and girls might experience, incest and rape were the most serious. Incestuous assault – carnal intercourse between near relations as described in Leviticus 18 – particularly exercised welfare officers because it occurred within the family domain where they could not pry.[7] Attitudes towards proprietorial men held that 'once their daughters reach the age of consent', they became 'legitimate sexual targets'.[8] This was of huge concern, especially if mothers were unwilling to report husbands for abuse of their children for fear of retribution as well as fear of losing the family breadwinner to prison. Ultimately, even if convicted, a father 'owned' his children and could not be 'divested of his rights over his child'.[9] However, power over children until they reached the age of majority, and a child's lack of agency in the home and wider society, did not always remove the prospect of a complaint of incest or rape if the victim of familial sexual abuse could summon the courage to seek help.

Case

In late summer 1928, the school headmistress noticed that a set of thirteen-year-old twins were not themselves.[10] One in particular – 'always a bad tempered girl' – was becoming even more so. A neighbour to the family had informed the headmistress that their father 'had been interfering with them'. She decided to keep an eye on them. Then one of the girls confided in a friend, after which the inspector for the Society for Prevention of Cruelty to Children visited the twins at school. One of them told the inspector everything, and then both girls were taken to Stobhill police office where they retold their story to a policewoman.

The girls had lost their mother at some point in 1923, leaving them with their Irish thirty-three-year-old stepfather. Their mother had married him in June 1919, six months after divorcing her first husband with whom she had had the twins in 1915. Before the War, their stepfather had worked at a brickfield, and his colleague spoke well of him both then and after he returned from war service, but both men had been suspended since the general strike in 1926. However, once their mother died, he had not deserted the twins, and now with two young girls to support, the stepfather had found alternative work as a boiler fireman for the Glasgow Corporation Gas Works earning £2 13s 6d per week. It was a reasonable wage for a single man, but not for a family of three. They were now living in a single-room house. There would have been a third sibling to accommodate, but their younger brother had run away from home when their mother died.

The girls described their sleeping arrangements. The house had two beds set into the wall with a partition between them, making it impossible to see from one bed to the other. Their stepfather received his pay on Fridays and was drunk by the same evening. At some point in June 1928, he had asked one twin into his bed where she told the precognoscer that 'he did dirty things to me'. By September, he had progressed to full intercourse with the other sibling. She told the policewoman that he often asked her to get into bed to 'scratch my head', but 'on various occasions between 1st September and 31st October 1928', he had asked her to lift her nightgown and to lie on top of him. She had refused, so he had climbed on top of her and had intercourse with her, which she confirmed had hurt and had made her 'wet'. He told her not to tell anyone,

ILLUSTRATION 12.1 *Street conditions Glasgow's central districts, early 1900s.* © Getty Images.

and then she returned to her own bed. He seems to have repeated the act most Friday nights across two months before the intervention of the school inspector. The girls confirmed he had been cruel to them, thrashing them 'with his hands and belt'. Forensic medical expert, Professor Glaister's examination of the girls reported that the one who claimed incest was 'relatively under developed' and did 'not bear evidences of approaching sexual maturity'. His intimate examination of her did not 'reveal evidence of complete intromission', and her hymen remained intact, although he confirmed that penetration had been likely. During his precognoscing, the Procurator Fiscal noted that one twin was 'a very unintelligent child', which was perhaps a comment intended to remind him not to rely on her testimony in court.

At trial in December 1928, their stepfather was charged with incest with one twin during September and October that year, and the combined indictment of lewd and libidinous practices and behaviour plus contravention of the Criminal Law Amendment Act 1922 section 4 (1) with the other twin in late June, just a fortnight before their thirteenth birthdays.[11] The panel pleaded not guilty with a peculiar defence: he claimed the twins were his illegitimate daughters by a liaison in 1915 with their mother four years before their marriage and during a period when she had been living apart from her first husband. His neighbour, also the sister of his wife's first husband, confirmed that her brother had always said he was not their father and had been sentenced to three months in prison for not supporting them during the war. It was anecdotal evidence, but if the testimony of his neighbour substantiated his claim, then the girls' illegitimacy would remove the charge of incest, because sexual relations with illegitimate blood relations was not a degree of relationship included in Leviticus 18. That would leave him facing the two lesser indictments of indecent assault, which were harder for the girls to prove and which attracted a shorter sentence if convicted. As usual with such indictments, the case was heard behind closed doors; there would be no news reports to depress Glasgow's citizens. After their deliberations, the jury returned a unanimously 'guilty as libelled' verdict, and Lord Moncrieff pronounced a sentence of twelve months' imprisonment.

Themes and analysis

The Legitimacy Act 1926 did not apply to Scotland, which would have automatically legitimized the twins after their parents' marriage in 1919 if their stepfather and his neighbour were correct about their conception.[12] However, by indicting the panel on one charge of incest, the Lord Advocate revealed his belief in the girls' legitimacy, which was confirmed by the jury's guilty verdict on both charges – incest and the Criminal Law Amendment Act 1922. Before the trial, the Procurator Fiscal had written to the Crown Agent confirming that the girls' birth had been registered under 'the subsisting marriage'; he provided extract birth and marriage certificates as evidence, which were listed as productions for the court. Thus, the twins were confirmed as the legitimate offspring of their mother's first marriage.[13] However, the panel's not guilty plea suggests he and his defence counsel continued to contest the matter. Whether the jury was convinced of the girls' legitimacy, either as the daughters of their mother's first husband making them legitimate stepdaughters to the panel, or legitimized by his marriage to their mother in 1919, is immaterial; they were legally his legitimate stepdaughters at the point when abuse began.

The panel's unusual defence had failed in its employment of contemporary Scots Law that it was not incest for a man to have intercourse with his wife's illegitimate daughter, even if that illegitimate daughter were his own child.[14] The possibility that the jury might not consider the twins to be legitimate probably persuaded the Crown to indict the panel on a combined charge of incest with lewd and libidinous practices and section 4 of the Criminal Law Amendment Act 1922. He would have had to be found not guilty on all charges to walk free; one count of guilty would have sufficed for a custodial sentence. Yet his paltry sentence for incest and sexual assault of two girls under the age of consent seems inconsistent with the severity of such crimes. However, socio-legal attitudes towards early teenage girls were hard to change, and the short sentence suggests either the attitude of the presiding judge on the girls' familial status, or it reflects the law's reluctance to view sexual assault of any girl over thirteen years of age as more serious than sexual abuse of girls twelve years old and under.

In Scotland the provisions of the 1567 Incest Act and the commentaries of the nation's eighteenth- and nineteenth-century lawyers prevailed. Both Hume and Alison denied 'any benefit of family life to the *filius nullius*', thereby denying an illegitimate child the right to make a complaint of incest against her paternal guardian.[15] Lord Moncrieff might have been aware of the recent English legitimacy legislation and the discrepancy with Scots Law, but he was powerless to direct the jury other than to return a verdict based on Scots Law as it stood. Similar cases of incest in the 1920s with children of similar ages acknowledged by their father attracted longer sentences. For example, in a case of a father and his thirteen-year-old daughter who was not yet showing signs of puberty in 1929, the father was found guilty and sentenced to four years' penal servitude.[16] However, in a similar case in 1928 where the father pleaded guilty, he received a twelve-month sentence of imprisonment.[17] The difference is that one pleaded guilty, whereas the other held out for the possibility of an acquittal, which makes the panel's sentence having pleaded not guilty on a legal technicality in this case appear even more lenient. The records do not detail why Lord Moncrieff did this; was he showing his disapproval of the verdict, by imposing a sentence more in keeping with a guilty verdict on either of the two lesser charges? A conviction on the Criminal Law Amendment Act charge allowed a maximum sentence of two years' imprisonment, and sentencing for lewd and libidinous practices in this period regularly resulted in sentences of months not years.[18] Or did Lord Moncrieff feel that the girls' ages needed to be reflected in his sentencing?

Amendments to the Criminal Law Amendment Act in 1922 had not revised the sentencing provision, thus Lord Moncrieff acted within his sentencing powers on the lesser charge for one twin, but this did not reflect the seriousness of the incest charge for the other. They were approaching their thirteenth birthdays when the assaults began and were definitely thirteen when the incest commenced. This placed both girls in a legal grey area where a felony against a child under twelve years became only a misdemeanour against a child over thirteen. Yet even that argument ignores the guilty verdict on the incest charge, which raises questions about the status of teenage girls in early twentieth-century society.

Historically, it is impossible to ascertain the average man's understanding of the details of the law, but the panel appears either to have possessed a greater grasp of Scots Law than is usually expected of someone of his background, or his counsel was testing the law with a convoluted defence. Whichever of them devised the illegitimacy defence, the panel was clearly aware of the age differentiation in law between a girl twelve years and under and one who had just turned thirteen. The evidence is in the timing of the commencement of his abuse of the first twin – two weeks before their thirteenth birthdays. Professor Glaister confirmed that the twin who had suffered incestuous assault was not yet sexually mature.[19] If the accused had sought sex with his stepdaughters in the absence of their deceased mother, he had not been seeking a woman replacement, because the twins were insufficiently developed to provide that attraction. His timing strongly suggests his assaults began when he knew the risk of lengthy imprisonment was reduced, and in conjunction with his possible knowledge of Scots Law and illegitimacy, the evidence further suggests the accused knew what he was doing.[20] It is unknown if or how he assuaged his sexual desires in the four years since his wife's death, but once they were of a less risky age to assault, the twins had become a source of sexual activity within the home.

Whether the twin who told her school friend about the abuse did so to confide, seeking solace in telling someone, anyone who would listen, is not recorded in her precognition. By deciding not to tell an adult – school teacher or female neighbour – it is reasonable to surmise that she felt unable to trust an adult not to take action. Not because she did not want help, but probably because she feared what her stepfather would do and possibly because she lacked faith in how a female adult could help in the face of his wrath. After all, as the Procurator Fiscal noted to the Crown Agent, the twin who had experienced indecent assault in June had not told her sister until a 'considerable time later'.[21] Had she been too scared of their father's reaction even to tell her closest confidante?

Barry Coldrey suggests that fear of the perpetrator is pivotal to non-disclosure but also distress that the victim may have, in some way, initiated or collaborated in the abuse is a contributory factor; 'genuine affection for the perpetrator' and fear of the consequences for the family also help to maintain silence.[22] However, the twins had been beaten by their stepfather, and they were old enough to remember their mother reporting him to the police for assault in October 1920 for which he received a fine, the equivalent of a week's wages. So, if they had learned from their mother's example, fear of losing the family breadwinner if convicted may not have been what prompted their reluctance to report him now for abuse. Arguably, what delayed their report was a lack of confidence in the adult system to support them.

Research on prosecuted cases of rape and incest during the 1920s in Scotland reveals that in all cases which reached the High Court of Justiciary, the mother, a female neighbour or an older sister had reported the crime to the police office. Adult women were the mediators for sexual abuse, spotting it and then reporting it if they felt able to do so.[23] Louise Jackson's research on child abuse in England in the nineteenth century confirms that mothers, undressing their children for bath and bed, might notice blood or discharge on their children's clothing and actively inspect their children for signs of abuse.[24] This suggests that the fear of child sexual abuse was endemic in British society in the nineteenth and twentieth centuries and that mothers anticipated it, either because they had heard it was common or because they had personal experience.

Jackson's research reveals that in 1886, when reporting of rape and sexual assault was at its highest in England after the introduction of the Criminal Law Amendment Act 1885, only 'four cases were tried nationally per 100,000 people'.[25] Coldrey agrees that cases which reached court were 'only the tip of the iceberg'.[26] Contemporary investigators were also sure that 'the full extent of this evil is not yet realized', and 'there is much more incest than ever comes to the surface'.[27] Thus, mothers who discovered evidence of sexual abuse on their children's bodies and clothing had to decide first if it was truly evidence of abuse; second, if they should report it to the police, and third, if they did, would they be listened to. From the statistics, clearly many parents sought justice for their children by lodging reports, but it is impossible to know the figures for those who decided to deal with it themselves and suffer in silence. Without a maternal protector in the home, the twins were vulnerable to their stepfather's continued predation unless someone intervened on their behalf.

In a society which perceived working-class girls of pubertal age as 'malicious and mendacious in sexual matters', the twins needed an advocate to reach help.[28] That person may have been the friend and confidante at school who told someone with the power to act or the headmistress who may have informed the authorities. However, after the first interview with the inspector, it was not a foregone conclusion that the case would proceed to prosecution at police, sheriff or High Court. The child's and others' supporting testimonies needed to align with judicial perceptions of 'the abused child'. Children under the age of thirteen were considered to be in greater danger of abuse, which resulted in a greater number of successful prosecutions.[29] Their innocence was also a factor, whereas a pubertal teenage girl could be construed as 'vicious' – someone who might trick a man into sex or be too alluring to resist, or simply be sexually curious for herself.[30] Against this stereotyped gendered prejudice, it is understandable that unprotected, unsupported girls would not anticipate assistance, but the twins did receive help after several months of suffering.

Child welfare and protection agencies in early twentieth-century Scotland, and elsewhere, were abundantly aware of the problem of child abuse, and although class-based prejudices existed among their inspectors, their aim was to help, albeit to reduce wider criminality among 'urban degenerates'. Louise Jackson's research on Scottish policing shows that the few female police employed by the Scottish forces in the early twentieth century required 'emotional literacy' to do their job. Their role was preventative as well as social, working within the community to protect girls at risk of sexual abuse. Their work was influenced by the National Vigilance Association, established in 1885 as a 'social purity' campaign group in response to the fears of 'white slave' trafficking by international criminals. By the 1920s, Scottish policewomen had carved out 'a special sphere of usefulness' complementing male officers' beat work by preventing, detecting and 'bringing to justice the vile and cowardly class of criminal' which preyed on young girls.[31]

In response to the moral panic concerning working-class sexual abuse, Scottish law officers 'fully utilized their authority to instruct Procurators Fiscal' to recommend such crimes to the High Court of Justiciary rather than for hearing at sheriff court.[32] If the twins' case was one that the Procurator Fiscal initially considered suitable for hearing at the sheriff court, with both twins' abuse being indicted on an indecent, non-penetrative assault charge, then the move towards hearing child sexual abuse cases at the High Court may have been sufficiently persuasive to increase one charge to incest. Thereby it was ensured to be prosecuted at the highest court. Because, if 'incest implied chaos', then 'its prohibition implied social order'.[33]

Professor Glaister's forensic medical report may also have contributed to the decision to prosecute at the High Court of Justiciary. Although unable to confirm 'complete intromission', his opinion that penetration had probably occurred supported one twin's complaint of incest. She confirmed that her stepfather had hurt her by 'moving up and down on top of' her, and he had ejaculated, which again supported a charge of incestuous intercourse. Since neither twin had witnessed the abuse of the other, Glaister's expert opinion provided sufficient evidence to corroborate the girls' stories. One twin also confirmed that 'no one else ever did anything to me'.[34] Neither twin used 'knowing' language in their precognitions. They did not know the correct anatomical terminology, nor did they use vernacular vocabulary to describe body parts or intercourse. This absence would have helped to construct them as innocent young girls at the mercy of a violent and drunken stepfather, further supporting the veracity of their complaint. As a body of evidence, the Procurator Fiscal had enough to recommend the case to the High Court of Justiciary, and the Lord Advocate agreed. As did the jury who convicted him.

Conclusion

As John Martine had done 220 years earlier, by not pleading guilty, the panel ensured that he faced a jury whereby he could challenge his victims with his masculine authority. Was he convinced of his innocence or his right to use his stepdaughters as he wished, or was he playing a wily game? His defence argument on convoluted points of illegitimacy and the timing of his assaults suggests the latter, which is why this case is important in 1920s Scottish history. Of all the prosecutions for incest heard at the High Court of Justiciary in the 1920s, this case penetrates the deepest into the psyche of men – fathers, brothers, grandfathers – so indifferent to the emotional and physical damage caused by their sexual abuse of their children that they perpetrated not only a legally constructed crime, but one that society has also always rejected as morally taboo.

Changing social attitudes, in the same period, to other forms of incestuous relationship emphasize the depravity of this man's crime. In 1927, a forty-one-year-old shepherd had begun a consensual sexual relationship with his twenty-four-year-old niece. She was the daughter of the shepherd's deceased wife's brother, which meant that the young woman was not a blood relation. However, in Scots Law, she was within the degrees of affinity to make their relationship incestuous. They had attempted to regularize their liaison by seeking the advice of two ministers, both of whom 'seemed to think it quite legal'. However, when asked if the sheriff would marry them, a solicitor had counselled them that their liaison was illegal. Their trial was held behind closed doors because of the sexual nature of the charge. Both panels pleaded not guilty, and after hearing defence counsel's argument concerning incest by affinity and explorations of what permutations of relationships had been included in Leviticus, the jury found them unanimously guilty as libelled. However, 'considering their crime was committed in ignorance and their conduct in voluntarily confessing', the jury also unanimously recommended 'them to the utmost leniency'. Before imposing sentence, Lord Fleming told the court he had 'considerable sympathy with many of the contentions put forward', presumably on points concerning their loving relationship and unawareness of the law, but he was bound by the statute of 1567. They had been found guilty of incest and must be sentenced. So, he admonished them and dismissed them from the court.[35] The jury's verdict and Lord Fleming's sentence reveal that attitudes were changing in late 1920s Scotland. The couple were technically guilty. But they were in love; they had had a baby and wished to marry, and there was not a shred of consanguinity between them. Lord Fleming's sentence had succinctly summed up the societal mood.

Their incest had been benign and consensual; the stepfather's was violent and coercive. As Jackson argues, 'shifts in attitudes, responses and behaviour patterns of prosecutors, police and magistrates' require 'close reading of newspaper reports and witness statements'.[36] In Scotland, that includes close reading also of thousands of preserved pages of court correspondence, trial transcripts and appeals to discover the opinions of those at the head of the judiciary who revealed their attitudes through sentencing. When the law of incest was broken by an unassuming, unrelated and loving couple, the judiciary could be compassionate, reflecting social attitudes. But when incest had been perpetrated as criminal violence against innocent children, then the law could be harsh and impose carceral punishment, although it might still reflect other social attitudes: young girls were not yet as valued by society as they should be.[37]

Notes

1 J. Laite, *The Disappearance of Lydia Harvey: A True Story of Sex, Crime and the Meaning of Justice* (London, 2022), 127.
2 Laite, *Lydia Harvey*, 149.
3 Laite, *Lydia Harvey*, 173.
4 *Report of the Departmental Committee on Sexual Offences against Children and Young Persons in Scotland* (Edinburgh, 1926), cmd.2592, 11–13.
5 Criminal Law Amendment Act, 1885 & 1922, 48 & 49 Vict., c.69, s.4.
6 *Committee on Sexual Offences*, 19.
7 R. M. Mitchell, *A Practical Treatise on the Criminal Law of Scotland by the late Honourable Sir J. H. A. MacDonald* (Edinburgh, 1929), 217–18.
8 L. A. Jackson, 'Family, Community and the Regulation of Child Sexual Abuse: London, 1870–1914', in *Childhood in Question: Children, Parents and the State*, ed. A. Fletcher and S. Hussey, (Manchester, 1999), 147.
9 C. Smart, 'Reconsidering the recent History of Child Sexual Abuse 1910–1960', *Journal of Social Policy* 29, no. 1 (2000), 64.
10 The names of the complainers in this case have been anonymized. The case occurred within 100 years, and it is possible the girls involved did not disclose the events of their early life to any descendants, who may still be alive.

11 The panel has not been anonymized; he did not share a surname with the twins.
12 Legitimation Act 1926 (16 & 17 Geo. 5), chapter 60.
13 Letter Procurator Fiscal to Crown Agent, 15 November 1928, confirming births and marriage register; AD15/28/93.
14 Mitchell, *A Practical Treatise*, 218.
15 Memorandum no. 44 'The Law of Incest in Scotland', Scottish Law Commission (April 1980), 18–19.
16 JC26/1929/12.
17 JC26/1929/1.
18 See L. Heren, *Sex and Violence in 1920s Scotland: incest, rape, lewd and libidinous practices, 1918–1930* (Bloomsbury, 2023), 42–43.
19 AD15/28/93.
20 Correspondence with Dr R. Shiels, retired solicitor, suggests that knowledge among men of the age difference in law may have been more common than historians have hitherto understood; email 9 January 2025.
21 Letter Procurator Fiscal to Crown Agent, 15 November 1928; AD15/28/93.
22 B. Coldrey, 'The Sexual Abuse of Children: the historical perspective', *Studies: An Irish Quarterly Review* 85, no. 340 (Winter, 1996), 376–7.
23 Heren, *Sex and Violence*, 80–3.
24 L. A. Jackson, *Child Sexual Abuse in Victorian England* (London, 2000), 33.
25 Jackson, *Child Sexual Abuse*, 24.
26 Coldrey, 'Sexual Abuse of Children', 372.
27 L. Fairfield, *Departmental Committee on Sexual Offences against Young Persons* (1925), Hansard Cmd 2561, 15 §18; D. Maitland, *Report of the Departmental Committee on Reformatory and Industrial Schools in Scotland, Minutes of Evidence taken before the Young Offenders Committee* (Edinburgh, 1925), NRS, Cmd 878/73, Q1408.
28 C. Smart, 'A History of Ambivalence and Conflict in the Discursive Construction of the "Child Victim" of Sexual Abuse', *Social and Legal Studies* 8, no. 3 (1999), 401.
29 See Jackson, *Child Sexual Abuse*, and Heren, *Sex and Violence*, for wider discussion of prosecution outcomes by age group.
30 Smart, 'Ambivalence', 399; L. Mahood and B. Littlewood, ' "The Vicious Girl" and the "street-corner boy": sexuality and the gendered delinquent in the Scottish child-saving movement 1850–1940', *Journal of the History of Sexuality* 4, no. 4 (1994), 557.
31 L. A. Jackson with N. Davidson, L. Fleming, D. M. Smale and R. Sparks, *Police and Community in Twentieth Century Scotland* (Edinburgh, 2020), 175, 178, 182.
32 R. Davidson, ' "This Pernicious Delusion": Law, Medicine and Child Sexual Abuse in Early Twentieth-Century Scotland', *Journal of the History of Sexuality* 10, no. 1 (2001), 66, 77.

33 W. Leeming, 'New Taboo: some Observations on the late Arrival of Changes to the Law of Incest in Scotland', *International Journal of the Sociology of Law* 24 (1996), 316.
34 AD15/28/93.
35 JC26/1928/91; JC14/40; JC15/39; JC34/140.
36 Jackson, *Child Sexual Abuse*, 30.
37 It is inappropriate to follow the lives of these victims of sexual abuse after their ordeal. However, the likelihood is that, without a legal guardian, the twins were removed from their home to an industrial school where they would have remained until their sixteenth birthdays. If no other guardian had stepped forward to care for them, then their reward for standing up to sexual abuse was a lengthy incarceration of hard work and discipline; C. Kelly, 'Continuity and Change in the History of Juvenile Justice', *Law, Crime and Society* 1 (2016), 70.

13

Peter Manuel 1958: 'Serial killer', mind and motive

Peter Manuel has become known as Scotland's first 'serial killer' for the murder of seven people in East Kilbride during Autumn 1956 to New Year 1958, crimes committed in widely different circumstances. His case allows exploration of the definition of serial killing, police ability to detect and link multiple murders and the arrogance of narcissism in the mind of a multiple murderer.

Context

Whereas multiple murder is an age-old human behaviour, serial killing is a late twentieth-century phenomenon, or at least the label 'serial killer' is. Philip Jenkins attributes this new terminology to the Federal Bureau of Investigation's (FBI's) Behavioral Science Unit's 'white-hot enthusiasm' in the 1980s to define the behaviour of a demographic group, predominantly white men, who killed serially with sexual motivation.[1] Thus, the multiple killers or stranger killers, who were undoubtedly recognized by society and law enforcement before the 1980s, were now serial killers for whom the credentials for definition continue to be debated by historians and criminologists. The key elements of the definition are: the commission of sexually sadistic murders of at least two victims; mostly young women and children or other 'vulnerables' such as the homeless or prostitutes become victims; there is no significant relationship between the perpetrator and the victims; a similar 'signature' or *modus operandi* exists for each murder in the series, and a 'cooling-off' period occurs between one murder and the next.[2] If caught after the first murder, a serial killer's potential is curtailed, but if he manages to continue to a second or third attack using similar methods, then trends or patterns become identifiable, allowing the police to piece together a possible series. The key question remains: are they looking for a single perpetrator or several perpetrators? Harbort and Mokros question the timeframes offered for serial killing definition. While some argue for a cooling-off period of a matter of hours, others employ intervals ranging from 'a few days, weeks, months or years' to formulate a series.[3] Thus, detection of serial killers becomes more difficult the longer the interval between murders. And if, like Peter Manuel, a multiple murderer now widely known as Scotland's first serial killer, their series is interrupted, and their *modus operandi* chaotic, then they can be especially difficult to apprehend.

A 'spree killer' is distinct again from a multiple murderer who kills with a recognizable signature, or a gangland or contract murderer who despatches more than one person at a time or across a period of time. A 'spree killer' is someone who walks into their workplace or school on a Monday morning and guns down a slew of colleagues in response to a personal or societal slight. Often, they commit suicide having killed their colleagues or are killed by law enforcement in the process of apprehension. Thus, using the thirty-day cooling-off criteria for the definition of a serial killer becomes problematic, because 'if a perpetrator murders three or more individuals in less than thirty days, the crime is usually defined as a *murder spree*'.[4]

A further key element of multiple murder behaviour is motive which can range from sexual gratification to torture gratification to monetary gain or a vicarious desire to help. This latter serial-killer type is often called 'an angel of death', someone whose impetus to murder is to put similar types of individual out of their pain, such as the elderly or terminally ill. Thus, many serial-killing categories appear on the psycho-criminal spectrum because their motivation for one murder, let alone several, is incomprehensible to society; it isn't normal.

The Whitechapel murderer, or Jack the Ripper, is often claimed as the first serial killer of the modern era. His sexual assaults and murders of at least five women within a few months in 1888 in Victorian London presented police with a set of signature behaviours that allowed them to link the women's individual murders. Jack the Ripper was profiled as a sexual maniac whose signature was evisceration of his female victims. Yet this linkage did not lead the police to the perpetrator, nor did it assist any efforts to prevent the next murder, until Jack the Ripper decided to stop. Sensationalist news reporting at the time aided the spread of societal fears: who would be the next victim? Who was he preying on? Could he be caught? Rather than Jack's activities being 'just a Victorian murder mystery', his actions shaped 'an enduring legacy', and arguably a widespread fascination with the behaviour of a serial killer.[5]

In Glasgow in the 1950s, the existence of serial killers was not yet properly understood, although the city was suffering a spate of unexplained and terrifying murders. In a city with a criminal underworld and gang culture, it would have been easy to consider these crimes as separate. Since the 'razor kings' of the 1920s, Glasgow had attracted a reputation as a dangerous city populated by hard men who would use their fists at the slightest altercation. Clydeside's culture of tough masculinity was born of its economic base in the shipyards and heavy industries where manliness and physicality were prized.[6] Thus, male interpersonal violence was an everyday occurrence for many in the workplace, on the streets and outside pubs, and inside homes where the particular variety of domestic violence occurred. However, by the 1950s, what journalists reported as a Chicago-style form of gang had developed in Glasgow. As Andrew Davies notes, the 'hooligan' of the 1920s had transformed into the 'gangster' of the 1930s, the latter operating protection rackets mostly around the city's working-class districts.[7] Was the identification of Glasgow's gang culture with Chicago's notorious gangsters journalistic rhetoric, or had Glasgow's poorer districts succumbed to gang rule? Davies argues that the police and police courts used the gangster terminology to 'secure convictions and then to persuade magistrates to impose harsher sentences'.[8] Glasgow's gangs gained national notoriety in 1936 for a 'gang-related murder trial' by the Savoy Arcadian gang. However, as Davies points out, in a city with over one million citizens, 500 'roughs' did not constitute the kind of criminality experienced by Chicago under Al Capone's tyranny, and Glasgow's so-called gangsters did not carry guns; they fought 'with broken bottles, razors, coshes, knives and bayonets', leaving behind disfiguring scars rather than bullet-ridden cadavers.[9]

Whether criminals operated individually, in hooligan gangs or as organized criminals, arguably no city has ever been without its share of murderers and thieves, and certain periods in history have promoted their behaviour. Poverty, unemployment and war have created circumstances of opportunity for criminal activity and victim selection. Amy Helen Bell argues convincingly for the opportunities provided for murder by night-time bombing raids on London during the Second World War. These were often not pub-brawl or gangland murders but were premeditated crimes – murderers seizing the moment to 'bump off' a rival or an unwanted partner or baby.[10] Gordon Cummins, the 'Blackout Ripper', murdered four women in 1942; John Reginald Christie raped and murdered a minimum of eight people before his arrest in 1953. Cummins had committed his crimes over a short period, whereas Christie's crimes stretched back to the war.

In late 1950s Glasgow, a spate of unexplained murders occurred. The victims included single women, married women, a daughter and a family. The methods of murder were bludgeoning, shooting and strangulation; in at least one event, sexual assault had occurred. The crimes were sporadically committed between January 1956 and January 1958, and the scenes of the crimes varied from a murder on waste ground to a family shot dead in their beds.

In 1957, fourteen murdered bodies were reported to the police in Scotland, of whom three were children. The Glasgow murderer accounted for four of those fourteen.[11] In 1958, eighteen bodies were reported to the Scottish police as murder victims, of whom five were children. The Glasgow murderer accounted for three of those eighteen.[12] Glasgow's police struggled to find the perpetrators. There was nothing apparently linking the murders, and while the city's police considered them separate events among the several others committed in the city, joining the dots was impossible. Any potential signature or motive was hidden because the killings were all so different. A multiple murderer, potential serial killer, operating in the city was not on the police radar.

Case

On Wednesday, 4 January 1956, the body of Annie Kneilands was discovered by a passing walker in a copse on the East Kilbride golf course. Her body was 500 yards from her home. She had sustained head injuries and was wrapped only in her coat. She had been missing since Monday, having told her family she was going dancing with a man she had met the previous Friday. When she did not return home, her father called her employer to ask if she had arrived for work, but she had not. He then telephoned the police. Detective Superintendent James Hendry of the Lanark County Constabulary was now investigating.[13]

Nine months later, Mr William Watts was recalled home from a short holiday to identify the bodies of his wife, daughter and sister-in-law who had been murdered in the family bungalow in Fennsbank Avenue, Rutherglen. Their bodies were found in the house's two bedrooms by the family's domestic help who witnessed the last breaths of the daughter. Mrs Marian Watts, her sixteen-year-old daughter Vivienne and her aunt Mrs Margaret Brown had all been shot in the head, and a glass panel in the front door was smashed. Mr Watts was a local businessman who owned a bakery, while his brother-in-law Mr George Brown was the owner of a dry-cleaning business in Falkirk, twenty-five miles away. The women had been alive when Mr Watts telephoned around 11.00 pm, and a young neighbour Diana Valenti had still been listening to the radio with them at 11.40 pm. Detective Superintendent Hendry confirmed that a 0.38 calibre revolver had been the murder weapon for which they were still searching, and a man's suede shoe had been found in the street. A few doors along Fennsbank Avenue, another break-in had occurred, and fingerprints were taken. No one had heard either disturbance.[14]

A little over a year later, on 28 December 1957, seventeen-year-old Isabelle Cooke was reported missing after leaving home to go to a dance on Saturday evening. The police put out a description of the teenager: '5ft. 5in. tall, with dark curly hair which hangs below her neck, and green eyes'. She had been wearing a blue raincoat, blue and white frock with a distinctive headscarf designed with a map of France.[15] Throughout 30 December, police searched for Isabelle and finally found her purse. Superintendent Miles Duncan was leading the case and divulged that the young man Isabelle had been going to meet had been stood up and had gone to the dance alone. Isabelle's parents were distraught, and her mother confirmed she had only had enough money in her purse for her bus fare, not enough to warrant stealing. That evening, Duncan ordered tracker dogs to assist police on the ground.[16] By 2 January 1958, any hope of finding Isabelle was vanishing. The police were now being aided by the Shettleston Harriers, an athletics club, who were ranging across the locale searching for her. A soldier returning to Aberdeen had reported seeing someone who looked like Isabelle at Morpeth, but he could not be sure.[17] Superintendent Duncan had a theory: had Isabelle been dropped over a railway bridge onto a moving goods train? Some of her clothing had now been recovered, but not her body, and two other young girls had gone missing: Maureen Kidd in Dundee missing since Hogmanay and Ann Noblett in Hertfordshire; both girls were in their teens.[18]

It was 6 January 1958 before the Smart family's bodies were discovered, shot in the head while in bed in Uddingston on New Year's Eve. The Chief Constable of Lanarkshire now asked the Glasgow Police for help to solve this 'latest evil episode in a wave of violent crime' affecting 'a small corner of Lanarkshire'. Unlike Scotland Yard which investigated crimes like this in England, Scotland did not have a similar body, although Glasgow's 'specialised criminal investigation department' could be called upon to use its 'superior facilities and equipment for scientific crime detection'.[19] On New Year's Eve, Mr and Mrs Peter Smart and their son Michael had been shot dead in their beds in a bungalow in Sheepburn Road, Uddingston. Superintendent Murdo Munro confirmed to the press that 'at the moment there is nothing to give us a lead'. The police did not know how the murderer had gained entry to the house, but they believed the motive was robbery. A family in a nearby street reported they had been disturbed during Friday night, 3 January 1958, and the police now had the description of the man seen running off. Were the murders of the Watts, then Isabelle and now the Smarts connected? It was reported that few women and girls were visible on the town's streets after dark, and homeowners were double-checking their locks to ensure their homes were secure. Meanwhile, the search for Anne Noblett continued as another body, of a Dutch girl, was found in Essex.[20]

Having so far treated the murders and disappearances as individual crimes, the final attack on the Smarts prompted Detective Chief Superintendent Muncie to recall a crime in 1946 when the perpetrator had slept in the property after breaking in. The evidence provided by the Smarts' neighbours suggested either that the killer had lingered in the house for a few days or that he had come and gone; there had been curtain movement and lights switched on. It was similar behaviour to that of Peter Manuel who Muncie had arrested twelve years earlier. The final clue was the discovery of banknotes stolen from the Smarts, which were being spent in local pubs. The perpetrator himself had unwittingly and carelessly provided the best piece of evidence yet. Thirty-one-year-old Peter Manuel was arrested on 14 January 1958. After which, Manuel voluntarily confessed to police to this string of recent crimes, which he would later construe as 'extracted unfairly', exploiting Manuel's 'worries about his father' who had been arrested with him.[21] In his confession, Manuel had connected a series of crimes – murders and break-ins – which the police had not.

Between arrest and trial which began on 12 May 1958 at Glasgow's High Court of Justiciary, Manuel confessed to the two group family murders, Annie Kneiland's and Isabelle Cooke's murders. He was indicted on eight separate charges; four covering the murder of eight people and four including details of various housebreakings during which Manuel had allegedly stolen anything from money to an odd assortment of items: an electric razor, a camera, one sock, gloves. The money stolen between January 1956 and 1958 amounted to £32 18 shillings.[22] Combined with his wages as a woodworker, it was still insufficient to fund a lavish lifestyle, although these may not have been the only housebreakings that Manuel had committed during this active period. The evidence for each indicted crime was circumstantial, based on grouping witness statements to build a compelling argument, and supported of course by Manuel's own confessions.

However, as his trial began, Manuel pleaded not guilty and accused William Watt of killing his own family, an accusation that was explored throughout the trial and for which Watt was exonerated. Represented by Harold Leslie Q.C., Manuel foisted the charge of stolen items from one property onto other persons and bizarrely used his presence in the Smart home as an alibi against the charge. The accumulation of stolen items as evidence productions were displayed on a table like 'jumble sale debris'.[23] As the evidence was heard, it became apparent Manuel had left 'disorder everywhere' at the murder scenes and break-ins.[24] By day two, evidence emerged of gun purchases, one of which Manuel had shown off to a workmate in the pub. The Watts' cleaner described hearing Vivienne letting out 'three or four big snores',

ILLUSTRATION 13.1 *Frontispiece*, The Trial of Peter Manuel: The Man Who Talked Too Much, *J. G. Wilson (Secker & Warburg, London, 1959)*.

proving she had been alive, barely, when discovered. Vivienne's torn clothing and the disarray in her room were also described, compared with the 'normal' state of her mother's bedroom which Manuel had left undisturbed.[25] On day seven of the trial, forensic medical evidence for Annie Kneilands was given. Dr Allison confirmed that at least four blows to the skull had killed Annie and that when her body was found her underwear was missing. Her body had been moved which tenuously might account for its absence. Dr Allison also confirmed there was no evidence of 'sexual interference'.[26] The evidence indicated that penetrative sexual assault of Annie, Isabelle or Vivienne Watts, among the young female victims, was unlikely, although the evidence from Vivienne's bedroom and the nature of Isabelle's death by strangulation with a bra suggested sexualized murders.

On day thirteen of the trial having earlier sacked his counsel, Manuel himself took the stand assisted by the judge, Lord Cameron, who offered to provide guidance to the panel, giving his own evidence. Manuel stood up, 'the paleness of his face was accentuated by his sleek, black hair', and he spoke 'rapidly, fluently, and with a wealth of detail' going back to meetings and events from 1955. Having recounted his version of events over his two years of criminal activity, Manuel then questioned his father about the night of his arrest and confession, insinuating that police questioning had suggested he had been insane. His father confirmed that he had 'not been himself' and that the police had almost dragged the confession out of him.[27] This line of questioning did not correlate with defence counsel's earlier attempts to insinuate 'careful interrogation' by the police playing on Manuel's concerns for his father.[28] The following day when the Advocate Depute and Lord Cameron questioned Manuel in the witness box, his arguments began to unravel. On the last day, Manuel's address to the jury took over three hours in which again he repeated his arguments about police coercion and his bizarre special defence concerning the Smarts.

Lord Cameron's summing-up was more succinct in which he called Manuel's case one 'without precedent in this country for very many years' and noted that Manuel's self-representation was unique but had been conducted with 'remarkable skill'. It was indeed remarkable given that he stood trial for four capital charges for which he would need to prove his innocence on every single one. Lord Cameron emphasized the need for corroboration in Scots Law, clearly a reminder that the evidence the jury had heard was circumstantial and uncorroborated unless one accepted Manuel's confessions as corroboration. He then removed the possibility of the jury returning an insanity verdict because no special plea nor special defence had been entered, and not 'one scintilla of evidence' supported any 'weakness of mind'; it was a 'matter you cannot and will not consider'. Lastly, Lord Cameron considered Manuel's allegations that the police had used him to cover their own incompetence in failing to solve a number of unexplained murders. He left the jury to decide whether such a 'devilish conspiracy to provide a solution to unsolved crimes' had left an innocent man in 'the dock on charges of murder'.[29]

When the jury returned with their verdicts after two hours' deliberation, they found Manuel unanimously not guilty of the murder of Annie Kneilands because Lord Cameron had directed that 'there is not sufficient evidence in law which goes beyond a matter of suspicion', irrespective of the panel's confession, to convict him of this murder.[30] However, their verdict was unanimously guilty of the Watts' murders, Isabelle's death and of shooting dead the Smart family. The clerk asked the jury foreman to confirm the degree of murder: the Watts' and Smarts' murders were capital crimes as differentiated by the Homicide Act of 1957, which had removed the death penalty from many forms of murder but had retained hanging for crimes involving the use of a firearm to kill or where murder had ensued during a theft; Isabelle's was simply murder.[31] The only sentence Lord Cameron could impose was doom.[32]

Themes and analysis

There were several ways for Lanarkshire and Glasgow police to connect the numerous crimes that occurred in and around the city during 1956–1958, although the key combinations were the Watts and Smart murders as two in a possible series of family attacks, and Annie's and Isabelle's murders in a potential series of assaults on single young women. Arguably, as the more usual type of assault, these two murders might have been linked to the other disappearances of young women reported around the country. However, the police made neither of these possible linkages. What led to Manuel's discovery was his lavish expenditure and continued presence in the Smarts' home after their murders; a link between two housebreakings recalled by Detective Chief Superintendent Muncie which were over a decade apart, followed by his confession to the other crimes in the series.

This suggests that the police did not consider the crimes connected by their murder type or crime scene details, or that they did not understand the nature of serial killing in this period. The recent Cummins and Christie murder series in London had been carried out under very different circumstances; one during wartime, the other committed by a controlling, misogynous man offering back-street abortions to entice vulnerable women into his home. The murders in these two series had obvious internal similarities, whereas those committed by Manuel appeared to be scattergun. The murders of Annie and Isabelle were unconnected by the police but appeared to be sexually motivated, although not rape; the Watts' murders were motiveless, whereas the Smart family's deaths on the surface looked like a violent break-in. The lack of serial characteristics connecting these crimes was, and is, unusual for a true serial killer.

Neither Annie nor Isabelle were prostitutes, a group which has often been targeted by serial killers along with other socially marginal types such as the homeless and homosexuals.[33] They were just single women intending to enjoy themselves on the evening of their deaths, but travelling alone after dark had made them prey to one, possibly two, opportunistic murderers. There is nothing in the evidence suggesting premeditated murder; the killer appears not to have planned these assaults, although he may have been prowling for victims to assuage some 'need' he had on those particular nights.

Recent scholarship by Lynes et al. on late twentieth-century serial killing suggests a new type of serial killer – a 'dark flâneur' – a peripatetic observer or man-about-town, 'always in full possession of his individuality', alienated from society, experiencing precarious employment and questioning his masculinity. Lynes et al. use the UK's serial killer, Levi Bellfield, to exemplify their theory, suggesting his peripatetic employment as a delivery driver aided his victim selection; he could attack young women across a wider geographical area using his van as the unobserved locus for his crimes. They argue that his innovative methods reaffirmed 'his dignity and status' in his own mind.[34] If Lynes's research team is correct in their analysis of Bellfield's crimes, Manuel may have been his precursor. He travelled around the East Kilbride area, observing victims and selecting them once he had ascertained their circumstances. For Annie and Isabelle, this was being unaccompanied after dark on deserted streets. For the Watts and Smart families, they were probably selected because Manuel believed he could gain access to their homes without disturbing them and take them by surprise as he shot all six of them; they may not have even known what had happened. Manuel's previous charges for a range of petty crimes and lesser assaults, and his self-representation at a previous trial and this one indicate a degree of self-possession and status beyond his socio-economic position. Clearly, he enjoyed spending Mr Smart's cash after murdering him and his family and did so with some panâche. Manuel's behaviour throughout his series of murders suggests some elements of the dark flâneur type.

Further, the two family group murders are unusual among 'classic' serial killers and the quick method of despatch by shooting leaves no room for sadistic torture, sexual or otherwise, another signature of 'classic' serial killing. Using a revolver was counter-cultural for Glasgow in this period, unless of course its owner was part of a shady criminal community which dealt in guns. Manuel's evidence on this point indicates that he knew in which pubs he could find men willing to sell guns, an increasing problem according to newspaper reports in the 1950s.[35]

The cooling-off periods between crimes are also uncharacteristic. Although there is no definitional rule for the time elapsed between incidents, the year between the Watts and the Smart murders is attributable to Manuel's incarceration in Barlinnie Prison during 1957 for petty crimes.[36] Within a month of his release, he had ransacked Reverend Houston's home, stealing the gloves, sock and camera, plus £2 on Christmas Day before strangling Isabelle three days later. Was this pent-up serial-killing rage or a housebreaking in search of funds followed by a disconnected murder to assuage some sexual desire? Sadly, the court records and other commentaries do not provide sufficient detail to answer these key questions. However, they suggest reasons why the police failed to connect Manuel's crimes: they were too dissimilar and too far apart. Thus, Manuel's behaviour should be considered more theoretically.

Manuel's not guilty plea followed by dismissal of his counsel in the early days of the trial illustrates important elements of his personality. He may have been advised to plead not guilty because his counsel was intending to rely on the shaky nature of the circumstantial witness evidence. However, even if his defence had counselled Manuel to plead not guilty for this reason, Manuel's confession to the police would have been difficult to refute, especially if Manuel took the stand for cross-examination by prosecution counsel. It must also be considered that by pleading not guilty to a series of crimes to which he had already confessed, Manuel ensured his day in court. Whether led through his statement by defence counsel or by the prosecution, 'his public' would hear him. As Bingham noted, 'these days were perhaps the most exhilarating in his life'.[37] And by dismissing his defence team and electing to represent himself, he guaranteed an opportunity to give the performance of – for? – his life.

Self-representation in court is a red flag for narcissistic behaviour and is acknowledged as 'characteristic of the arrogance' of many serial killers.[38] Manuel displayed several of the criteria for what is now recognized as narcissistic personality disorder: grandiosity, fantasizing, lack of empathy and arrogance; otherwise 'risky behaviour' fluctuating between covert shyness and overt superiority.[39] In Scots Law, being a party litigant, by representing himself, Manuel's behaviour suggests mental imbalance and, in a capital case, a lack of understanding of the importance of professional representation. As Lord Cameron said in his direction to the jury, 'you must scrutinise the evidence with most particular and scrupulous care' because 'by his voluntary action', Manuel had 'deprived himself of the most distinguished forensic abilities and technical skill' of his defence counsel.[40] Any chance of acquittal or a reduced verdict based on insanity or diminished responsibility required the accused to recognize his own mental illness.

Manuel's use of the Smarts' murders as an alibi for one of the housebreaking charges suggests not only that he did not understand the severity of the outcome if found guilty of any one of the murders, but that he also insisted on his counsel adhering to his instructions rather than following counsel's professional advice. As Robert Shiels argues, an effective defence depends on 'clear and unequivocal instructions from a lucid and informed client'.[41] Arguably, Manuel was a poorly informed client in that his narcissism precluded him from understanding the gravity of his situation, or his narcissism had convinced him of the inevitability of a successful outcome. After all, he had represented himself on a charge of aggravated sexual assault some years before and been acquitted.[42] It is unlikely considering the severity of the charges that defence counsel provided Manuel with sub-standard legal advice. Thus, was Manuel actually insane, either at the time of the offences or more generally?

By definition, multiple murder may be considered an act of insanity by the general public, particularly when accompanied by sadistic behaviour, but Lord Cameron had indicated that an insanity verdict would not be accepted. This was due to a legal technicality because a special defence of insanity had not been entered; also, Manuel did not satisfy the definition of diminished responsibility in Scots Law. His self-defence did not acknowledge any deranged behaviour at any of the murder scenes, although staying in one property along with his victims and feeding the family cat suggest mental instability. In fact, Manuel's arguments appear rational if one accepts his police conspiracy line. At no point did his counsel's or his own arguments indicate diminished responsibility; he had acted knowing what he was doing at the time of the commission of the crimes as well as in court. That the murders of the three young female victims were not sexual may further have distanced the police from linking these crimes as the work of a deranged individual. Obvious evidence of deviance, including rape, was absent. Thus, the police were not looking for a sexual maniac loose in East Kilbride, and so they engaged the assistance of the newspapers to help them track down a culprit or several culprits, thereby creating a mini moral panic.

If the police did not connect the crimes as the actions of a single perpetrator, the press connected them as evidence of a violent crime wave as suggested by the *Glasgow Herald*'s 8 January edition.[43] Yet even journalists did not link the crimes together as a murder series. As Jenkins argues, 'the relative obscurity' of early and mid-twentieth-century serial killers can be attributed to the 'full scale of an offender's crimes' only becoming apparent at 'the end of his or her career' after arrest.[44] Press reporting of Jack the Ripper's 1888 crimes created a moral panic over a period of months because he was given a readily useable nickname while he was still operating, and his crimes followed a signature pattern. Whereas Manuel's crimes appeared to be the product of several criminals operating within a certain locale and therefore did not become a journalistic sensational series. Often the police employ news reporting to aid their investigations prompting readers to report suspicious activity, and in the case of Isabelle Cooke, Lanarkshire police put out her description in an attempt to discover her (living) whereabouts. Yet without obvious linkage the police could not ask the public to assist with finding a single serial murderer. The fascination of reading salacious murder details was denied to the public, although the *Glasgow Herald* suggested that a pervasive fear had spread among women and girls and homeowners. These were distinctive groups, and the coalescence of public fear into a moral panic prompting increased police surveillance did not occur.

However, despite often colourful press reporting from the court, Manuel did not attract public sympathy in the immediate aftermath of the verdict and sentence. Only fifty-nine people signed a petition requesting a reprieve of the death sentence.[45] His case went to appeal on 24 June. But on 20 June, Manuel had already taken grains of barbiturate 'sufficient to consist of a fatal dose' which had been smuggled into Barlinnie Prison for Manuel's use if his appeal failed. Perhaps his pre-appeal suicide attempt was intended to postpone the appeal, thereby delaying his execution, or he had intended it as a display of his 'unsound mind', another tactic to delay execution since capital punishment could not be carried out on a mentally unstable prisoner. However, Manuel's stomach was pumped the same day, and the appeal went ahead. Yet even after the appellate court upheld the original verdict, Manuel wrote to the prison governor claiming that his 'QC carried out the appeal on grounds not fully formulated' and that 'advantage was taken of me by Counsel while I was in no position to do anything about it'.[46] Arrogantly, he was still claiming greater legal skill than his counsel as well as attempting to blame him, as he had originally accused the police.

A note between legal officers on 15 July 1958, four days after Manuel's execution, remarked on the increasing difficulties surrounding 'psychopaths who are not suffering from diminished responsibility' if the 'Mental Care and Treatment Bill makes it possible for the courts to order psychiatric care and treatment for all psychopaths'.[47] This suggests further that Manuel's suicide attempt had been a bid to prove insanity, thereby respiting but not commuting his death sentence. He would have languished in Barlinnie Prison until such time as he was declared sane again, became eligible for parole or until natural death.

Conclusion

Peter Manuel's activities during 1956 and 1958 do not completely satisfy the credentials for serial killing as defined in the 1980s by the FBI. However, his enforced hiatus during 1957 while in prison disrupted his behaviour, and arguably, he may have carried out more murders if he had had his freedom. The jury did not find him guilty of Annie Kneiland's murder, although the *modus operandi* was sufficiently similar to Isabelle's murder for there to have been initial linkage. Jenkins argues that 'the British police have always been far more centralized than their American counterparts', which has aided criminal detection across 'separate jurisdictions'.[48] But Scotland has always been a separate jurisdiction from England, and the conflation of England with Britain is unhelpful in this regard. In the 1950s, Scottish police constabularies relied on Glasgow's police for their superior skills in violent crime investigations, although collaboration with forces south of the border did occur. Perhaps these separate jurisdictions and police forces delayed Manuel's apprehension. If he had not confessed, would the police have ever linked all the crimes?[49]

Jenkins's research shows that after the abolition of the death penalty in 1965 in England and Wales, and Scotland, defence counsel's imperative to attempt an insanity defence was removed.[50] Proving an insanity defence became the difference between imprisonment and incarceration in a specialist hospital facility, although the hope of eventual freedom remained vanishingly small. Capital punishment of a capital crime was removed for good. Jenkins remarks that England is particularly sceptical about insanity defences and remains reluctant 'to attribute insanity to extremely violent offenders'.[51] As Scotland's first 'serial killer' of the modern era, it was too early to characterize Peter Manuel's particular brand of killing with insanity. He did not consider himself to be insane, at least not until his arrogance and narcissism failed him at his appeal.

In the twenty-first century, it has become the norm to consider all serial killers as sexual killers to a degree that if sexual motivation is absent, the public is less engaged with the 'story'. Angel of death killers such as England's Lucy Letby and those who murder for financial gain such as Harold Shipman rarely attract public interest until the latter stages of the judicial process. Sexual deviancy is a key attribute introduced by the FBI and promoted by Hollywood depictions of infamous American serial killers. Peter Manuel's series of murders, while they have gained him notoriety as Scotland's first serial killer, have not accumulated the fame and fascination of his sexual serial-killing colleagues. He would probably be devastated to know that.

Notes

1. P. Jenkins, 'Catch me before I kill more: Seriality as Modern Monstrosity', *Cultural Analysis* 3 (2002), 3–4.
2. C. Grover and K. Soothill, 'British Serial Killing: towards a structural explanation', *British Criminological Conferences: Selected Proceedings*, vol. 2, Belfast, 15–19 July 1997 (1997), 2–3. Kevin Haggerty argues for a serial killer qualification of three or more victims; K. Haggerty, 'Modern Serial Killers', *Crime Media Culture* 5, no. 2 (2005), 169. While Kelleher and

Kelleher require three or more victims in a period of thirty days or more; M. D. Kelleher and C. L. Kelleher, *Murder Most Rare: the female serial killer* (Westport, 1998), 4.

3 S. Harbort and A. Mokros, 'Serial Murderers in Germany from 1945 to 1995: a descriptive study', *Homicide Studies* 5, no. 4 (November 2001), 312.

4 Kelleher and Kelleher, *Murder Most Rare*, 4.

5 A. Warwick and M. Willis, *Jack the Ripper: Media, Culture, History* (Manchester, 2007), 3.

6 R. Johnston and A. McIvor, 'Dangerous Work, Hard Men and Broken Bodies: Masculinity in the Clydeside Heavy Industries', *Labour History Review* 69, no. 2 (August 2004), 138; J. Begiato, 'Between Poise and Power: Embodied Manliness in Eighteenth and Nineteenth Century British Culture', *Transactions of the Royal Historical Society* 26 (2016), 135.

7 A. Davies, 'The Scottish Chicago?: from 'hooligans' to 'gangsters' in inter-war Glasgow', *Cultural and Social History* 4, no. 4 (2007), 516–17.

8 Davies, 'Scottish Chicago?', 519.

9 Davies, 'Scottish Chicago?', 521, 519.

10 A. H. Bell, *Under Cover of Darkness: Murders in Blackout London* (New Haven, 2024).

11 *Criminal Statistics Scotland 1957, Statistics relating to Police Apprehensions and Criminal Proceedings for the Year 1957* (Edinburgh, 1958), cmnd. 426, 10.

12 *Criminal Statistics Scotland 1957, Statistics relating to Police Apprehensions and Criminal Proceedings for the Year 1958* (Edinburgh, 1959), cmnd. 746, 10.

13 'Golf Course Murder', *Glasgow Herald*, 5 January 1956, 5.

14 'Triple Murder in Bungalow', *Glasgow Herald*, 18 September 1956, 7.

15 'Police Enquiries for Girl', *Glasgow Herald*, 30 December 1957, 5.

16 'Police find purse of missing girl', *Glasgow Herald*, 31 December 1957, 5.

17 'Hope dwindling in Search for Girl', *Glasgow Herald*, 2 January 1958, 5.

18 'Dropped in Wagon?', *Glasgow Herald*, 4 January 1958, 5, 6. Maureen Kidd was found three days later lost in a Dundee department store.

19 'Epidemic of Murder', *Glasgow Herald*, 8 January 1958, 6.

20 'Glasgow Detectives join Murder Investigations in Lanarkshire', *Glasgow Herald*, 8 January 1958, 7.

21 J. Bingham with Detective Chief Superintendent, W. Muncie, Lanarkshire County Police, *The Hunting down of Peter Manuel, Glasgow Multiple Murderer* (London, 1973), 156–7, 187.

22 A. M. Kilday, *Crime in Scotland 1660–1960: the Violent North?* (Abingdon, 2021), 57–60.

23 'Manuel Trial begins in Glasgow', *Glasgow Herald*, 13 May 1958, 7.

24 'First Day of Manuel's Trial for Murder', *Glasgow Herald*, 13 May 1958, 8.

25 'Murder Scene in Watt's Home described', *Glasgow Herald*, 14 May 1958, 12–13.

26 'Club Manager's Meeting with Manuel', *Glasgow Herald*, 19 May 1958, 3.
27 'Solicitor accused by Manuel', *Glasgow Herald*, 27 May 1958, 7–9.
28 Bingham, *Hunting down*, 187.
29 'Manuel Trial', *Glasgow Herald*, 29 May 1958, 7–9.
30 'Tragic Mistake', *Glasgow Herald*, 30 May 1958, 6.
31 Homicide Act, (1957), section 5, 5 & 6 Eliz. 2., c.1.; L. Blom-Cooper & T. Morris, *With Malice Aforethought: a study of the crime and punishment for homicide* (Oxford, 2004), 113.
32 'A Damaging Admission on Smart Killings', *Glasgow Herald*, 30 May 1958, 7.
33 D. Wilson, 'Late Capitalism, vulnerable populations and violent predatory crime', ed. S. Hall and S. Winlow, *New Directions in Criminological Theory* (London, 2012), 221.
34 A. Lynes, C. Kelly & P. Kapil Singh, 'Benjamin's 'flâneur' and serial murder: an ultra-realist literary case study of Levi Bellfield', *Crime, Media, Culture*, vol. 15, no. 3 (2019), pp.524, 528 & 532.
35 Bingham, *Hunting down*, 213–16; J. G. Wilson, *The Trial of Peter Manuel: The Man who talked too much* (London, 1959), 223.
36 Wilson, *Trial*, 23.
37 Bingham, *Hunting down*, 188.
38 D. Wilson, *Signs of Murder, a Small Town in Scotland, a Miscarriage of Justice and the Search for the Truth* (London, 2020), 23.
39 S. Tinetti, 'Me, Myself and I: Narcissistic Personality Disorder and Criminal Sentencing', *University of Illinois Law Review* 5 (2020), 1611–12; P. Allen, 'Narcissistic Personality Disorder: anatomy and risk', https://www.theseusrisk.com/insight-post/narcissistic-personality-disorder-anatomy-and-risk/ (accessed March 2025).
40 Wilson, *Trial*, 200.
41 R. Shiels, 'Historic Defective Representation: The Defence Case for Oscar Slater', *Scots Law Times* (2025), 166.
42 Kilday, *Violent North*, 57.
43 'Epidemic of Murder', *Glasgow Herald*, 8 January 1958, 6.
44 Jenkins, *Intimate Enemies*, 55–6.
45 Kilday, *Violent North*, 64.
46 HH60/703/1, Note Manuel to Governor at Barlinnie Prison, 10 July 1958.
47 HH60/703/1, Note 15 July 1958.
48 Jenkins, *Intimate Enemies*, 49.
49 Among murders of several women to which he confessed while in prison, the murder of a taxi driver in York in 1957 has also sometimes been attributed to Manuel, but he was never indicted for it; Kilday, *Violent North*, 64–5.
50 P. Jenkins, 'Serial Murder in England 1940–1985', *Journal of Criminal Justice* 16 (1988), 4.
51 Jenkins, 'Serial Murder', 12.

14

Henry John Burnett 1963: Murderer, state execution and abolition

If the jury could have stretched to accepting the expert witness testimony in Henry John Burnett's case, he would not have been executed. But as the last person to hang in Scotland, Burnett was prosecuted at a pivotal moment in British and Scottish judicial history, in the midst of the inquiry on capital punishment and on the cusp of its abolition, when an individual's murderous behaviour was tied up in moral debate and political grandstanding on crime.

Context

The so-called Scottish serial killer, Peter Manuel, was executed the year after the Homicide Act 1957 differentiated between murder and capital murder, and seven years before the UK abolished capital punishment altogether. In that seven-year interval, Henry John Burnett would be the last person to hang in Scotland.

The Homicide Act 1957 has been described as 'fundamentally flawed' in its attempts to 'limit the extent of capital punishment'.[1] The Homicide Act had served only to reform the law on murder after a Royal Commission on Capital Punishment, established in 1948 to 'discover whether the use of capital punishment could be limited or modified', had not been permitted to investigate arguments for total abolition.[2] Why the Commission had been restricted on matters concerning abolition is multifarious and began in the mid-nineteenth century before public executions ceased after 1868.

As James Gregory argues, abolition 'was not high up on the agenda' as an election issue before or after 1868, and the late nineteenth-century minority abolition movement failed to capture the public's attention; also, 'support of the gallows was always too strong' among the elites who implemented the law.[3] However, despite being considered inhumane by public figures such as Charles Dickens, the issue of deterrence was a continuing debate as agitation for abolition grew: if hanging ceased, would murder increase? Across the first half of the twentieth century as murder statistics fluctuated, interrupted by two world wars, it was almost impossible to substantiate arguments that the death penalty either deterred murderers or was no deterrent at all.

In 1925, the Howard League for Penal Reform began 'the modern attack on capital punishment' with Roy Calvert leading the charge. He believed that not only was the death penalty wrong, but it was also no real deterrent. His campaign forced the appointment of a Select Committee on Capital Punishment in 1929 which aimed to suspend hanging for a 'trial period of five years'. While no action was taken, his work spurred the abolition movement onwards. In 1938, the House of Commons 'carried a motion in favour of abolition' during that year's debates on the Criminal Justice Bill, which subsequently failed to include an abolition clause. Then the Second World War intervened. In 1948, the House of Commons carried a free vote on abolition which was quashed by the House of Lords, but it was 'this culminating point in the campaign' that gave birth to 1948's Royal Commission. However, after five years of research and debate, restricted by the parameters it had been set, all the Commission could recommend was that juries should be allowed discretion in murder trials to request the death penalty for particular types of murder offence. Its recommendations were rejected, but the Commission had posed one essential question: 'whether capital punishment should be retained or abolished'. Finally, a focussed and concise question had been asked.[4]

Between 1953 and 1957, a new campaign led by Sydney Silverman, MP, succeeded in another motion carried in the House of Commons but was yet again refused by the House of Lords. Eventually, the Homicide Act 1957 contained some of the clauses suggested by the Commission earlier in 1953 to differentiate between types of murder. The use of a firearm as a murder weapon was retained as a capital offence, a distinction which would lead the jury foreman in Manuel's 1958 trial to confirm their verdict on capital murder. As barrister Louis Blom-Cooper argues, before 1957 sentence of execution was a certainty if convicted of any type of murder, a situation that continued between 1957 and 1965 if convicted of capital murder, despite the 'embarrassingly transparent' deficiencies of the 1957 Act. The 'distinction between capital and non-capital murders aroused such hearty disapproval among the judiciary' that several judges who had been on the fence came down on the side of 'outright abolition'.[5] By removing capital punishment from many categories of murder, the 1957 Act had brought abolition a step closer and gathered more elite support.

Once the Act was passed, some tabloid newspapers suggested that a 'sensational increase in murders' had occurred, particularly sexually motivated murders of children, a topic bound to capture attention. Public opinion – or rather journalists' opinions – kept the abolition debate alive but as the chair of the General Council of the Bar of England and Wales, Gerald Gardiner stated, government statistics for England and Wales proved that, in particular, child murders were comparable between 1955 and the first six months after 1957. In 1959, Gardiner concluded, 'there is no evidence that the changes made by the Homicide Act are having any effect whatever on the homicide rate'.[6]

In Scotland, the statistics collated for panels proceeded against on a charge of murder had risen from seven in 1951 to twelve in 1953, before decreasing to seven again throughout 1954 and 1955.[7] Statistics for 1958 in Scotland revealed that fourteen persons had been proceeded against for murder, although which were capital charges was not explained. However, of an eventual six found guilty, only two were sentenced to death, of whom one was reprieved.[8] Thus an upward trend was not apparent in the murder or conviction statistics in England and Wales, and Scotland. Gardiner confirmed his belief that whatever the outcome of the next general election in 1963, 'the remains of a punishment which an increasing number of people feel cannot be shown to be necessary' would be abolished because capital punishment 'no longer accords with the degree of civilization to which we feel we have attained'.[9]

When Sydney Silverman reintroduced the Murder (Abolition of Death Penalty) Bill to the House of Commons in 1964, he argued that abolition had actually been debated in 1957; what remained now was to decide whether execution for capital murder should also be removed from that statute, irrespective of what he acknowledged was public opinion for its retention. Ultimately, he called on the moral consciences of Members of Parliament to act on what they knew to be correct without fear of losing their seat at the next general election if they voted against the majority will of their constituents.[10] He declared the death penalty to be a 'callous, brutal, coldhearted ritual' with no social purpose.[11] The Commons debate was heated and lengthy. Brigadier Clarke asked how Silverman would respond when prison officers were killed by murderers in their care who now might only be sentenced to life imprisonment; what about the increased threat to police officers who would face murder by bank robbers because of the removal of the deterrent.[12] A female doctor Member of Parliament used the Hippocratic oath to argue that 'unnecessary killing is morally wrong and that death authorised by law is morally wrong'. Dr Shirley Summerskill also introduced a point that would become pivotal to those on trial for murder until the complete abolition of the death penalty: 'who can say any murderer is beyond hope of a cure?'. If psychiatrists could find the causes of crime, they might one day cure psychopathic murderers. Therefore, detain them in 'maximum security provisions' because 'their safety and not their punishment' was of greater concern.[13]

The moral argument was a key aspect of the debate surrounding abolition irrespective of what the newspapers considered to be 'public opinion'. Yet, while numerous MPs and lords changed their minds during the course of the Bill's passage through the two Houses, some were concerned that if abolition became law there could be no reversal. Writing in 1966, Dawtry argued that abolition had not been politically motivated because MPs had been allowed a free vote which had carried the motion for abolition by 355 votes to 170. He noted that the 'most effective speeches in support' were given by a member of the Conservative front bench and a former Conservative Home Secretary, members of the party which had previously argued to dilute the reforms contained in the 1957 Act.[14] However, the insertion of a sunset clause by Henry Brooke, a Conservative MP, meant that the debate and the Bill would be revisited by 30 July 1970 'unless Parliament by affirmative resolution of both Houses otherwise determines'.[15] Brooke did not agree that 'the taking of life by the State is contrary to moral principle', and he adhered to the death penalty's unique deterrent effect.[16] By introducing a sunset clause into the Murder Bill, effectively he gave a get-out to those Conservatives who had voted for abolition as a temporary measure, which had been supported by some lords as only 'an experiment and not a final act'.[17] Despite the Labour Prime Minister Harold Wilson's lifelong commitment to the abolition cause and Labour Lord Chancellor Lord Gerald Gardiner's attempt in the House of Lords to scotch the sunset clause, it was defeated by fifty-nine votes to fifty-five.[18] In November 1965, the Murder (Abolition of Death Penalty) Act received royal assent.

By the time the Murder Act came up for its sunset review, the Labour Government which had seen through abolition had been replaced by a Conservative administration, still containing many of its pro-hanging adherents. However, the liberal attitudes of the Swinging Sixties had become entrenched in British society, and it is debatable whether the death penalty's reintroduction would have now met with public approval. Complete abolition was confirmed in 1970, although the debate lingered into the 1980s under another Conservative Government with the prime minister 'regularly' voting 'in favour of restoration'.[19]

Interestingly, between 1955 and 1957, while the Homicide Act was debated, the Conservative Home Secretary had reprieved all capital sentences for convicted murderers. It had been a humane response to the undetermined outcome of a political and moral debate. Yet, while many legal advisers and government officials recognized the 'moral shabbiness' and 'professional incompetence' of the final Homicide Act and the probable need for its revision in the near future, no such moratorium on capital sentencing was extended to those found guilty of capital murder between 1957 and 1965.[20]

The Swinging Sixties were not to everyone's taste; sexual promiscuity, free love and adultery were severely frowned upon by many of the elites, particularly when indulged by the working classes. Thus, if one committed murder in a moment of impassioned jealousy, if one had a history of mental instability and a shotgun had been one's weapon of choice, 1963 was a most dangerous year to stand trial for capital murder.

Case

It is not that he did not mean to do it, but he had been insane in the moment he had shot Thomas Guyan at point blank range, or at least that was the special defence entered by his counsel Dr R. R. Taylor Q. C., a defence with which a majority of the jury of ten women and five men disagreed.

Henry John Burnett had met Margaret Guyan in 1961 while working at a local Aberdeen fish-curing firm. Margaret was married to Thomas with two young children, the second of whom was allegedly by another man, and although Thomas had agreed to support them as a family, Margaret had asked for a divorce. Her husband, a merchant seaman, was often away at sea for long periods, and she had decided to live with Henry, whom she called Harry, as man and wife. But then Thomas returned. Growing increasingly jealous of this new situation, Harry locked Margaret in their home on 31 May 1963, but not before they had fought and he had cut her neck with a knife. Their landlord freed Margaret who then sped after Harry; he had headed to his brother's home to fetch a gun.[21] That evening as Margaret sat watching the television with her newly returned husband at their family home, Harry knocked on the door. Thomas answered, but the two men had never met, and Thomas asked who he was. Harry replied, 'I've got you now' and fired at Thomas who fell down dead. Harry reloaded and threatened the rest of the family, including Margaret's grandmother who witnessed the scene. Quickly, Margaret agreed to go with Harry to prevent him from shooting anyone else.

Later in court, she testified that Harry 'did not look in his right mind'; his eyes were 'staring out of his head'. Harry took Margaret to a nearby petrol garage where he threatened John Irvine who was having his vehicle filled. Having stolen Irvine's car, they drove off but were intercepted by police not far away in Peterhead. As Harry emerged from the vehicle with his arms held out 'as if to show that he was not armed', he said 'It's me you want'. On the back seat of the car was the shotgun with one barrel loaded.[22]

At trial, Harry pleaded not guilty to two counts of assault, one on Margaret and the other against John Irvine, and also pleaded not guilty to capital murder. However, according to the Advocate Depute, Mr W. R. Grieve Q. C., not only was Harry's murderous jealousy on trial for 'being unable to bear seeing his mistress's favours being given elsewhere' but 'the sordid background of a sailor's wife being unfaithful to her husband when he was at sea'. Grieve argued he had proven beyond reasonable doubt that Harry had had 'a deliberate intention of shooting Thomas Guyan'. Yet, Harry's mother had testified that he had attempted suicide in 1961 when a girlfriend left him, and Dr Ian Lowit, a consultant psychiatrist at the Sick Children's Hospital, had examined Harry using 'an electric brain-testing machine' which had found an 'abnormality'.[23] Lowit considered Harry to be a psychopath under the definition described by the Mental Health Act 1959, whose 'whole life is comprised of impulsive unconsidered acts'.[24] He concluded that intermittently Harry had been incapable of 'rational decision'. On this basis, defence counsel asked the jury to consider that Burnett had been insane at the time, or 'at least they must say that he was partially insane and suffering from a state of diminished responsibility'.[25] The judge, Lord Wheatley's guidance to the jury emphasized that point: if they 'rejected the special defence of insanity, they then had to consider the secondary defence of diminished responsibility, but only in relation to the charge of capital murder'.[26] Twenty-five minutes later the jury had found Harry unanimously guilty of both charges of assault and, by a majority, guilty of murder. Lord Wheatley sentenced him to death.

Burnett declined to appeal his sentence, although Aberdeen's city magistrates appealed on his behalf and his family sent a telegram directly to the queen. On 15 August 1963, Burnett's execution was the first in Aberdeen for over 106 years – the last one had been held in public – and was the last time that 'judicial hanging' was recorded on a Scottish death certificate.[27] Burnett was the last man ever to hang in Scotland. Interviewed in Autumn 1963, Professor Millar, who held the Chair of Mental Health at Aberdeen University, told the press that 'he might refuse to give evidence at future murder trials where the degree of responsibility was a main issue ... because of the differing views of human responsibility held by doctors and lawyers', and clearly by jurors.[28]

Themes and analysis

There was no denying Burnett's guilt because there were witnesses to the murder; because the murder weapon on the back seat of his vehicle belonging to his brother fitted with the story that he had visited his brother's home to fetch it and there had been an altercation, and because on apprehension, Burnett had told the police it was him they wanted. Thus, the jury had only to decide: was Burnett insane at the time of the shooting or at least of diminished responsibility? Under the 1957 Homicide Act, using a gun to kill was classed as a capital offence; therefore, if found guilty, Burnett's only sentence would be execution. Only expert evidence on his mental state might save him.

Burnett was not considered so insane that he could not stand trial – insanity in bar of trial. However, in defence, Dr Taylor argued that Burnett had been insane at the moment of commission of the crime and employed expert psychiatric witnesses and Burnett's mother to provide evidence of mental instability. This was a special defence of insanity in bar of pleading; an insane person could not plead guilty to a crime which they had committed but for which they were not responsible. Scots Law on this point found 'guilty but insane' an illogical argument, because being insane at the time of the crime meant being unfit to plead.[29] Thus, Burnett's plea of not guilty was logical. However, this had been problematical to the Royal Commission in 1948, which seemingly could not grasp the particularity of Scots Law that not 'all insane persons are irresponsible', which ignored 'the question of volition'.[30] In this case, Burnett had intended to kill Guyan; there was volition. Further, while the death penalty remained a possibility if indicted for capital murder, in Scots Law, a guilty plea would not be accepted even for someone not entering an insanity defence; a thorough trial must be held. And if found guilty but of diminished responsibility, then the panel 'should not suffer the full pains of the law'.[31]

In a 1960 murder case, *HM Advocate v. Kidd*, Lord Strachan had directed the jury to consider the panel's 'alienation of reason'; 'there must have been some mental defect ... by which his reason was overpowered, and he was thereby rendered incapable of exerting his reason to control his conduct and reactions'. Lord Strachan argued that the test of knowing whether the act being committed was right or wrong had long passed and that now the law directed that 'A man may well know very well what he is doing, and may know that it is wrong, and he may none the less be insane'. Lord Wheatley accepted Lord Strachan's interpretation of the law when summing up to the jury in Burnett's case two years later.[32] Hence, his acknowledgement that Burnett knew what he had done was neither proof of sanity nor insanity. Thus, as T. B. Smith, professor of civil law, argued in this period, 'the jury is charged in the circumstances of the case, having particular regard to the evidence led by specialists in mental illness', which in Burnett's case was Drs Lowit and Taylor.[33]

Both psychiatrists for the defence were of the opinion that Burnett was insane and 'was suffering from psychopathy', making him incapable of 'assessing his actions'.[34] As psychiatrists argued in 1961, 'the definition of psychopathy in the Mental Health Act of 1959 was likely to lead to further difficulties' than those already posed by the Homicide Act 1957 once the English courts adopted 'the concept of diminished responsibility'.³⁵ However, diminished responsibility had been evolving within Scots Law since the nineteenth century, and Scottish juries, like that at Robert Handley's 1926 trial, were accustomed to its discussion, although the definition of what now constituted 'psychopathic disorder' was obscure. Understanding this particular diagnosis of mental illness and its impact on individual behaviour was not helped by the Mental Health Act which described it as 'a persistent disorder or disability of mind (whether or not including sub-normality of intelligence)' causing 'abnormally aggressive or seriously irresponsible conduct' which could be 'susceptible to medical treatment'.³⁶ However, the Homicide Act had specifically included language that would exclude from a defence of diminished responsibility 'persons who committed murder as a result of sudden outbursts of passion or rage'.³⁷ Thus, was Burnett psychopathic or just enraged?

Prosecuting counsel did not introduce a psychiatric expert to argue for Burnett's sanity; thus, the jury's understanding of his mental state was left to the defence to explore. The impulsive nature of Burnett's assault on Guyan could not be considered a 'crime of passion' since this was no defence in Scots Law, although that may not have prevented some jurors from sympathizing with his romantic predicament. Therefore, any evidence adduced for insanity or diminished responsibility rested on Burnett's medical history and psychiatric opinion for psychopathy. His mother and two psychiatrists confirmed Burnett's long-term mental instability, and one doctor specifically used the diagnosis of 'psychopathy'. As Smith argued in this period, the courts, 'while not surrendering their control of the doctrine [of diminished responsibility] to psychiatrists' would consider the 'consensus of expert opinion'. Yet, writing in 1961, Smith confirmed that the Scottish courts had yet to accept 'psychopathic personality' as 'justifying a plea of diminished responsibility'.³⁸ When summing up, Lord Wheatley had directed the jury to consider diminished responsibility and with little else in this trial for juridical debate, their verdict by a majority reflects a lack of consensus on this point. Either the psychiatrists had not argued convincingly for Burnett's psychopathic disorder, or the jury was not yet as informed as they might have been of an expanding area of medical knowledge sympathetic to the impacts of mental illness on culpability. The jury's division will rightly never be known and their majority verdict was guilty. However, among the fifteen jurors, some or perhaps just one believed Burnett had diminished responsibility for his actions.

Conclusion

Whether capital punishment is right or wrong or is a deterrent to murder remains a hot debate. Even in the early 1960s when discussing the statistics before and after the 1957 Homicide Act which differentiated capital from other types of murder, politicians could not decide whether the murder figures had declined. It was a matter of interpretation, which year range one selected and the removal of anomalous years. Further, as Sir Edward Boyle argued in Parliament, there was growing recognition that juries would not convict where the death penalty was the only sentence, and in the past in England, they had acquitted rather than condemn. That was an argument that had persisted in Scotland since the late nineteenth century. Sir Edward preferred that juries might convict without having to test their personal moral judgement on capital punishment, and removal of the death penalty would mean all murder cases would receive equal consideration. He believed the death penalty to be 'a somewhat sickening and barbarous ritual'.[39]

Yet, the debate for and against the death penalty will not go away. In 2011, a Member of Parliament who would become Britain's Home Secretary told a national television audience that she 'would actually support the reintroduction of capital punishment' as a deterrent to violent crime. Her statement was ambiguous as to whether that was solely for murder or would include rapists and other violent criminals.[40]

However, when the 1970 sunset clause came up for review, the reintroduction of judicial murder was rejected. Further reintroduction attempts were made up to 1994 when a House of Commons vote on an amendment to the Criminal Justice and Public Order Bill was rejected by 403 votes to 159. As Knowles' research confirms, every time the subject has arisen, the majority against the death penalty has increased. He attributes this to the revelations of miscarriages of justice revealed in the 1980s and 1990s.[41] If Burnett had in fact been of unsound mind or of a psychopathic personality, then his execution was indeed a miscarriage of justice, but the concept of mental illness is a developing discipline as psychiatrists gain greater understanding of the (mal)function of the human brain. What was known in 1963 has been greatly superseded. As Blom-Cooper avows, 'all law is the product of particular philosophical, religious and political views' and since what constitutes 'crime is a social construct', thus the law becomes a product of its time reflecting judicial mores in that moment.[42] Arguably, the law also reflects current scientific and medical expertise, as well as the judiciary's ability to accept that expertise.

Henry John Burnett's trial remains a sensitive issue for all those closely involved. In 2014, his body buried within the confines of Craiginches Prison in Aberdeen was exhumed after the prison was sold for development, and he was reburied in a private ceremony.[43] Burnett confessed his guilt and requested that no petition for a reprieve of sentence should be raised. It might be that he had achieved his goal of erasing his adversary in love and viewed his situation as futile, or it might be argued that his rejection of a petition was in itself a sign of mental instability.

ILLUSTRATION 14.1 *Craiginches Prison, Aberdeen 1963. Used by kind permission of DC Thomson & Co Ltd.*

On a national scale, a general election was looming in late 1964, and the incumbent Conservative Government would not have wished to be seen by its electorate as soft on violent crime. Further, if political division on the final debate remained too close to call in the few years between 1957 and 1965 and public opinion was perceived still to be in favour of execution for capital murder, this may further explain why the Conservative Government, hopeful of a third term in office, did not suspend the death penalty in the lead-up to its abolition as it had done before 1957.

Burnett was the last man to hang in Scotland, but he was not the last to hang in the UK. The continuation of judicial execution up to its final abolition was not a great moment for British civilizing tendencies. However, while 'in a mature democracy it is possible to tell the difference between public clamour and the persuasiveness' of rigorous investigation and debate holds true, then capital punishment has no place where proper and humane government persists.[44]

Notes

1. L. Blom-Cooper and T. Morris, *With Malice Aforethought: A Study of the Crime and Punishment for Homicide* (London, 2004), 109.
2. F. Dawtry, 'The Abolition of the Death Penalty in Britain', *British Journal of Criminology* 6, no. 2 (April, 1966), 189.
3. J. Gregory, *Victorians against the Gallows: Capital Punishment and the Abolitionist Movement in Nineteenth Century Britain* (London, 2011), 146 , 229.
4. Dawtry, 'Abolition', 188–9.
5. Blom-Cooper and Morris, *With Malice Aforethought*, 110, 114.
6. G. Gardiner, Q.C., 'Criminal Law: Capital Punishment in Britain', *American Bar Association Journal* 45, no. 3 (March, 1959), 261.
7. Table 4 'Persons proceeded against after full committal: analysis by type of crime', *Criminal Statistics Scotland 1955*, cmnd. 9750 (1955), 25. There is a large discrepancy in data reported in the *Criminal Statistics Scotland 1956* in the table shown on page xviii 'Persons found guilty of the different offences'. However, the higher total numbers of convicted murderers do not show a greatly different trend in convictions between 1954 and 1956.
8. *Criminal Statistics Scotland 1958*, cmnd. 746, 10.
9. Gardiner, 'Capital Punishment in Britain', 261.
10. Hansard, 21 December 1964, vol. 704, col. 870–1010.
11. Hansard, 21 December 1964, vol. 704, col. 884.
12. Hansard, 21 December 1964, vol. 704, col. 948.
13. Hansard, 21 December 1964, vol. 704, col. 950–1.
14. Dawtry, 'Abolition', 183–4.
15. Dawtry, 'Abolition', 184.
16. Hansard, 21 December 1964, vol. 704, col. 909.
17. Dawtry, 'Abolition', 184.
18. Dawtry, 'Abolition', 184.
19. J. B. Knowles, Q.C., 'The Abolition of the Death Penalty in the United Kingdom: how it happened and why it still matters', published by The Death Penalty Project (2015), 56.
20. L. Radzinowicz, *Adventures in Criminology* (London, 1999), quoted in Blom-Cooper and Morris, *With Malice Aforethought*, 110.
21. N. Adams, *Blood and Granite: true crime from Aberdeen* (Edinburgh, 2003), 59–60.
22. 'Widow's Evidence in Seaman's Death', *Glasgow Herald*, 24 July 1963, 5.
23. 'Close of Evidence in N.-E. Murder Trial', *Glasgow Herald*, 25 July 1963, 5.
24. Adams, *Blood and Granite*, 64–5.
25. 'Close of Evidence in N.-E. Murder Trial', *Glasgow Herald*, 25 July 1963, 5.

26 'Burnett sentenced to Death', *Glasgow Herald*, 26 July 1963, 8.
27 'City's first hanging for 106 years', *The Times*, 16 August 1963, 5; 'Grim Day', *Press and Journal*, 11 August 2020; https://www.pressandjournal.co.uk/fp/past-times/2389519/grim-day-when-the-last-man-hanged-in-scotland-was-executed-at-craiginches-prison/ (accessed February 2025).
28 *Scottish Daily Mail* 1963, quoted in Adams, *Blood and Granite*, 70.
29 T. B. Smith, *British Justice: The Scottish Contribution* (London, 1961), 105.
30 G. H. Gordon, *The Criminal Law of Scotland*, 2nd edition (Edinburgh, 1978), 10, 39, 373.
31 Smith, *British Justice*, 107.
32 Gordon, *Criminal Law*, 10:40, 374–5.
33 Smith, *British Justice*, 106.
34 'Close of Evidence', *Glasgow Herald*, 25 July 1963, 5.
35 D. Curran, 'Psychiatric Evidence in Court', *British Medical Journal* 1, no. 5228 (March, 1961), 817.
36 Mental Health Act, (1959), 7 & 8 Eliz. 2., c.72., 4 (4).
37 J. E. Hall Williams, 'The Psychopath and the Defence of Diminished Responsibility', *The Modern Law Review* 21, no. 5 (September 1958), 544.
38 Smith, *British Justice*, 107–8.
39 Hansard, 21 December 1964, vol. 704, col. 984–7; Hansard, 26 March 1968, vol. 761 col. 1330–1.
40 'Home Secretary Priti Patel, I want criminals to feel terror', BBC interview, 3 August 2019, https://www.bbc.co.uk/news/uk-49213743 (accessed February 2025).
41 Knowles, 'Abolition of the Death Penalty', 56–7.
42 Blom-Cooper and Morris, *With Malice Aforethought*, 31–2.
43 'True Crime: the story of the last man to hang in Scotland', *The Herald*, 1 July 2023.
44 Blom-Cooper and Morris, *With Malice Aforethought*, 32.

15

S. v. HM Advocate 1989: Marriage, rape and abuse

When is rape not really rape? When perpetrated within marriage. But in 1989, a marital rape case – previously a charge almost impossible to bring – forced the judiciary and society to reflect on a two-centuries-old common law concept that on marriage, a woman's right to consent or not consent to sex with her husband was expunged; she had become her husband's property to do with as he wished. In 1989, that absurdity was removed from Scots Law, which led the way to similar legislation across the UK.

Context

As a socio-legal concept, marital rape contains so much that requires explanation concerning gender, masculinity, property rights and female agency. As a form of domestic abuse, marital rape is arguably only one step behind the ultimate in domestic violence which is spousal murder. It is only in the late twentieth century that anyone with the power to rectify this form of criminal violence against women has done anything about it. Scotland's Law Commission has argued that marital rape as opposed to all forms of extra-marital rape is 'particularly offensive' because it is 'an abuse of an act which has been or should have been' a husband's way of 'expressing love for his wife'.[1] As research by the Scottish Parliament has discovered, domestic abuse including marital rape does not only occur among 'the rougher elements of society'; women do not 'ask for it' and often even when marital violence becomes intolerable, they are unable to escape abuse by leaving their family home.² However, history has not always seen sexual intercourse within marriage – consenting or non-consenting – in this way.

In Corinthians 1:7, St Paul discusses what has been termed the 'marital debt': the wife does not rule over her own body, yet neither does the husband rule over his own. However, St Paul's assertion of 'reciprocity' and 'mutuality' within marriage has not always been adhered to by Christians in the intervening two thousand years or so.³ In the early eighteenth century, the *History of the Pleas of the Crown* by England's great Stuart jurist, Sir Matthew Hale, was published. Hale confirmed the 'old common law rule' that 'a husband cannot be guilty of a rape committed by himself upon his lawful wife, for by their mutual matrimonial consent and contract the wife hath given up herself in this kind unto her husband, which she cannot retract'.⁴ By 1797, adherence to this ancient attitude towards sexual inequality in marriage had been reshaped in Baron Hume's enduringly authoritative treatise on Scots Law. Hume added the caveat that, although a woman became the property of her husband on marriage and she surrendered herself to him and revoked her right to dissent, a husband could not do quite what he wanted with his wife because he could be charged as 'art and part' of her rape if he acted as an accessory.⁵ As more recently emphasized, throughout the nineteenth century 'women were virtually voiceless chattels with little control over their persons or property'.⁶ The situation remained uncontested until the end of the twentieth century when the first cases of marital rape were prosecuted.

Scotland's first criminal trial for marital rape at the High Court of Justiciary began in 1982 with a trial for rape alleged against a husband who was living apart from his wife but with 'no judicial order of separation' yet in place. The panel's counsel objected to the charge on the grounds that no such law existed in Scotland: a man could not rape his wife because she belonged to him and could not withdraw her consent.⁷ The implied consent to intercourse within marriage, and its removal, had never been tested. However, as the eminent voice in Scots Law in the twentieth century, Sir Gerald Gordon K.C. argued, 'there is no good reason for treating this implied consent as an irrebuttable presumption of the law in every case', particularly where the spousal parties were separated, even if not yet judicially so.⁸ Thus, with no case law to guide him and applying logic during the appeal hearing, Lord Robertson concluded, 'I do not think it can be affirmed as a matter of principle that the law of Scotland today is that a husband in no circumstances can be guilty of the crime of rape upon his wife'. If a husband could be charged with assaulting his wife, then logically he could be charged with rape if it was accepted that rape was a form of aggravated assault in Scots Law.⁹ The accused man was acquitted by a majority.

In 1984, another case was brought. This time, the couple appear to have been wavering between separation and reconciliation, and the alleged rape occurred in the man's home. The same objection to the charge was raised: it was not a crime for a man to rape his wife in Scots Law. This time Lord Cameron followed a similar argument that separation was 'the clearest form' of indication that consent to spousal sex under marriage was withdrawn, because marriage was only '*prima facie* evidence of consent'; 'because the parties lived apart the conclusion that there had been surrender was not acceptable'.[10] As Gordon had earlier commented, a husband's 'irrevocable privilege' to sex was no longer recognized by 'contemporary *mores*', and the law needed to 'take contemporary attitudes' into account.[11] The charge against the panel was found not proven.[12]

As usual, the juries' deliberations in both cases remain unknown. Whether both panels were acquitted because of an unconvincing Crown case or because social and juridical attitudes lagged behind the judges' arguments is a point of conjecture. Despite the delays while objections were entered and appeals were heard, it must be assumed that the evidence gathered by the Procurator Fiscal and presented to the Crown was sufficiently compelling and corroborated for both cases to proceed to the High Court of Justiciary. Therefore, evidence for the women's lack of consent had also been sufficiently determined, although not proved, for the prosecution to proceed. However, consent did not only rest on the complainer's testimony of saying 'no', but the man's understanding of her willingness to participate in intercourse had also to be established. The man's *mens rea* – did he know the woman was unconsenting or was he reckless as to whether she did or not – was critical to the jury's decision-making, because if the man believed she had consented and the jury believed that to be proved, then he could not be guilty of rape.[13] Thus in both cases, besides the possibility that the respective juries held conservative values, it is also feasible that they were unconvinced that both women had actively withdrawn consent to marital intercourse.

As societal attitudes towards women were clearly changing, evidenced not least by the fact that marital rape could now be prosecuted, as Lindsay Farmer has argued, 'the whole basis of the law' was shifting 'from a requirement of force to one of absence of consent'.[14] However, a legal conundrum would be presented by the next case to hit the headlines in 1989. A two-centuries-old argument had rested on the contention that if assaulting a wife was criminal but raping her was not because her consent was inherent in the marriage contract, then the husband was immune from a charge of rape. But as it was about to be argued, 'if a woman cannot consent to an assault and if rape is a form of assault then the immunity [to a husband] cannot be justified'.[15] Which would mean that in the forthcoming case, Hume's espousal of the husband's exemption from prosecution for the rape of his wife would be challenged. This time the circumstances were that the husband and wife were definitely still cohabiting when the assault occurred. However, yet again the trial began with an objection and appeal against the charge.

Case

The indictment alleged that on 24 August 1988, the couple had had an argument in which the forty-one-year-old unemployed lorry driver slapped his twenty-eight-year-old wife because he had discovered that she was stealing pills from the psychiatric clinic she visited, and her drinking was 'making her brain scattered'. He had decided he was 'going to embarrass her' by demanding she undress, knowing that she was uncomfortable with her naked body. Having humiliated her, he left the house to sign on at the unemployment office, but when he returned, he found her wearing handcuffs which they had bought as a joke some years earlier. He said, 'She was a nutter'. That was his version of events.

The wife's version, partially corroborated by a concerned neighbour, was that he had 'ordered her into the bedroom' where he had used the handcuffs and then tied her to the bed with ropes, forced a sock into her mouth and taped her face with Sellotape before raping her. The neighbour described their 'pact' that if the wife were in trouble, she would rap on the wall. Having heard banging noises, the neighbour had spoken to the wife through the letterbox of the locked house and could see 'gauze' around the naked woman's neck. At this point, the husband returned, and she challenged him with tying up his wife 'like a dog'.[16]

Before the trial could commence, in early March 1989 the man's defence counsel objected to the charge of rape. Lord Mayfield had 'held the libel relevant' and had declared that 'It is clear, on the authorities, that rape is an aggravated form of assault and equally clear that it is a criminal offence to assault a wife', but he gave leave for the panel to appeal further.[17] In due course, an appeal was lodged and in 'a historic ruling', Lord Emslie upheld Lord Mayfield's decision on the point that 'he did not believe it had ever been the law of Scotland that a woman in marriage surrendered herself ... to violation by force against her will'. Defence counsel's attempt to use Hume's 1797 interpretation was rejected. Yet having acknowledged that a husband did not have the right to 'sexual relations with his wife when he wants and whatever his wife's feelings', defence counsel argued that 'a wife has no absolute right to say no whenever she wants'. If a wife was that reluctant to have sex with her husband, it should become 'the subject of a divorce action'. Whether the courts should intrude into 'the intimate personal relations of marriage' was called into question as well as 'the difficulties in bringing a rape charge against a husband'.[18] But this was the end of the twentieth century; society had come a long way in two hundred years. Or as the law report on the appeal stated, 'whether or not the reason for the husband's immunity from a charge of rape committed upon his wife was a good one in the 18th and early 19th century, it had since disappeared altogether'.[19] Scotland's Solicitor General adhered to the 'modern understanding' of a wife's rights and that 'there was no such thing as an irrevocable submission to intercourse' within marriage.[20] Thus, the entire matter now rested on whether it could be proven at trial that the wife had withdrawn her consent, rather than that the husband could be found guilty of rape.

Between the appeal and the trial, the press published several letters commenting on the debate. In London, the Scottish appeal outcome had been met with 'disquiet', the letter's author stating, 'There is an unbridgeable difference' between this kind of rape and 'when a rapist leaps out of the unknown ... in a lonely place, late at night'. She went on to discuss the 'trauma' of a 'surprise rape' being more severe than if the woman had been out socially with the man beforehand, and she asked readers to consider the 'total destruction' suffered by a man charged or convicted of rape when the assault may have been 'a clumsy miscalculation on his part'. The female author was writing from London's legal quarter.[21] The backlash was swift. A female solicitor asked whether the writer was 'seriously suggesting' that going out for a drink with a man constituted consent to sex, and if marriage meant consenting to sex for 'the rest of her life'. Another woman asked readers to consider how a wife should be expected to spend the rest of her life with her rapist who should have cherished her 'above all others'.[22]

Eventually, the trial began on 25 April 1989, and the panel entered a plea of not guilty. The police surgeon confirmed finding bruising on the wife's wrists 'consistent with abrasions caused by handcuffs', and the neighbour testified with her eyewitness corroboration of events after the alleged rape. The complexities of the legal debate notwithstanding, the trial lasted three days, at the end of which defence counsel submitted to the jury that 'there must be very few married couples where one or the other of them had not gone a wee bit over the top from time to time'. He added, 'It is, in my submission, at least a basic assumption that the parties to a marriage are willing to have sexual relations' and that 'You do not have to ask your wife for permission every time sexual intercourse is on your mind'. The judge, Lord Sutherland summed up the key arguments for the jury of nine men and six women: a wife must make it 'abundantly clear' that she is unconsenting to intercourse with her husband; 'forcible taking of a woman' was an 'essential element of rape'; being married was 'neither here nor there' if a woman was forced into sex, and if the panel had 'an honest and genuine belief' that consent was given, then it was not rape.

The jury's verdict was not proven, and the panel was acquitted, but not before being admonished for a breach of the peace a month before the alleged rape and for the assault of striking his wife on the day of the alleged rape. Speaking after the trial, a representative from Scottish Women's Aid stated, 'It is unlikely that this woman's treatment at the hands of the court will encourage other women to use the law to protect themselves'.[23]

Themes and analysis

Studies conducted in the United States in the 1980s reveal that a 'pervasive fear among political and legal professionals' was that repeal of the marital rape exemption would 'ultimately flood the courts with vindictive wives' prosecuting their husbands, using a rape allegation as revenge for any number of spousal disagreements.[24] This connects to an older assumption associating false accusations of sexual assault with attempts to blackmail elite men.[25] However, more modern judicial and juridical attitudes towards the removal of the marital rape exemption range across a number of concerns. There is the assumption that marital rape is not as serious as 'classic rape'. 'Because a woman has previously had *consensual* intercourse with her partner,' this diminishes 'the gravity of any subsequent *non-consensual* intercourse' [emphasis in original].[26] Historical 'cultural bias' has suggested that marital rape is 'less serious,' and the 'victim is more to blame than in cases of stranger rape'. Bennice and Resick argue this is because marital rape 'does not fit the cultural schema of the stranger in the dark alley'. There is also the culturally reinforced idea that men have a greater need for sex than women and therefore, when refused, may force themselves upon their partner.[27] Other reasons for not criminalizing marital rape in the past have included the intrusion into the private sphere of family life and undermining 'the institution of marriage'.[28]

None of these arguments has stood the test of time, but in the 1970s and 1980s they were real impediments to gender equality within marriage, and arguably indicative of wider societal attitudes towards women. Where women lacked agency, men could take advantage, and as the US studies of the 1980s reveal, where wives were uneducated, had not been employed before marriage and had several children keeping them in the family home, marital rape was more prevalent. Frieze's 1983 study of communities in Pittsburgh revealed that wives believed their husbands raped them because of their desire to prove their manhood.[29] Forced violent sex was manly. Some wives attributed their rapes to their husbands' drinking, external frustrations and others to their husbands' jealousy and unfounded notions of unfaithfulness. More mundanely, some women believed they had been raped because they had simply been reluctant to have sex. There was a correlation between husbands' drinking and raping, between other domestic abuse and raping and between a first rape leading to repeated raping.[30] Bennice and Resick attributed this repetition to the 'trust and proximity' that exists within the marital home, where rapes were more likely to be 'completed rapes' than in cases of stranger rape.[31] All the women surveyed attributed their rape 'as the responsibility of the husband'; they had done nothing to provoke him.[32] If indeed there exists any female behaviour to provoke rape.

The US studies also suggested that wives who were raped had experienced rapes outside of marriage, either stranger rapes or rapes from fathers, grandfathers and male in-laws, and that a wife's past rape experiences may have precipitated marital rape.[33] However, Frieze and Bennice and Resick concluded that, when reports of marital rape gained through their studies were extrapolated, marital rape was 'actually the most common type of rape'; it 'occurred at a far higher frequency than non-marital rape'.[34] Commenting in the immediate aftermath of the 1989 trial, Lindsay Farmer noted that 'to be properly aware of the potential for reform', it was necessary to recognize 'the extent of marital rape' which required everyone from men to 'the police to prosecutors and defence counsel' to change their behaviour. Thus, it was not just 1980s United States but also 1980s Scotland where the incidence of marital rape was alarming.

Further, Bennice and Resick comment that 'widespread legal, cultural and professional invalidation of marital rape' has limited 'the identification and treatment' of raped wives.[35] Such official blindness has also restricted punishment for those brought to justice. Sentencing for marital rape has continued to attract shorter carceral penalties than stranger rape, primarily because marital rape has been considered not so upsetting as 'classic rape'. As Kelly and Shiels quote from an English case in 1988, the judge reduced the sentence to three years because 'the element of degradation which a victim of rape suffers simply from the act of intercourse forced upon her by a stranger is absent'.[36]

Conclusion

As usual in a Scottish trial, so much evidence had been agreed by the legal parties before reaching court that it took only three days to acquit the panel accused of marital rape in 1989, but the legal debate that followed changed the law in Scotland. Of the constituent countries of the UK and Great Britain, Scotland was the first to make marital rape a competent criminal charge whether the parties were separated, going through a separation or indeed still cohabiting. As Farmer noted, 'it should not require separation for the revocation of consent to be recognised by the law'.[37] It had taken 150 years – arguably 2,000 years – to reach this point. However, one significant element of *any* rape trial persists, and that is the introduction of a woman's sexual history as 'evidence' for the defence case. Because rape is a predominantly private violence, it is difficult to corroborate and remains largely a 'contestation' of her word against his.[38] The introduction of the complainer's sexual past as defence 'evidence' has been used to discredit the woman, when all the jury is actually directed to consider is evidence presented by the Crown and in defence of the panel's behaviour.

Despite Scotland's strenuous judicial endeavours to prohibit this humiliating, embarrassing and intimidating strategy through the implementation of the 2002 Sexual Offences (Procedure and Evidence) (Scotland) Act, there remains the option for defence counsel to apply to the Crown to bring the complainer's sexual history evidence as part of their case. There must of course be reasons for this request, and the 'nature and relevance of proposed questioning' must be submitted in writing before the trial. Equally, where the defence has made such a request, the Crown is obliged 'to disclose any previous analogous convictions that the accused may have'. Thus, if he has done it or anything like it before, the jury will be informed. Further, the panel can no longer cross-examine the complainer, a practice loaded with the possibility of the woman having to relive her rape experience led through the details by the man who allegedly committed the assault.[39] These are tremendous developments in Scots Law, but perhaps there is work still to do within society.

For cases which come to trial, the conviction rate remains woefully low, although this largely depends on what statistics are employed. For all rapes reported to the police, the number of which has increased by 451 per cent between 1977 and 2007, there has only been a 15 per cent increase in the number of prosecutions.[40] Further, of those cases which make it to court, the number of convictions has fallen. The same research discovered that Scotland's arrest and custody rates 'were the highest of all countries' studied.[41] However, the picture improves if one considers the conversion of prosecutions to convictions. More recent data indicate that of all prosecuted rape cases, 43.3 per cent secured a conviction.[42] That is a more encouraging statistic. Yet it suggests that poor evidence and little corroboration – his word versus hers – as well as the possibility of a complainer withdrawing her complaint, for numerous reasons having had her report recorded, make getting to court a difficult process.

The fear of a wave of prosecutions inundating the law courts never happened. A study conducted in 1996 found that of 450 rape reports, only twenty-two concerned marital rape.[43] Whatever the reluctance of the judiciary and society more generally to accept that marital rape happened, that it was a criminal offence, it became the law in Scotland before elsewhere in the UK that marital rape should and would be prosecuted. That law rested on the interpretation of the common law by judges with the insight to realize that society had moved on from Hume's days. However, the discussion morphed into a debate on the appropriateness for the judiciary to make new laws that should otherwise be enacted by Parliament. Farmer has commented that the Parliamentary route may be preferable to enacting new law 'in terms of speed and democratic legitimacy' when addressing social problems, although the risk is that Parliament may 'legislate in a way which is inconsistent with established principles or rules of common law'.[44] Criminalizing marital rape was a 'liberalising reform' which expanded the criminal law.[45] Which begs a tangential question: is the expansion of the criminal law a good or a bad thing?

Perhaps the best way to sum up how far Scottish society has come regarding women's agency and protection in law is to return to the words of Lord Emslie in the appeal for this now notorious 1989 marital rape case: 'The fiction of implied consent [in marriage] has no useful purpose to serve today. ... It would be an understatement to say that this authentic example of male chauvinism fails to accord with current opinion as to the rights of husbands'.[46] He was right in 1989, and Lord Emslie remains right today.

Notes

1 Law Commission, *Rape within Marriage*, no. 205 (London, 1992), para 3.12, 8–9. Note all cases have been anonymized due to their close proximity in time to the current day.

2 'Violence against Women', Debate, Meeting of the Parliament, 9 November 2006, 29224.

3 D. MacCulloch, *Lower than the Angels: A History of Sex and Christianity* (London, 2024), 90–1.

4 M. Hale, *Historia Placitorum Coronæ* (London, 1736), 629; D. Kelly and R. Shiels, 'Marital Rape in Scots Law', *Journal of the Forensic Science Society* 28 (1988), 253.

5 D. Hume, *Commentaries on the Law of Scotland, respecting the description and punishment of crimes*, vol. 2 (1797), 10.

6 Lord Advocate's Reference no. 1 of 2001 v. Edward Richard Watt, Opinion of Lady Cosgrove, Appeal Court (Edinburgh, 2001), para 13.

7 Kelly and Shiels, 'Marital Rape in Scots Law', 254–6.

8 G. H. Gordon, *The Criminal Law of Scotland*, 2nd edition (Edinburgh, 1978), 33:12, 888.

9 Kelly and Shiels, 'Marital Rape in Scots Law', 255; *S. v. HM Advocate*, 1989, *Scots Law Times*, 469.

10 Kelly and Shiels, 'Marital Rape in Scots Law, 256; *S. v. HM Advocate*, 1989, *Scots Law Times*, 469.
11 Gordon, *Criminal Law*, 33:12, 888–9.
12 Kelly and Shiels, 'Marital Rape in Scots Law', 254–6.
13 Lord Advocate's Reference no. 1 of 2001, Opinion of the Lord Justice General, para 28.
14 L. Farmer, 'Criminal Law', in *A Compendium of Scottish Ethnology: Scottish Life and Society*, vol. 13, ed. M. Mulhern (Edinburgh, 2012), 186.
15 L. Farmer, 'Recognising Marital Rape', Scottish Legal Action Group, bulletin (1989), 103.
16 'I wanted to humiliate my wife, says rape trial husband', *Glasgow Herald*, 26 April 1989, 3.
17 *S. v. HM Advocate*, 1989, *Scots Law Times*, 469; 'Court upholds marital rape charge', *The Times*, 16 March 1989, 3.
18 'Judges rule on rape within marriage', *Glasgow Herald*, 16 March 1989, 3.
19 *S. v. HM Advocate*, Case Digest, 1989, S.C.C.R. 248.
20 'Judges rule on rape within marriage', *Glasgow Herald*, 16 March 1989, 3.
21 'Letters to the Editor', *The Times*, 20 March 1989, 17.
22 'Letters to the Editor', *The Times*, 23 March 1989, 17.
23 'Husband's rape charge not proven', *Glasgow Herald*, 27 April 1989, 3.
24 J. A. Bennice and P.A. Resick, 'Marital Rape: History, Research, and Practice', *Trauma, Violence & Abuse* 4, no. 3 (July, 2003), 229.
25 A. M. Kilday, *Crime in Scotland 1660–1960: the Violent North?* (Abingdon, 2021), 83–4.
26 P. N. S. Rumney, 'When rape isn't rape: court of appeal sentencing practice in cases of marital and relationship rape', *Oxford Journal of Legal Studies* 19, no. 2 (Summer, 1999), 248.
27 Bennice and Resick, 'Marital Rape', 232–3.
28 Rumney, 'When Rape isn't Rape', 245.
29 I. H. Frieze, 'Investigating the Causes and Consequences of Marital Rape', *Signs* 8, no. 3 (Spring, 1983), 544.
30 Frieze, 'Investigating the Causes', 544, 538, 535.
31 Bennice and Resick, 'Marital Rape', 238
32 Frieze, 'Investigating the Causes', 544.
33 Frieze, 'Investigating the Causes', 545, 535.
34 Bennice and Resick, 'Martial Rape', 238; Frieze, 'Investigating the Causes', 536.
35 Bennice and Resick, 'Marital Rape', 243.
36 *The Times*, 11 June 1988 quoted in Kelly and Shiels, 'Marital Rape in Scots Law', 257.
37 Farmer, 'Recognising Marital Rape', 104.

38 S. Brindley and M. Burman, 'Meeting the Challenge? Responding to rape in Scotland', in *International Approaches to Rape*, ed. N. Westmarland and G. Gangoli (Bristol, 2012), 154.
39 Brindley and Burman, 'Meeting the Challenge?', 157.
40 This may be partially attributed to greater ease in reporting, improvements in police practice or a real number increase in sexual violence complaints.
41 Brindley and Burman, 'Meeting the Challenge?', 159–60.
42 www.rapecrisisscotland.org/help-facts/ (accessed February 2025).
43 J. Harris and S. Grace, *A Question of Evidence? Investigating and Prosecuting Rape in the 1990s* (London, 1999), 6.
44 Farmer, 'Criminal Law', 188.
45 Farmer, 'Recognising Marital Rape', 104.
46 *S. v. HM Advocate*, 1989, *Scots Law Times*, 469.

Conclusion

In her book *Crime in Scotland*, Anne-Marie Kilday concludes that Scotland is no more violent than the rest of Britain; it is hard to disagree.[1] But does a reducing trend in the level of violence equate with being a civilized society? An improvement in interpersonal behaviours over time should be obvious in a nation which has attached its name to the eighteenth-century Enlightenment. Yet, women and girls cannot walk the country's streets without fear of molestation; young men continue to become embroiled in fist fights outside pubs, and New Year's Eve celebrations occasionally dissolve into rowdy affairs. But that is not just Scotland; it could be any country.

The study of criminal violence is hugely informative of a nation's developments towards societal and judicial improvement and social inclusion of all strata. By viewing violent crime through a societal, judicial and gendered lens, it is possible to trace historical advances, where they responded to national events, local pressures or changing social attitudes. Acting for the public good has meant different things across time and class, but essentially the public good is defined as 'what is best for society as a whole … to right wrongs; uncover and then expose corruption' and to treat all of society 'fairly, irrespective of race, class or gender'.[2] The abolition of the death penalty is probably the most prominent example of a centuries-long debate, responding at times to national and local pressures, coming to fruition for the combined benefit of the individual and society. Yet the ultimate measure of that society's advances is more probably its equal treatment of women. 'While men's prerogative over women expanded' in some social spheres during our period of investigation, in others it contracted. Tolerance of domestic violence endured longer than public acts of gendered violence, because notions of masculinity – workplace toughness and domestic authority – persisted in all classes.[3] In 2006, the members attending a meeting of the Scottish Parliament debated, 'too often, we talk about violence against women as if it happens in the absence of anyone else and we do not mention the men'.[4] Many of the criminal cases described here have involved male abuse of women, whether through criminal violence or through judicial process. While men continue to use violence – sexual or otherwise – against women to prove their masculinity, to enhance their standing among their peers, to impose their status and power, it reflects a society wedded to the past and suggests that German sociologist Norbert Elias's *Prozess der Zivilisation* of a linear decline in violence was too optimistic. Like other nations, Scotland has revealed moments in its history of exceptional advances in interpersonal behaviours as well as confounding reversals.

In 1708, Elspeth Martine was acquitted of the charge of incest with her uncle and did not hang as he did. She had offered the court sufficient evidence for the jury to understand that she had been forcibly sexually assaulted despite the more authoritative voice of her older male relation. This was a point of hope for women and girls sexually assaulted by abusive men exercising their supposed 'rights' to female bodies. Arguably, Elspeth's community had shown empathy and had used the law to right a wrong, and the law had judged Elspeth's and her uncle's case on its merits, not their prejudices.

However, by 1727, in remote Dornoch, Janet Horne was burned, possibly alive, for witchcraft. When the newly united Great Britain had moved away from superstitious beliefs in malefice, the community in this rural area of northern Scotland held tight to misogyny, wrapped up in fear of the Devil walking among them. Janet and her family were vulnerables, poor, unprotected by a male figure, elderly and disabled, and it appears that no one sought the authority of the judiciary to conduct a fair trial – if there ever could be a fair trial for witchcraft. It appears that someone helped Janet's daughter to escape; an empathetic individual who did not hold with witchcraft superstitions? But Janet suffered gross injustice, fuelled by her superstitious, misogynistic neighbours and a group of elite men who obliged their fears.

By 1808, Barbara Malcolm's prosecution for murdering her daughter reveals that support for a beleaguered unmarried woman only extended so far. An employer might be happy to look the other way to engage her wet-nursing services, and a foster family might take in an illegitimate child to augment their family income. But the societal condemnation of single motherhood led to the judicial murder of a woman who had no motive to kill her child. No one considered the possibility of a mistake made by the apothecary who appears to have been overly eager to conduct an autopsy on a child to whose mother he supplied medicine. Single motherhood and unlucky circumstance combined to ensure that Barbara 'fitted' the crime perfectly, whereas the elite male apothecary was never considered as a perpetrator of, even accidental, crime.

CONCLUSION

By 1811, the exuberance of youth with a little bit of money in their pockets, testing the limits of their juvenile masculinity at Hogmanay, got out of hand. Coordinated gang behaviour, petty criminality and what appears to have been a beating rather than the motivated murder of a policeman resulted in the execution of young boys who, due to their ages, might otherwise have been shown mercy. The growing voice of the middle classes pushing for recognition among the elites who had previously looked the other way after a rowdy New Year's Eve changed how Edinburgh's enlightened society viewed its youth; they had become a recognizable group to be controlled.

The murders committed by Burke and Hare in 1828 for financial gain exploited recent advances in medical science and the need for cadavers for medical students to practise on. The latter reflects socio-medical improvements that would eventually benefit all society, whereas the former reveals the grasping, licentious nature of some men, capable of monetizing the murder of society's least protected individuals. The political debate on where to source more bodies suggests the beginning of an elite move away from barbarous punishments with the worst – execution and dissection – reserved only for the most violent criminals. The differentiation of capital punishments by crime may be seen as the earliest step towards total abolition of the death penalty. But Burke's and Hare's crimes reveal a pocket of society tethering hopes of a universal civilizing trend to humanity's darkest behaviour.

Margaret Paterson's rape-murder in 1830 reflects a different species of toxic masculinity. Dobie's and Thomson's disregard for Margaret's sexual autonomy as a woman, their continued disdain for her welfare once they became aware of her suffering all indicate a gendered fissure in mid-nineteenth-century society: some men believed they could do as they liked with women's bodies without fear of the law. However, by mid-century, the elites and therefore the judiciary could look beyond the underprivileged background of an impoverished woman who liked a drink to see further into the criminality of an underclass of men capable of such violence. Sexual assault, among other violent crimes, had become a social problem that the elites were determined to address. It had no public place in nineteenth-century Scotland, although in private, sexual abuse with limited recourse to the law would continue for another 160 years.

Margaret's case might be seen as recognition for every woman's rights in Scottish society; however, Madeleine Smith's acquittal suggests that once more, social privilege might buy judicial privilege. When the middle classes committed criminal violence, 'offenders received punishment, but only when their actions proved impossible to ignore or redefine'.[5] Madeleine's punishment was the public ignominy of a trial, while her crime, although not redefined as anything other than murder by poison, was debated as a social ill rather than a criminal act. Madeleine's case reveals that Victorian Scotland was not yet prepared to see a young middle-class woman convicted of a crime that exuded immorality and sexuality. Indeed, it would have been unconscionable to countenance the reaction of the lower classes if she had been found guilty and hanged, let alone that of her own class.

From the late nineteenth century, rapid urbanization and industrialization have been identified as key drivers for higher rates of crime.[6] At this point, Scottish violence became focussed on Glasgow. While Patrick Higgins's prosecution for same-sex child abuse coincided with the notorious trial of Oscar Wilde, it is not a case of homosexual abuse. Apart from the licentious circumstances leading to the appalling abuse of six-year-old Thomas, Higgins's case reveals the social inequalities and poor living conditions of Scotland's working classes before the turn of the century, the result of immigration, urbanization and industrialization. This might have led to abundance for all, but instead it created slums and precarious employment, particularly for the unskilled like Thomas's father who was unable to support his family without the extra income earned from a lodger.

Only thirteen years later, that same society pulled together to petition for the reprieve of the death sentence for Oscar Slater. Law enforcement, the judiciary and the jury appear to have assumed that this 'foreigner' was guilty of the brutal murder of an old lady because his type fitted the crime. The evidence was circumstantial, and the persistence of Glaswegians with the assistance of one notable celebrity whose dogged campaigning on Slater's behalf resulted in the creation of Scotland's criminal appeal court. Slater suffered an injustice, which resulted in improved justice for all.

Yet Susan Newell's conviction and execution reveal a reversal in empathy when circumstances pointed towards an alcoholic, difficult woman as the perpetrator. Elite recognition of juries' reluctance to convict when execution was the only sentence was debated by the legal officers involved in Susan's case, but among the jury, no such reluctance was apparent. Neither was a petition raised by her neighbours nor much intervention offered by elite men, except to request the Scottish Secretary not to make them execute a woman. It was less about Susan and more about their reputation.

Only three years later, Robert Handley, on trial for rape-murder, was convicted of culpable homicide. Circumstantial evidence and an insanity plea, this time entered ahead of the trial, and his good 'character' in court combined to return a conviction on a non-capital charge. Sympathy for the victim and empathy for the accused were both evident.

In 1928, 220 years after John Martine was hanged for incestuously raping his niece, Thomas Lutton was sentenced to twelve months' imprisonment for incestuous assault against his two stepdaughters. His sentence reveals a huge step forward in judicial punishment, but his personal behaviour suggests that nothing had changed when it came to the power relations between adult men and young girls.

CONCLUSION

Peter Manuel's mindless murder of several victims is an anomaly. His case cannot be seen as an instance of toxic masculinity, nor can it be viewed as a reversal of a civilizing trend. Post-war Scottish society was as flummoxed by his behaviour as any society is when a serial killer stalks among them. Another Scottish serial killer – known as Bible John – active in the 1960s came and went without arrest or explanation. It is only post-prosecution when the evidence is analysed that an understanding of the morally incomprehensible can be attempted. Despite criminologists' best efforts, no one has yet provided a wholly convincing explanation for why serial killers do it.

In cases where an insanity plea or one of diminished responsibility is entered, this is an indication that either defence counsel is convinced of the accused's mental instability or they are grasping at any plea that will avoid their client's conviction, particularly when there is the potential for capital sentencing. In Henry John Burnett's case, the jealous killing of a love rival is nothing new in history, but his trial allows insight into nearly twenty years of judicial debate concerning the death penalty, its deterrent effect and its abolition. Sadly, too late for Burnett, the abolition of barbarous judicial punishment came to an end across Great Britain in the mid-1960s. Its timing was later than some countries and sooner than others, but it is a line in the sand across which no civilized society should reverse.

Being the first nation in the UK to criminalize marital rape in 1989 is considered, by this author, the pinnacle of Scottish enlightenment.

The survey of detailed studies of violence in this book suggests that, generally, everyday life is safer than it has been, that individuals can rely on the law to protect them and to deal with them without social bias if prosecuted. The judicial system has arguably achieved the ultimate in civilized behaviour – the abolition of the death penalty – and changes in the law over 300 years have addressed numerous societal issues which have had a great impact on the creation of a largely law-abiding society. However, the evidence makes it abundantly clear that we cannot take progress for granted; regression always remains possible, either regionally, locally or individually.

While Scotland's political, intellectual and judicial history has been exceptional, Scotland's uniqueness appears not to have isolated it from the continued pestilence of violent crime experienced by other, less remarkable countries over the past three centuries.

Notes

1 A. M. Kilday, *Crime in Scotland 1660–1960: the Violent North?* (Abingdon, 2021), 289–94.

2   D. Wilson, *Signs of Murder: a small town in Scotland, a miscarriage of justice and the search for the truth* (London, 2020), 211.
3   P. Knepper, *Writing the History of Crime* (London, 2017), 192.
4   Meeting of the Parliament, 9 November 2006, 29214.
5   Knepper, *Writing*, 190.
6   Knepper, *Writing*, 120.

Glossary

Advocate Depute Members of the Scottish Bar selected personally by the Lord Advocate to appear in court on his or her behalf; on a commission lasting for a few years or for individual cases, as a prosecutor for the most serious cases.

Art and part The concept of shared responsibility in the commission of a crime, but not necessarily the main participant; correlates broadly with the concept in English law of principal and accessory.

Assoilzied and dismissed An order of a court dismissing the panel from the bar on a verdict of acquittal, either not guilty or not proven.

Compeared To be called to be present at a Scottish trial.

Complainer Scots Law term for an individual reporting a crime, comparable in English law to complainant.

Contra bonos mores Against good morals.

Crown Agent A solicitor who is the head of the civil service department for public prosecutions, based in the Crown Office, Edinburgh, and staffed by permanent civil servants.

Crown Counsel The collective term for those who, at the most senior level, advise the Lord Advocate; *viz.*, the Solicitor General for Scotland and Advocates Depute.

Declaration Statement made voluntarily by an accused when brought before a Sheriff and which in the time before an accused could give evidence in court on his own behalf at his own trial (Criminal Evidence Act 1898) was the only means of stating his side of events.

Depute-Sheriff, also Sheriff-Depute (historical) Regional judicial officer with powers to hold trials.

De recenti Evidence of events and words spoken at the time of the incident, often evidence given to a person not present, but in whom the witness has particular confidence; otherwise known as hearsay testimony.

Dittay A statement of the charge or charges against an accused person.

Dole An individual's knowledge of right from wrong, and guilty mind in law, crucial to determining criminal liability.

Escheat (property) Ownerless property that is forfeited to the Crown as a result of natural death or judicial execution.

Exculpation/exculpatory evidence Testimony provided as to character or facts about the panel as part of the defence case.

Forfeited Estates Property confiscated from Scottish aristocrats and others deemed guilty of treasonous involvement in the Jacobite Rebellions of 1715 and 1745.

Hogmanay Scottish New Year's Eve celebrations.

Justice-Depute (historical) Appointed by the Justice General to exercise judicial functions on their behalf.

Libel The criminal charge in Scots Law.

Lord Advocate The principal prosecutor and legal officer for the Crown.

Lord Justice-Clerk Scotland's second most senior judge after the Lord President of the Court of Session and also Lord Justice General of the High Court of Justiciary.

Lord President In modern times, alongside being head of the Court of Session, also holds the title of Lord Justice General of the High Court of Justiciary.

Mens rea The modern term often used in place of dole; the panel's intention or knowledge of wrongdoing at the point of perpetration of a crime.

Not proven One of two verdicts of acquittal in Scots Law.

Panel/pannell The old term in Scots Law for an accused (in English law, a defendant); spelling has been variable across time.

Precognition statement Pre-trial written testimonial statement from the complainer, witnesses and experts. Taken by the Procurator Fiscal or his clerk and signed by the witness.

Precognoscer Person tasked to take down a complainer's and witnesses' testimonies.

Privy Council The executive of the Scottish government.

Procurator Fiscal Public prosecutor.

Resetter Individual who takes in stolen goods to sell on.

Solicitor General The second most senior principal public prosecutor and legal officer for the Crown.

Further and Extended Reading

The titles suggested here are intended to complement research for each chapter as well as extend understanding of the key topics of each chapter into different time periods and geographies.

Chapter 1 – John Martine, 1709

Kennedy, C. 'Criminal Law and Religion in Post-Reformation Scotland'. *Edinburgh Law Review*, vol. 16, no. 2 (2012), 178–97.

Leeming, W. 'New Taboo: Some Observations on the Late Arrival of Changes to the Law of Incest in Scotland'. *International Journal of the Sociology of Law*, vol. 24, no. 3 (September 1996), 313–36.

Chapter 2 – Janet Horne, 1727

Buchan, J. *Witch Wood*. London, 1927.

Gaskill, M. *The Ruin of All Witches: Life and Death in the New World*. London, 2021.

Gibson, M. *Witchcraft: A History in 13 Trials*. London, 2023.

Goodare, J. 'The Scottish Witchcraft Act'. *Church History*, vol. 74, no. 1 (March 2005), 39–67.

Levack, B. P. 'The Great Scottish Witch Hunt of 1661–1662'. *Journal of British Studies*, vol. 20, no. 1 (Autumn 1980), 90–108.

Machielsen, J. *The Basque Witch-Hunt: A Secret History*. London, 2024.

Stanmore, T. *Cunning Folk: Life in the Era of Practical Magic*. London, 2024.

Chapter 3 – Barbara Malcolm, 1808

Brennan, K., and Milne, E., eds. *100 Years of the Infanticide Act: Legacy, Impact and Future Directions*. London, 2023.

Callahan, K. 'Women Who Kill: An Analysis of Cases in Late Eighteenth- and Early Nineteenth-Century London'. *Journal of Social History*, vol. 46, no. 4 (Summer 2013), 1013–38.

Hyman, R. 'Medea of Suburbia: Andrea Yates, Maternal Infanticide, and the Insanity Defense'. *Women's Studies Quarterly*, vol. 32, no. 3/4 (Fall-Winter 2004), 192–210.

Porter, T., and Gavin, H. 'Infanticide and Neonaticide: A Review of 40 Years of Research Literature on Incidence and Causes'. *Trauma, Violence & Abuse*, vol. 11, no. 3 (July 2010), 99–112.

Chapter 4 – Tron Riots, 1811

Carruthers, G., Gallagher, K. T., Lamont, C. and Smith, G. *1820: Scottish Rebellion, Essays on a Nineteenth-Century Insurrection*. Edinburgh, 2022.

King, P. 'The Rise of Juvenile Delinquency in England 1780–1840: Changing Patterns of Perception and Prosecution'. *Past and Present* 160 (August 1998), 116–66.

Magarey, S. 'The Invention of Juvenile Delinquency in Early Nineteenth-Century England'. *Labour History* 34 (May 1978), 11–27.

Chapter 5 – Burke and Hare, 1828

McCracken-Flesher, C. *The Doctor Dissected: A Cultural Autopsy of the Burke and Hare Murders*. New York, 2012.

Rosner, L. *The Anatomy Murders: Being the True and Spectacular History of Edinburgh's Notorious Burke and Hare and of the Man of Science Who Abetted Them in the Commission of Their Most Heinous Crimes*. Pennsylvania, 2010.

Stevenson, R. L. *The Body Snatcher*. London, 1884, new edition issued 2019.

Chapter 6 – Dobie and Thomson, 1830

Conaghan, J., and Russell, Y. *Sexual History Evidence and the Rape Trial*. Bristol, 2023.

Harper, R., and McWhinnie, A. *The Glasgow Rape Case*. London, 1983.

Stanko, E. A. *Intimate Intrusions: Women's Experience of Male Violence*. London, 1985.

Tomaselli, S., and Porter, R. *Rape: An Historical and Social Enquiry*. London, 1990.

Chapter 7 – Madeleine Smith, 1857

Abrams, L., Gordon, E., Simonton, D. and Yeo, E. J. *Gender in Scottish History Since 1700*. Edinburgh, 2006.
Cheadle, T. *Sexual Progressives: Reimagining Intimacy in Scotland, 1880–1914*. Manchester, 2020.
MacGown, D. *The Strange Affair of Madeleine Smith: Scotland's Trial of the Century*. Edinburgh, 2007.

Chapter 8 – Patrick Higgins, 1895

Cleves, R. H. *Unspeakable: A Life Beyond Sexual Morality*. Chicago, 2020.
Kirby, M. 'The Sodomy Offence: England's Least Lovely Criminal Law Export', ed. C. Lennox and M. Waites, in *Human Rights, Sexual Orientation and Gender Identity in the Commonwealth: Struggles for Decriminalization and Change*, 61–82. London, 2013.
Smith, H. *Masculinity Class and Same-Sex Desire in Industrial England, 1895–1957*. Basingstoke, 2015.
Weeks, J. *Queer Trades, Sex and Society: Male Prostitution and the War on Homosexuality in Interwar Scotland*. London, 2023.

Chapter 9 – Oscar Slater, 1909

Jackson, L. A. et al. *Police and Community in Twentieth Century Scotland*. Edinburgh, 2020.
Rossini, B. *Oscar Slater, a killer exposed*. London, 2023.

Chapter 10 – Susan Newell, 1923

Barclay, K., Cheadle, T. and Gordon, E. 'The State of Scottish History: Gender'. *The Scottish Historical Review*, vol. XCII, supplement no. 234 (2013), 83–107.
Wilson, J. *Medicine, the Penal System and Sexual Crimes, in England, 1919–1960s: Diagnosing Deviance*. London, 2018.

Chapter 11 – Robert Handley, 1926

Report on Insanity and Diminished Responsibility: Report on a reference under section 3(1)(e) of the Law Commissions Act 1965 Laid before the Scottish Parliament by the Scottish Ministers, *Scots Law Commission* (July 2004).

Rice, F. J. 'Madness and industrial society: a study of the origins and early growth of the organisation of insanity in nineteenth century Scotland c.1830–70', doctoral thesis, University of Strathclyde, 1981.

Chapter 12 – Thomas Lutton, 1928

Salvesen, E. I. 'The Law of Incest in Scotland: A long overdue reform'. *Juridical Review*, vol. 53 (1941), 112–17.
'The Law of Incest in Scotland', Report on a Reference under Section 3(1)(e) of the Law Commissions Act 1965, Scottish Law Commission (Edinburgh, 1981), Cmnd. 8422.

Chapter 13 – Peter Manuel, 1958

Garcia, F. *We all go into the dark: the hunt for Bible John*. London, 2023.
McArthur, A., and Long, H. K. *No Mean City*. London, 1989.
Mina, D. *The Long Drop*. London, 2017.
Summerscale, K. *The Peepshow: the Murders at 10 Rillington Place*. London, 2024.

Chapter 14 – Henry John Burnett, 1963

Banks, S. *The British Execution, 1500–1964*. London, 2013.
Low, P., Rutherford, H. and Sandford-Couch, C., eds. *Execution Culture in Nineteenth Century Britain: From Public Spectacle to Hidden Ritual*. Abingdon, 2021.
Webb, S. *Execution: A History of Capital Punishment in Britain*. Cheltenham, 2011.

Chapter 15 – *S. v. HM Advocate*

Bourke, J. *Rape: A History from 1860 to the Present*. London, 2007.
Eskow, L. R. 'The Ultimate Weapon?: Demythologizing Spousal Rape and Reconceptualizing its Prosecution'. *Stanford Law Review*, vol. 48, no. 3 (1996), 677–709.
Yliö, K., and Torres, M. G., eds. *Marital Rape: Consent, Marriage and Social Change in Global Context*. Oxford, 2016.

Bibliography

National Records of Scotland archive papers

In chapter order

John Martine: JC26/90, JC11/1
Barbara Malcolm: JC26/1808/27, JC4/4, JC26/1886/266
Tron Rioters: AD14/12/101, JC8/9
Burke and Hare: JC26/1828/469, JC8/23
Dobie and Thomson: AD14/30/334, JC26/1830/346, JC4/20
Madeleine Smith: JC26/1857/371/1
Patrick Higgins: JC26/1895/35, AD14/95/31, JC8/80
Oscar Slater: HH15/20/1, HH15/20/2, HH16/109
Susan Newell: JC36/43, AD15/23/71, HH16/180
Robert Handley: JC13/137, AD15/26/81, JC15/37
Thomas Lutton: AD15/28/93, JC26/1928/54, JC15/39

Other contemporary archive sources

Webster, A. *An Account of the Number of People in Scotland in the Year One Thousand Seven Hundred and Fifty Five* (Edinburgh, 1755).
Criminal Statistics: statistics relating to police apprehensions, criminal proceedings, and Reformatory and Industrial Schools, for the year 1925 (Edinburgh, 1928).
Criminal Statistics Scotland 1955, Statistics relating to Police Apprehensions and Criminal Proceedings for the Year 1955 (Edinburgh, 1956), cmd. 9750.
Criminal Statistics Scotland 1957, Statistics relating to Police Apprehensions and Criminal Proceedings for the Year 1957 (Edinburgh, 1958), cmd. 426.
Criminal Statistics Scotland 1958, Statistics relating to Police Apprehensions and Criminal Proceedings for the Year 1958 (Edinburgh, 1959), cmd. 746.
Departmental Committee on Sexual Offences against Young Persons (1925), Hansard cmnd. 2561.
Law Commission, *Rape within Marriage*, no. 205 (London, 1992).
Lord Advocate's Reference no. 1 of 2001 v. Edward Richard Watt (Edinburgh, 2001).

Report of the Departmental Committee on Reformatory and Industrial Schools in Scotland, Minutes of Evidence taken before the Young Offenders Committee (Edinburgh, 1925), NRS, cmnd. 878/73.

Report of the Departmental Committee on Sexual Offences against Children and Young Persons in Scotland (Edinburgh, 1926), cmnd. 2592.

Report of an Inquiry by the Board of Trade into the Earnings and Hours of Labour of Workpeople of the United Kingdom (1906), cmnd. 6556.

Report on the Judicial Statistics of Scotland for the Year 1909: Statistics relating to Police Apprehensions, Criminal Proceedings, Prisons, Reformatory and Industrial Schools, Criminal Lunatics etc. (1910), cmnd. 5417.

Report of Committee to consider Overtures from the Presbytery of Glasgow and from the Synod of Glasgow and Ayr on 'Irish Immigration' and the 'Education (Scotland) Act, 1918', 29 May 1923, 750–6.

Acts of Parliament: Scottish and British

Incest Act 1567.
Witchcraft Act 1563.
Act anent Murthering of Children (1690), 1 Wm & Mary, c.20, s2.
An act for altering and amending an Act of the forty-fifth year of His present Majesty, for regulating the Police of the City of Edinburgh, and the adjoining districts, and for other purposes relating thereto, 1812: 52 George III, c. clxxii.
An act for better preventing the horrid crime of murder (1751), 25 Geo II, c.37.
Criminal Law Amendment Act (1885), 48 & 49 Vict., c.69.
Homicide Act (1957), 5 & 6 Eliz. 2., c.11.
Legitimacy Act (1926), 16 & 17 Geo.5, c.60.
Married Women's Property Act (1887), 33 & 34 Vict., c.93.
Mental Health Act (1959), 7 & 8 Eliz. 2., c.72.
Offences against the Person Act (1828), XVIII, 9 Geo. IV, c.31.
Offences against the Person Act (1861), 24 & 25 Vict., c.100.
Representation of the People Act (1867), a.k.a. Reform Act 1867, also Second Reform Act, 30 & 31 Vict., c.102.
Sale of Arsenic Regulation Act (1851), 14 Vict., c.13.
Sexual Offences (Scotland) Act (2009).

Supplementary legal cases

R v. Sweenie (1858), 8 Cox CC 223.
HM Advocate v. Duffy (1982), *Scots Law Times* (1983), 7.
HM Advocate v. Paxton (1984), *Scots Law Times* (1985), 96.

Contemporary newspapers and periodicals

Caledonian Mercury.
Edinburgh Annual Register.
Glasgow Herald.
Morning Post.
Narrative of Some Interesting Particulars respecting Hugh M'Donald, Neil Sutherland, Hugh M'Intosh, who were executed at Edinburgh on 22nd April 1812 (Edinburgh, 1812).
Scots Magazine & Edinburgh Literary Miscellany.
Sheffield Independent.
The North Briton.
The Times (of London).

Contemporary sources: Books and articles

Anonymous. *An Account of the Crime, Trial, and Behaviour of Barbara Malcolm*, John Johnson Collection: An Archive of Printed Ephemera, Crime (1808).
Bingham, J., with Detective Chief Superintendent W. Muncie, Lanarkshire County Police, *The Hunting down of Peter Manuel, Glasgow Multiple Murderer*. London, 1973.
Burr, C. W. 'Burke and Hare and the Psychology of Murder'. *Annals of Medical History*, vol. 1, no. 1 (April 1917), 75–82.
Burt, E. *Letters from a Gentleman in the North of Scotland to His Friend in London.* Edinburgh, 1876, facsimile of 1754 first edition.
Cockburn, H. *Memorials of his Time.* Edinburgh, 1856.
Doyle, A. C. *The Case of Oscar Slater.* London, 1912.
Cox, E. W. *Principles of Punishment.* London, 1877.
Gibb, A. D. *Scotland in Eclipse.* Edinburgh, 1930.
Gibb, A. D. *A Preface to Scots Law.* Edinburgh, 1944.
Gibbs, P. *Now it can be told.* London, 1920.
Hamilton, C. *Modern Scotland.* London, 1937.
Hollander, B. *Psychology of Misconduct, Vice and Crime.* London, 1922.
King James Holy Bible.
von Krafft-Ebing, R. *Psychopathia sexualis: with especial reference to the antipathic sexual instinct a medico-forensic study.* London, 1931.
MacGregor, G. *The History of Burke and Hare and the Resurrectionist Times.* Glasgow, 1884.
Pennant, T. *A Tour in Scotland, 1769*, 2nd edition. London, 1772.
Pennant, T. *A Tour in Scotland and Voyages to the Hebrides 1772.* Edinburgh facsimile edition 2019.
Pryde, G. S. *Social Life in Scotland since 1707.* London, 1934.
Sharpe, C. K. *A Historical Account of the Belief in Witchcraft in Scotland.* London, 1884.

Sinclair, J. *The Statistical Accounts of Scotland, 1791–1845*, vol. VI. Edinburgh, 1793.
Wilson, J. G. *The Trial of Peter Manuel: The Man who talked too much.* London, 1959.

Contemporary sources: Legal works

Alison, A. *Principles of the Criminal Law of Scotland.* Edinburgh, 1832.
Anderson, A. M. *The Criminal Law of Scotland.* Edinburgh, 1892.
Arnot, H. *A Collection and Abridgement of Celebrated Criminal Trials in Scotland from AD1536 to AD1784, with historical and critical remarks.* Edinburgh, 1785.
Gordon, G. H. *The Criminal Law of Scotland*, 2nd edition. Edinburgh, 1978.
Gray, J. ed. *Scottish Population Statistics including Webster's Analysis of Population 1755.* Edinburgh, 1952.
Hume, D. *Commentaries on the Law of Scotland, respecting trial for crimes*, vol. 1 (Edinburgh, 1797).
Hume, D. *Commentaries on the Law of Scotland, respecting the description and punishment of crimes*, vol. 2 (Edinburgh, 1797).
Hume, D. *Enquiries concerning human understanding and concerning the Principles of Morals* (1748), ed. L. A. Selby-Bigge. Oxford, 1902.
Hume, D. *Essays, moral, political and literary* (1758), ed. E. F. Miller. Indianapolis, 1989.
MacKenzie, G. *The Laws and Customs of Scotland, In Matters Criminal: Wherein is to be seen how the Civil Law, and the Laws and Customs of other Nations do agree with, and supply ours.* Edinburgh, 1678.
Mitchell, R. M. *A Practical Treatise on the Criminal Law of Scotland by the late Honourable Sir J. H. A. MacDonald.* Edinburgh, 1929.
Smith, T. B. *British Justice: The Scottish Contribution.* London, 1961.
'Violence against Women', Debate, Meeting of the Parliament, 9 November 2006, 29206–44.

Secondary sources: Books and chapters

Adams, N. *Blood and Granite: true crime from Aberdeen.* Edinburgh, 2003.
Arnot, M. L. 'Understanding Women committing newborn child murder in Victorian England', ed. S. D'Cruze, in *Everyday Violence in Britain, 1850–1950: Gender and Class*, 55–69. Harlow, 2000.
Barclay, K. 'From Rape to Marriage: Questions of Consent in Eighteenth-Century Britain', ed. A. Greenfield, in *Interpreting Sexual Violence, 1660–1800*, 35–44. Abingdon, 2016.
Bates, L. *The New Age of Sexism: How the AI revolution is reinventing misogyny.* London, 2025.
Block, M. R. '"For the Repressing of the Most Wicked and Felonious Rapes and Ravishments of Women": Rape Law in England, 1660–1800',

ed. A. Greenfield, in *Interpreting Sexual Violence, 1660–1800*, 23–33. Abingdon, 2016.

Blom-Cooper, L. and Morris, T. *With Malice Aforethought: a study of the crime and punishment for homicide*. Oxford, 2004.

Brindley, S. and Burman, M. 'Meeting the Challenge? Responding to rape in Scotland', ed. N. Westmarland and G. Gangoli, in *International Approaches to Rape*, 147–68. Bristol, 2012.

Burgess, K. 'Workshop of the World: Client Capitalism at its Zenith, 1830–1870', ed. T. Dickson, in *Scottish Capitalism: Class, State and Nation from before the Union to the Present*, 181–243. London, 1980.

Cheadle, T. *Sexual Progressives: Reimagining Intimacy in Scotland, 1880–1914*. Manchester, 2020.

Clark, A. *Women's Silence, Men's Violence: Sexual Assault in England, 1770–1845*. London, 1987.

Cocks, H. G. *Nameless Offences: homosexual desire in the 19th century*. London, 2010.

Conley, C. *Certain Other Countries: Homicide, Gender and National Identity in Late Nineteenth-Century England, Ireland, Scotland and Wales*. Ohio, 2007.

Cook, M. *London and the Culture of Homosexuality, 1885–1914*. Cambridge, 2003.

Daly, M. and Wilson, M. *Homicide*. New Jersey, 2014.

Davidson, R. *Illicit and Unnatural Practices: The Law, Sex and Society in Scotland since 1900*. Edinburgh, 2019.

Davies, A. *City of Gangs: Glasgow and the Rise of the British Gangster*. London, 2014.

D'Cruze, S. and Jackson, L. A. *Women, Crime and Justice in England since 1660*. Basingstoke, 2009.

Devereux, S. *Execution, State and Society in England 1660–1900*. Cambridge, 2023.

Edwards, S. S. M. 'Provoking Her Own Demise: from common assault to homicide', ed. J. Hanmer and M. Maynard, in *Women, Violence and Social Control*, 152–68. London, 1987.

Emsley, C. *Crime and Society in England 1750–1900*. Harlow, 2010.

Emsley, C. *The Elements of Murder: A History of Poison*. Oxford, 2005.

Farmer, L. *Criminal Law, Tradition and Legal Order: Crime and the Genius of Scots Law 1747 to the Present*. Cambridge, 2005.

Farmer, L. 'Criminal Law', ed. M. Mulhern, in *A Compendium of Scottish Ethnology: Scottish Life and Society*, vol. 13, 177–90. Edinburgh, 2012.

Farmer, L. 'Notable Trials and the Criminal Law in Scotland and England, 1750–1950', ed. P. Chassaigne and J. P. Genet, in *Law and Society in France and Great Britain, XII-XX centuries*, 149–70. Paris, 2003.

Farmer, L. 'Responding to the Problem of Crime: English Criminal Law and the Limits of Positivism', ed. M. Pifferi, in *The Limits of Criminological Positivism: The Movement for Criminal Law Reform in the West, 1870–1940*. Abingdon, 2021, chapter 8.

Fiske, A. P. and Rai, T. S. *Virtuous Violence*. Cambridge, 2015.

Flinn, M. W., ed., *Scottish Population History, from the seventeenth century to the 1930s*. Cambridge, 1976.

Fraser, W. H. 'Patterns of Protest', ed. T. M. Devine and R. Mitchison, in *People and Society in Scotland*, vol. 1, 1760–1830, 268–291. Edinburgh, 1988.

Gatrell, V. A. C. *The Hanging Tree: Execution and the English People, 1770–1868*. Oxford, 1996.

Glaister, J. *A Text-Book of Medical Jurisprudence and Toxicology*. Edinburgh, 1913.

Goodare, J. 'Witch-hunting and the Scottish state', ed. J. Goodare, in *The Scottish Witch-hunt in context*, 122–45. Manchester, 2002.

Gray, D. D. *Crime, Policing and Punishment in England, 1660–1914*. London, 2016.

Harris, J. and Grace, S. *A Question of Evidence? Investigating and Prosecuting Rape in the 1990s*. London, 1999.

Heren, L., *Sex and Violence in 1920s Scotland: Incest, Rape, Lewd and Libidinous Practices, 1918–1930*. London, 2023.

Heren, L. and Barclay, G. *Tanks on the Streets? The Battle of George Square, Glasgow 1919*. Barnsley, 2023.

Jackson, L. A. *Child Sexual Abuse in Victorian England*. London, 2000.

Jackson, L. A. 'Family, Community and the Regulation of Child Sexual Abuse: London, 1870–1914', ed. A. Fletcher and S. Hussey, in *Childhood in Question: Children, Parents and the State*, 133–51. Manchester, 1999.

Jackson, L. A. with Davidson, N., Fleming, L., Smale, D. M. and Sparks, R. *Police and Community in Twentieth Century Scotland*. Edinburgh, 2020.

Jenkins, P. *Intimate Enemies: Moral Panics in Contemporary Great Britain*. New York, 1992.

Kavanagh, S. '"The Most Loyal of Towns": Greenock and the Radical War of 1820', ed. G. Carruthers, K. T. Gallagher, C. Lamont and G. Smith, in *1820: Scottish Rebellion, essays on a nineteenth-century insurrection*, 93–110. Edinburgh, 2022.

Kelleher, M. D. and Kelleher, C. L. *Murder Most Rare: the female serial killer*. Westport, 1998.

Kilday, A. M. '"Angels of the House" or "Angel-Makers": Problematizing Murderous Mothers in the Nineteenth Century', ed. D. Nash and A. M. Kilday, in *Beyond Deviant Damsels: re-evaluating female criminality in the nineteenth century*, 69–101. Oxford, 2023.

Kilday, A. M. '"Circumstances of Unexplained Savagery": The Gilchrist Murder Case and Its Legacy, 1908–1927', ed. A. M. Kilday and D. Nash, in *Fair and Unfair Trials in the British Isles, 1800–1940: microhistories of Justice and Injustice*, 137–73. London, 2020.

Kilday, A. M. *Crime in Scotland 1660–1960: the Violent North?* Abingdon, 2021.

Kilday, A. M. 'Desperate Measures or Cruel Intentions?: Infanticide in Britain since 1600', ed. A. M. Kilday and D. Nash, in *Histories of Crimes: Britain 1600–2000*, 60–79. Basingstoke, 2010.

Kilday, A. M. *Women and Violent Crime in Enlightenment Scotland*. Woodbridge, 2015.

King, P. 'Moral Panics and Violent Street Crime 1750–2000: A Comparative Perspective', ed. B. Godfrey, C. Emsley and G Dunstall, in *Comparative Histories of Crime*, 53–71. Cullompton, 2003.

King, P. *Punishing the Criminal Corpse 1700–1840: Aggravated Forms of the Death Penalty in England*. London, 2017.

Kingsley-Kent, S. *Making Peace: The Reconstruction of Gender in Interwar Britain*. Chichester, 1993.

Kirby, M. 'The Sodomy Offence: England's Least Lovely Criminal Law Export?', ed. C. Lennox and M. Waites, in *Human Rights, Sexual Orientation and Gender Identity in the Commonwealth*, 61–82. London, 2013.

Knox, W. W. *Industrial Nation: Work, Culture and Society in Scotland, 1800–Present*. Edinburgh, 1999.

Knox, W. W. *Lives of Scottish Women: women and Scottish society, 1800–1980*. Edinburgh, 2006.

Knox, W. W. and McKinlay, A. 'Crime, Protest and Policing in Nineteenth-Century Scotland', ed. T. Griffiths and G. Morton, in *A History of Everyday Life in Scotland 1800–1900*, 196–224. Edinburgh, 2011.

Laite, J. *The Disappearance of Lydia Harvey: A True Story of Sex, Crime and the Meaning of Justice*. London, 2022.

Larner, C. *Enemies of God: the witch-hunt in Scotland*. Baltimore, 1981.

Levack, B. P. 'The Decline and End of Scottish Witch-hunting', ed. J. Goodare, in *The Scottish Witch-hunt in context*, 166–81. Manchester, 2002.

Levack, B. P. *Witch-hunting in Scotland: Law, Politics and Religion*. London, 2008.

Logue, K. J. *Popular Disturbances in Scotland, 1780–1815*. Edinburgh, 1979.

MacCulloch, D. *Lower than the Angels: A History of Sex and Christianity*. London, 2024.

MacDonald, C. '"The ebbing of the old shallow tide": The civil context of the Radical War', ed. G. Carruthers, K. T. Gallagher, C. Lamont and G. Smith, in *1820: Scottish Rebellion, essays on a nineteenth-century insurrection*, 1–17. Edinburgh, 2022.

McDiarmid, C. *Childhood and Crime*. Dundee, 2007.

Maver, I. 'The Catholic Community', ed. T. M. Devine and R. J. Finlay, in *Scotland in the Twentieth Century*, 269–84. Edinburgh, 1996.

Meek, J. '"That Class of Men": Effeminacy, Sodomy and Failed Masculinities in Inter- and Post-War Scotland', ed. L. Abrams and E. Ewan, in *Nine Centuries of Man: Manhood and Masculinities in Scottish History*, 242–57. Edinburgh, 2018.

Meikle, H. W. *Scotland and the French Revolution*. New York, 1969.

Mitchison, R. and Leneman, L. *Girls in Trouble: sexuality and social control in rural Scotland 1660–1780*. Edinburgh, 1998.

Nash, D. S. 'The use of a martyred blasphemer's death: the execution of Thomas Aikenhead, Scotland's religion, the enlightenment and contemporary activism', ed. A. M. Kilday and D. S. Nash, in *Law, Crime & Deviance since 1700: micro-studies in the history of crime*, 19–35. London, 2017.

Overy, R. *The Morbid Age: Britain and the Crisis of Civilization, 1919–1939*. London, 2010.

Polk, K. *When Men Kill: Scenarios of Masculine Violence*. Cambridge, 1994.

Pugh, M. *We Danced All Night: A Social History of Britain between the Wars*. London, 2008.

Raffe, A. 'Scotland Restored and Reshaped: Politics and Religion, c.1660–1712', ed. T. M. Devine and J. Wormald, in *The Oxford Handbook of Modern Scottish History*, 251–67. Oxford, 2014.

Roberts, D. 'The Paterfamilias of the Victorian Governing Classes', ed. A. Wohl, in *The Victorian Family*, 59–81. New York, 1978.

Rodger, R. 'Urbanisation in Twentieth Century Scotland', ed. T. M. Devine and R. J. Finlay, in *Scotland in the Twentieth Century*, 122–52. Edinburgh, 1996.
Rosner, L. *The Anatomy Murders: Being the True and Spectacular History of Edinburgh's Notorious Burke and Hare and of the Man of Science Who Abetted Them in the Commission of Their Most Heinous Crimes.* Pennsylvania, 2010.
Roth, R. 'Gender, Sex and Intimate-Partner Violence in Historical Perspective', ed. R. Gartner and B. McCarthy, in *Oxford Handbook of Gender, Sex and Crime*, 183–90. Oxford, 2019.
Settle, L. *Sex for Sale in Scotland: Prostitution in Edinburgh and Glasgow 1900–1939.* Edinburgh, 2016.
Simmons, C. 'Modern Sexuality and the Myth of Victorian Repression', ed. K. Peiss and C. Simmons, in *Passion and Power: sexuality in history*, 157–77. Philadelphia, 1989.
Singh, F. B. *Scandal and Survival in Nineteenth-Century Scotland: The Life of Jane Cumming.* Woodbridge, 2020.
Smith, L. M. 'Sackcloth for the Sinner or Punishment for the Crime? Church and the Secular Courts in Cromwellian Scotland', ed. J. Dwyer, R. A. Mason and A. Murdoch, in *New Perspectives on the Politics and Culture of Early Modern Scotland*, 116–32. Edinburgh, 1982.
Smith, R. *Trial by Medicine: Insanity and Responsibility in Victorian Trials.* Edinburgh, 1981.
Smout, T. C. *A History of the Scottish People 1560–1830.* London, 1985.
Smout, T. C. 'Aspects of Sexual Behaviour in Nineteenth Century Scotland', ed. A. A. MacLaren, in *Social Class in Scotland: Past and Present*, 55–85. Edinburgh, 1976.
Spierenburg, P. 'Long-Term Trends in Homicide: Theoretical Reflections and Dutch Evidence, Fifteenth to Twentieth Centuries', ed. E. A. Johnson and E. H. Monkkonen, in *The Civilization of Crime: Violence in Town and Country since the Middle Ages*, 63–105. Chicago, 1996.
Thomas, K. *Religion and the Decline of Magic.* London, 1971.
Tosh, J. 'Domesticity and Manliness in the Victorian Middle Class', ed. M. Roper and J. Tosh, in *Manful assertions: Masculinities in Britain since 1800*, 44–73. London, 1991.
Toughill, T. *Oscar Slater: the mystery solved.* Edinburgh, 1993.
Warwick, A., and Willis, M. *Jack the Ripper: Media, Culture, History.* Manchester, 2007.
Whatley, C. 'An Uninflammable People', ed. I. Donnachie and C. Whatley, in *The Manufacture of Scottish History*, 51–71. Edinburgh, 1992.
Whittington-Egan, R. *The Oscar Slater Murder Story.* Glasgow, 2001.
Whorton, J. H. *The Arsenic Century: how Victorian Britain was poisoned at home, work and play.* Oxford, 2011.
Wilson, D. 'Late Capitalism, Vulnerable Populations and Violent Predatory Crime', ed. S. Hall and S. Winlow, in *New Directions in Criminological Theory*, 216–37. London, 2012.
Wilson, D. *Signs of Murder: A Small Town in Scotland, a miscarriage of justice and the search for the truth.* London, 2020.
Wormald, J. *Court, Kirk and Community: Scotland 1470–1625.* London, 1981.

Young, A. F. *The Encyclopaedia of Scottish Executions 1750–1963*. Orpington, 1998.

Secondary sources: Journal articles

Anonymous. 'The Sale of Poisons', *British Medical Journal*, vol. 2, no. 35 (August 1857), 742–4.

Barclay, K. 'Love, Care and the Illegitimate Child in Eighteenth-Century Scotland', *Royal Historical Society Transactions*, 6th series, vol. 29 (2019), 105–25.

Barrie, D. 'Naming and Shaming: Trial by Media in Nineteenth Century Scotland', *Journal of British Studies* 54, no. 2 (April 2015), 349–76.

Begiato, J. 'Between Poise and Power: Embodied Manliness in Eighteenth and Nineteenth Century British Culture', *Transactions of the Royal Historical Society*, vol. 26 (2016), 125–47.

Bennice, J. A. and Resick, P. A. 'Marital Rape: History, Research, and Practice', *Trauma, Violence & Abuse*, vol. 4, no. 3 (July 2003), 228–46.

Bingham, A. '"It Would Be Better for the Newspapers to Call a Spade a Spade": The British Press and Child Sexual Abuse, c. 1918–90', *History Workshop Journal*, no. 88 (March 2019), 89–110.

Bingham, A. and Jackson, L. A. 'Scandals and Silences: The British Press and Child Sexual Abuse', *History and Policy* (August 2015).

Blaikie, A. 'Scottish Illegitimacy: Social Adjustment or Moral Economy?', *Journal of Interdisciplinary History*, vol. 20, no. 2 (Autumn 1998), 221–41.

Coldrey, B. 'The Sexual Abuse of Children: the historical perspective', *Studies: An Irish Quarterly Review*, vol. 85, no. 340 (Winter 1996), 370–80.

Crosby, K. 'Keeping Women off the Jury in 1920s England & Wales', *Legal Studies* 37, no. 4 (2017), 1–23.

Curran, D. 'Psychiatric Evidence in Court', *British Medical Journal*, vol. 1, no. 5228 (March 1961), 763–824.

Dabhiowala, F. 'Lust and Liberty', *Past and Present*, vol. 207, no. 1 (May 2010), 89–179.

Davidson, R. '"This Pernicious Delusion": Law, Medicine and Child Sexual Abuse in Early Twentieth-Century Scotland', *Journal of the History of Sexuality*, vol. 10, no. 1 (2001), 62–77.

Davies, A. 'The Scottish Chicago?: From "Hooligans" to "Gangsters" in Inter-war Glasgow', *Cultural and Social History*, vol. 4, no. 4 (2007), 511–27.

Dawtry, F. 'The Abolition of the Death Penalty in Britain', *British Journal of Criminology*, vol. 6, no. 2 (April 1966), 183–92.

Dempsey, B. '"By the law of this and every other well governed realm": investigating accusations of sodomy in nineteenth-century Scotland', *Juridical Review*, no. 2 (2006), 103–30.

Egger, S. 'A Working Definition of serial murder and the reduction of linkage blindness', *Journal of Police Science and Administration*, vol. 12, no. 3 (1986), 348–57.

Farmer, L. 'Arthur and Oscar (and Sherlock): The Reconstructive Trial and the "Hermeneutics of Suspicion"', *International Commentary on Evidence*, vol. 5, no. 1 (2007), 1–17.

Farmer, L. 'Recognising Marital Rape', *Scottish Legal Action Group*, Bulletin 89, no. 154 (1989), 102–5.

Friedman, D. 'Torture and the Common Law', *European Human Rights Law Review*, no. 2 (2006), 180–99.

Frieze, I. H. 'Investigating the Causes and Consequences of Marital Rape', *Signs*, vol. 8, no. 3 (Spring 1983), 532–53.

Goodare, J. 'The Scottish Witchcraft Act', *Church History*, vol. 74, no. 1 (March 2005), 39–67.

Goodare, J. 'Women and the witch-hunt in Scotland', *Social History*, vol. 23, no. 3 (October 1998), 288–308.

Goodman, N. M. 'The Supply of Bodies for Dissection: A Historical Review', *British Medical Journal*, vol. 2, no. 4381 (December 1944), 807–11.

Grant, I. F. 'Law of Incest in Scotland', *Juridical Review*, vol. 26 (1914), 437–47.

Grover, C. and Soothill, K. 'British Serial Killing: towards a structural explanation', *British Criminological Conferences: Selected Proceedings*, vol. 2, Belfast 15–19 July 1997 (1997), 2–3.

Haggerty, K. D. 'Modern Serial Killers', *Crime Media Culture*, vol. 5, no. 2 (2009), 168–87.

Hamlin, C. 'Scientific Method and Expert Witnessing: Victorian Perspectives on a Modern Problem', *Social Studies of Science*, vol. 16, no. 3 (August 1986), 485–513.

Harbort, S., and Mokros, A. 'Serial Murderers in Germany from 1945 to 1995: a descriptive study', *Homicide Studies*, vol. 5, no. 4 (November 2001), 311–34.

Hartman, M. S. 'Murder for Respectability: the Case of Madeleine Smith', *Victorian Studies*, vol. 16, no. 4 (June 1973), 381–400.

Harvey, A. D. 'Prosecutions for Sodomy in England at the beginning of the nineteenth century', *Historical Journal*, vol. 21, no. 4 (December 1978), 939–48.

Jenkins, P. 'Catch me before I kill more: Seriality as Modern Monstrosity', *Cultural Analysis*, vol. 3 (2002), 1–17.

Jenkins, P. 'Serial Murder in England 1940–1985', *Journal of Criminal Justice*, vol. 16 (1988), 1–15.

Johnston, R., and McIvor, A. 'Dangerous Work, Hard Men and Broken Bodies: Masculinity in the Clydeside Heavy Industries', *Labour History Review*, vol. 69, no. 2 (August 2004), 135–51.

Kelly, C. 'Continuity and Change in the History of Scottish Juvenile Justice', *Law Crime and History*, vol. 1 (2016), 59–62.

Kelly, D. and Shiels, R. 'Marital Rape in Scots Law', *Journal of the Forensic Science Society*, vol. 28 (1988), 253–8.

Kenefick, W. 'Comparing the Jewish and Irish Communities in Twentieth Century Scotland', *Jewish Culture and History*, vol. 9, no. 2–3 (2007), 60–78.

Kilday, A. M. 'Hell-Raising and Hair-Razing: Violent Robbery in Nineteenth-Century Scotland', *Scottish Historical Review*, vol. XCII.2, no. 235 (October 2013), 255–74.

King, P. 'The Rise of Juvenile Delinquency in England 1780–1840: Changing Patterns of Perception and Prosecution', *Past and Present*, no. 160 (August 1998), 116–66.

King, P. and Ward, R. 'Rethinking the Bloody Code in Eighteenth-Century Britain: Capital Punishment at the Centre and on the Periphery', *Past and Present* 228, no. 1 (August 2015), 159–205.

Knowles, J. B. 'The Abolition of the Death Penalty in the United Kingdom: how it happened and why it still matters', published by The Death Penalty Project (2015), 1–67.

Knox, W. W. '"The Attack of the Half-Formed Persons": the 1811–12 Tron Riot in Edinburgh Revisited', *Scottish Historical Review*, vol. 91, no. 232, part 2 (October 2012), 287–310.

Knox, W. W. 'Homicide in Eighteenth-Century Scotland: Numbers and Theories', *Scottish Historical Review*, vol. XCIV, no. 238 (April 2015), 48–73.

Leeming, W. 'New Taboo: some Observations on the late Arrival of Changes to the Law of Incest in Scotland', *International Journal of the Sociology of Law*, vol. 24 (1996), 313–36.

Leneman, L. and Mitchison, R. 'Scottish Illegitimacy Ratios in the Early Modern Period', *Economic History Review*, vol. 40, no. 1 (February 1987), 41–63.

Levack, B. P. 'The Prosecution of Sexual Crimes in Early Eighteenth-Century Scotland', *Scottish Historical Review*, vol. 89, no. 228 (October 2010), 172–93.

Lynes, A., Kelly, C. and Singh, P. K. 'Benjamin's "flâneur" and serial murder: an ultra-realist literary case study of Levi Bellfield', *Crime, Media, Culture*, vol. 15, no. 3 (2019), 523–43.

Mahood, L. and Littlewood, B. 'The "vicious" girl and the "street-corner" boy: sexuality and the gendered delinquent in the Scottish child-saving movement, 1850–1940', *Journal of the History of Sexuality*, vol. 4, no. 4 (April 1994), 549–78.

McColgan, A. 'Common Law and the Relevance of Sexual History Evidence', *Oxford Journal of Legal Studies*, vol. 16, no. 2 (1996), 275–307.

McCullagh, C. B. 'Bias in Historical Description, Interpretation and Explanation', *History and Theory*, vol. 39, no. 1 (February 2000), 39–66.

Meek, J. 'Boarding and Lodging Practices in early twentieth-century Scotland', *Continuity and Change*, vol. 31, no. 1 (2016), 79–100.

Neill, W. N. 'The Last Execution for Witchcraft in Scotland, 1722', *Scottish Historical Review*, vol. 20, no. 79 (April 1923), 218–21.

Neill, W. N. 'The Professional Pricker and hist Test for Witchcraft', *Scottish Historical Review*, vol. 19, no. 75 (April 1922), 205–13.

O'Keeffe, E. '"A natural passion?": The 1810 reflections of a Yorkshire farmer on homosexuality', *Historical Research*, vol. 94, no. 263 (February 2021), 181–90.

Philp, J. 'Bodies and bureaucracy: The demise of the body snatcher in 19th century Britain', *Anatomical Record*, vol. 305, no. 4 (April 2022), 827–37.

Ralston, A. G. 'The Tron Riot of 1812', *History Today*, vol. 30, no. 5 (May 1980), 41–5.

Reid, A., Davies, R., Garrett, E. and Blaikie, A. 'Vulnerability among illegitimate children in Nineteenth century Scotland', *Annales de demographie Historique*, no. 1 (2006), 89–113.

Rumney, P. N. S. 'When Rape isn't Rape: Court of Appeal sentencing practice in cases of marital and relationship rape', *Oxford Journal of Legal Studies*, vol. 19, no. 2 (Summer 1999), 243–69.

Sauer, R. 'Infanticide and Abortion in Nineteenth-Century Britain', *Population Studies*, vol. 32, no. 1 (March 1978), 81–93.

Sewell, A. and Oxley, J. 'An Overview of Benign and Premalignant Lesions of the Foreskin', *Diagnostic Histopathology*, vol. 25, no. 10 (October 2019), 390–7.
Shiels, R. 'Historic Defective Representation: the defence case for Oscar Slater', *Scots Law Times*, News (2025), 163–7.
Shiels, R. 'The Mid-Victorian Codification of the Practice of Public Prosecution', *Scottish Historical Review*, vol. 98, supplement 248 (October 2019), 410–38.
Shiels, R. 'Reassessing the Criminal Appeal of Oscar Slater', *Scots Law Times*, News (2024), 37–43.
Smart, C. 'A History of Ambivalence and Conflict in the Discursive Construction of the "Child Victim" of Sexual Abuse', *Social and Legal Studies*, vol. 8, no. 3 (1999), 391–409.
Smart, C. 'Reconsidering the Recent History of Child Sexual Abuse 1910–1960', *Journal of Social Policy*, vol. 29, no. 1 (2000), 55–71.
Smith, F. B. 'Labouchere's Amendment to the Criminal Law Amendment Bill', *Historical Studies*, vol. 17 (1978), 165–73.
Smyth, J. and McKinlay, A. 'Whigs, Tories and Scottish Legal Reform, c.1785–1832', *Crime, Histoire & Societes*, vol. 15, no. 1 (2011), 111–32.
Stevenson, K. 'Unearthing the Realities of Rape: utilising Victorian newspaper reportage to fill the contextual gaps', *Liverpool Law Review*, vol. 28 (2007), 405–23.
Stone, L. 'Interpersonal Violence in English society, 1300–1980', *Past and Present*, vol. 101 (November 1983), 22–33.
Strauss, M. 'Victims and Aggressors in Marital Violence', *American Behavioural Scientist*, vol. 23, no. 5 (1980), 681–704.
Sullivan, S. '"What's the Matter with Mary Jane?": Madeleine Smith, Legal Ambiguity, and the Gendered Aesthetic of Victorian Criminality', *Genders 1998–2013* (February 2002), 1–20.
Taylor, A. '"In Glasgow but not of it"'? Eastern European Jewish immigrants in a provincial Jewish community c.1890 to c.1945', *Continuity and Change*, vol. 28, no. 3 (2013), 451–77.
Taylor, K. J. 'Venereal Disease in Nineteenth-Century Children', *Journal of Psychohistory*, vol. 12, part 4 (1985), 431–64.
Tinetti, S. 'Me, Myself and I: Narcissistic Personality Disorder and Criminal Sentencing', *University of Illinois Law Review*, vol. 5 (2020), 1603–36.
Tod, M. C. 'Gonorrhoeal Vulvo-Vaginitis in Children', *British Journal of Veneral Diseases* (1927), 113–21.
Williams, J. E. H. 'The Psychopath and the Defence of Diminished Responsibility', *Modern Law Review*, vol. 21, no. 5 (September 1958), 544–9.
Wood, A. 'Sale of Poisons Bill', *British Medical Journal*, vol. 1, no. 116 (March 1859), 237–8.

Unpublished materials, theses and online resources

Allen, P. 'Narcissistic Personality Disorder: anatomy and risk', https://www.theseusrisk.com/insight-post/narcissistic-personality-disorder-anatomy-and-risk/

Anonymous, *Town Jail Craft Centre: a brief history* (Dornoch, 1974), 1–16. https://www.historylinksarchive.org.uk/pictures/document/5365.pdf?r=527437

Armitage, D. 'The Impulse of the Present', *Historical Transactions*, blog post 26 July 2023: https://blog.royalhistsoc.org/2023/07/26/the-impulse-of-the-present/

Cudney, A. 'Social Control and Disciplinary Bias: Bute, 1642–1702', unpublished doctoral thesis, University of Edinburgh (2025).

Haider, S. 'Female Petty Crime In Dundee, 1865–1925: Alcohol, Prostitution and Recidivism in a Scottish City', doctoral thesis, University of St Andrews (2013).

Merry, K. J. 'Murder by Poison in Scotland During the Nineteenth and Twentieth Centuries', unpublished thesis, University of Glasgow (2010).

Population statistics www.visionofbritain.org.uk/census/

Watson, C. 'The Trouble with Eyewitness Identification', *Legal History Miscellany*: https://legalhistorymiscellany.com/2024/09/27/the-trouble-with-eye witness-identification/

UK population data: https://www.visionofbritain.org.uk/unit/10061325/cube/TOT_POP

Index

1603 – *see under* Union of the Crowns
1707 – *see under* Act of Union (Parliamentary)

Aberdeen 10, 46, 202, 219, 235–6, 239
  Craiginches Prison 239
  Millar, Professor, chair of mental health 236
  University of 236
Abercrombie, John, surgeon – *see under* Edinburgh
Act anent the Murthering of Children 1690 – *see under* infanticide
Act for the Queen's most gracious general and free Pardon (1708) 23
Act of Union (Parliamentary) 1, 2, 15, 22, 24, 65
Adams, Arthur 154
Advocate Depute 10, 18, 142, 173, 188, 189, 190, 222
  Balfour, Patrick, Lord Kinross 170, 171, 173, 174, 177–8, 179, 181
  Elphinstone 17–18
  Grieve, W. R., Q. C. 236
  Mackenzie, Donald 122
Aitchison, Craigie, K. C. 186, 188, 189, 194, 195
alcohol – *see also* drink 5, 90, 109, 168, 169, 170, 178, 188, 189, 190, 193, 195, 196
  alcoholism/addiction 91, 175, 178, 179, 180
  delirium tremens 178, 196
  inebriation 110, 193, 194
  inebriety 169, 179
Alexander, Walter 67
Alexander, Thomas, apothecary-surgeon 50, 53, 55–7

alienation of reason – *see under* insanity
Alison, Sir Archibald 10, 46, 52, 56, 74, 102, 206
Allison, Archibald, prisoner 109
Allison, Dr 222
Alness, Lord, Munro, Robert – *see under* Lord Justice-Clerk
America 2, 3, 4, 5, 152, 228
  New York 8, 154–5, 157
anatomization/anatomizing – *see also* dissection 52, 74, 81, 85, 92–4, 108
Anatomy Act (1832) 94, 95
Anderson, A. M., lawyer 135
Anderson, Dr 172, 173, 178, 179
Andersonian University – *see under* Glasgow
Annan, James – *see under* Sheriff
antisemitism 152, 161
Appellate court 160, 197, 227
Atlantic 1, 154, 157

Balfour, Patrick, Lord Kinross – *see under* Advocate Depute
Bamberry 103, 105
  Ann 103–4
Barlinnie Prison – *see under* Glasgow
Barrowman, Miss 154, 157, 159
Beck, Adolf 156
Belgium – *see under* Europe
Bellfield, Levi 224
Bible 17
  Corinthians 1:7 244
  Leviticus 18 16–18, 23, 202, 205, 210
'Bible John' 259
Birrell, George Gilchrist – *see under* Gilchrist, Marion

INDEX

Birrell, Wingate – *see under* Gilchrist, Marion
bloody code 63, 94
body-snatchers 82, 84, 92
Borders 3
Boyle, Lord – *see under* Lord Justice-Clerk
Boyle, Sir Edward MP – *see under* Parliament
British Tube Works – *see under* Glasgow
   Birmingham factory – *see under* England
Brooke, Henry MP – *see under* Conservative Party
Brown, Janet 90
Brown, George 218
   Margaret 218
Bruce, Peter 69
Bryden, Euphemia, Nurse 186–9, 190–4, 196, 197
   Mrs, mother of 190
Buccleuch, Duke of 111
Burke, Constantine 90
Burt, Captain Edmund 31–2, 33, 35, 37
   Receiver General 31
Bushey – *see under* England
Bute 34, 36

Calvert, Roy – *see under* Howard League for Penal Reform
Cameron, Lord John – *see under* Judges
Campbell's Close – *see under* Libberton
Campbell, Dugald – *see under* Police
Campbell, James 67
Cannoway, John 86
capital case(s) 10, 159, 225, 228
   charge 173, 175, 189, 222, 233, 258
   conviction 82
   crime(s) 7, 15, 16, 83, 94, 223
   felons 82
   indictment 84
   offence 135, 232, 237
   punishment 8, 11, 63, 94, 95, 126, 156, 181, 185, 186, 197, 227, 228, 231, 232, 233, 238, 240, 257

sentence 10, 11, 63, 81, 84, 143, 150, 151, 156, 159, 173, 234, 235, 259
death penalty 9, 11, 18, 47, 94, 127, 150, 158, 194, 195–6, 223, 228, 232–4, 237, 239, 240, 255, 257, 259
   abolition 9, 11, 228, 231–4, 240, 255, 257, 259
execution 2, 7, 28, 30, 32, 33, 37, 39, 57, 61, 63, 68, 69, 81–5, 88, 91, 93–4, 95, 101, 108, 150–1, 156, 157, 177, 181, 193, 227, 231, 233, 236, 237, 239–40, 257, 258
day boisterousness 150
executioner 70
indoors 1868 150, 231
judicial cruelties 62
   hanging 63, 71, 150, 155, 197, 223, 232, 234, 236
   murder 231, 232, 233, 235–7, 240
   Royal Commission on Capital Punishment 231
   Select Committee on Capital Punishment 232
child murder – *see* infanticide
Chisholm, John – *see under* Police
Christie, John Reginald – *see also* London 217, 223
Christison, Dr 127
Clarke, Brigadier MP – *see under* Parliament
Clyde, Clydeside – *see under* Glasgow
Coatbridge – *see under* Glasgow
   Burgh Police – *see under* Police
Cockburn, Henry 10, 62, 87, 93, 94
Combination Acts (1799 & 1800) 63
Company of Scotland 1
Conan Doyle, Arthur 159
consent (sexual) 20, 21, 22, 100, 109, 110–11, 134, 142, 143, 243, 244–5, 247, 250, 251
   age of 16, 20, 134, 202, 206
   legislation 201
Conservative Party 234
   Brooke, Henry MP – *see also* Parliament 234
   Government 234, 240

INDEX

Home Secretary 234, 239
Cooke, Isabelle 219, 220
Cooper, Harriet 56
Corinthians 1:7 – *see under* Bible
Cornwall – *see under* England
Corporation Gas Works - *see under* Glasgow
Covenantors 16
Cox, Edward 21
Craiginches Prison – *see under* Aberdeen
Criminal Evidence Act (1898) 11, 158
Criminal Justice and Public Order Bill (1994) 239
Criminal Justice Bill (1938) 232
Criminal Law Amendment Act (1885) 134, 135–6, 143, 185, 201, 202, 208
   Labouchère's Amendment 134
   Revisions (1922) 185, 202, 205, 206
   section 4 205
   section 11 134, 135
Criminal Lunatics Act (1884) 176
Crown Counsel/Agent 10, 101, 138, 143, 205, 207
Culloden, Battle of 2
Cummins, Gordon, 'Blackout Ripper' – *see also* London 217, 223
Cunningham, James 123

'Daft Jamie' – *see under* Wilson, James
Dalkeith 102, 103, 108, 111
Darien Adventure 1, 2, 12, 24
Deas, Lord George – *see under* Judges
death penalty – *see under* capital punishment
Depute-Sheriff (also Sheriff-Depute) 31, 32, 33, 36, 39
de recenti – *see also* hearsay 101, 108
diminished responsibility 167, 175, 177, 190, 193, 194, 196, 197, 225, 226, 227, 236, 237–8, 259
Dingwall, William 103, 105
HM v. Dingwall - *see under R v. Dingwall*
dissection – *see also* anatomizing 81, 82, 83–4, 88, 94–5, 108, 129, 257

Docherty, Mary or Madgy 85, 86–7, 88, 90, 91, 93
dole – *see also* mens rea 73–4
Donald, the pensioner 89
Dornoch 31, 32–3, 35, 36–7, 39, 256
   Thane's Croft 32
Douglas, Lord Alfred – *see under* Wilde, Oscar
drink – *see also* alcohol etc. 85, 87, 90, 91, 103, 109, 110, 112, 167, 168, 169, 170
   problem 5–6
Dublin – *see under* Ireland
Dumbarton 3
Duncan, Miles, Superintendent – *see under* Police
Dundas, Robert – *see under* Lord Advocate
Dundee 4, 10, 17, 179, 219
Dykebar Mental Hospital – *see under* Glasgow

Eastern Police office – *see under* Police
East India Company 1
East Kilbride 215, 218, 224, 226
Edinburgh 1, 3, 4, 9, 23, 29, 32, 33, 35, 36, 39, 40, 48, 50, 52, 62, 63, 64, 65, 67, 70, 71, 73, 74, 75, 76, 81, 82, 83, 84, 90, 91, 92, 93, 95, 103, 107, 110, 113, 120, 122, 202
   Blair Street 67
   Calton Hill 32
   Canongate 69, 71, 73
   City guard 65
   Cowgate 75
   Elites, middle class 61, 63, 64–5, 70, 72, 73–4, 75, 76, 257
   Fleshmarket 67
   Grassmarket 49, 75, 85, 91
      gang 69, 71, 73
   High Street 67, 75
   Incorporation of Surgeons and Barbers 81–2
   Lady Lawson's Wynd 49, 50
   Lawnmarket 75
   Leith 50, 156, 172
      Walk 50

medieval town 64
New Town 48, 64, 65, 74
  Charlotte Square 64
Niddry Street 68, 75
  gang 69, 71, 73
Old Town 64, 65, 71, 73, 75, 85, 90
Princes Street 64
Royal College of Surgeons 50, 52, 53, 54
  Abercrombie, John, fellow of 50
  Farquharson, William, president of 50
Stamp Office Close 69
Surgeons' Square 86, 87, 89
Tanner's Close 85, 90
Tolbooth 105
Tron church 65, 68
University of 51, 95, 188, 197
'Volunteers' 64, 69, 70
West Port 85
Edmonston, George 67
Effy, the cinder raker 90
Elias, Norbert 7–8, 9, 256
  Civilizing process 8
  Über den Prozess der Civilization 7, 256
Eliot, Gilbert – *see under* Judges
Ellenborough, Lord 47
Elphinstone, Advocate Depute – *see under* Advocate Depute
Emslie, Lord – *see under* Judges
England 15, 22, 23, 28, 30, 31, 35, 45, 47, 48, 56, 63, 64, 65, 71, 83, 94, 100, 134, 143, 144, 150, 152, 156, 208, 219, 228, 233, 239, 244
  Birmingham 172
  Bushey 181
  Cornwall 151
  English 2, 4, 6, 206
    courts 237
    juries 179
    language 153, 202
    law 10, 15, 22, 28, 110
  Essex 83, 220
  Liverpool 154, 161
  Tweed, south of 3
Enlightenment 12, 22, 32, 36, 39, 76, 82, 91, 120, 255, 259

Erskine, James, defence advocate 17, 18, 23
Essex – *see under* England
Europe 3, 24, 27, 45, 152, 153
  Belgium 134
  European 152, 153, 158
  Lithuanians 152
  Low Countries 24
  Poles 152
  Russians 152
execution – *see under* capital punishment

Faculty of Advocates 122, 123
  Inglis, John, Dean 122, 123, 125, 127, 128
Falkirk 175, 218
  Redding Pit disaster 175, 181
Farquharson, William, president – *see under* Edinburgh
Federal Bureau of Investigation Behavioral Science Unit (FBI) 215, 227, 228
Fennsbank Avenue – *see under* Glasgow
Ferguson, Mrs, servant 154
Fleming, Lord – *see under* Judges
Forfeited Estates 31
Foucault, Michel 144
France 12, 219
  French
    characteristics 128
    clothes 120
    consul, Méan, Auguste de 124
    Frenchman 125
    French Wars 2, 47
    Revolution 61, 62
Freud, Sigmund 135

Galt, Dr 154, 159
gangs
  Al Capone 217
  Chicago-style 217
  Grassmarket – *see under* Edinburgh
  Niddry Street – *see under* Edinburgh
  razor – *see under* Glasgow
  Savoy Arcadian – *see under* Glasgow
Gardiner, Lord Gerald, K. C., Lord Chancellor – *see under* Labour Party

INDEX

Garrey, Dr 174, 177
General Council of the Bar of England and Wales 233
Gentles, Mr, K. C., advocate 173–5, 177–9
Gilchrist, James 68
Gilchrist, Marion 149, 153–4, 155, 156, 159, 160, 161, 162
   Birrell, Wingate, nephew 162
   Birrell, George Gilchrist, nephew 162
Gillan, Violet 104
Gillon, William 103
Gilmerton 90, 102, 103, 105, 106, 108, 109, 110
   carters 110
Glaister, John, Professor 154, 155, 159, 160, 172, 173, 177–8, 191, 196, 204, 207, 209
Glasgow 1, 3, 4, 10, 63, 64, 70, 90, 120, 122, 124, 127, 138, 149, 152–4, 155, 157, 161, 168, 171, 172, 174, 176, 180, 181, 202, 217, 218, 219, 223, 224, 228, 258
   Andersonian University 127
   Barlinnie Prison 225, 227
   Blythswood Square 122, 124
   British Tube Works 172
   Clyde(side) 3, 152, 167, 168, 169, 217
      heavy engineering 152
   Coatbridge 171–2, 175, 179, 180
   Corporation Gas Works 203
   corridor 170
   Eastern Police office 172
   Fennsbank Avenue 218–19
   Glasgow Police 219, 223
   Gorbals 152
   Govan 140
   High Court of Justiciary 170, 220
   Lord Provost 62, 63
   Maryhill 180
   Newlands Street 171
   New Sneddon Street 140, 142
   Paisley 32, 136, 140, 186
      Dykebar Mental Hospital 186
   Penny, Professor of Chemistry 127
   Queen's Terrace 153–4
   razor 'kings' gangs 6, 217
   rent strikes 168
   'Rowaleyn' 124
   Rutherglen 218
   Sauchiehall Street 122
   Savoy Arcadian gang 217
   'second city of empire' 4, 152
   University of 169, 191
   West Princes Street 153, 155
Glorious Revolution 22
Gorbals – see under Glasgow
Gordon, Sir Gerald, K. C. 10, 197, 244, 245
Gordon, defence advocate 68
Gordon, Adam 49–50, 53, 56
Govan – see under Glasgow
Graham, Dr 138, 141, 144
Granger, James 62–3
Gray, Anne 85, 86, 87
   James 86
Great War 4, 149, 167, 197
Greenock prison 188
Grieve, W. R., Q. C. – see under Advocate Depute
Grotto, John 68, 69
Gunn, Robert 69
Guthrie, Lord Charles John – see under Judges
Guyan, Margaret 235
   Thomas 235–7

Haldane, Margaret 90
Hale, Sir Matthew 244
Hamilton, Cicely 3, 169
Hamilton, Mrs, employer 48, 51, 55
Handyside, Lord – see under Solicitor General
hanged – see under capital punishment
Hanover, House of 2
   Prince Regent 68
Hardie, Keir 4, 5
Hare, Margaret 85, 86, 87, 90, 93
hearsay – see also de recenti 31, 101, 108
Henderson, Dr 188, 194
Hendry, James, Detective Superintendent – see under Police

INDEX

High Court of Justiciary 9, 10, 100, 193, 196, 208, 209, 210, 244, 245
   Edinburgh 30, 35, 36, 40, 70, 72, 107, 122
   Glasgow 138, 143, 170, 220
   Perth 17, 22, 24
Highland 4, 9, 33, 152
   Clearances 3
   and Islands 30
   line 3
H. M. Advocate v. Kidd 237
Hogmanay 61, 65, 70, 71, 73, 74, 76, 219, 257
   New Year 65, 68, 215
home rule 4, 61
Home Office 175
Home Secretary 2
Homicide Act (1957) 223, 231, 232–5, 237, 238, 239
Hope, John Rt Honourable – *see under* Lord Justice-Clerk
Hostler, Mrs 90
Houston, Reverend 225
Howard League for Penal Reform 232
   Roy Calvert 232
Hume, Baron David 10, 16, 18, 35, 36, 43, 73, 74, 100, 206, 244

illegitimacy 45, 47, 205, 207, 210
   pregnancy 45, 46, 101, 110
   rates 45
   stigma 45
incest 6, 256, 258
   Incest Act (1567) 10
   Revisions (1649) 16, 18
   incestuous conception 48
infanticide
   Act anent the Murthering of Children (1690) 43
   revisions (1809) 48, 56
Inglis, John Dean – *see under* Faculty of Advocates
Inglis, Sir Robert, Tory MP 94
insane/insanity
   'alienation of reason' 174, 237
   defence 127, 174, 194, 228, 237
   lunacy 53
   'mental unsoundness' 189, 193
   plea 48, 258, 259
   post-partum psychosis 47
   psychopathic disorders 238
      murderers 234
      personality 239
   psychopaths 227, 236
   psychopathy 237–8
   special defence 54, 167, 170, 188–9, 193–6, 222, 226, 235, 236, 237
Inverness 10, 30
Inverness-shire 39
Militia 48
Ireland 3, 45, 65, 83, 84, 85, 86, 90, 91, 169
   County Tyrone 91
   Dublin 83
   Irish 85, 91, 169, 181, 203
      Catholics 152, 169
      immigrants 152, 169
Irvine, John 235–6

Jack the Ripper – *see also* Whitechapel murderer 216, 226
Jacobite 2, 39
   cause 2
Jacobins 23
   rebellions, rising 2, 12, 61
      (1715) 2, 31, 61, 262
      (1745) 2, 31, 61, 262
Jenkins, Ann Duthie 123
Jews 153, 154
   Jewish 152, 158
Johnston, James 68
Johnston, John, child 170–1, 180
Joseph, the lodger 89
Judges
   Cameron, Lord John 222–3, 225, 226, 245
   Deas, Lord 193, 196
   Gilbert, Eliot 17
   Emslie, Lord 246, 251
   Fleming, Lord 210–11
   Guthrie, Lord Charles John 155–6, 158, 160–1
   Kines, Lord 45
   Mayfield, Lord 246
   Meadowbank, Lord 92
   Moncrieff, Lord Alexander (1928) 205, 206

INDEX

Ormidale, Lord 186–7, 189
Robertson, Lord 244
Strachan, Lord 237
Sutherland, Lord 247
Wellwood, Lord 138
Wheatley, Lord John Thomas 236–8

Kelly, John 109
Kidd, John 71
Kidd, Maureen 219
Kines, Lord – *see under* Judges
King's evidence 67, 68, 72, 87, 93, 106
Kirk 22, 23, 30, 31, 34, 35
   Church of Scotland 22, 75, 169
   General Assembly 23, 30
   Presbyterian 16, 22, 23
   Puritan 23
   Session 22, 23, 28, 29
Knox, Dr Robert 84–5, 87, 90
Kneilands, Annie 218, 222, 223

Labour Party 4
   Gardiner, Lord Gerald – *see also* Parliament 233, 234
   Government
      Independent 4
      Scottish Parliamentary 4
   Lord Chancellor 234
   Prime Minister 234
   Wilson, Harold PM – *see also* Parliament 234
Laing, Andrew 23, 24
Lamb, John – *see under* Scottish Office
Lambie, Helen 154–5, 157, 159
Lanark County Constabulary – *see under* Police
   Chief Constable – *see under* Police
Lanarkshire 122
Lancaster 143
Legitimacy Act (1926) (England) 205
Leith – *see under* Edinburgh
Leslie, Harold, Q. C. 220
Letby, Lucy 228
Leviticus 18 – *see under* Bible
Libberton 103
   Bridgend Coal Depot 103
   Campbell's Close 103

Pentland's public house 103, 105, 108, 109
Lithuanians – *see under* Europe
Liverpool – *see under* England
London
   Christie, John Reginald 217, 223
   Company of Surgeons 82
   Cummins, Gordon, 'Blackout Ripper' 217, 223
   Middlesex Assize courts 82, 134
   Tring 32
   Westminster 1, 2, 4
      Members of Parliament, MPs - *see* under Parliament
Lord Advocate
   Dundas, Robert 62
   MacKenzie, Sir George 10, 18, 29, 39, 74
   Moncreiff, Lord James 87, 122
Lords Commissioners of Justiciary 87
Lord Justice-Clerk 51, 69, 87, 94, 107
   Boyle, Lord 74
   Hope, John Rt Honourable 122, 123, 124, 129
   Munro, Robert, Lord Alness 173–4, 177, 179, 180–1, 195, 197
Lord President 22, 100
Lord Provost – *see under* Glasgow
Loth 32–4, 35, 36–7, 38
Louis, King XVIII 119
Low Countries – *see under* Europe
Lowit, Dr Ian 236, 237
Lowlands – *see under* Europe
lunacy – *see under* insanity
Lusitania 154

M'Allister, Dr 188, 194
McAllister, Susan 179
McAuley, Louis 187
McClure, Mr, K. C., advocate 155, 156
McCulloch, John 287
MacDonald, Alexander 69
MacDonald, Hugh 67, 69, 71–4
M'Dougal, Ann 90
M'Dougal, Helen, (Burke) 85–6, 87, 88, 90, 93
McIntosh, Hugh 65, 67, 68–9, 71–4, 81
McKay, Margaret 49, 54

INDEX

Mackenzie, Donald – *see under* Advocate Depute
McKenzie, Kenneth 68
McKenzie, Mary 134, 136, 137, 138, 140, 142, 144, 145
  Mr 137, 140, 141
  Thomas 136, 138
MacKenzie, Donald – *see under* Advocate Depute
MacKenzie, Sir George – *see under* Lord Advocate
M'Lean, Alexander 187, 194
McLeod, Angus – *see under* Sheriff's officer
McLeod, Janet 171
  father 175, 180
Maiden, Peter 67
Maitland, Edward – *see under* Solicitor General
Mamroth, Dr 160
Married Women's Property Act 1870 117
Marsh's Test 127
Maryhill – *see under* Glasgow
masculinity 12, 129, 133, 181, 195, 210, 217, 224, 243, 255, 256, 257
  capital 109
  hyper 170
  'rights' 170
  toxic 111, 113, 259
Mayfield, Lord – *see under* Judges
Meadowbank, Lord - *see under* Judges
Méan, Auguste de – *see under* French consul
mens rea 195, 245
Mental Care and Treatment Bill 227
Mental Health Act (1959) 236, 237, 238
Middlesex Assize – *see under* London
migration 3, 46, 64
  internal 3
  Lowlands 3
Millar, Professor – *see under* Aberdeen
Minnoch, William 123–4
misogyny 12, 34, 37, 99, 111, 113, 223, 256
Moncrieff, Lord James – *see under* Lord Advocate

Moncrieff, Alexander, advocate 122
Moncrieff, Lord Alexander – *see under* Judges (1928) 205, 206
Moncrieff, Scott, advocate 111
Monypenny, David – *see under* Solicitor General
Monro, Alexander, Professor, *primus* 83
Montgomerie, William 100
Morpeth 219
Morrison, Dr 104, 106, 111
Muncie, Detective Chief Superintendent – *see under* Police
Munro, Murdo, Superintendent – *see under* Police
Munro, Robert, Lord Alness – *see under* Lord Justice-Clerk
Murder Act (1751) 82, 83, 94
Murder (Abolition of Death Penalty) Act (1965) 234
Murder (Abolition of Death Penalty) Bill (1964) 233
Murdoch's Apothecary 122, 123
Musselburgh 49

Napier, George 68, 69, 72
Newbigging, Mr, surgeon 68
New World 1
New Year's Eve – *see under* Hogmanay
New York – *see under* America
Noblett, Ann 219–20
North Britain 1, 3
  Britishness 3
Novak, Lord – *see under* Secretary of State

Oban 173, 178, 179, 180
Offences against the Person Act (1828) 100
Ormidale, Lord – *see under* Judges

paedophilia 135
paedophile 135, 138, 144
Paisley – *see under* Glasgow
Pall Mall Gazette 134
Parliament
  Boyle, Sir Edward MP 239
  Brooke, Henry MP 234

INDEX

Gardiner, Lord Gerald, Lord Chancellor 233, 234
House of Commons 4, 39, 94, 135, 232, 233, 239
House of Lords 232, 234
Members of 4, 233–4
   Scottish 255
Clarke, Brigadier MP 233
Silverman, Sydney MP 232–3
Summerskill, Dr Shirley MP 233
Wilson, Harold PM 234
Paterson, David 86, 87
Paterson, Margaret 9, 102–8, 196, 257
Paterson, Mary 90
Paterson, William 104
Pearce, Charles and Bella 120
Pennant, Thomas 2, 32
Penny, Professor – *see also* Andersonian University, Glasgow 127
Pentland, Colin 103
Perry, Miss 132
Perth 10, 15, 17, 23, 24
Peterhead 235
  gaol 159, 160
Pittsburgh – *see under* United States
pogroms 152
Poles – *see under* Europe
Police
  Act (1812) 75
  Campbell, Dugald 67, 68, 69, 75
  Chisholm, John 68
  Coatbridge Burgh Police 172
  Courts 138, 208, 217
  Duncan, Miles, Superintendent 219
  Eastern Police office – *see also* Glasgow 172
  Glasgow Police 219, 223
  Hendry, James, Detective Superintendent 218
  as instrument of elite discipline 90
  Lanark County Constabulary 218, 223, 227
    Chief Constable 219
  Muncie, Detective Chief Superintendent 220, 223
  Munro, Murdo, Superintendent 219
  Renfrewshire Constabulary 188

  Stobhill Police office 203
  Trench, John Thomson, Detective 160
  Watt, James, Detective Inspector 137
Ponton, Alexander – *see under* Procurator Fiscal
'Popery' 16
potato famine 3, 6
presentism 11
Privy Council 2, 28, 29–30, 35
Procurator Fiscal 10, 101, 102, 105, 106–9, 111, 123, 124, 138, 145, 172, 180, 188, 205, 207, 209, 210, 245
  Ponton, Alexander 65, 71, 72
  Scot, William 50, 53, 65
Proudfoot, Grace 103
Protestant 2, 16, 152, 158
psychopathic
  disorders – *see under* insanity
  murderers – *see under* insanity
psychopathy – *see under* insanity

Queen Anne 2, 23, 24

R v. Dingwall 196
R v. Sweenie 22, 100
Ramage, William 103
razor gangs – *see under* Glasgow
Redding Pit disaster – *see under* Falkirk
Reform Act 1832 76
  1867 150
Reformation 16, 34
Renfrewshire Constabulary – *see under* Police
Renton, Dr James 104, 105
Rescissory Act 1661 16
Restoration 16, 22
Resurrectionists 82, 83, 91
Richmond, Dr 136–7, 140, 141–2
Riot Act 62
Robertson, Lord – *see under* Judges
Robertson, Robert, minister 32, 36
Robertson, Mr. defence advocate 93, 94
Roman Catholics 2, 152, 169, 169, 176
'Rowaleyn' – *see under* Glasgow

INDEX

Royal College of Surgeons – *see under* Edinburgh
  Abercrombie, John, fellow of – *see under* Edinburgh
  Farquharson, William, president of – *see under* Edinburgh
Royal Commission on Capital Punishment – *see under* capital punishment
Russians – *see under* Europe
Rutherglen – *see under* Glasgow

Sale of Arsenic Regulation Act (1851) 117–18
Scots Law 2, 6, 9, 10, 15, 18, 21, 22, 36, 50. 63, 71, 94, 100, 101, 111, 135, 136, 149, 177, 189, 190, 196, 197, 206–7, 210, 222, 226, 237–8, 243, 244, 245, 250
  Commission 243
  'thin skull rule' 191
Scottish
  Diaspora 3
  Office 157, 175, 176, 181
    Lamb, John 175–6
  Parliament 243, 251, 255
  Women's Aid 248
Scott, William – *see under* Procurator Fiscal
Scouller, Nurse 187, 190, 193, 194
Second World War 5, 8, 217, 232
Secretary
  Novak, Lord 176, 181
  for Scotland 2, 156, 258
  of State 176, 181
Select Committee on Capital Punishment – *see under* capital punishment
serial killing/killers 6, 89, 91, 215–18, 223, 224, 225–7, 228, 231, 259
Sex Disqualification (Removal) Act (1919) 7, 179
Sexual Offences (Procedure and Evidence) (Scotland) Act (2002) 250
Sharpe, Charles 33
Sheriff
  Annan, James 50
  Auld, John, of Leith Walk 50
  court 135, 138, 208, 209
  Sheriff's officer 106, 109
    McLeod, Angus 111
  Sheriff-Depute - *see* also Depute-Sheriff 31, 32, 33, 36, 39
    of Caithness 33
    Ross, Captain David 33, 35, 36, 39
  Sheriff-Substitute
    Smith, Archibald of Lanarkshire 122
    Tait, George 85
Shettleston Harriers 219
shipbuilding 3
  America 4, 152
  Germany 4, 152
Shipman, Harold 228
Silverman, Sydney, MP – *see under* Parliament
Simpson, Abigail 90
Skelton, John 67–8, 69, 70, 72
slum(s) 170, 258
  dwellings 4
  living 3–4
  'slumdom' 169
Smart, family 219, 220, 222, 223–4, 225
  Michael 219
  Peter 219
Smith, Archibald – *see under* Sheriff-Substitute
Society for Prevention of Cruelty to Children 203
Solicitor General 2, 67, 68, 72, 188, 247
  Handyside, Lord Robert 122
  Maitland, Sir Edward 122
  Monypenny, David 72, 74
St Andrews 15, 23
St Paul 244
Statistical Account of Scotland 32, 36, 37
Stead, W. T. 134–5, 201
  Maiden Tribute of Modern Babylon 134
Steel, Gerard 175
Stevens, Dr 127
Stewart, James 67, 72
Stirling 10
Stobhill police office – *see under* Police
Stonehaven 3

Strachan, Lord – *see under* Judges
Strang, James 18
Stuart
   James VII (II of Britain) 2, 23
   jurist – *see under* Hale, Sir Matthew
   monarchy 1, 2, 23, 61
Summerskill, Dr Shirley MP – *see under* Parliament
Sutherland 32
Sutherland, John 48, 49, 52, 55
   Margaret, daughter 48
Sutherland, Lord – *see under* Judges
Sutherland, Neil 65, 67–70, 71, 72–4
Swan, John 69
Swan William 65, 67, 69, 72
Swinging Sixties 234, 235

Tait, George – *see under* Sheriff-Substitute
Tait, James, surgeon 50, 53
Tasker, John 65, 68, 69, 71
Taylor, Dr R. R., Q. C. 235, 237
Tennent, Thomas, Dr 188
thin skull rule – *see under* Scots Law
   eggshell skull rule – *see under* Scots Law
Thomson, Dr 127
Thomson, James 103
Thomson, John, Detective – *see under* Police
Torrence, Helen 84
torture 8, 27, 28, 29, 30–1, 34, 35, 36, 39, 216, 224
Tring – *see under* London

Uddingston 219
   Sheepburn Road 219
UK 1, 4, 113, 152, 168, 224, 231, 240, 243, 249, 251, 259

Union of the Crowns 1
United States 8, 248, 249
   Pittsburgh 248
University of Aberdeen – *see under* Aberdeen

Valenti, Diana 218
volunteer units – *see under* Edinburgh
'vulnerables' 7, 56, 84, 91, 95, 215, 256

Waldie, Jean 84
Wales 15, 47, 56, 143, 151, 228, 233
Watt, James, Detective Inspector – *see under* Police
Watts, family 219, 220, 223, 224, 225
   Marian 218
   Vivienne 218, 220, 222
   William 218
Webb, Beatrice 180
Webster's census 3
Wellwood, Lord – *see under* Judges
West Indies 1
Wheatley, Lord John Thomas – *see under* Judges
Whitechapel murder – *see also* Jack the Ripper
Wilde, Oscar 143–4, 145
   Douglas, Lord Alfred 143
Wilson, Harold PM – *see under* Labour Party
Wilson, James, 'Daft Jamie' 85, 87, 90, 93
Witchcraft Act (1563) 27, 39

Yorkshire courts 134
Young, Annie 171, 175, 177, 178
Young, George, advocate 122